MY TIMES WITH DOGS

At ringside. - *Klein*

My Times With Dogs

by WALTER R. FLETCHER

FIRST EDITION
First Printing - 1980

HOWELL BOOK HOUSE Inc.
230 Park Avenue
New York, N.Y. 10017

Library of Congress Cataloging in Publication Data

Fletcher, Walter R
  My times with dogs

  Bibliography: p. 320
  1. Fletcher, Walter R   2. Dog shows.   3. Dogs.
     4. Journalist: United States: b. I. Title.
SF422.82.F47A33   636.7'.08'   880973   79-245-75
ISBN 0-87605-664-8

To my wife,
Vera
and my sons,
Carey and Winston.

Contents

Foreword
by Red Smith

*(Dog items are generally reported upon in the sports pages, and introducing Red (Walter W.) Smith to readers of sports pages is like introducing bread to butter; they've already been romancing all our lifetime. Red is probably the best known and most respected writer on sports in America today. He began covering fun and games with the Philadelphia Record back in 1928 and is still going strong as a three-times-a-week featured sports columnist with **The New York Times.** His multitude of honors include a Pulitzer Prize in 1976 and an honorary degree from his alma mater, Notre Dame. — **The Editor.**)*

"THE DOG has got more fun out of Man than Man has got out of the dog," James Thurber wrote, "for the clearly demonstrable reason that Man is the more laughable of the two animals."

This is one of those half truths or three-quarters-truths or seven-eighths truths which, like the varnished blonde in the chorus line, looks good until examined at close range. Walter Fletcher is as warm, friendly and companionable a man as you could catch if you set a bear trap in the aisle of a cathedral, but no reader of this book could possibly believe that dogs have got as much fun out of him this last half-century as he has got out of dogs. He is one of those rare beings fortunate enough to have found a job he loved, and to have loved it his whole adult life.

Dogs do, indeed, get a lot of fun out of Man, but how many dogs would trouble to learn that a certain judge of German Shepherds could work in the show ring from 8 A.M. to 7:30 P.M. without once going to the men's room or, having learned it, would derive the pleasure Walter Fletcher gets from the knowledge? Clearly, Walter Fletcher's life has been better than a dog's life.

I have had the good fortune to work on the same paper with Walter and benefit from his knowledge. One afternoon at the Westminster Kennel Club show I mentioned to Walter that I had been watching a judge working with Old English Sheepdogs. I especially admired his ability to distinguish one end of the dog from the other, a gift that I thought was reserved to ferryboat captains.

Oh, Walter said, sure, he knew that judge. Fine fellow. Some years back, Walter said, the judge had been doing some work at Harvard and had fallen for a Radcliffe lady who owned a Great Pyrenees, a breed that is named for a mountain range, aptly. The Harvard man and Radcliffe lady had married and gone off on their honeymoon in a Volkswagen bug, with the dog in the rear seat, more or less.

They lost the dog in Yellowstone Park. Probably he just spilled out of the Volks. They were frantic for a day or so. Then a park ranger phoned. ''I think we've got a line on your dog,'' he said. ''A tourist just reported sighting a polar bear.''

To Walter Fletcher, this was just an anecdote to be tossed off in the press room in Madison Square Graden. For me, it was raw material that made a whole column, bless his generous heart.

I am deeply indebted to Walter Fletcher. If it weren't for him, I would not know that the Holy Roman Emperor Rudolf II preferred dogs to girls. In 1603 Rudolf, then 51, was jilted by the 17-year-old daughter of the Duke of Bavaria. As a peace offering, the duke sent Rudolf a dozen dogs. ''These great animals are my joy and comfort,'' Rudolf said. ''My admiration for them is stronger and bigger than my understanding of marriage.''

If it weren't for Walter, I wouldn't know about the judge from England who frequently dropped to all fours and barked at the dogs he was judging.

Describing the accomodations provided for dogs traveling to shows, Walter tells us about the trailers with housekeeping facilities, exercise pens and barber chairs for hair-styling Poodles. He mentions in passing that breeding is not necessarily confined to Doberman Pinschers. ''Even I,'' Walter writes, ''despite my square manner, have been approached with erotic hints by several ambitious women eager for special publicity.''

It is good to know that there are groupies who follow dog shows. It is good, too, to learn how Walter encouraged the airlines to allow dogs to travel first class, and how the French Line had a special menu for *chien* when the grand ship, *France,* was still afloat—Consomme de Boeuf, Epinard, Legume and assorted cookies.

From no one else but Walter Fletcher can one learn that Alf Letourner, the six-day bike rider, had a dog that sang so well he was permitted to carry the melody when the band played in the grand salon of the *France.*

Then there was the time Oliver Holden, a copyreader on *The New York Times,* got into Norwegian Elkhounds. He sent one to President Herbert

Hoover, who liked it so much he wanted another. The White House called *The New York Times* but it was Oliver Holden's day off. Sorry, the *Times* operator said, it was against policy to give out home phone numbers.

"This is the White House," a voice said. "This is for the President."

"I'll put you on hold," the operator said, "while I ask Mr. Holden if it's all right to give you his number."

Dave Anderson and I do the sports column in *The New York Times* on alternate days. We consult frequently on which subjects we're going to cover, and there is a tacit understanding that the first to stake a claim owns the topic.

One winter I thought I'd probably go scratch for a column at the Westminster show, but Walter Fletcher happened to mention that Dave had asked for working credentials. This told me Dave had put his bid in for the dog show as column material, so I backed off.

A day or so later somebody was asking me how Dave and I managed to avoid conflict. It was no problem, I said. We consulted often on the phone, and at other times we had a pretty good idea of what the other would be doing.

"For example," I said, "I happen to know that today he's writing about the dog show." I did not know that a hockey player had scored a gang of goals, prompting Dave to write about him instead of the dogs.

I opened the paper to show my friend how Dave and I worked. "Why, the son of a bitch!" I said.

Walter Fletcher always thought it was language suitable to dog people.

Dog Writers' Association of America

presents this certificate of award to

Walter R. Fletcher
New York Times

Best Column, Best News Report, Best Feature Story

Best Syndicated Column ~ A Clean Sweep!

_____
PRESIDENT

_____
CONTEST CHAIRMAN

_____
SECRETARY

February 13, 1977
DATE

The Dog Writers Association of America has honored me many times, including this sweep of newspaper category awards for 1977. To one of the dinners at which I was to be saluted—

```
RELAY MOFOO4 PD

            MO NEWYORK NY FEB 14 730PM EST

CH. WALTER FLETCHER

     DOG WRITERS DINNER STATLER-HOTEL NYK

WHO'S WALTER FLETCHER?

              JAMES ROACH   SPORTS EDITOR   NEW YORK TIMES

                                                        731P
```

My boss sent this congratulations.

Introduction

FOR YEARS I've read dog books, some good, some bad, but all dealing with canines. For some reason, the people who are closely associated with the sport—judges, breeders, exhibitors, handlers, club officials—have been brushed aside. During five decades I had the good fortune to cover more events and interview more dog show people than any other reporter in America. So I determined my book would be a work about the *homo sapiens* at ringside, as well as the *canis familiaris* inside the ring. However, it is not to be a Who's Who of dog show people but rather choice morsels from my notebooks of some of the thousands I've encountered in my half-century in the sport.

In culling, many noteworthy episodes about dedicated fanciers had to be left out, otherwise this book would have grown to three volumes.

It's been a fascinating experience to witness the motivation, dedication, persistence and enthusiasm of the aficionados. As a newspaperman, I tried to be objective while I watched hopes rise and fall, exhibitors laughing and crying.

Invariably I'm asked, "How did you start to write about dogs?" It's a rather prosaic story. I arrived at *The New York* Times as a full-fledged staff member in 1927, the year that Charles Lindbergh flew the Spirit of St. Louis across the Atlantic on his epochal flight from New York to Paris. One day the sports editor, Bernard Thomson, called me to his desk and asked if I ever had covered a dog show. When I said "No," he replied, "Well, you are doing your first tomorrow."

Now I had been reporting on a variety of sports—basketball, track, tennis, golf, hockey, yachting and hunts meets—and the thought of a dog show wasn't too exciting. I went to the files of previous editions of the *Times,* read a dog story or two and studied the style of the summaries; in those days winners dog, winners bitch, best of winners and best of breed were carried in addition to the groups and best in show.

My first show was Queensboro at the old Aqueduct race track in New York. Being a youngster and worried about an expense account, I took an elevated train that left me a half-mile from the course. Toting a typewriter, I set off in the direction of the track, only to reach it a good distance from the gates. When I asked some kids for the entrance and learned how far I still had to walk, they heard a few choice words from a cub reporter. "There are a couple of bent iron bars," said one. "When we want to get in, we squeeze through." I was a tall, gangling youth weighing 145 pounds, so this *New York Times* reporter squeezed into his first show.

To me it was bedlam. Much barking and people all over the place. There was a great deal of movement and sound, certainly no order, or at least that's how it appeared to this tyro. Actually, of course, a dog show is one of the most systematized of all sports competitions. Everything has been spelled out by the American Kennel Club, dogdom's ruling body. Each animal has an assigned role, as have also the judges, stewards and superintendents.

I had been told by Bryan Field, a reporter on the *Times* staff who had covered dog shows, to ask for the superintendent, and he would tell me what to do. It was George Foley, a pioneer in the sport, and he provided me with a catalogue, explained where I could get the results and then I was on my own.

Early Days

My journalistic career had started when I was a 14-year-old boy in my junior year at Manual Training High School in Brooklyn. I was writing for the school paper when *The Evening World*, long since dead, in an effort to increase its circulation, started a Brooklyn edition. Getting up my courage, I went to the paper's editorial offices and offered my services as a reporter for news of the school. Paul Lockwood, who later was to become an assistant district attorney under Thomas E. Dewey, was handling the school news section and hired me. I was to be paid on a space basis—$5 a column.

Then I heard the *New York Call*, long defunct, was looking for a school reporter, and I was signed up by a second daily. My first "big" assignment was a high school football game, between Manual and Erasmus Hall, played at Ebbets Field, the home of the old Brooklyn Dodgers. It drew 19,000 fans, a huge crowd for a school game. When I reported to the sports editor of the *Call*, he pointed to a typewriter and said, "Give me 400 words and a line-up."

Never having learned to type, I was in a bit of a quandry. Certainly I didn't want to admit it. So laboriously, using just the index finger of the right hand, I hunted for the keys as I pecked out the story. Several times the editor passed the desk and asked if the story was ready. Either he was very kind or just too busy but nothing was said about my one-finger typing. Incidentally, I have improved considerably since that day. Now I use two fingers—adding the middle finger of the left hand. But I can pound it out at a good speed.

That day I received a letter signed by Walter Liggett, the *Call's* managing editor, requesting I be admitted to all school sports events. Liggett, who was to become my brother-in-law, was a brilliant newspaperman, magazine editor and author, and an idealist. He later went to Minnesota with my sister, Edith, an accomplished writer on her own, and bought a weekly newspaper. Exposing corruption and mob rule in the state, he was murdered in 1934 by the underworld, to silence him.

The smell of ink, which permeates so many of the smaller newspaper plants, has always been perfume to me. Leaving the *Call,* after writing my first big story, I got into a crowded elevator and heard reporters using such esoteric expressions as "I sent the story up in takes," and "Did you read the AP and UP stories?" I felt as though I had been knighted and admitted to the Round Table; that I now was a Fourth Estate fledgling. Little did I realize that later, and for many years, I was to be a copy editor, sit at a horseshoe desk and use the same phrases I had overheard.

When I entered City College of New York in 1923, I quickly became a member of the college paper. But having had a taste of reporting on metropolitan dailies, this was small game and I inquired how one became a college correspondent. I was told those were plums reserved for upperclassmen on the college weekly.

In my sophomore year, the sports editor of the college paper, who was also a correspondent for *The Evening Post,* an arch conservative paper in those days, found he was too busy with his duties and his college work. He asked if I would like the job. So when I was 18 I was hired by the *Post* to cover City College athletic activities.

The *Post* had a small staff and in no time I was handling other sports assignments for it. Whereas my classmates spent their free hours together in bull sessions at college, I would rush to the *Post* and sit listening to the staffmen and reveling in the excitement of the office. Soon the sports editor was giving me releases and asking me to rewrite them. Between my junior and senior years, I spent my summer at the *Post.* It was on-the-job training.

One day the sports editor called me over and said, "Go to the composing room and make up the edition." I didn't know where the composing room was and had no idea of make-up. When I asked a staff man, he told me the room was up on the next floor, that I should get a list of new or running stories from the head of the sports desk (called a "slotman") and that I was to send the edition to press. He saw I looked rather bewildered and added, "Just ask for Mac, when you get to the composing room. He does the sports make-up. Give him the list of stories and he will do the rest." Mac turned out to be an elderly Scotsman. He showed me where to stand and said, "You are now the editor and should tell me where you want the stories." Whereupon he placed the stories himself but had the decency to ask, "Is this all right with you?" Then he said I should return to the sports department and tell the editor we had gone to press on time.

That was my composing room initiation and it served me in good stead, for relatively few newspapermen on a big city daily ever have the opportunity to do make-up.

I was graduated from City College in February of 1927 and immediately was hired for the sports staff of the *Post.* After a few weeks of editing copy on the day side, being the junior member of the department, I was given the night hitch. I worked from midnight until 9 A.M. and was alone until the day staff reported. It was a grueling assignment. I had to read all the copy for the first edition, decide on and write the headlines for the stories and finally go to the composing room and do the make-up. It was far too much work for one man —when I left they hired two newspapermen— but it gave me invaluable experience.

I had an explosive transfer to the *Times*. In August I had seen someone off at Grand Central Station at 11 P.M. and having some time to spare, started to walk downtown. As I reached 28th street, there was a blast. The pavement shook, the grating on the sidewalk rattled, black smoke began pouring through—a bomb had exploded in the station. I was among the first to run down to the platform and I assisted people to the street. The *Times,* in its usual efficient manner, had a half-dozen reporters on the scene quickly. As they phoned in their stories, I made notes and I accompanied them to Bellevue Hospital, which had dispatched ambulances, and to a local police station. I didn't reach the *Post* until 4 A.M. and reported immediately to the city editor. He told me to write as much as I could. The story, which led the paper, was run two-column measure on the first page under my byline. An introduction, in italics, told of how I had been among the first on the scene and that this was an eyewitness account.

The story attracted a great deal of attention. The next morning I received a call from the *Times,* saying the sports editor wanted to see me. He asked whether I would like to join the staff. I did and must have liked it, for I was to remain until forced to abdicate, because of age, a half-century later.

On the *Times,* I was to serve in a variety of capacities—reporter, copy editor and make-up editor for the sports department and for a half-dozen years as night picture editor for the news section. At one time or another I covered practically every sport, from auto racing to yachting.

A few memories of my days as picture editor. For a month before D-Day, the *Times* had been alerted that an invasion was contemplated. Each night the paper would stay open until 5 A.M., awaiting word. There were two of us on the night picture desk and we divided the vigil. When the invasion became a reality, it was early enough but since no actual pictures of the landing came in, we went with a 4-column map of the area on page 1.

Another memory is of the day President Roosevelt died and was succeeded by Vice President Truman. I had to choose two photos for the first page. There was a plethora of photos of Roosevelt but very little choice of his successor. A vice president of that era commanded little attention. It was rather like, ''Harry who?''

Then a night I'll never forget concerned Mussolini's death. The Duce had been captured and executed by Italian partisans in 1945 and our correspondent had obtained the pictures. At great risk, and after a wild chase through Italy, he managed to get them out of the country. When the negatives arrived at the picture

16

desk and were printed, we rushed them to the managing editor. They were exclusive and worth a fortune, for the *Times* could have syndicated them and made a handsome profit. The managing editor called the publisher, Arthur Hays Sulzberger, who promptly answered, "Give them to the services free. I want everyone to see what happens to a dictator."

Occasionally celebrities visited the paper and were given a VIP tour. My desk always was piled high with photos. Whenever anyone passed the desk and picked up a picture he promptly, and in no uncertain tones, was told to put it down. One late afernoon, busy at the desk, out of the corner of my eye I saw someone looking over my photos. I just checked myself in time. It was Field Marshal Bernard Montgomery, commander of the British Armies in World War II, being taken through the *Times* on a tour.

On occasion, as picture editor, I had been called upon to judge such diverse activities as beauty contests and bartender championships. The first beauty contest, at the Advertising Club on Park Avenue, was for "Mrs. America" and I had visions of viewing gorgeous girls. It was a rude shock when I was told merely to choose from photos of the candidates, with their measurements and an accompanying letter. Fortunately another judge arrived and he acquainted me with the facts of life—that the ideal measurement was the same for bust and hips, with 10 inches less for waist. He cited a good figure would be 36-26-36. So I searched for that ideal. There were four judges and we were supposed to choose 15 from the several hundred photos submitted. The real judging was done by the professionals—heads of modeling schools and artists.

For two years I judged the contest and apparently word spread that I was an authority on female pulchritude for I was asked to help select Miss America Big Girl in New York's Tavern-on-the-Green in Central Park. All the contestants were six feet tall and upward. They all wore cowgirl outfits and I staggered through this one, lassoing a winner.

I, who couldn't tell a Martini from a Manhattan, three times was called upon to help pick the bartenders of the year. The contest, in the grand ballroom of the Waldorf-Astoria Hotel in New York, was in three categories—best cocktail, best long drink and best after-dinner concoction. The bartenders came from all over the United States and qualified for the final, after surviving a series of regional tests. The judges had to sample six drinks. After each, we would write a score, from 0 to 10, on a small blackboard and hold it up so all could see. I quickly learned that to be considered a connoisseur one should mark low—a 4 to 6. So at the beginning, where I had been giving 8 or 9, I soon dropped my scores. Thus, I became an authority. I always felt sorry for the poor contestants. Several thousand dollars went to the winners and if the other judges had taste buds as poor as mine, the public was having some weird drinks foisted upon it.

But it was dogs that played a major role in my life at the paper; I became a voice and pen pal for the doggy set. Not only did I write about canines but for

At the shows, I was constantly interviewing. Sometimes it was a judge, as at top with John G. Laytham. Sometimes it was an owner, as at right, with Mrs. M. D. Hooks, following the win of the Toy Group by her Chihuahua, Ch. Snow Bunny D Casa de Cris, at Denver 1976. And sometimes it was a handler, as below with Richard Bauer.

years, at each Westminster show, my dulcet tones were heard over the air reporting the classic for the CBS radio networks. Col. Frank Huyler, who had ridden jumpers at the National Horse Show in Madison Square Garden, an event I also covered, phoned me after one broadcast to say he had been driving from North Carolina to New Orleans when he heard all about Westminster from one of my broadcasts. We hadn't seen each other for years and it was a nice reunion over the phone.

In the fall of 1965, I was master of ceremonies for the Long Island Fair's dog exhibitions at Roosevelt Raceway. During the six days of the fair I described the action over the track's loudspeaker system, so not only did the 12,000 spectators hear about the dogs in my hour-long spiel, but so did all the villagers whose houses rimmed the track.

As a boy I had been brought up with a Golden Retriever. Then, later, I successively had a Dachshund, Dalmatian, Boston Terrier and Cocker Spaniel. A pesty, overgrown Wire Fox Terrier, belonging to my sister, was a frequent visitor to the house. The Dalmatian was my only showdog. We showed her during the period when I was picture editor and not writing about dogs, so there was no conflict of interest. The Dal had been the runt of a litter and the breeder, Capt. Alfred Nicholson, had given her to my younger son, Winston, as a pet. The captain called her Runty but that offended her young master, who promptly changed it to Rundy.

When she was six months old, there were two shows a few miles from where we lived and Nicholson urged us to show her. Neither the Dal nor my wife ever had been in a ring and it must have been apparent. As my wife strived to imitate the professional handlers in stacking the pup, the judge, Evelyn Nelson, then president of the Dalmatian Club of America, came over and said, "Leave the bitch alone, she sets herself up very nicely."

Rundy, in her very first show, was winners bitch for 3 points. The next day she added another 3 points. My son Winston had trained her to lick his face when he put his head close to hers. When the judge, and it was the great Alva Rosenberg, bent down to go over her, Rundy promptly kissed him. Alva, grinning from ear to ear, gave her the blue ribbon for the class and the purple for winners.

Rundy was to gain her championship as an 11-month-old pup and then was retired, since it was as expensive to show her as to keep my son Carey at Cornell. If I could have afforded to campaign the Dal, she would have done very well, for she had the potential to be a best-in-show winner. As it was, she had a couple of group placements as a puppy in her brief career in the ring.

There have been many changes over my years in the dog show world. In 1927 there were 290 all-breed and specialty events across the country. The shows were benched and typical entries were Philadelphia, a two-day affair, 509; Devon, 490; Westchester, 438; Long Island, 331, and Del Monte, 250. There were exceptions, of course. Westminster, a three-day show in Madison Square Garden in New York, had 2,133. The year I retired, 1976, saw 1,653 all-breed and specialties, and an entry of 1,000 was commonplace. The leading show that year was Santa Barbara, with 3,995, and all the fixtures in the top ten surpassed 3,000 dogs.

When I started, there were five groups. Sporting and Hounds were shown together and comprised the largest division, with 28 breeds. To those fanciers who complain about today's large Working group, there were then only 13 breeds, including Dachshunds and Eskimos. The Eskimos are no longer registered with the AKC and Dachshunds are in the Hound group. In the miscellaneous class were Miniature Pinschers, Salukis, Giant Schnauzers, Skye Terriers and Italian Greyhounds.

Boston Terriers led the AKC registrations, having displaced the German Shepherd the previous year. The Boston was to stay No. 1 until 1936, when the Cocker Spaniel pushed to the fore. The Cocker reigned supreme until the Beagle ran to the head of the pack in 1953, where he stayed through 1959. Then along came the ubiquitous Poodle to become top dog. The Poodle's rise was spectacular, for in 1927 only three were on the books. A half-century later, 139,750 were registered for the year.

The years I covered the dog beat have left a regret or two. Although the *Times* was extremely liberal in sending me to shows around the country, it was a New York paper and most of the events I attended were in the East. International, in Chicago, was as far West as we ordinarily covered. So rarely did I get out to the West Coast, which in the mid-seventies took over as the focal show center of America, with such great fixtures as Santa Barbara, Beverly Hills, Ventura and Santa Clara. In 1978, the top three shows based on actual dogs in competition, were in California.

Still, the *Times* was the only paper in the world that gave dog news international coverage and ran the stories on the sports pages. In 1976 the *Times* devoted the equivalent of 27 complete pages, that is, 216 full columns of space, to dog articles. I did stories from England, Portugal, Spain, France, Monaco, Austria, Czechoslovakia, Italy, the Caribbean, Central and South America. And the fanciers were hungry for news.

At a Santa Barbara show, which was the largest in the United States that year, the only other paper represented was from Oxnard, Calif., and the reporter was so intrigued that a New York paper would send a writer to the Coast for a show that he devoted his column to me and not the dogs. At a Denver fixture, a local paper sent a photographer but no reporter. Its coverage was a "framed" picture of a Bulldog with a cake of ice on its head, so it could be comfortable in the heat. Rocky Mountain exhibitors had to buy a New York paper for the results of the show. At city after city, fanciers would tell me they bought *The New York Times* every Sunday for the dog stories. As a result, I always strived to write as much national news as possible in those columns. I remember one in which I gave the best in show at 21 events the previous weekend, covering every area of the country.

Frequently I was the only reporter at an event. When someone would be assigned, invariably it was a youngster covering for the first time. Rather than try to explain what was happening, I'd give him or her a copy of my summaries and then my story, stressing it should be rewritten. And each year, when I would take a vacation in this country or in foreign lands, I always made a point of getting in touch with local fanciers, so I could get material for future columns about doggy doings in the area. It made good reading and spread good will.

So I would like to spread the good will further among my readers to make you better acquainted with each other.

One of my most prized awards. When the chair concessionaire wanted to take a chair from under me while I was typing the story of the final at a Monmouth County show, club president Dr. Ed McGough bought it from him. The following year the club presented me with the chair (with my name imprinted on it) in a formal ceremony. - *Philps*

The dog show scene may appear hectic to the unfamiliar eye. Bronx County show at Kingsbridge Armory, New York City.

Purebred Potpourri

ONCE UPON A TIME, there was a great stud dog. He was looked upon with awe and longing eyes by all the bitches in the kennel and with envy by other dogs. There came a day when he was struck with a strange malady. His owner summoned a veterinarian, who took the dog to his hospital. Then came the bad news! The dog had contracted a disease which involved the reproductive tract. Unless he was castrated, it could be fatal. The surgery performed, the dog returned home. The mood in the kennel was tense. But he strode haughtily into his run and looked over his domain as if nothing had happened. Finally one of the dogs, no longer able to contain himself, said, "Come on, we know what happened to you. Now what are you going to do?" Looking down with great disdain, the former stud replied, "Now I am going to be a consultant."

A dog is a dog is a dog.

That's the feeling of the average man on the street. But the fancier knows otherwise. The showgoer will tell you there's a world of difference, and not only in size. Every breed was developed for a purpose, rarely just for its good looks.

Since the Stone Age, when man and dog are believed to have joined forces, the *canis familiaris* proved his worth as a hunter, herder and a guardian against predators. But today, particularly in the city, the dog gets little or no opportunity to pursue game, drive cattle and round up flocks. Most of his hunting is confined to the kitchen, where he looks for goodies. When it comes to sheep, his master or mistress is probably familiar only with the bedtime counting variety. With the mounting crime wave, however, the family pet still plays a watchdog role, guarding against human, rather than animal predators.

The owner has an opportunity to display his dog's worth and that's in the competition of the show ring. And for all the tensions and regrets connected with the sport, there is still the satisfaction in proving "my dog is better than yours."

I always told people with purebreds if they wanted to make new friends all they had to do was start showing their pets. Each weekend they could join the motorcade en route to the show grounds. Never would they be lonely. Whereas years ago, the sport was dominated by the wealthy with large kennels, now the one-or-two dog exhibitor is in the majority. And if the owner dreamed of a stage career, here was a chance to perform. Should the would-be thespian get the jitters, there was always a professional handler, who for a fee would walk Rover into the ring. Should the dog win, there's the pleasure of seeing its name and the OWNER'S in print. And that first trophy is as precious as the Kimberly diamond.

One invariably learns something at a dog show and perhaps that is one of the great attractions of the sport. There is no season, such as baseball or football. It is a year-round endeavor, in which the entire family can participate, whether it be in the show ring, obedience training or field trial. And there is the hidden ingredient—companionship. After a show, trial or just a hike, when you return home you have a loyal companion.

What Breed for Me?

While I was at the *Times,* I had the heaviest mail in the sports department. The question I was most frequently asked was, "What breed of dog would you recommend that I buy?" My answer was always emphatic — "That depends." Then I would explain that not every dog is right for everyone. With show people, of course, it was quite different. Some would choose a breed because of a driving desire to win.

I was always intrigued by the psychological motives that moved a person to get a particular breed. Such as the aggressive man who wanted a Bull Terrier or Doberman Pinscher. Others found in their dogs a substitute for children or friends. For some years it has been fashionable to own a Poodle. This even is true behind the Iron Curtain. I received a phone call from a Soviet diplomat of the United Nations, who wanted me to get him a White Toy Poodle. "It will be the only one in Moscow," he told me, "and I want that little dog so my daughter can walk with it across Red Square." In Czechoslovakia, when I asked a dog writer what breed would command the greatest attention on the streets of Prague, the response was, "An Afghan. There are very few in the country."

The First Dog Show?

Although it is generally accepted that the first organized dog show was held in Newcastle-upon-Tyne, England, in June of 1859, with one class for Pointers and one class for Setters, on one of my trips to Czechoslovakia I learned from Karel Stepansky, editor of that country's leading dog magazine, that a public dog show took place in Prague in 1791.

Said he: "According to Ignaz Cernov, who lived from 1740 until 1822, and was a history professor at Charles University, and a priest, Father Martin Pelcl (1734-1801), the show was held in a garden owned by Josef Emanuel Malabatla Canal. There were 12x12-foot runs, with five-foot-high fences. As a humorous note, there was a sign above the gate to the garden, 'No Dogs Allowed.'

The show lasted three days. There were 128 dogs—28 Pyrenees Shepherds, 18 Spitz, 16 Butcher Dogs (probably Rottweilers), 14 Dachshunds, 12 Mountain Dogs, 10 Poodles, 9 Pugs, 7 Pyrenees, 8 Russian Wolfhounds and 6 St. Bernards. There were many spectators, some of whom sat on a ring of benches under the trees until darkness, when oil lamps were lit. All of this is historically documented.''

Then, from the memoirs of Jan z Vresovic, head of the Imperial Forestry Department in 1603, we learn of a field competition held that year. The Holy Roman Emperor, Rudolf II, had received a gift of a dozen dogs from Maximilian, the Duke of Bavaria, in 1603, as appeasement for his 17-year-old daughter's refusal to marry the 51-year-old Rudolf. Apparently the bribe worked, for, according to Vresovic, when Rudolf saw the dogs in the courtyard of his Hradcany Castle in Prague, he exclaimed, ''These great animals are my joy and comfort. My admiration for them is stronger and bigger than my understanding of marriage.''

Rudolf was so taken with the gift that a few weeks later he organized the first documented field trial in Central Europe, when 480 dogs competed for eight days on the grounds of the castle. Twenty-six of the dogs came from as far as Spain. The emperor then organized what was probably the world's first field trial club. Vresovic writes, ''The Society of Experienced Hunters was composed of 12 gentlemen, who met every Thursday in the Emperor's private chambers and he was its chairman. The members described to him the experiences of what happened during the hunts. The society had its own insignia—silver circular badges with a miniature design of a hunting dog.'' The group met weekly for five years until the Emperor's health failed.

Family Affair

I never ceased to be amazed at the tremendous number of people taking part at the shows. Few sports are as demanding. This is a participation activity for dad, mom and the kids, in which the odds are all against them. Take a show with 3,000 dogs. Only 10 percent are going to do any meaningful winning, whereby they get points toward championships or take the breed to advance to a group. And there is only one best in show. The others get nothing, save a ribbon or two and perhaps a token trophy.

For those fortunate enough to have a top winner, there are headaches as well as prizes. Skyrocketing motel prices, food, rising gasoline costs, high insurance rates, entry fees, basic veterinarian expenses make it an expensive hobby. Should there be a professional handler, and the owner attend the shows, it runs into big money. Peggy Westphal, whose Ch. Sagamore Toccoa was the top-winning Cocker Spaniel in history, told me she never again could afford to campaign a major victor.

Trophies have changed considerably over the years. A look at the 1877 Westminster catalogue shows that among the prizes were an ivory, enamelled

The trophy cases bulge at Mr. and Mrs. Joe Longo's home in Harrison, N.Y. Her Poodles have won dozens of handsome obedience prizes and he's a top golfing pro (Westchester PGA champion in 1972).

The ribbons pile up fast, too, when you've a winner of the scale of the Vizsla, AKC Dual and Can. Ch. Sir Lancelot, owned by W. F. Goodman. Sir Lancelot set a record for his breed with 234 field trial points.

opera case; a gold-and silver mounted, pearl-handled revolver; a case of stuffed American game birds; a silver-mounted split bamboo fly rod; and a double-barrelled breach-loading shot gun. Later we went through a period of the Winged Victory abominations, some three feet tall, topped by the figure. During the boom years there were sterling silver trays, cups, coffee and tea services. Some practical trophy chairmen then hit upon pewter, which required no polishing. In the 1970s, when there was a bit of a recession, silver plate, rather than sterling, became the rule.

Eleanor Cole, who showed most of her own German Shepherds —she owned or bred 75 champions—had 60 three-foot-high glass cabinets built, so she could exhibit the ribbons and rosettes. Mrs. Cole was the exception. Mimi Denton, whose Dachshunds and Whippets were big winners through more than 25 years, said she had most of the ribbons stored in boxes, a practice common with owners of famous dogs, being awarded them week after week.

As to trophies, many are either relegated to the attic or if they haven't the initial or name of the sponsorship club, they are donated to other organizations for their shows.

Michael Weissman, who with his mother.Florence, co-owns the Wire Fox, Ch. Aryee Dominator, who in 1978 became the greatest winning terrier in American dog show history with 76 best-in-show awards, explained it this way: "If we wanted to put all the silverware on display, we would need a huge trophy room. And have you ever polished silver?"

Walter Goodman and his octogenarian mother, Adele Goodman, whose Skye Terriers dominated rings for four decades, keep only the Westminster Bowl their Ch. Glamoor Good News won in 1969, and one or two other trophies, on display. Mrs. Walter M. Jeffords, Jr. and Mrs. Charles Engelhard had even more of a problem. Their husbands' horses triumphed in big stakes on both sides of the ocean, and the dog prizes had to be worked in with the turf awards.

The Judging Problem

Meanwhile each year we see more shows which necessitate more judges, and there is an ever-increasing problem of obtaining sites. Fortunately, the AKC in 1978 selected as its president a man acutely aware of the situation. He is William (Bill) Stifel. When I asked him what the AKC proposed to do, Bill responded, "Since 1971, entries have increased 36 percent. We are re-evaluating our stand on all-breed clubs holding shows on a common site. There is no problem with specialty clubs, since the AKC can approve up to 20 specialty shows to share one common site."

When I pointed out how exhibitors are constantly complaining about the judging, he replied, "Approving judges is one of our most important jobs. We are having personal interviews with all applicants. We would like to expand the whole program, with more testing—both oral and written."

27

Since judging is subjective, it will always be controversial. I remember the second show I covered. It was a specialty and the judge was putting on quite an act. He would frequently drop to his hands and knees and bark at the dogs. Since it was getting late, when he finished a class, I went into the ring, introduced myself and said I was afraid we were going to miss the edition. "My boy," said he, taking me to the far corner of the ring, away from the steward, "Is this your first dog show?" "No sir, my second." "Well, I'm what is known as a professional judge. I come from England. These people have paid to see me put on a show, and by God, I put on a show. Now I know who I am going to make best. You can go back to your paper and write the story. But be sure to call me, to check that the dog hasn't died or gone lame."

I went to the paper, wrote the story, and then phoned the Briton, "It's all right, you can print it. He won," said he.

With anything as flagrant as that, it is pretty hard to write about the good old days and how much better the judging was in the past.

More Is Not Necessarily Better

The AKC, starting in 1924, tried a five-year experiment, when it used multiple arbiters for the groups and best in show. The first year, at Westminster, there were two judges for best. They had difficulty in agreeing, so in 1925, four were in the ring. Then for the next three years, there were three judges for each group and five for the top award. In 1928, it took an hour and 20 minutes for the quintet to make a decision. It finally leveled down to Reggie Lewis's Wire Fox Terrier bitch, Ch. Talavera Margaret, and the Giralda Farm's German Shepherd, Ch. Cito v.d. Marktfeste. Both were recalled to the platform used by the judges and all five arbiters took turns going over them, finally giving the decision to the Terrier.

The AKC, in announcing its decision to revert to one judge only for the group and best, said, "When three or more judges officiated, it was quite frequently found that they could not agree, each one being in favor of a different dog and holding out determinedly for it. Hence, a compromise was effected and another dog, entirely different from those favored by each individual judge, went to the top . . . Some have suggested two judges and, if necessary, a referee. It is very seldom two men will agree on the merits of different dogs, no matter how well versed each one may be in the knowledge of different breeds. So the one with the most able and persuasive powers of argument will most frequently win the other over and so we have in this case a one-man decision, if not in the letter, at least in the spirit. Again, suppose that each is equally firm in his convictions and refuses to yield ground, and the referee is called in to settle the question, again will the decision in the final analysis not be that of one man? Therefore, the License Committee argued, why not have one man from the beginning and let the exhibitors and spectators know squarely whose was the responsibility of the award.''

So how do we get better judging?

I always have felt the AKC should follow the example of the livestock shows, for at least the groups and best, whereby the judge would evaluate each animal over the loudspeaker, so all could hear the reasons for the selection. A written report of each dog that had been judged also would be a great aid for future breeding.

Dr. E. S. Montgomery, who in a 30-year span owned 21 different Terrier breeds, and is a longtime arbiter, was outspoken in his criticism of the judging system. ''Lack of training for judges is one of the serious ailments affecting dog shows,'' the physician said to me. He agreed that all good sportsmen accept an official's decison. However, he pointed out that in all sporting events a reason is given for the judge's decision. ''In football, the referee signals the penalty, so that the teams, coaches and spectators are aware of an infraction,'' he added. ''A referee and two judges at a prize fight score their decisions. But the dog show judge makes his decision without answering to anyone and without giving his reasons, whether his placings are good, bad or just indifferent. What judge is so superior in knowledge that he or she can expect a decision to be accepted without question? Written or oral reports should be made by the judges.''

Training and Testing Judges Abroad

Australia and Austria have very stringent regulations in making judges. I remember when I was discussing the situation with Derek Rayne, the all-rounder, who said, ''Judges should attend classes and then have to pass examinations, as in Australia.''

''In 1964, in New South Wales, we decided something had to be done about our judging,'' Dr. Harold Spira, a veterinarian from Sydney told me. ''It took three years to come up with a satisfactory system. It purports to train fanciers to become breed, group and eventually all-round judges. A fancier must have been active with a breed for five years, either as an owner, exhibitor or breeder to be eligible. The candidate enrolls in a nine-month course, with a series of lectures every two weeks conducted by the Australian KC. Then he takes a written examination—one hour on anatomy and two more hours on the breed standards for which he is applying and ring technique. If the examiners are in doubt, the candidate is recalled for a practical test, judging a class and discussing his selections with the experts. The successful candidates become eligible for the group course. These sessions last a year, with fortnightly meetings. Then there is a three-hour examination. Those who pass take a practical test, placing from four to six dogs, in at least four breeds chosen at random by the examiners. After six group assignments, the judge is eligible to start with another group. So, theoretically, after six years, he could become an all-rounder.''

How testing the system is was further explained by Noel Butler of Sydney, who like Spira is a judge. Said he, ''In the state of Victoria, in 1975, of 104 who applied for licenses, only 20 passed the three-hour oral and written and went on to the practical test. Of those, seven received licenses. Speaking of judging in the United States, your judges only can take 175 dogs a day. In Australia, we have no limit. I've judged as many as 430, starting at 9 A.M. and finishing at 8, with an hour for lunch.''

When I was in Austria in 1970, I interviewed Ida E. Bublik, at that time the only all-rounder of 250 judges iń the country. To become an arbiter, an aspirant must be a member of the Austrian KC for at least five years and have been a successful breeder and exhibitor. All candidates take a course in Vienna, consisting of anatomy, bone structure and the standards of the breeds the aspirant is seeking to judge. After working in a ring at three shows, each supervised by a different licensed judge, the candidate takes an examination. The president of the Austrian club and two other officers do the questioning. If the candidate is successful, he must judge at two more shows. He also writes a critique of each dog he has ruled on. The reports are studied and if satisfactory, the candidate is certified.

However, despite these regulations, I have seen some very questionable judging by Australians in this country and I heard plenty of complaints from members of the Austrian club.

I was very impressed with the judging system in Czechoslovakia. In each ring there was a table with a typist. As the judge went over each dog, he dictated his findings—''Good head but poor topline; powerfully muscled legs, with good bone; feet strong and rounded.'' The critique went to the exhibitor, with copies for the club and the breed publication. For the judging, the FCI system is used—excellent (blue ribbon), very good (red), good (green), satisfactory (violet) and unsatisfactory.

I found exhibitors the same the world over, when it came to the judging. At the finish of a Collie specialty on the grounds of Konopiste Castle (once the home of Archduke Francis Ferdinand of Austria, whose assassination precipitated World War I) there was a knot of people, with one man gesticulating and shouting. When I asked Vera to translate, she said he was extremely irate and was asking, ''How could the judge say my Collie is unsatisfactory? He should never be allowed to judge again. He knows nothing about dogs.'' When the president of the club appealed to him to quiet down, since there were visitors from America, he screamed, ''Let them go home and tell what thieves we have judging.'' It all sounded so familiar.

30

Common Show Sites

Now, back again to what Bill Stifel said about the AKC studying requests for multiple all-breed clubs using a common show site. With the great concern of getting gasoline for travel and the difficulty of getting locations, I think this is a solution. Westchester and Tuxedo share Lyndhurst, the beautiful national landmark at Tarrytown, N.Y., and certainly neither club has lost its identity, one of the reasons given by the AKC for denying clubs the same site. In 1976, the Colorado Centennial Canine Circuit was held with six clubs from all over the state staging their events in the Hall of Education Building in Denver, over a period of nine days. The circuit celebrated the nation's bicentennial and Colorado's 100th anniversary as a state. It was a tremendous success. Ordinarily the six clubs would have drawn from 800 to 1,200 dogs for their all-breed events. However, being at the one site, entries were attracted from coast to coast and the shows had from 3,133 to 3,551. Several exhibitors told me ordinarily they would have had to drive 1,000 miles to get a major. This way there were majors in most of the breeds.

Channel City and Santa Barbara, since 1975, have been holding their shows at the University of California at Santa Barbara, although on different parts of the campus. Channel City has its event on Friday and Santa Barbara, the nation's largest fixture, on Sunday. In between is Ventura, just a short drive away. California has taken over as the land of the big show. In 1975, Channel City set a record for a first-time event, when it had 3,376 entries. That year, Santa Barbara had 4,442 and Ventura 3,500, giving a three-day total of 11,318.

Here an updating note is in order. Because the university site would not be available to them after the 1979 show, Santa Barbara has proposed (pending AKC approval) a two-day show for the future, to be held at the Earl Warren Showgrounds, which would be limited to 750 dogs each day and further limited to dogs that are champions or that have a major win (3 points or more) toward their title.

Tom Crowe, whose Moss-Bow organization superintends more than 400 shows a year, is another who advocates multiple shows on one site. "Expenses are reduced for the participating clubs and since exhibitors don't have to drive from one place to another, energy is conserved," he said. The North Carolina entrepreneur criticized some judges. "There generally are five or six dogs that stand out in a group and the judge, after gaiting the entire field, should concentrate on these," he added. "I've seen judges gait every dog in the group several times. That's a sheer waste of time." Tom berated clubs for failing to plan ahead, when preparing a judging panel. "A man will draw 175 dogs," he explained, "and that means seven-and-a-half hours of judging, with another half-hour for lunch. So he cannot start a group until 5 P.M., which makes for a late show. Clubs should have more judges, and if they are doing groups, should see that they are not loaded with breed assignments."

Carriages and Carrying Ons

Fanciers are getting a lot fancier in the way they attend shows. More and more are arriving in recreational vehicles. Exhibitors, who in the past had to be up in the wee hours of the morning to get a show on time for the early judging, are finding it much easier to load their dogs and crates in the big rigs the day before and park overnight at the site of the event.

After the initial expense, it is also much cheaper. "We were tired of expensive motels and the hassle of unloading and loading," Leonard Ripley, a Lhasa Apso breeder and member of the motor-home set, told me. "No longer do we have the aggravation of arriving at a motel only to learn it has been overbooked and has no room for us."

In 1972, when Trenton drew a crowd of 50,000, the superintendent of Washington Crossing State Park drove me around the grounds so I could see the parking facilities. "We have at least 100 campers or trailers here," he said, "whereas last year we had only a half-dozen." There is no doubt that the recreational vehicles are causing problems for show chairmen. At Santa Barbara, I counted more than a thousand in the over-27-foot variety. At Westchester, Wallace Owen, a club member, estimated the total value of the big rigs on the grounds at $2-million.

The motor homes continue to get longer and longer. The handlers bring rigs to accommodate from 10 to 14 dogs, with complete housekeeping facilities, tables for private "hair-styling", at least two exercise pens for their dogs and chairs for themselves. On a stroll down "Handlers' Row," a habachi for the gourmet's indulgence can be spied, if the camper doesn't provide kitchen facilities, or if the fancier has a date with friends or clients. Many of the exhibitors set up canopies and have luncheon parties under them. During the afternoon, the pop of champagne bottles signals the return of a winner.

Not surprisingly, there is also a bit of extra-marital activity and gossip abounds about who is sleeping with whom. If I only remembered all the stories I had been told, it would make another book, although on the risque side. To many a professional handler, marrying a wealthy client is a side benefit. The divorce rate is high among the doggy set, what with all the traveling, parties and overnight stays. Even I, despite my square manner, have been approached with erotic hints by several ambitious women, eager for special publicity.

Although I rarely was the first to a dog show, I always was the last to leave, for my main story started when the judging ended. So frequently I had to seek out-of-the-way, late-serving restaurants. And all too often, I tried to duck my face into the soup or look the other way, for there would be a couple of exhibitors, married but not to each other, having a snack.

In the summer, I would hear fanciers complaining to the show chairman about the noisy air-conditioning units in the big motor homes, insisting that the vehicles should be parked in a soundproof area so as not to disturb the sweltering, cranky, less fortunate. Alice Ladd and Rodney Sachs came up with a solution at the Somerset Hills show, when it moved to North Branch, N.J. The area assigned to the recreational vehicles was at least a morning's jog to the rings. So a shuttle service was set up, with chauffered pick-up trucks to carry dogs and equipment from rig to ring.

Aerial view of the Montgomery County all-Terrier show on Temple University's suburban campus at Ambler, Pa.

Woman's Lib Comes to Dogdom

The show ring is a great leveler. Long before women's lib became a cause célèbre, members of the fair sex were competing on an equal footing with men. Numerically, they have taken the lead in the sport, being active in club work, stewarding, breeding and handling. Years ago, I interviewed the president of a leading club, who said, "When I took over this club it was badly run down. It had a woman president before me and she didn't know what she was doing." When he saw me taking notes, he shouted, "Don't print that. Do you want me to be in bad with every woman in America?" That day is long over.

As in so many clubs around the country, on Long Island women play a major role at three of the major organizations—Westbury, the Ladies Kennel Association and the LIKC. Mrs. William Tabler, whose husband is one of the country's leading architects, in 1979 was serving her fourth term as president of the Long Island club. Her Ch. Chaminade Syncopation was the first Bichon Frise to become a champion and before he was retired he had taken the top award seven times. With her daughter, Judith Kelsey, Mrs. Tabler also breeds Cocker Spaniels.

Pat Spear, long a Doberman enthusiast, had been hospitality chairman for Westbury while Selma Tucker was entrusted with the club's publicity. Both Pat and Selma have been leaders in the humane movement. Pat, who comes from England and was a nurse during World War II, long has dabbled in photography and she covers several of the leading Eastern shows for American and Canadian magazines. Selma is a horticulturist, and for Westbury she prepares flower arrangements that would win prizes. Mrs. Eben Pyne, club president for a number of years, Mrs. Alan Corey, Muriel Higgins and Peggy Adamson are prominent members of LIKC ladies. Mrs. Corey, who at one time bred top winning Golden Retrievers, has served in a number of top posts. Muriel, who won fame with her Dalmatians, is judging, as is Peggy, a former president of the Doberman Pinscher Club of America, whose Dobes have been big winners here and overseas.

Mrs. Geraldine Lee Hess, a member of Westbury and Long Island (where she was show chairman) and a prominent Pekingese breeder for many years, is now a well-respected Toy and Non-Sporting judge. Barbara Danis, a radiation therapist, and an officer at Westbury and a Long Island board member, is also a judge. An so is Mrs. Philip S. P. Fell, who also belongs to both clubs and is a leading Norfolk Terrier breeder, one of her drop-ears having taken the Norwich Terrier Club Specialty three years in a row, starting in 1976.

Another feminine VIP of the sport is Betty Gribbin of New Jersey. Betty's parents helped to reorganize the Trenton club in 1927, so her affiliation with the club was well established. When she stepped down in 1976, she had been the club's president for six years. Her great Great Dane, Ch. Heidere's Kolyer Kimbayh, shown in the early '70s, had 237 breeds, 227 group placements (of which 87 were firsts) and 28 bests. After a period away from the rings, Betty was

34

back in 1979 with a Kimbayh son, Sweep-On, who fittingly enough earned one of his majors at Trenton and then became champion at Queensboro.

Not all business leaders in dogs are men. The top winning black and tan Minpin in America in 1976 and 1977 was Ch. Reapage's Toma, owned by Rose Radel, also of New Jersey. Toma is also an FCI international champion, and owns titles in Canada, Bermuda, Mexico and Monaco, as well as points in Italy and France. When Toma's attractive blonde owner isn't involved showing him, she is busy analyzing and setting policy for field service personnel in over 500 Prudential Insurance Company offices throughout the United States and Canada.

I take pride in having played a role so that women officially would have a voice at AKC. In June, 1972, I wrote a story telling how the organization was considering a change in its constitution, which then specified that "the voting power of each member club or association can and shall be exercised only by a male delegate." I wrote that should a woman be elected, she could eventually become a member of the board, on which 12 directors serve.

Not being a delegate, I couldn't attend the meeting in December 1973, when the motion was put to a vote. But I spoke to several delegates who were good friends, and asked them to take notes for me. So I was able to report "sex discrimination continues at the American Kennel Club." I told how, in 1952, a motion had been defeated and again this time by an all-male assembly of 202, who voted it down by 25 ballots. I used names, telling who led the fight to support and who were opposed. I wrote that of the 2,664 AKC judges, 40.7 percent were women; that a spot check at four shows revealed that 60 percent of the exhibitors were women; that Hilda Pugh was president of the Canadian KC, the third woman to hold that post, and Princess Antoinette, the sister of Prince Rainier, headed Monaco.

Finally, in March 1974, the delegates, in an open roll call—the previous one had been a secret ballot—voted 180 to 7, to accept the motion. Apparently my stories had been read, for John C. Sheahan of the Delaware County KC said his club had voted against the measure, which I reported, and that he had taken a great deal of abuse because of it. He said he still would vote against the proposal. But at the conclusion of the roll call, when President John Lafore asked whether any delegate wished to change his vote, Sheahan rose and joined the majority, "For the sake of peace, harmony and the women," he said. So in June, Julie Gasow, representing the English Springer Spaniel Club, Carol Duffy, the Mid-Hudson, and Gertrude Freedman, the Bulldog Club of New England, were seated. But it had taken 90 years from the time the AKC was founded. Since then, the three women delegates have been joined by many others.

There was one discordant note that again I brought into the open. The following December, Mrs. Billie McFadden, who had been chosen by Trenton to represent it at the AKC, was rejected by the delegates. I wrote how the "dirty tricks" era had been carried over to the dog world. "I have the distinction at least of being the first woman to be turned down by the AKC," Billie told me.

Kay Jeffords' Pekingese and Boston Terriers have been in the forefront over many years. Kay also shares her husband's (Walter M., Jr.) keen interest in horses. - *Spear*

Mrs. Charles W. Engelhard, wife of the late industrialist, with Ch. Cragmount's Hi-Lo, top winning Golden Retriever of the late '60s. A prominent society figure, Mrs. Engelhard has been on the "best-dressed" list many times.

However, this was not a sex issue but rather a battle within the Trenton club and several of its members resigned in a shake-up after the affair. Mrs. McFadden had run for the seat vacated by Adolph Kunca, when he became a member of the AKC board, and had won by a single vote. Her name had been posted in the AKC *Gazette* for two consecutive issues, giving readers an opportunity to write to the organization if they had any objections. Apparently the AKC was satisfied with Billie's credentials for its board approved her and submitted her name to be placed before the delegates.

When the delegates gathered at the Biltmore Hotel in New York City, many found under their luncheon plates a slip of paper saying, "Billie McFadden to represent the Trenton Kennel Club, Inc. (vote no)." When this was brought to the attention of Lafore, he castigated the action. He told the members he considered it highly improper, reminding them that the directors had approved the proposed delegate. But the "dirty work" had already been done. Many of the delegates gathered at the bar before luncheon and several reported they had been asked to cast negative votes. Some also had received phone calls. Whereas the 17 other delegates were accepted by acclamation, a secret ballot was demanded for Mrs. McFadden. Of the 174 delegates at the meeting, 91 voted for her, 77 against and 6 abstained. She needed a four-fifths vote to be seated. Dr. Armour Wood, Trenton president from 1961 to 1971, told me, "It's unfortunate that there has been a power struggle within the club. It's also too bad last June's election results were tardily sent to the AKC. As a result, there was an opportunity for dirty politics."

Another controversy I spotlighted was that over the proper feminine costume for the show ring. No one expects a judge or an exhibitor to wear high heels into the ring, but the worry over excessive exposure, while bending to have a close look at a short-legged dog, is equally uncomfortable and distracting. James Trullinger, an all-round judge, brought the issue to the fore at a dinner. "I believe hot pants, slacks and pants suits for lady judges do not have a place in the show ring," said he. "This also applies to women handlers and the exhibitors. The ring should not be a burlesque stage."

I conducted a survey, which showed a sharp diversity of opinion. Jeannette (Jerry) Cross led the opposition. "I wore a tailored pants suit into the ring at Westchester in 1970," said Jerry, "and several people congratulated me, calling it a first for a woman judge in the East. They also expressed their approval. Since then, I've made it a practice when I'm judging. I find it extremely comfortable."

Anne Rogers Clark added, "As long as fashion dictates women wear slacks or pants suits to the theater or any good restaurant, there is no reason why they shouldn't be worn in the ring." For Westminster, which she judged in 1978, Annie wore a blue-and-beige evening dress she had designed.

Capt. Arthur Haggerty, a noted dog trainer and a Bronx club official, thought "slacks very practical. However, when a girl appears in a miniskirt, the crowd always appears around the ring."

Joe Mellor, a judge, was "in favor of women wearing slacks or pants suits. We all have been exposed to too much exposure with abbreviated apparel." Arlene Thompson, another arbiter, commented, "I'm not in favor of women judges wearing slacks, since they are not flattering and are warm. But I would like to see them wearing narrow, ankle-length skirts."

I probably could have kept the controversy going by pointing out how at some of the Canadian shows, formal clothes are worn for the groups and best show by both judge and exhibitor. The long dress is certainly attractive in the ring but it must be a chore to show a German Shepherd, where so much running is required.

Which leads us to conclude that since either a dress or a pants suit can be decorous enough in the ring, it might be left entirely to the women to decide if and how much they want their slips showing.

Mr. and Mrs. G. L. K. Morris's Dog, Miss Rose, Is Enshrined in Social Register as 'Junior'

The pages of the Social Register have at last gone really doggy. In its 1936 Summer issue a 4-year-old red-haired Pekingese dog has achieved the recognition for which social climbers without number have struggled and intrigued in vain.

On page 288 of the current volume there appears the listing of Mr. and Mrs. George L. K. Morris of 14 East Ninetieth Street and Brookhurst, Lenox, Mass., followed a line below by the entry "Junior Miss Rose." It developed yesterday that Rose is Mrs. Morris's pet Pekingese, named by her after Rosa Ponselle, the singer.

When the news reached the offices of the Social Register Association at 381 Fourth Avenue yesterday there was a gasp of horror, followed by silence. The association "has absolutely nothing to say," its spokesman told reporters.

Mr. Morris, who is a painter and a brother of Newbold Morris, Republican candidate for President of the Board of Aldermen, was at the Morris Summer place in Lenox early yesterday, but as long-distance telephone calls from newspapers kept coming in ever-increasing numbers he took to flight. The butler at Brookhurst said last night that he had no idea where Mr. Morris had gone or when he would return.

Mrs. Morris, who was said by members of the family to have perpetrated the listing of "Rose" as a joke, is now in Europe studying music. She is a soprano who had appeared on the concert stage before her marriage to Mr. Morris Jan. 30, 1935.

Mrs. Morris is the former Estelle Condit Frelinghuysen, daughter of the late Frederick Frelinghuysen, president of the Mutual Benefit Life Insurance Company, and granddaughter of the late Frederick T. Frelinghuysen, who was Secretary of State under President Arthur. Mr. Morris is a descendant of General Lewis Morris, a signer of the Declaration of Independence, and of Lewis Morris, the first native-born Chief Justice of New York State.

Not all the dog stories in the *Times* have been in the sports section. This one, unearthed by a news reporter, created quite a stir when it appeared on the front page, July 31, 1936.

Skyes in the Sky

Again it was a story that I wrote in the *Times* that did much to get airlines to accept dogs in the cabins. Pan American World Airways and Trans World Airways for a quarter of a century had permitted people to take their pets in the cabin, but they didn't publicize it. The TWA public relations department told me that on each flight two small dogs were permitted in the cabin, one in first class, the other in economy, and that TWA charged only single excess baggage. "We have a policy of first come, first served," said a TWA official, "so it's advisable to book ahead." Pan Am said, "If the plane isn't crowded, we try to keep the seat next to the passenger with the dog vacant." The "friendly skies" of United then opened to live animals in the cabin. Allan B. Wayne, then PR director, phoned to tell me that United not only would carry one dog in first class and one in economy but on the giant 747s, it would permit four. "We did a spot check for two months and found we were carrying an average of 60 small animals systemwide daily," he told me. "This included cats and birds. On the basis of the present revenues realized from passengers accompanying the small animals, it is projected that an average of more then $1-million will be realized annually." A special meeting of the directors of American Airlines was called, and that carrier agreed to fly two pets in the cabin. A year later, Eastern joined the parade. I always felt that $1-million figure I quoted had something to do with it.

Schipps on Ships

When the ocean liners were on the trans-Atlantic run or on long cruises, all of the big ships had kennels. Probably the most luxurious was that aboard the *France,* where M. Chien and Mme. Chienne traveled first class, with wall-to-wall, or cage-to-cage, carpeting. The French line, which always prided itself on its fine cuisine, didn't forget the pets.

On the *France* a daily menu was prepared—in French, of course—for the canine passengers. There was a choice of five entrees. A typical menu would offer Consomme de Boeuf-Toasts-Legumes (beef consomme, toast and vegetables); Carottes—Viande Hache—Epinards—Toasts (carrots, chopped meat, spinach and toast); Haricot Verts—Poulet Hache—Riz Nature, Arrose de Jus de Viande et de Biscottes en Poudre (green beans, hashed chicken, rice and crumbled biscuits with gravy); Os de Cote de Boeuf, de Jambon and de Veau (a ham or veal bone); and les Legumes Frais et les Patés Alimentiares (fresh vegetables and nourishing patés).

If the owner preferred, he could order a special dinner for his pet. "We have had requests for filet mignon," Andre Ozenne, the kennel master told me, "and for black coffee, with sugar. The owner said the dog always had coffee with him in the morning."

On the giant liner was a turquoise-colored tiled air-conditioned kennel, with 32 stainless steel compartments. Each had carpeting of a material that could quickly be removed and replaced. The *chenil* (kennel) was situated on the port side of the sun deck, just aft of the captain's quarters. There were three separate exercise areas and a long promenade, where the more ambitious hound could do a little running. In the exercise rings, familiar to any French or American dog, were a lamp post, a fire hydrant, and two red-and-white highway stones—one marked Le Havre and the other Paris.

Andre explained how he joined the line when he was 17 years old. "I first worked in the kitchen. Then I became a waiter. I was on the *De Grasse* and they needed someone to handle the kennel. I always liked animals, so I asked for the job. That was in 1950. I handled the kennel on the *Flandre* before the *France*." When I asked M. Ozenne did he have any favorite passenger, he replied, "There was a dog owned by Alfred Letourner, the French six-day bicycle rider, who liked to sing. He was so good the ship's entertainment director let him sing in the middle of the grand salon, while the band played."

England has long been famous for its roast beef and Yorkshire pudding. Dogs being shipped aboard the *Queen Elizabeth* would get the beef but not the pudding. Into their dishes went the same succulent meat served the passengers aboard the 86,673-ton Cunard liner. But it wasn't seasoned. "Makes them drink too much," explained Jack Garret, the chief butcher, who was the overseer of the kennel. Garrett's role, however, was simply that of an executive. In direct charge was Michael Porter of Southampton. "I signed on as a butcher in 1959," said Porter, "but never worked in the galley. I had handled the kennel on the Royal Mail's *Andes* and the Cunard's *Saxonia,* so Mr. Garrett told me to take over on the *Elizabeth*."

The kennel was on the starboard side of the sports deck in the lee of the massive red-and-black funnel. The animals had their own "Dog Deck," a 16 × 30 foot area, where the owners could come and walk their pets. However, more frequently it was Porter, garbed in his butcher's uniform, who did the exercising. "The owners were too busy," he said. "Most of the time they would look in for a couple of minutes. I exercised the dogs four times a day." The *Elizabeth* had 24 cages but they never had been all occupied with dogs. "The most we ever carried was 23 dogs, a skunk and a shearwater," recalled Porter, "and the shearwater wasn't a paid passenger." The *Elizabeth* was a day out of New York when the bird crashed into the rigging and fell to the deck. "When I went to pick it up," said Porter, "it pierced my middle finger with its beak." Now I'd never been bitten by a dog but I was by a bird." He kept the shearwater in a cage for a day and then released it. "But I was taking no chances," said he, "I wore heavy gloves."

Reviving a Breed

In the frozen tundra of northern Canada, in the land of the polar lights, the value of the Eskimo dog has been known for centuries. And if William J. Carpenter has anything to say about it, the *Canis Familiaris Borealis,* or Kingmik as he is known to the Inuit (Eskimo) people, will be appreciated on a much wider scale. "In 1972, when I started the project of saving the Eskimo dog from extinction," the 35-year-old red-haired Canadian told me in 1976, "things looked pretty bleak. The Canadian Kennel Club, which had recognized the Eskimo as a breed 85 years ago, hadn't registered one since 1966. The AKC, because of lack of interest, had discontinued listing in 1959."

Carpenter, a biologist, had moved to Yellowknife, capital of the Northwest Territories, in 1971, while working for the territorial government. "My first observation," he told me, "was the precipitous decline in the number of sled dogs in many of the Inuit settlements. Dogs were being replaced by snowmobiles and the purebred Eskimo had been severely affected by the introduction of various cross-bred sled dogs." The next year, Carpenter met John McGrath, then Economic Development Officer for the Government, and very shortly the two embarked on the project. "We began to buy dogs through friends in widespread locations, sight unseen," said the scientist. "We had the dogs sent to Yellowknife, where I had built a kennel. The results were disastrous. All we received were cross-breds." Carpenter then decided on a new tack. He checked with the CKC and tracked down fanciers, who had been Eskimo owners. But they all told him they no longer had any.

"In the fall of 1974, we hit pay dirt," said the Canadian. "Fred Nagel, a friend in Yellowknife, while working on some electrical contracts in remote communities on the Arctic coast, found a purebred white male and a gray bitch. Then Dave Turner, who had lived in the Chantry Inlet area, south of Spence Bay, for 35 years, came up with a few purebreds and they were flown to me."

The Inummarit Cultural Society of the Baffin Region also produced some dogs from near the Melville Peninsula. "They were excellent specimens," recalled Carpenter, "and formed the foundation stock for the project. An Inuit, Idlout, who lived in an isolated part of the world, 100 miles from Resolute Bay, far north of the Arctic Circle, traveled to Resolute by dog team to offer me one of his best bitches."

When I met Carpenter at the Montreal show in 1976, he had a big white Eskimo with him and two puppies. It was the first time any of the dogs had been under a roof. They attracted much attention. This dedicated and articulate man told me how he had resigned from his government job, so he could devote full time to his project. "I spent $6,000 of my own money, purchasing the dogs and feeding them," he said. "However, I then had the good fortune to receive a $6,600 Canadian Council grant, and $10,000 from the Northwest Territories Government toward traveling expenses and purchasing additional Eskimo dogs from the Inuits." He stressed the dogs would be given away and not sold. A number would go to fanciers selected by the CKC to insure continued breeding of pedigreed animals. The rest would remain in the north, with some of the dogs being sent to remote camps, settlements or cultural societies, where they were needed.

The Eskimo, long used as a draft animal, has developed a powerful body with a thick neck, broad chest and heavy coat. The male weighs from 65-to-85 pounds and measures up to 28 inches at the shoulders. The ears are carried erect. The paws are large, with thick pads, so the dogs can haul heavy loads for miles over rough ice and crusted snow, without getting footsore. The outer coat runs from three to six inches in length, with a dense one to two inch undercoat. Colors range through white, wolf gray, blue gray, black on white, and all shades of tan or buff. The animal has unusual strength.

"I've been on a 400-mile expedition with a team of seven dogs and we did from 50-to-70 miles a day, hauling 600 pounds," said Carpenter. "The dogs are almost totally carnivorous and eat four pounds of walrus, seal meat or fish a day. I've seen a dog devour a four-and-a-half pound codfish in two minutes. They don't seem to be able to handle carbohydrates and do not have the ability to digest commercial dry meal. The period of gestation is longer than normal— from 64-to-70 days—and the puppies develop very quickly. Their eyes open on the seventh day. When they are two-and-a-half or three-weeks old, they are weaned on fish or meat, since they refuse puppy chow. They develop much faster than the ordinary dog. In size and weight the pup is fully mature by the time it is seven or eight months old and can work in harness on a team. Bitches come into heat as young as five months old."

I wrote a story that appeared in *The New York Times,* telling about the project and how the Eskimo Dog Society of the Northwest Territories had been organized with McGrath as president. I told how Carpenter at that time had 45 Eskimo dogs at the kennel. However, only nine were bitches and five had been bred. He was having so many problems raising funds, I wrote that readers could send $5 and become full members of the society, or $1 and be associate or junior, with all money going to the project.

It was gratifying when I received a letter from him saying they had more than 300 requests for membership and another 1,000 letters seeking information.

When I phoned the Canadian early in 1978, he said he now had 90 Eskimos, including 20 bitches. "Every dog must be part of a working team, if it is going to be used in the breeding program," he said. "We now have two generations of our breeding and in the Fall the pups will be three generations. Then McGrath and I will present the stud book to the CKC."

Carpenter told of a nine-month youth project, Katimavik (Inuit for Meeting Place), sponsored by the Government, aimed at providing learning by doing. "Ten youths have been assigned to our project," he said. "In addition to the kennel work, they fish to provide food for the dogs, and after brushing the Eskimos, collect the hair so it can be spun. I now have more time for my administrative and research duties. My biggest problem is raising funds."

The scientist told of how he already had presented ten of the dogs, as working stock, to a newly established Inuit outpost on the Arctic coast, southeast of Cambridge Bay. "These camps are being set up under a Government program to promote that life style for Inuits, who choose to return to their former land-oriented society," he explained.

Mrs. Herbert Hoover with the Norwegian Elkhound, Ronnie av Glitre.

Advancing a Breed

Another Northern breed dog I, indirectly, helped bring to the fore was the Norwegian Elkhound. In the late 1920s, Oliver Holden, a copy editor on the foreign desk of *The New York Times*, asked me for a pass to Westminster, which I procured for him. But Holden watched none of the judging. Instead he spent the entire day wandering from bench to bench. A few days later, he told me he had come up with a breed that he felt had possibilities. At the time, the German Shepherd was enjoying great popularity. So Holden wanted a dog that resembled the Shepherd.

At Madison Square Garden, he met Amory Coolidge of the Kettle Cove Kennels and bought an Elkhound from him. He also imported a number from Johnny Aarflot of Norway. Now Holden decided if he could promote the breed sufficiently, he could leave journalism and make a living raising Elkhounds. He walked his dogs on Park Avenue and if questioned by a passer-by would extol the virtues of the breed. He also gave one to President Herbert Hoover and another to Commander C. E. Rosendahl, as a mascot for the dirigible, Akron. Soon the dogs were seen in newsreels and their pictures were in the papers. The President liked his Elkhound so much, he wanted another, so a phone call was placed from Washington to the *Times* for Holden. The *Times* operator rang the foreign desk, only to be told it was Oliver's day off. When the White House asked for his home telephone number, it promptly was informed it was against *Times* policy to give home numbers. "But this is the White House calling," said a harried press secretary. "This is for the President." Back snapped the answer, "I'll put you on hold, while I ask Mr. Holden if it is all right to give you his number." Needless to say, that gentleman agreed to speak to Mr. Hoover and soon a second Elkhound was dispatched to Washington.

Prior to addressing the Dog Fanciers' Club in New York, AKC president William F. Stifel (left) and vice-president William M. Schmick (right), share a pleasant story with Elsworth S. Howell, president of the Fanciers'. —*Spear.*

John A. Lafore, Jr., then president of the AKC, pictured outside the Chalfonte-Haddon Hall in Atlantic City, site of the first "A Day with the AKC" symposium in 1973. The symposium was quite a success and set the pattern for others throughout the country. The Chalfonte also went on to some success of its own - it became the site of the first gambling casino in the resort.

The Governing Bodies

A TALL, SLENDER, graying man, who smiles easily, in March 1978 became the most powerful individual in the dog show picture in this country when he was elected president of the American Kennel Club. But don't be deceived by the ready smile, for William F. Stifel is a man of determination, who brooks no nonsense. And, few, if any, of his predecessors had as much training or background with the AKC.

Bill, as he is known to his associates, had two decades behind him before he was elected to the top post and during that time learned every phase of the operation. Stifel, a serious man, is a good listener. He seeks ideas from his colleagues and gives credit rather than taking it himself. Until the year before he was elevated, Stifel wasn't known too well among the fanciers. His days were spent at 51 Madison Avenue, in the AKC offices. But then this soft-spoken man, who dresses conservatively, started to attend the major shows. He also was a member of the management team and a speaker at the AKC symposiums that were held around the country.

The son of a doctor, who for years served as chief of staff of a hospital in Toledo, Ohio, Stifel was a member of the class of 1944 at Harvard. But World War II intervened and he joined the Coast Guard. Following the cessation of hostilities, Bill studied abroad, majoring in Russian and French. Returning to New York, he became a free-lance writer. There he met Carolyn Graham, who had her master's degree in educational administration. Now free-lance writing is a rather hazardous living, so in 1957 Bill took a part-time job with the AKC in the show-plans department. A few weeks later, Stifel was offered a full-time post. He accepted and the next year the couple was married. He rose steadily in the organization, becoming supervisor of show plans and records, then executive secretary in 1964 and in March 1976, executive vice president.

The Stifels, who live in Irvington on Hudson, a Westchester suburb of New York, have two daughters. They also have a Scottie and a cat. There is a sincerity, decency and integrity about Bill and Carolyn. You get the feeling the AKC is in good hands. Determined and honest, Bill is steering the right course for the staff of more than 400 that oversees 9,000 dog events and approves 12,000 judging assignments.

Stifel's predecessor, John A. Lafore, Jr., is very different in personality. Whereas Bill is on the quiet side, Jack is very much an extrovert, "the life of the party." Lafore, who continues active as a member of the AKC Board, tells an amusing story about his introduction to his successor. "Twenty years ago," said he, "I had an appointment to meet for the first time a young executive at the AKC. I arrived on time, only to be kept waiting some 25 mintues before Bill Stifel showed up, breathless, rushing to keep his appointment with me. Bill apologized for being late and explained he was delayed because his Scottie puppy had chewed up his shoes. On that auspicious note began my long and valued association with William F. Stifel."

An alumnus of Swarthmore and the University of Pennsylvania, Lafore was in the Pennsylvania legislature for four terms. Then, in 1957, he was elected to Congress, where he served two terms. Defeated in the primary of 1961, Jack returned to private life and became president of an aircraft firm for five years. His next move was to a big Philadelphia engineering company as financial vice president, which he left to become executive vice president of the AKC. Lafore had become affiliated with the AKC 16 years earlier, as a delegate from the Devon Dog Show Association and in 1963 was elected a director. After three years as executive VP, Lafore was chosen as the 13th president.

Under Lafore the image of the club was to change radically, and for the better. Whereas in the past, under Alfred M. Dick, who ruled with an iron fist, it had been a one-man operation, with the AKC a distant and remote leader, out of touch with the day-to-day problems, now the door was thrown open. The public was invited to visit 51 Madison Avenue. There was much more effective communication between the fancy and the ruling body. Films were produced and made available to the clubs. Meetings were held all over the country and Lafore made a point of going to the major shows. "Today's leadership must be aware of more response to the concerns of the fancy," stressed Lafore. "There is no substitute for communication between people who have a common interest."

Jack and his wife Peg were longtime breeders and exhibitors of Collies and Keeshonds. "We started to show in the 1950s," he told me, "and suddenly we found we had a lot of Collies. At one time we had as many as 123. Someone asked me, 'Do you breed them?' I replied, 'Of course we breed them, but the trouble is we don't sell them!'" In 1956, the Lafores acquired a couple of Kees and that breed became their chief interest until Jack joined the AKC in 1968, and they stopped showing. "We had finished 22 champions," he recalled. They kept their home in Haverford, Pa., and Jack commuted five days a week. "I'd get up at 5 A.M., catch the 6:06 from Haverford to Philadelphia, and the 6:50 to New York," he told me. "I'd be on the 5:30 from New York and be home at 8 o'clock. The commuting didn't bother me at all. I had a chance to read the newspapers, catch up on some paper work and sleep."

Three months after Lafore became president, a full-time paid job, a new position was created, chairman of the board, which was unpaid, and Alexander

Feldman, who had been AKC treasurer, was moved up to it. "Having a chairman of the board is in line with modern corporate structure," Jack told me. "The organization has grown to such an extent, I feel we have taken a great step forward in establishing the new office."

The chairman had a rich, varied background—a lawyer, a successful business man (he gave up his law practice to take over the family business of wholesale news distribution when his father died) and a devotion to the sport of dogs. He and his wife, Poppy, have had Great Danes for four decades. In their Glen Cove, L.I., home are many beautiful bronzes, paintings and a doll collection of Poppy's. Al's affiliation with the AKC started in the fifties, as a delegate for the Great Dane Club of America. Later, he was the Saw Mill River Club's delegate and he became president of the Dane club, whereupon he stopped showing. When he was elected an AKC director in 1964, Poppy practically stopped showing, taking only one bitch through the classes. She gave it up entirely, when her husband was named chairman.

Feldman devoted many hours to help make the AKC more responsive to the fancy, to bring it out of an ivory tower. I always had a good relationship with him and knew if I phoned, and he was there, I'd get a clear and immediate answer to my queries. "The sport of dogs no longer is for a few but for everyone now," he said, upon his retirement from the board. "We have no caste system. Your friends represent every phase of society. So the sport today has a meaning and is a benefit to more people and so must the AKC." In 1977, Al stepped down as chairman and was replaced by August Belmont, whose grandfather had served as the organization's president from 1888 to 1916. Belmont served two years, and was followed by the chairman at this writing, Haworth F. Hoch.

Said Feldman: "I think the greatest achievement of my administration has been that women were approved as delegates for the first time in AKC history. I had hoped that I would see a woman on the board, provided she had the qualifications and not just because she was a woman. But that is another area and will take more time." Now Al is judging Great Danes, something he always wanted to do.

A precedent was set when Al Dick became president in 1968, for he was the first paid chief executive. The top man not only was greatly feared by the fancy but also by his colleagues. He ran an extremely tight ship. Al had a violent temper and at least on one occasion shattered the glass top on his desk. A chain cigarette smoker, he also favored cigars and a cloud of smoke hovered over his desk. However, even with his explosive temper, members of his staff always said, although he really would chew them out, he held no grudges. A dedicated man, Dick had little patience for stuffed shirts. He wanted to get the job done quickly and efficiently. He had the reputation of being a man who did not like to relegate authority, preferring to try to do everything himself.

Club officials trembled when he appeared at their shows. I remember Trenton when that fixture moved to Washington Crossing State Park the first time. Here was where the Continental Army had crossed the Delaware to defeat the Hessians at Trenton on December 26, 1776. It was almost two centuries later when an army of motorized fanciers clogged the highways leading to the park and it made much slower progress than Washington's foot soldiers. There was only one entrance to the grounds and traffic was backed up for four miles. And in one of those cars was Mr. Dick. It took him 45 minutes to cover the last mile. "Where's Wood?" (Dr. Armour Wood, the club president), the red-faced AKC chief roared, when he finally arrived. "Worst mess I've ever seen." Needless to say, the next year there were five entrances, two reserved for exhibitors and their dogs, and a map depicting the location of the rings and parking area was sent to each exhibitor.

Mr. Dick, a Dachshund fancier, had been a president of the Kennel Club of Philadelphia and did much to make its show a major attraction. He came to the AKC as a delegate from the Dachshund Club of America and in 1947 was appointed a field representative. In that capacity, he met hundreds of club officials as he traveled from coast to coast.

The first president of the AKC whom I knew was Dr. John deMund, actually the organization's seventh chief executive. The physician, a Borzoi breeder and a judge, brought the AKC through the depression years, resigning in 1932 because of poor health. He did much to build the club and was associated with it from 1909, being one of the 27 members when the organization was incorporated.

The doctor's successor, Charles T. Inglee, was president only a few months, since there was a complete reorganization with the post of executive vice president created, which was a full time paid position. Inglee, born in Brooklyn, where he had been a successful realtor, told me that he had become interested in dogs during a period of ill health when he was a teenager. To build him up, the family moved to the country and he did quite a bit of hunting. "I had Irish Setters, Foxhounds and Beagles," he remembered. "The first dog I ever showed was an English Setter at Brooklyn's Clermont Rink." But the breed with which he has always been associated is the Gordon Setter. Indeed, he was called the "father" of the American Gordon. His Inglehurst Kennel sent out many top black and tans. In 1921, he organized the Gordon Setter Club of America and became its delegate to the AKC. Seven years later, he was elected vice president of the national body.

Russell H. Johnson, a Philadelphian, took over as president in 1933. He had come to the AKC as a delegate from the Wissahickon KC in 1905. His Bolton Kennels were famous for Airedales and Wire Fox Terriers. An authority on Terriers, he did much judging. Johnson was fond of saying, "I've been a dog fancier since I was four years old, when I had my first dog," which was a bit of an exaggeration. The Philadelphian would come to New York to run the delegates' and directors' meetings, with Inglee handling the day-to-day work. Johnson died suddenly, in 1940, and a special meeting of the board was called to elect a successor.

Dudley P. Rogers assumed the helm, a position he was to hold for 11 years. It was a new dynasty, for he chose Henry D. Bixby as his executive vice president. Rogers was a Sealyham Terrier breeder, the owner of the Brecknock Kennel. He was active in club work, not only in dogs but also in polo. It was as the Eastern Dog Club's delegate that the Massachusetts fancier made his AKC appearance and he promptly was chosen a member of the board. During the Rogers-Bixby regime, registrations tripled and the number of dog shows and field trials doubled. In 1951, the top duo threw a bombshell into the organization, announcing neither one would stand for re-election.

In came the team of William E. Buckley, a corporation lawyer from Huntingdon, L.I., as chief executive, a post he was to hold until 1968; John C. Neff, executive vice president, and Al Dick, executive secretary. Neff and Dick were both fulltime paid administrators, Buckley receiving no remuneration.

Buckley had arrived at the AKC in 1944, as the Westbury delegate. He was a Terrier man from 'way back. "As long as I can remember, I had an Airedale," he told me. So it was no surprise he eventually became president of the Airedale Terrier Club of America. He was also head of the Suffolk County club. His Marbuck Kennels was known for its good Airedales, although he always maintained its success was due more to his wife's efforts than his own. The Buckleys also bred Wire Fox Terriers, Kerry Blues and Scotties.

I remember an AKC party for a nine-month-old Golden Retriever, Eddie's Ginger, who although she never was shown became one of the most celebrated pups in purebred dog history. For she was the 10-millionth dog to be registered in the AKC stud book. Said Buckley, who presented a framed certificate to the Golden's owner, an 11-year-old boy, Edwin L. Miller 3d of Pawling, N.Y., "It took 57 years to reach our first million and 15 years for the second. In 1965 alone we had three-quarters of a million. Based on the present trend, we will soon be registering one million annually." That goal was reached four years later in 1970. It was a far cry from 1927, the year I started in the field, when the AKC registered 57,598.

The AKC president insisted that his executive staff attend shows on weekends. "Some of them didn't even know the breeds," he complained. Buckley judged just once, doing Airedales at Westbury. "That's the first and last time," said the lawyer, and although he was on the books as a judge until his death, he never took another assignment.

Neff had a remarkable career with the AKC. An Irish Setter breeder, he became a delegate in 1942 and although he retired in 1977, he was still a delegate. Elected a director in 1942, he served in that capacity for 32 years. As executive vice president, Neff started a pension plan, revised the stud book and the registration procedure, began microfilming important records and instigated the move from Park Avenue South to Madison Avenue.

A Degree in AKC

Dr. Adrian Tiemann professionaly is a sociologist. In the dog show world, she is known as a Shetland Sheepdog breeder and a working-breed judge. She is unique in that she obtained her doctorate at the State University of New York, in Albany, by writing her thesis on the American Kennel Club.

Dr. Tiemann pointed out that the AKC is voluntary and regulatory . . . it represents a new institutional area—purebred dogs . . . it arose from various social movements, such as animal husbandry, animal and child welfare, eugenics and leisure life styles . . . it represents a successful endeavor in that it has persisted, changed in response to changing conditions, done a good job of regulating dog breeding and show activities, and yet has managed to retain its original image—thus it provides grist for the mill of organizational theory . . . it demonstrates how man's need to develop ''social realities'' become adapted to particular areas under particular social needs.

The sociologist said ''the dog world began as an upper class interest but quickly became less than upper class. Because the AKC was a regulatory body, it supervised the activities of fanciers in particular ways while explicating its purpose and rationale for such regulation. It brought people from all walks of life together at dog shows and in clubs, where high status characteristics could be seen and copied by those less endowed.''

United Kennel Club

The second oldest and second largest all-breed dog registry in the United States is the UKC, based in Kalamazoo, Mich. It was founded in 1898 (14 years after the AKC) by Chauncey Z. Bennett, who was determined to establish a registry where in-breeding and line-breeding would be discouraged. Upon his death in 1936, his daughter, Frances Ruth, took over. She married Dr. E. G. Fuhrmann, who gave up his practice and joined the kennel club, in time becoming president. In 1973, the Fuhrmanns sold UKC to Fred T. Miller, who became president.

Although the club has an all-breed registry, with a half-dozen breeds not recognized by the AKC, more than half the dogs in the book are Coonhounds. Wheras the AKC lists only Black-and-Tan Coonhounds, the UKC also registers Bluetick, English, Plott, Redbone and Treeing Walker.

The Coonhounds are specialists in trailing game that takes to the trees. ''The sport of Coonhunting is widespread throughout the United States and Canada,'' Miller told me. ''We recognize 975 clubs located in 42 states and Canada, with 3,285 licensed events held annually.''

The licensed Coonhound events are Nite Hunts, in which the raccoon is tracked and treed. The first dog that gives voice, when he has found the trail, is awarded points, as is the first that trees the game. The killing or taking of the raccoon is not allowed under UKC rules. There are also bench shows, field trials and water races.

In the water races, six Coonhounds are in starting boxes, from 15 to 25 feet from the pond's edge. When they are released, they plunge into the water and pursue a cage in which there is a live raccoon. On a cable, it is suspended a couple of feet above the water and it is kept moving just ahead of the swimmers, then being drawn to a tree or post. The first hound to cross a line, as it emerges from the water, scores points, and the first to tree the caged raccoon and bark also gets points. If there are 36 or more dogs, each line and tree winner advances to the semi-finals and then to the final, earning additional points toward a championship.

A dog can become a titleholder in all four categories—nite hunt, bench, field trial and water. After the animal becomes a champion, it competes against other titleholders to work toward a Grand Champion degree. In 1978, something new was introduced, a tournament of champions, with a four-day final, the winner to be declared World Champion, with the designation World Ch. placed in front of its name.

In the early thirties, the UKC came up with the Purple Ribbon (PR), a designation much coveted by breeders. To earn such a rating a pup, when it is whelped, must have at least three generations of ancestors (14) registered with the UKC. The organization offers a certified six-generation pedigree (126 ancestors) and a seven-generation (254).

The American Field

The American Field, in Chicago, keeps a field dog stud book and is the leader in the bird dog phase of the sport. The American Field Publishing Company has been publishing the weekly, *American Field,* since 1874, the bible of the field trial and hunting set. "We opened a free kennel registry for all dogs in field sports on March 11, 1876," William F. Brown, the *American Field's* editor told me while we chatted in his office, on whose walls were oil paintings of national champions. "This was done to supplement the work of Arnold Burges in his book, *American Kennel and Sporting Field.* The first three volumes we gave to the American Kennel Club and this was the start of their stud book."

With the majority of dogs being registered with the AKC and that organization staging most of the dog shows, field trial sportsmen, who had been running dogs since 1874, felt they were being neglected. So in 1900, American Field established the Field Dog Stud Book (FDSB). Although it is an all-breed registry, the book specializes in the sporting breeds. It has on file records of two million pedigreed dogs. All the field records of a dog or bitch and the progeny are listed in the stud book. This is a boon to the breeder, since it gives complete information about performance and production.

More than 825 trials are held annually under the jurisdiction of the Amateur Field Trial Clubs of America and American Field. Unlike the AKC trials, where championships are awarded to a dog scoring 10 points, a FDSB title must be earned by winning a championship stake. "The criteria of a FDSB champion is quality, rather than quantity," Brown stressed. "We want the field dog to demonstrate his inherent instinct to hunt, accept and retain training and show speed, class and stamina. We are looking for a dog with the unquenchable desire to win and find birds. We advocate breeding dogs for their field qualities rather than just for conformation. Bird dogs, like race horses, run in all shapes and sizes.''

Some Other Organizations

Then there are: the International Dog Sled Racing Association; the American Sight Hound Field Association, with coursing and lure-racing trials; American Working Terrier Association, which encourages terrier owners into the field with their dogs; American Rescue Dog Association, volunteer search and rescue dog operatives; Working Dogs of America and North American Working Dog Association, schutzhund groups; the United States Professional Dog Trainers Association, which sponsors training; Owner Handler Association of America, which strives to teach the inexperienced owner how to handle his dog.

The universality of the sport of dogs is embodied in the Federation Cynologique Internationale (FCI), for it is represented on six continents. Although the United States isn't a member, or wasn't by the time I ended my career writing for *The New York Times,* 46 countries were enrolled, either as full or associate members of the organization, with headquarters in Thuin, Belgium. The FCI was founded on May 22, 1911, with Austria, Belgium, France, Germany and the Netherlands as charter members. Each year, a president and vice president are elected and the General Assembly is held in the president's homeland. There are mutual agreements on breed standards, stud books, recognition of judges, control and scheduling of shows, reciprocal agreements concerning disciplinary measures, and awarding of the CACIB (Certificate of Aptitude, Championship International, Beauty) and international titles.

All the organizations work to promote man's best friend, about whom Samuel Butler, the 19th century British novelist, wrote: *''The great pleasure of a dog is that you make a fool of yourself with him and not only will he not scold you, but he will make a fool of himself, too.''*

It Takes All Kinds

I N FEW SPORTS do the participants represent as wide a range of backgrounds and interests as do those of the dog game. Rich men, poor men, bakers, candlestick makers . . . shake down an exhibitors' list and any or all are apt to pop out.

In this chapter we've chosen to group some exhibitors and judges who share a similar interest away from the show rings. One group are all doctors, another are all educators. A third all have a ''show-biz'' background, and a fourth all fly. But even within these groups, we'll still find plenty of variety—variety in age, size, nationality and most especially—in choice of favorite breed.

Let's start with some who reach for the heights.

High Steppers

The biggest judge I have known is a Pennsylvania lawyer, Alvin Maurer. He is six feet seven inches tall and weighs 320 pounds. ''That's about 70 too much,'' he admitted. For years Derek Rayne, the Californian, insisted he was the tallest. One day the two stood back to back and the attorney from Minersville had the advantage.

It was hunting that started the big man on the show trail. He bought a German Shorthaired Pointer pup he would train to shoot over. One day Maurer drove to Philadelphia with his wife, who wanted to do some Christmas shopping. Rather than spend hours in department stores, Maurer went to his first dog show, the Philadelphia. ''I watched the Shorthairs and decided my pup was as good as any of the others,'' he recalled.

So at Harrisburg, he entered the dog in a puppy class and left with the blue. ''That did it. I was hooked,'' said he. ''But I was pretty much of a loss as a handler and the poor pup lost many times when he shouldn't have. One day Tom Crowe, then a handler, in exasperation said, 'Come here, I want to show you how to set up your dog.' He gave me a lesson I'll never forget and it paid off, for my dog became a champion.''

Living in the center of town, Maurer never could do much breeding, but his

Shorthair did have four litters. "The last dog I finished was in 1968 at Boardwalk," he said. "Two years earlier I had received my judging license and I was beginning to get more breeds and assignments. Now all I have is one Miniature Pinscher, a house pet. I enjoy judging; it's an absorbing hobby. You view the dogs entirely differently from when you show."

James Vaughters is a big, soft-spoken man but he speaks and acts with authority both in and out of the ring. For the imposing six-foot-three-inch judge was a police lieutenant for almost two decades in Memphis. He was the dominating force behind the Centennial show in the Tennessee city on the Mississippi in 1974.

Vaughters for many years owned Boston Terriers and Bulldogs. "I never showed the Bostons, just kept them as pets," he said.

A judge since 1967, I watched him do his first assignment at a BCA specialty on Long Island. He drew 140 entries, such confidence did bulldoggers have in his judgment. Not that judging was anything new for him, for Big Jim had been ruling on pigeons for a quarter of a century.

Five days a week, David C. Merriam presides over a San Bernardino County Municipal Court in Ontario, Calif., where he is a judge. On weekends, when he isn't showing, Dave, who is six-feet-four, is towering over a ring in various parts of the country as a judge of dogs.

"I've had my license to judge since 1966. That was the same year I was graduated from law school and admitted to the California bar," said the jurist. "I find a great similarity when I'm a judge. At a show, a dog is brought into the ring and I weigh the physical evidence, evaluating the animal with the breed standard. In criminal law, should John Doe be accused of committing burglary, the evidence is presented in court and is then compared with the legal standard."

In 1979 Merriam was appointed to the AKC's Board of Directors, the youngest of the Board's 12 members.

The judge has a long background in Bull Terriers. He received his first when he was 14 years old. "Mars Gigi, a white bitch, was only four months old when she was given to me," he recalled. "Six months later, I showed her at the Golden State specialty in Los Angeles and she was best of breed in the largest Bull Terrier show held that year."

College, law school and a short hitch in the Army kept Merriam away from the show rings but he did some breeding and was active in club work. After graduating from law school, he went abroad. In England, Dave met Raymond Oppenheimer, that country's Mr. Bull Terrier. "I acquired a bitch in whelp of Oppenheimer's breeding," said the Californian. "That was the start of my Broadside Kennel and I have done reasonably well over the years with homebreds and imports. We have developed very good heads over the last two decades, but both the white and colored are having problems with undershot jaws. Overall, the breed is much better than when I started."

High on the Bull Terrier. Left, Dr. E. S. Montgomery and his homebred best-in-show winner of the early '60s, Ch. Dancing Master of Monty-Ayr. Right, David C. Merriam, a judge in the California courts as well as in Terrier rings, with his Ch. Goldfinger, also a '60s standout.

However, he really surprised me when I asked if he preferred judging to showing, since he ruled for the latter. "If the AKC ever declared breeders no longer could judge, I'd be saddened to give up judging but I wouldn't hesitate for a minute. One can do far more creative work in breeding and exhibiting. I feel judging makes one a better breeder and exhibitor. It makes one more cognizant of what has to be achieved in a breeding program."

The Waldorf Towers was the site for one of my most unusual interviews. Dr. Edward S. Montgomery was in New York to deliver a luncheon speech. By appointment I arrived at the hotel at 8:45 A.M. Mrs. Montgomery greeted me, saying, "Edward is still in the shower, won't you join me for a cup of coffee?" Suddenly from the next room the physician appeared. Now the good doctor is an imposing figure, in or out of the ring. He is six-feet-four-inches tall and in those days weighed 350 pounds. But I must confess, I was taken aback. For there he stood, stark naked except for a towel draped around his middle, and wearing a straw hat. Absolutely at ease, he assured me he would be ready in a few minutes. "Edward always wears a hat when he steps out of the shower," explained Mrs. Montgomery, "to try and flatten his curly hair."

Curly or flat, the physician has been known for years as "Mr. Bull Terrier." He told me, "I've been a Bull Terrier aficionado since I was five years old, when I found a bedraggled white pup that was lost and brought it home." That led to Dr. Montgomery, at one time, having the largest Bull Terrier kennel in the country, with 60 dogs. In the forties, fifties and sixties his Bull Terriers made show history.

During his career, the physician owned 20 other Terrier breeds. But it was the Bull Terrier which was his greatest love. And the doctor was very much like the gladiator of the dog world. Both as an exhibitor and judge, he was a controversial figure. When I asked him to evaluate the various Terrier breeds, he pulled no punches, using such phrases as "in a period of distress" . . . "Must have a firm hand or the breed will fall into disrepute because of unsoundness of conformation and movement" . . . "oversize, rubbery legs and poor rear quarters are plaguing this breed." My columns on him evoked more letters of protest and indignation than any I ever wrote.

Unlike so many judges who can do nothing but talk dogs, the physician was a well-rounded man with an avid interest in the theater, a love for horses and he was an astute cattle breeder. He always paid his own expenses when he was judging and any fee he received went to a charity.

Strongly opinionated, the doctor could be relied upon to stir up a commotion when he talked. And he wasn't one to talk off the record, so when he delivered a speech, there was always a good turnout.

"Lack of training for judges is one of the serious ailments affecting dog shows," he told an audience at a Dog Fanciers Club luncheon. "The increase in the number of shows has created a problem, for it necessitates the use of inadequately trained and inexperienced judges. The older hierarchy is not being replaced." He deplored judges' lack of knowledge of what is proper movement in the breeds. "This lack of emphasis of the dog in motion," he complained, "is rapidly deteriorating a half-dozen breeds into unsound entities. It is only in motion that the true anatomical structure of an animal can be observed. In motion the conformation faults cannot be concealed by clever handling."

Regarding breeding programs, he maintained there has been too much emphasis on the new champion, without thought of the genetic makeup or improvement of the breed. Long a champion of the breeder, he urged that the bred-by-exhibitor class should be made a major event at shows. "Trophies and ribbons should go not only to the owner but also to the breeder of a dog that achieves such top places as winners, reserve winners and best of opposite sex," he maintained.

When I asked the physician what he considered the greatest danger to the sport, he promptly replied, and with no uncertainty, "There is the all-too prevalent symptom of the sickness that is becoming an international malady—the emphasis on winning." In the 1970s, Montgomery pretty much dropped out of the dog show picture. He long since has stopped showing and only on rare occasions does some judging. It is unfortunate for he was so knowledgeable and one of our better arbiters.

Don Coss is a retired major in the Air Force. For the last eight years of the 22 he spent in the service, the big man—he stands six-feet-two-inches and weighs 270 pounds—was engaged in earth-satellite tracking. But now he is very much down to earth in Colorado dog show circles, where he is engaged in all phases of the sport—breeding, exhibiting, judging and club work. Perhaps because of his size, Coss likes big dogs. That's the reason he turned from Boxers to St. Bernards.

The Air Force played a major role in the major's show career. In 1960, he was stationed at Moses Lake Wash., and a new kennel club had been organized there. "We had just bought a Boxer pup," he recalled, "so we joined."

The next year the major was moved to Wichita Falls, Tex., to train for the missile program. There he went to his first dog show and soon had his Boxer in the ring. "We did a little breeding and exhibiting but realized we weren't doing too well with our Boxers," said Coss, "so in 1964, when I was transferred to the Strategic Air Command headquarters at Omaha, my wife, Pauline, suggested we switch to Saints." It proved a good move. Buying three brood bitches, they finished two, not showing the third. Indeed, they made champions of four of their first five Saints. At the South Colorado Club show in 1976, Bonney's Legacy, a fourth generation Coss Saint, became their 10th champion. The 170-pound red, orange and white was shown by Pauline, who is five feet two and weighs 115 pounds.

Coss, who judges a half-dozen Working breeds, insists on a well-balanced dog "that can move well, fore-and-aft." Two of their Saints, Mrs. Coss has obedience trained and they have their CDs. "The Saint is a very individual dog," said Don. "He is going to work at his own speed and there's nothing you can do about it. Pauline took Hickory Knolls Eleasah to a CD when she was only 10 months old. Then I showed her in the breed ring and she had her championship six months later."

The Colorado couple joined the Flatirons Club in Boulder in 1971. "Our club is very community-minded," said the major. "We give obedience and breed-handling exhibitions in the schools, work with the 4-H clubs, consult with the city commissioner on animal control and meet with the sheriff, so we can discuss dog problems and hear both sides. We also donate to a spaying and neutering clinic, where there is a very nominal charge, or if the owner cannot afford to pay, it is free."

In addition to the Saints, the Cosses have a Yorkie, Scottie, Smooth Fox Terrier and a white Bull Terrier, who are the house dogs. Their 17 Saints are in the kennel. "They all get along very well," said Don, "with the 5-pound Yorkie keeping them in line."

High Flyers

A former Navy pilot, who flew missions over Iwo Jima and Truk in World War II, now is flying all over this country on a more pleasant assignment— judging dogs. He's Jim Frank of El Cajon, Calif., and he's engaged in almost every phase of the sport. As a breeder, he had success with Boston Terriers. As a clubman, he's been president of Silver Bay for more than a decade. Then Frank has been an ardent hunter since boyhood. "As a kid, I'd go after rabbits," he said. "Later, when I had Labs and Springers, I'd hunt pheasants, quail, duck and geese."

It was in the mid-fifties that Jim and his wife bought a Boston. Like so many first purchases, she didn't fare too well. "We then went out and bought a good one," he recalled. "She was Hey Look Me Over and that's what she told the judges. She finished quickly. I'm an electrical contractor and developer and busy all week. I found showing dogs relaxing. It enabled me to get away from a busy work schedule."

The Franks never were big breeders and had only a few champions. When he began to accept judging assignments, Jim decided it was time to stop showing. As an arbiter, he's been busy not only in this country but south of the border, for he's ruled in Mexican rings five times. "It's a thrill to find a good animal, for then you feel you really are helping to improve the breed," he observed. "And that's what the sport is all about."

"It's getting increasingly difficult to find a place to hold a show," Frank complained, "but we are lucky." And lucky they are, for Silver Bay is held in Balboa Park, San Diego's pride. Right in the heart of the city, exhibitors can run over to the zoo and even see a performance of Shakespeare. Vera and I had the good fortune to watch a dress rehearsal.

Joe Tacker is a man accustomed to making split-second decisions. For a quarter of a century, he's been at the controls of planes, flying passengers on the inter-islands run in Hawaii. For the handsome man with the far-off look is a captain with Hawaiian Airlines. Indeed, he's the senior airman and serves as a check pilot for the other captains. When he is not at the controls of a plane, the pilot is likely to be in control of a dog show ring, since he's in great demand as an arbiter and he's had assignments at all the big ones.

Tacker had a rather incongruous start in the dog world. "I was at the Naval air base in Pensacola (Fla.) in 1951," he recalled, "and bought a red-and-white Cocker Spaniel bitch. She probably set a record for reserve ribbons. Never won a point. But the next year I came up with Grymesby Dapple Dawn. She became a champion and was the foundation bitch for my Tackertown Kennel in Hawaii. I bred three or four champions but there were coat problems because of the warm climate, so in 1958 I turned to Boxers. Because there were so few shows in Hawaii, in addition to a quarantine, it was difficult to get points. Not a Boxer finished there from 1952 till 1962." Later the pilot acquired some English Setters and in the 1960s added Norwich Terriers. His Jericho Dirk and Jericho Sparkle were two of the top-winning Norwich in America in 1967 and 1968.

Tacker attributes much of his success as a dog show judge to the fact that he did a lot of riding, being particularly interested in dressage. "In dressage, one has to analyze a horse's movements," said Tacker. "I've been able to transfer that knowledge when I watch a dog gait."

In Hawaii, the pilot had the advantage of handling a great many breeds. "We were all amateurs and some would get stage fright when they were supposed to take a dog into the ring. I probably handled 30 breeds for friends. It was a tremendous experience for I learned a great deal. I prefer the judging to the showing. It's a challenge to study what you see and then make your choice."

A little seven-year-old girl, with a "near Sheltie," made her debut in the dog show world at St. Petersburg, Fla., and a spectacular one it was. For she swept the boards, taking three first places—best trick dog, best groomed and the best-informed owner. "That was my start, and it's pretty hard to top it," said Michele Leathers Billings, better known as Mike, who went on to gain fame as an exhibitor, club official, handler and finally judge. "Dogs always have played a part in my life. My father had English Springers, Foxhounds and Beagles. As you can gather, he was a sportsman and would hunt everything from rabbits to bears."

Mike really started in 1950, when she bought a German Shepherd dog and bitch. But it was Beagles that brought the Floridian to the fore. From 1954 until 1969, her Kings Creek kennel turned out more than 60 champions. One Beagle, King's Creek Triple Threat, whom she sold to Tom and Marcia Foy, made history for the breed. Trippi was best Beagle 396 times, more than any dog of any breed; had eight top awards, 84 blue rosettes, 261 other placements and in 1976, had sired 47 champions.

Two prominent figures of the fancy — Bob Forsyth, ace professional handler, and Bill Kendrick, veteran all-rounder judge—spot something that tickles them. — *Spear*

Another prominent veteran of the show scene, Porter Washington, with Ch. Flakkee Instant Replay, one of the more recent of his kennel's long string of best-in-show Keeshonds.

Mike has always been a high flier and she came by it naturally. Her father owned a chain of flying services in Florida and she was actually piloting a plane when she was 14. But she had both feet on the ground as she grew up.

From 1950 until 1962, she was in the political picture in Georgia, serving as secretary to Ben W. Fortson, Jr., the Secretary of State. On weekends, she would take to the dog circuit, showing first Shepherds and then Beagles. Mrs. Billings helped to organize the German Shepherd Dog Club of Atlanta and was its first president. She was also secretary of the Atlanta KC. At the show ring, she frequently would take a friend's dog in for the judging. "I enjoyed the competition so much, I decided to give up my secretarial position and to become a professional handler."

In 1962, Mike received a license and demonstrated so much skill that twice she was nominated for an award as best woman handler of the year. Ten years later, she turned in her handler's license and became a judge. "Since I no longer own any dogs, it is a great thrill being able to judge those of others. I feel I'm still very much a part of the sport," she told me.

Bob Wilson is a busy judge. He flies all over the country making decisions. As a matter of fact, he does far more flying than other arbiters for he's a captain with American Airlines and pilots the big planes on transcontinental runs. During World War II, Wilson flew 55 missions in the Pacific. I interviewed him just before he went into the ring at a Longshore-Southport show years ago, when he was showing St. Bernards. Bob was chain-smoking and more than a little tense. "I still get butterflies when I walk into a ring," he confessed. "It's much easier flying a jet."

He recalled when he started to show dogs in the early 1960s. "I had a good bitch, Mardonhof's Stormy Mortgage, and I was living on Long Island at the time. There were so few Saints in the area that when Stormy had 14 points, I had to go to four shows with her, so she could finish. It wasn't that she didn't win but there weren't enough to get a single point."

Bob was the first president of the St. Bernard Club of Greater New York, organized in 1967, and he made a great drive for members. "We managed to get 135, and then I pushed them into showing puppies. I explained it would give them both experience and they would have a better chance of gaining a championship, once the pup had matured, two or three years later."

When there was an earlier severe fuel shortage in this country, Wilson was flying a run to Mexico. South of the border, the planes would take on as much fuel as possible. "I had a big plane, and was on the runway at Mexico City, ready to take off," said Wilson. "We had a large passenger list and with all the fuel, we needed most of the runway to be skyborne. Just as we were rolling down, I saw a German Shepherd slowly trotting toward the plane. I had a split second to make a decision. Should I continue, and kill the animal, or should I slam on the brakes and delay my passengers. I chose the latter but with the extra weight of the fuel, it was like stopping a freight train. I just managed to stop before hitting him. He looked up at me defiantly and then trotted away. I couldn't help but size him up with a judge's eye and he had poor hindquarters. I apologized to my passengers and told them the cause of the delay. At least a half dozen, when they were disembarking at Dallas, came forward to thank me for what I had done.''

Showing dogs is one activity in which the family can, and often does, participate. Take the Brewsters. Since Joy and Sari were tiny tots, they and their mother, Mary, have been around rings. Mary's initiation to the sport was quite accidental. She was at a dog show in Salt Lake City and someone asked her to walk a Dalmatian into a ring, an experience that led to nearly a half-century of breeding, exhibiting and judging.

But it wasn't the coach dog that was to be this high-flying woman's first breed. She had English Springers and Great Pyrenees. Later she owned dogs in all the groups, except Terrier. Her Robwood Kennels, which go back to the 1940s, sent out many top breed winners before she retired from showing and breeding in the sixties. As to her high-flying, Mrs. Brewster was an instructor for the Civil Air Patrol and flew all over the world. ''I had a pet Pomeranian, whom I would take into the cockpit,'' she admitted. After the war, Mary came down to earth, had a TV program, ''Tailwaggers,'' in Washington, D.C., and received her law degree from George Washington University. Now she has a few Chin and Standard Poodles as housepets and spends her weekends judging. In between, Mary researches champion pedigrees for dog clubs.

Joy started in 1955, working at shows for Anne Hone Rogers, now Mrs. James Clark. Later, while working as an executive secretary during the week, she ran Anne's kennel on weekends. In 1965, Joy bought her own kennel property in Newtown, Conn., and received her handler's license. And why did she choose handling as a profession? ''Handling always was my goal,'' she responded. ''I knew dogs, had shown and conditioned them and managed a kennel.'' When I asked what she regards as her greatest achievement in handling, she responded, ''I guess my biggest thrill has been the success of Pinto (Ch. Funfair's Pinto O Joe Dandy, a Pomeranian, who finished by going best in show from the classes). Not merely because I have handled him, but I co-bred him.''

As a breeder, Sari Brewster Tietjen believes her greatest success was in establishing four generations of group-placing Japanese Chin, a breed seldom considered in the groups. It was the ''horses,'' who paid for her start with the Chin. ''I went to England and bought two dogs from the Rui Gu Kennels. They became my foundation studs. I paid for them with money I won betting on the 'horse races' held aboard ship, on the way.''

But her goal always was to become a judge. On her 21st birthday, she applied for two Toy breeds—Poms and Japs. As she was approved for additional breeds she phased out her showing-and-breeding program. ''I took a year's sabbatical from dog shows and it gave me a fresh perspective about the sport.''

62

Edna Joel is a well known judge in both Canada and this country. Edna has been an all-breed judge for three decades, having started in London in 1948. She's the only judge to have twice been called upon to select best in show at Leeds—in 1966, when there were 6,600 entries, and in 1973, with more than 7,500.

It should not be surprising that she moves smoothly and gracefully in the ring, for she is a graduate of a physical education college in Newcastle-upon-Tyne (where the first dog show in England was held, in 1859.)

Edna's father bred Smooth and Wire Fox Terriers, so naturally enough her first dog was a Fox Terrier, a Smooth, when she was four years old. "I learned to pluck, when I was very young, for I would help my father with the Wires," she recalled. When she was 14, her father bought her an Irish Setter. "That was much easier," she said. "It just meant brushing, not plucking."

Following the war, Edna married Tommy Joel, a civil engineer, and they lived in Scotland. "We bought a pair of Kerry Blue pups, a dog and a bitch, and that was the start of our Dinmohr Kennel," she recalled. "On New Year's Day we entered the two pups at Aberdeen. I handled the dog and he was best puppy in show. I still have the silver cake dish I received, and it's one of my most cherished possessions."

The Joels did very well with Kerry Blues and Dinmohr Terriers were very much in demand. Edna also finished some Poodles, Fox Terriers, English Setters and English Cocker Spaniels. Six years later, Tommy was transferred to Canada and the kennel was dispersed. In Toronto, the Joels joined the Canadian Kennel Club and both began to judge, receiving licenses as all-rounders.

Judging north of the border led to another career. "In 1969, while I was doing a show in Alberta, I had to fly from Calgary in a very small plane, where I sat right next to the pilot," she said. "I enjoyed it so much, a week later I was taking flying lessons and in eight months I had my wings." She now owns and flies a Piper Cherokee and is a member of the Ninety-Nine, an international organization of women pilots. Said Edna, "I find there's a similarity in both my avocations—flying and judging—for there is an international cameraderie among pilots and dog show people."

Dorothy Stevens never has walked on a Hungarian puszta, but the ancestors of her Komondors trotted over many of the grassy plains. Actually, the Bedford Hills, N.Y., fancier and her husband, Arnold, a New York lawyer, started with Old English Sheepdogs. "We bought a puppy bitch in 1968," recalled Dorothy. "I took her to Plainfield for our first show and we failed miserably. It was my fault. I was much too nervous. So we hired Monroe Stebbins to handle and he quickly finished her."

At Westbury, the couple saw their first Komondor. "Arnold was taken with the breed and when he learned you never use a brush on a Komondor, he said that was the dog for us," recalled Dorothy. "And I agreed, for we both had our fill of constantly brushing the Old English." So in 1970, the couple bought a six-month-old Komondor dog and a four-month-old bitch from a Canadian breeder. Dorothy handled the dog, Krampampuli Flash, to his championship in a dozen shows.

In 1972, they imported Borsodi Mancsos from Hungary and Dorothy finished her. Bred to Flash, Mancsos (mop in Hungarian) had eight pups. Only two were shown, Mrs. Stevens finishing one. The other, Summithill Baba, was sold as a seven-week-old pup to Alice Lawrence of Syracuse. At Bucks County, in 1976, I watched Baba become the first Komondor bitch in the history of the breed in the United States take best in show. "Slopping through the mud in the rain, she never faltered and was showing all the time," said Carl Tuttle, the judge. Said her owner: "She's a working lap dog and have you ever tried to hold a 75 pound dog. She sleeps on my bed."

"Bucks County was tremendous," said Dorothy, "but I really was pushed. I bathed three Komondors the day before the show. It takes two quarts of shampoo for each dog, two hours to bathe them and eight hours to dry them—using commerical dryers, so I wasn't through until 10 in the evening. I then had to bottle-feed nine pups. I managed to get to bed at midnight but was up again at five to feed the pups. When I heard Baba went best in show, I burst into tears."

Now Dorothy's Ch. Summithill Csontos, winner of six bests in show, has become the top winning Komondor of all time. At the 1977 Westminster of the 10 Komondors, six were of Dorothy's breeding. "I had to take two of them into New York to appear on a TV program," she said. "Crossing Ninth Avenue, my Komondors stopped traffic. Everyone wanted to have a look."

The big, white corded mops are high fliers. Arnold Stevens has a Cessna. "There is just room for the two of us and one Komondor," said Dorothy.

Although Pan American World Airways probably isn't aware of it, that international carrier played a role in the rise of the Silky Terrier in America. "I started to work for Pan Am in 1943," said Mrs. Merle Smith of Mill Valley, Calif. "My husband, who is a captain on the Oriental run, joined us immediately after World War II, when we were still using the old flying boats."

The Smiths saw their first Silky in 1950. "We were having dinner in San Francisco when a woman came in with a pup. I made such a fuss over it, my husband promised to get me one in Australia. We knew absolutely nothing about dogs so he went to a pet shop in Sydney. It didn't have any but said it would get us one. We were extremely lucky for the one it did get for us proved to be exceptionally good. She was Brenhill Splinters." When the Smiths decided to breed her, they couldn't find a stud in this country. So when the captain flew to Australia, he brought back Wexford Pogo. "Again we were lucky," said Mrs. Smith, "for of the first 450 Silky champions, 75 per cent were descendants of our original pair."

Mrs. Smith was a leader in the movement to gain AKC recognition for the breed. The Silky Terrier Club of America was organized in 1951 and she served as president. Then she was secretary for five years.

Pogo was seven years old when he became the couple's first champion. "It was I, not Pogo, who was doing the losing. I knew nothing about showing and it was strictly trial and error." Still she learned quickly, breeding a dozen Silkies who became titleholders and buying six more, which she finished. Pogo sired 15 champions from 30 litters. A son, Ch. Redway Buster, did even better, with 16 from 27.

Mrs. Smith is now busy judging and her showing days are over. But she did a masterful job in putting over the Silky. To gain recognition, the breed club has to present a stud book to the AKC, with all its registrations. Mrs. Smith started one in 1955. Although the Silky was formally accepted in May 1959, she continued the compilations as a hobby. "I stopped when we reached 10,000," she said. That's high flying for any breed in a short time.

Covering a dog show, I noticed a Massachusetts license on a car. It said CORGI 1. This was a plate that really registered, so I went in search of its owner. She was Mrs. Clayton L. Thomas, a demure, charming woman who was president of the Pembroke Welsh Corgi Club of America. She was certainly flying high. When she wasn't in a show ring with one of her champions, she was up in the clouds. For she was also secretary-treasurer of a balloon school.

Born in Tientsen, China, where her father was an exporter and her mother taught English at the university, Mrs. Thomas was brought up in Canada. "I suppose it was natural for me to want Corgis," she said, "because my mother was Welsh. After I married, we decided to get one, just as a pet." The Thomases bred their bitch to a champion, feeling certain they would have some truly sensational pups.

"We were quite disillusioned," she recalled, "it was just an ordinary litter. I then began to attend shows and speak to Corgi breeders. Since my husband is a physician, we felt we could use his knowledge of genetics and perhaps be more successful the next time. We bought another bitch, bred her, and from the litter came our first champion, Festiniog's Autumn Bounty."

The Thomases are not big breeders, having only a litter or two a year. But their dogs are known for good temperaments. "As far as I'm concerned, no dog, regardless of how beautiful, means anything if it isn't good-natured and happy," said the balloonist.

And how did she become interested in ballooning? "My husband was a flight surgeon in the Navy for seven years and then did some parachuting," said Mrs. Thomas. "I felt the jumping was too dangerous, so he gave it up and turned to ballooning. We both find it interesting and exciting. Now we have a school and are teaching others to enjoy the sport."

All's right with the world for Maurie Lewis when she can
be where she can do her lovely oils and also enjoy her
Scottish Deerhounds.

Dr. Bud McGivern and wife Diane bring youthful zip and an
evident enjoyment of their Vizslas to the show rings. Bud is a
very active member of the Westminster and Westchester clubs.

Doctors In The House

I first met Dr. Buris Boshell at Putnam County, where he gaited a Miniature Pinscher to best in show. We soon grew to be good friends, for the Birmingham physician was active in the show ring and his little Minpins were big winners. I particularly remember his Bo-Mar's Drummer Boy. Dr. Boshell proudly held that not only was the Drummer a multi-best-in-show winner but that he left his stamp on the breed, siring many champions.

The doctor started in the show world shortly after he was graduated from Harvard Medical School. A patient gave him a Boxer.

"He suggested that I show the pup," said the Alabaman. "He told me about a match in nearby Lowell and I entered Dixie's Bama. After the ribbons were handed out I spoke to the judge and he was kind enough to tell me that although I had a lovely pet, it was no show dog." Now the doctor had been brought up on a farm and liked animals. He even had contemplated being a veterinarian and had attended vet school at Auburn before switching to medical school. "I decided if I was going to get a good dog, I'd go about it scientifically," he said. "I spent hours studying pedigrees and finally bought a Bang Away daughter. She won the open fawn class at Westminster and finished quickly." One of her grandsons, Skyrealm's Bubbling Over, became the Grand Futurity winner in 1964. "That was the end of my Boxer days," continued the doctor. "I had accomplished what I intended to do—breed a top one—and Bubbling Over was all of that."

Seven years earlier the Boshells had started with Miniature Pinschers. "We wanted a small dog but we wanted one that looked and acted like a Working dog," said the physician. They bought a nine-week-old pup, Rebel Roc's Cora von Kurt, and she gained her title when she was only 11 months old. Cora has been the foundation bitch for the Bo-Mar Kennel. One of her pups, Bo-Mar's Ginger Snap, became the first Boshell homebred Minpin champion. Since then there have been more than 80, almost all handled by the physician himself.

The doctor, a world authority on diabetes, is director of the first public diabetes hospital in America. It is located at the University of Alabama medical school complex, where Dr. Boshell also heads the internal medicine department. He has ruled in rings not only in this country but in Australia, Japan, India, Singapore, Formosa, the Philippines, and Europe. "Whenever there was a medical convention overseas that I had to attend, I'd try and line up a judging assignment," he said. "I do enjoy it but I've been so busy with my medicine, I've had to curtail my judging."

Dr. Wolfgang Casper, a dermatologist from Staten Island, N.Y., as a young man in Germany had fiery red hair. "Perhaps that influenced my choice of breeds, when I started in the sport here," said the physician. "I went to a show, saw a flashy red Irish Setter and fell for it." The first time he showed an Irish Setter, he literally fell. "I tripped over the leash," he chuckled, "and fell on my face. When I managed to regain my feet, the judge gave me a blue ribbon for having the best pup in the class.''

The doctor has come a long way since then. For almost two decades he staged the combined Setter fixture, at which English, Gordon and Irish are shown on the day before Westminster. He's a former president of the Eastern Irish Setter Association and for years has been a leading figure in the Staten Island club, serving as its delegate to the AKC.

Each year, at his house, the physician holds a judges' party the night before the show. ''Too many clubs leave the judges in a hotel with nothing to do,'' said the physician. ''Staten Island has always been friendly and we want to keep it that way.'' The physician never had a large kennel but he bred more than six generations of the mahogany-coated Irish. A firm believer in obedience training, several of his dogs gained titles. ''By careful breeding, dedicated Irish Setter fanciers have been able to get away from the broad head and produce the beautifully chiseled, long and lean head,'' Dr. Casper explained. ''Still, there is plenty of brain room, with a well-defined occipital protuberance.

The doctor said he was able to apply knowledge from treating humans as a dermatologist to his care of his Setters. He said dogs have many of the same skin ailments and allergies as people.

''As to training, you cannot use force with the Irish Setter. You must use gentleness and psychology. He's an affectionate dog who thrives on kindness. I'd never sell a puppy to a loud-mouthed or short-tempered person. Training should begin at nine months. Just as a child must be taught how to get along with the family, a puppy must be educated. You can have delinquency among young untrained animals as you have juvenile delinquency among humans.''

Walk around the campus of Rutgers Medical College and you are likely to see some short-coated, short-legged dogs, who back in their native Wales would be herding cattle. They are Cardigan Welsh Corgis and a half-dozen members of the faculty now own the little dogs, not as herders but as pets. It all started with Dr. W. Edward McGough, head of the department of psychiatry, who owns four champion Cardigans, including Springdale Droednoeth. The 12-year-old (in 1978) tri-color had the distinction of being the first, and up to when I retired, the only Cardigan to ever go best in show. ''Several of my colleagues saw Droed and couldn't wait to get a Cardigan,'' said the good doctor.

McGough was introduced to the breed when he was a medical student at Georgetown. In Washington, D.C., he met Mrs. Henning Nelms, whose Brymore Kennels produced so many good Cardigans, and he became intrigued with the breed. He transferred to Duke, where he received his M.D., went on to a residency at Yale, and then returned to Duke to teach psychiatry.

''As soon as I had a home at Durham (N.C.),'' said the physician, ''I acquired Springdale Brangwyn. I now had the time and money to go to dog shows, so I entered her at Roanoke. I was shaking when the judge handed me a ribbon, for she had gone winners bitch. Then I decided I wanted a really top dog and I had the good fortune to get Droed.'' The black, white and tan proved to be a great one. In addition to his best, five years in a row (starting in 1966) he was best of breed at Westminster.

The white-haired doctor now lives in a small house in Colt's Neck, N.J. that dates back to the Revolution, and which he has had restored. A music lover, he has a large collection of records and some unusual tapes of Toscanini, made while the maestro was rehearsing.

Ed has been active in club work, serving as president of Monmouth County for 10 years. This is a show I always liked and it rates as one of the best in the East. The doctor is also a trustee of Camden County and for a decade has been the AKC delegate for the Rock River club, in Rockford, Ill., which stages one of the few benched shows still in existence.

The handsome, distinguished-looking psychiatrist is doing more and more judging, although his medical duties somewhat restrict him. Not only is he a professor at the medical school but he is the psychiatrist at a nearby hospital. In Britain, he's twice judged at the mammoth Birmingham show, and also at Coventry.

It took pulling teeth for Dr. Leon Seligman to acquire his first showdog. A Baltimore dentist for 45 years, Dr. Seligman recalled that in 1937 one of his patients was William Todd, a Smooth Fox Terrier breeder. "I bought one of his dogs, a grandson of the great Nornay Saddler, and that started me. Until the War, I bred and showed smooths, even finishing one,'' he said.

During World War II, his time was taken up by the Air Force, where he served as a major in the dental corps. In 1945, while he was still in the service, he received his license to judge. "I was stationed in Columbia, S.C., and a club there asked me to do a match show for them. The next thing I knew I was asked back to judge my first point show. I did Fox Terriers, Airedales and Welsh, and I still have the catalogue.''

Once out of the service, the little dentist had little time for dogs, since he had to rebuild his practice. But gradually he started to breed, and show, branching out to Irish Terriers, Cairns and Scotties, as well as Fox Terriers. "I was friendly with James Austin, the owner of Saddler, and he gave me the best Fox Terrier bitch I ever owned, Ch. Side Saddle of Wissaboo,'' said the dentist. "In the oil painting of Saddler and his famous seven, hanging in the AKC gallery, Side Saddle is one of the seven.'' In the early sixties, Dr. Seligman stopped showing since he was getting so many judging assignments. "There has been a great change over the years,'' he said. "Most of the breeds have improved and the presentation of the dogs is far better. I'm not one to say it was better in the old days.''

Dr. David Green Doane, a leading breeder and judge of Dalmatians, literally walked his way into becoming a dog owner. "I was interning at the Naval Academy,'' he reminisced. "Almost every night I strolled around the grounds to get a bit of air. On the walks I'd meet a Dalmatian, who was being exercised. I decided if I ever owned a dog, that would be my breed."

So when he moved to the Chelsea Naval Hospital in Boston, the doctor bought a Dal. Not only did he buy, but he began to show. He had the usual first-dog experience. "I accumulated loads of reserve ribbons but never a point," he said. "However, I was learning. By the time I bought my third dog, Beloved Scotch of the Walls, I knew what I was doing. I finished him quickly and he proved to be a tremendous sire. Among the champions he sired was Ch. Green Starr's Masterpiece, the first American-bred liver-and-white Dal to take a best in show."

The physician, an Army colonel, in 1979 was stationed at Fort Belvoir in Virginia. Now that he is doing a great deal of judging, he does very little breeding. Not that he ever had too large a kennel, for he averaged 15 adults. Still, he bred some 40 champions. Dogs sired by Scotch of the Walls were the foundation stock for several kennels. "I always strived for the short-bodied, close-coupled and balanced Dal, as opposed to the long-bodied Whippet type," he told me. The doctor was also successful with some Irish Terriers he bred. Ch. Green Starr's Gold Stripe was one of the few Irish Terrier bitches ever to go best in show in the United States.

The Colonel had been scheduled to judge at Westminster in 1971 but was excused so that he could attend a ceremony at the White House. He received the Congressional Medal of Honor from President Nixon, awarded posthumously to his 22-year-old son, Lt. Stephen Doane, killed in action in Vietnam. While he was training at Fort Benning, the lieutenant showed Dalmatians. Among the effects the Army sent home from Vietnam were a half dozen ribbons his dogs had won.

The doctor, who became a Dalmatian fancier because of a walk, now has moved up to a jog. He jogs from 15 to 20 miles, three times a week, and in 1978 ran in the Boston Marathon.

"It was either a shotgun or a dog," said Dr. Roscoe B. Guy, director of health services at Metropolitan Hospital and a dean at New York Medical College. "We live in West Nyack (N.Y.) and Jacqueline (Mrs. Guy) and our children are alone a great deal," he said. "She wasn't enthusiastic about a shotgun, so we decided on a dog and a big one."

The physician wasn't exaggerating when he said a big one, for their Caesar, more formally known as Ch. Willowedge Caesar III, is a Mastiff and weighs 219 pounds. "We bought him in 1973, when he was eight weeks old and he weighed 25 pounds," recalled Jackie. "By the time he was six months old, he was 125." At the urging of some friends, Jackie took him to a nearby match. "In my ignorance, I walked into the ring wearing high heels," she said. "Then I started him in point shows and I made every mistake in the book handling him. I tried to show Caesar like a German Shepherd, Afghan or a sporting dog, racing him around the ring. I thought the faster he and I ran the better it was. But I watched and learned, so when we really started, he finished in two months with five majors.'' They became a familiar team and Caesar, in 1975, won more breeds than any Mastiff in America.

I remember the first time I met the team. It was an indoor show in upstate New York. There were two telephone booths. I had just completed phoning some summaries to the *Times* and was leaving, when I saw this huge Mastiff, with a little girl trying to hold him, as he strived to get into the other booth, where Jackie was phoning her husband to say they had won the breed and would have to stay for the group. The girl was the Guys' daughter, Allison. I grabbed the leash and held the dog until Jackie could complete her call. Mrs. Guy, who comes from Paris, proceeded to thank me in both French and English.

In June 1976, at Twin Brooks, Jackie ran over to me and said I should go to the Mastiff ring, I'd see something interesting. There was Allison, all of 64 pounds, handling Caesar. And the little girl gave her seniors a lesson, for she gaited the giant dog to best of breed. ''They made a good team,'' said Ted Wurmser, and his words carried weight for he had been judging 30 years. ''The youngster did a really professional job and deserved to win.''

Occasionally at a dog show there's an urgent call over the public address system for a doctor. In 1973, at the Newton, N.J., fixture, the physician who responded, ran from a ring where she was showing a Skye Terrier to care for another exhibitor. She was Dr. May Leong and at the time, she was a comparative newcomer to the circuit. Indeed, she never had been to a show until three years previously.

''I grew up in Chinatown in New York,'' she recalled, ''and there were very few dogs there. My mother said that in China animals were kept for their utilitarian value, cats to handle the mice and dogs for protective purposes, to sound an alarm. It was considered especially good to have a dog whose tail curled into a corkscrew, for there was a superstition that this brought wealth and good fortune to a household. In Chinatown, the utilitarian principle was carried over, with almost every store having a cat. I never thought about dogs until shortly after I had graduated from Smith. I was working in Washington and saw a most unusual dog. When I asked what breed it was, I learned it was a Skye Terrier. I vowed right there and then, if I ever had a dog it would be a Skye.''

But it was another dozen years before she was to fulfill the vow. For she went to medical school, and upon graduating served a six-year internship and residency. Settling in a garden apartment in Brooklyn Heights, she finally obtained her Skye, as well as a Siamese and a Burma cat. The Skye she bought as a pet from an ad in *The New York Times*. While walking with her little dog she met Bart Murphy, who owned the first drop-eared Skye to have finished in 11 years. At his suggestion, she joined the Skye Terrier Club of America and so became initiated to the show world. In 1970, she flew to St. Louis to attend the club's national specialty. ''I was in the grooming area,'' she said, ''and mentioned to one of the exhibitors I'd love to own a cream-colored drop-ear. The next thing I knew I was the owner of Twin Town Sweet William, who the year before had been the reserve winners dog at the speciality.''

William was two and a half years old and had been a country dog. He had a hard time adjusting to city life and it took six months of constant work by the physician to make a city dog of him. Dr. Leong and William made their show debuts at Saw Mill in March 1972. ''Neither of us knew what we were doing,'' she said, ''so I decided I'd go to a handling class and learn what it was all about.'' She proved an apt pupil. In May 1973, William finished. ''As far as I can ascertain, he was the first drop-eared cream male to become a champion in America,'' said the physician.

Dr. Leong moved to New Canaan, Conn., and so she can have her weekends free to attend shows, she has given up her private practice and turned to industrial medicine. The highlight of her Skye career was reached at the 1977 specialty, when Bellwethers Romach, whom she owns with William Bouton, went best of breed. When she isn't curing people's ailments or showing Skyes, Dr. Leong is off on a safari to Africa. ''The only shooting I do is with a camera,'' she said.

What started as a very modest venture, with the purchase of a $25 pet, mushroomed until a physician had a kennel of 125 and was buying two tons of dog food every six weeks. ''I was then living in Council Bluffs (Iowa),'' said Dr. Arthur Pedersen. ''A druggist's Collie had a litter and he sold me a pup. Hearing about a dog show in Omaha, we entered our pup, and with my wife doing the handling, he did nothing. The poor animal had every fault in the book.'' Buying another ''bargain'' pup, the Pedersens again had no success.

Then the doctor met Stephen Field and that proved the turning point. ''He was the Mr. Collie of those days,'' said Dr. Pedersen, ''and he taught us so much about dogs. Through his influence, we acquired some really good Collies. In the sixties, we finished three of them.''

In 1966, the physician received his license to judge. ''I was the first Council Bluffs KC member to become a judge,'' he recalled. The next year a virus swept through the kennel and 15 Collies were lost plus a Bouvier des Flandres that had been bought for the doctor's son, Bill.

For a Bouvier replacement, Dr. Pedersen went to Dorothy Walsh, a pioneer in the breed in this country, and obtained a 12-week-old bitch. She was Bibarcy's Job's Daughter and young Bill showed her to a championship. In her first litter, she produced five titleholders and in her second, three. One of the pups was Bibarcy's Soldat de Plomb (French for lead soldier), the top-winning American-bred male in the history of the breed in this country. In 1972, he was best of breed 73 times, with 49 group placements, including 20 firsts and six best-in-show awards.

The doctor served for a term as president of the Bouvier des Flandres Club of America and for three years was on the board. In 1975, he had 20 Bouviers, one of the largest kennels of the breed in America at the time.

Now that he is so involved in Bouviers, what has happened to the Collies? ''In

1971," said Dr. Pedersen, "I accepted a post in the Emergency Department of Gastonia (S.C.) Memorial Hospital. Before going we gave away some 60 Collies, including one champion, to friends where we were assured they would have good homes." Dr. Pedersen, who now lives in Bessemer, Alabama, is winning recognition as a judge of Working breeds.

The Giant Schnauzer, although an old breed, was little known outside of Bavaria until the turn of the century. So when Dr. Klaus Anselm, a gastroenterologist in Pueblo, Colorado, decided to get a dog for protective purposes, he remembered the breed from his native Germany and went in search of one. From an ad in *The New York Times,* he and his wife, Joan, bought a bitch. "She was too small for the show ring," he recalled, "so we turned to obedience and put a CD on her. She also has been our foundation bitch."

In two generations, the Anselms had their first champion, Lutz von Gestern. It was Lutz who made the couple known to the fancy. He finished as an eight-month-old pup. In the first litter he sired, there were eight pups. Three never were shown but all of the others finished. One of the pups who wasn't shown in the breed ring was Doric Mannix von Gestern, the top Giant Schnauzer of 1975 in obedience.

As a physician, Anselm insists the dogs be in peak condition. "We have a 35-acre ranch," he said, "and we have horses. The dogs accompany us when we ride."

A dedicated breeder, the doctor is very concerned about the problem of hip dysplasia and won't use a dog for breeding unless it has been X-rayed and received a certificate. "Even with great care, breeding clear to clear," he said, "one may come up with a dysplastic. When that's the case, the pup should be spayed or neutered and given away as a pet. When we sell a pup, we pay the buyer's dues for a year's membership in the Giant Schnauzer Club of America. That way he is assured expert advice."

Both the doctor and his wife are active in the national club. She was president in 1973 and he held the top post in 1975 and 1976. Under the guidance of the couple, the organization increased its membership from 200 to 375. The physician also was president of the South Colorado KC in 1976. Joan teaches obedience and a half-dozen of the Anselm dogs have earned CDs. "And that's no small achievement," said Klaus, "for the Giant Schnauzer tends to get bored with the exercises."

The couple have visited Giant Schnauzer kennels in Germany. "We found the dogs here are just as good as any we saw overseas," said the doctor.

"You can't teach an old dog new tricks" is an adage to which Dr. Daniel Horn does not subscribe. The psychologist, who in 1977 was appointed Director of the National Clearing House for Smoking and Health, a government agency to control health problems that result from smoking, believes that most people bring out their dogs entirely too early, particularly in the big breeds.

"A Chesapeake Bay Retriever, with which I am most familiar," said the Marylander, "doesn't reach his peak until he is between four and six years old. This is an age when most fanciers have retired their dogs from the ring." Horn, who is a well-known obedience judge and has done much teaching among the educated dogs, said that in his classes the top "graduate" frequently was the oldest animal.

The psychologist added that age also is an advantage for the field dog and cited a top-winning Chesapeake of years ago, Ch. Nelgard's Baron, who when he was 10 years old was one of only four retrievers to complete all 12 series in the national trials.

Horn started with the Chesapeake just after World War II when he was at Langley Air Force Base, in charge of a study to determine the psychological factors in aircraft accidents. He bought a pup for his wife and Janet trained her by reading a book.

Before the pup ever attended an obedience class, she had two of the three legs needed for a CD. "Despite what so many people think about the Chesapeake being a one-man dog, we have always found him to be a family dog," declared Horn. "We have trained them in obedience, shown them in the breed ring and they all hunt. That's what you call an all-round dog."

I met Dr. Horn at Genesee Valley in Rochester, N.Y., in the summer of 1977. He was showing Ch. Eastern Waters Supercharger and he took the blue. "This is the 50th Chessie to have our kennel name (Eastern Waters)," he said proudly, "and 37 of them have had obedience degrees, as well." He had just returned from Switzerland, where he had spent a year in Geneva, as a consultant to the World Health Organization. Horn said he and Janet took two Chesapeakes over with them and the dog won seven CACIB certificates and the bitch six, scoring at shows in Switzerland, France, Germany and Italy. "They had a litter and there were four pups. Two are in France, one in Finland and one in Sweden," he said.

In 1954, *The New York Times* ran a picture of Horn on Page 1, with the American Cancer Society's report on smoking, to which he was a principal contributor. When I phoned to congratulate him, he had a complaint. "How could the *Times* say I was a Labrador Retriever breeder?" That was his only comment on the story.

There are relatively few veterinarians in the sport of dogs. One of them is Dr. Charles P. Gandal, a field trial enthusiast. "It all began when I was an undergraduate at Cornell," he recalled. "After graduating from the veterinary college, I was in large animal practice for a year. Visiting in New York, I went to the Bronx Zoo and dropped in on the vet. 'I haven't had a vacation in 10 years,' said he. 'How would you like to substitute here for two weeks?'" Gandal protested he knew nothing about exotic animals, but to no avail. When the regular veterinarian returned, he suggested Gandal stay on as an assistant. Three years later, the older man left and Gandal was in charge.

Meanwhile, Gandal had bought a German Shorthaired Pointer, Biff Bangabird, and he had begun to run the dog at field trials. When I visited the veterinarian at the zoo, there was Biff sleeping beside his desk.

In 1961, Gandal and eight other field trialers organized the Long Island German Shorthaired Pointer Club. "Our motto," said he, "was to promote the Shorthair in the field, the water and in the show ring." That is what he did with Biff, for he made him a dual champion. "There was no trouble in the field," he confided, "but both he and I were bored in the show ring." Biff was a real ham. When we took him outside the building, in which the veterinarian had his office, so that I could take a picture, I said I would like him posing on point. "No problem," said Gandal. "There are plenty of pigeons around." Sure enough, one alighted near us and Biff froze as though he had found a pheasant.

"If a person is going to have one dog, here is an opportunity to have an all-rounder," declared Gandal. "Biff is a good example. He has won many trials, finished in the ring, and he romps around the house with my son. My wife's only complaint is that Biff still thinks he's a puppy. He wants to sit on her lap. Biff weighs 70 pounds and my wife is only 98."

The first woman veterinarian graduated from the University of Pennsylvania was Josephine Deubler. She can be called Doctor-Doctor for she also has her Ph.D. in pathology. Jo, as she is known to her friends, comes from a family of veterinarians, her father, uncle, brother and two cousins all holding VMD degrees. Even more remarkable is the fact that since early childhood, Jo has been almost totally deaf and had to learn by reading lips. This courageous and determined woman for many years has been doing research at the University of Pennsylvania Veterinary School. All her life Jo has been with animals, her father's practice having been farm animals. Her first love was horses and the doctor won any number of ribbons, riding hunters over the jumps. Indeed, her thesis was written on the recurrent ophthalmia in the eyes of the horse.

In the dog world, she long was known for her Terriers, particularly Dandie Dinmonts. She also had Irish Terriers, Smooth Fox and Kerry Blues. In 1956, she imported a Dandie, Salismore Silversand, and Jimmy Butler, her handler, quickly finished him. Silver was best of breed at Westminster and three years in a row took the national specialty. In 1961, Ch. Salismore Playboy was Dandie of the year. The same year, Jimmy persuaded her to start judging, which she did on a very limited scale. When Butler retired in 1966, Jo retired from the show ring and she began to accept more judging assignments. She was chosen to name best of breed at the national specialty that year and in 1967 was invited to do the British specialty at Carlisle.

Now she has no dogs but plays a leading role in club work, being show chairman for Bucks County. Each year Bucks grows larger. Located between the Delaware River and the old ship canal, just north of New Hope, it has become one of the most attractive of the May shows in the East. In 1976, Dr. Deubler received a well-deserved Fido from the Gaines Research Center, as the Dog Woman of the Year.

Center Stage

Howard Atlee is a well known figure on the Broadway scene. He has been a publicist for some top theatrical hits. On the dog show stage, Atlee plays a leading role and a diversified one. He has starred as a breeder, owner, handler, founded a specialty club—the Knickerbocker Dachshund—and served as a judge at match shows.

"I was a press agent for a summer repertory theater at Camden, Me., in 1956," he recalled. "One day, driving to the theater, I saw a kennel. I stopped and when I left I owned a smooth Dachshund." The next summer, Atlee was with a road company and had to board the little badger hound. "A professional handler took her to his kennel and asked if I wanted her shown. I visualized a champion overnight. But although she managed a point or two, she was no real show dog."

Atlee, meanwhile, had become much more knowledgeable. He bought two really good Wirehaired Dachshunds. One, Zelediah of Sharondachs, already was a champion. The other, Wilhelmina of Sharondachs, was a bitch of show quality. Now Howard began to handle his own dogs. "Wilhelmina was the first dog I ever showed to a championship," he said. That was in 1962. The Dachshund bitch who really brought Atlee on the big stage was Ch. Celloyd Virginia Woolf, the top-winning Dachshund bitch of 1966. "I named her after the hit show, *Who's Afraid of Virginia Woolf* which I was handling. The play ran for 18 months and my little Dachshund was constantly in the headlines, for she was doing her big winning." Early in 1967, Virginia was bred and her six pups all were given operatic names. Three became champions—Penthouse Salome, Penthouse Steurman and Penthouse Siegfried.

Penthouse is Atlee's kennel name. "As I bought and bred more dogs and began to do more handling, I realized larger quarters were needed, so I rented a penthouse," said the publicist. "My penthouse soon was too small. Then I bought a 250-year-old stone house in Stone Ridge, N.Y. I had the stable converted into a kennel, with radiant heat in the floor. I also have radiant heat in the outdoor runs. That way I never have to shovel snow and with 25 runs, that's a relief."

Howard's wife, Barbara, has won signal success with her Salukis. But the most publicized of her dogs was not a champion. In August, 1978, she saw an ASPCA ad, with a picture of a Saluki, captioned, "Please save me!" Rushing to the shelter, she saved the animal, who was "sheer skin and bones." Two months later, with tender loving care, she brought Karena Saga along to where she entered him at Monticello, where he went best of winners. Saga's heartwarming saga gained national attention.

It was in the Brown Derby restaurant in Hollywood, California, that I interviewed Don Wilson. The big, gray-haired rotund announcer, for 32 years the butt for Jack Benny's barbs on radio and TV, played a straight role when it came to dogs. Amid a parade of celebrities who came over to our table, Don said, "Showing dogs is one of the most satisfying hobbies I know. All dog owners have to be a little bit crazy, but Poodle owners are positively insane. I've often wondered what folks thought when they saw my wife, Lois, and me walking our dogs along Sunset Boulevard before sunrise."

Then, as he chuckled, he recalled, "We really were green, when we started. Neither Lois nor I had ever heard about dog shows, and cared less. All we wanted was a miniature Poodle. We were told that Frank Sabella knew more about Poodles than anyone on the Coast, so we drove to his place. He showed us a black standard bitch, Bel Tor Hussar Le Joyeuse, owned by Becky Mason of Pine Orchard, Conn. We didn't know the difference between a miniature and a standard. All we knew was that we wanted Joy. Sabella told us Mrs. Mason would sell the Poodle, but with one proviso—that she be shown. We quickly agreed and Sabella said he would do the handling."

Shown in puppy trim, Joy made her debut when she was nine months old and went best of variety. She was still a pup when she became a champion. "She was well named," added big Don, "for she was a joy to have around the house and was part of the family. She was never beaten in the breed."

Mrs. Wilson, meanwhile, had become interested in apricot-colored Poodles. "We bought an English import and his success belonged to my wife," said the announcer. "He had a very difficult coat to get going. She would work from six to eight hours a day, brushing and grooming him. Trigger was three years old before he ever walked into a ring. When he walked out, he had 5 points and we had a beautiful silver trophy. All of our Poodles have been a great joy, but one, with the name of Wo, had a special meaning for me. I had heard of a black standard pup Mrs. Mason owned, who had been a sensation at the William Penn Club's futurity in Philadelphia, but it was not for sale. When I was East, I rented a car and drove to the kennel to see the dog. He was everything that we'd heard and then some. I was determined to buy him but Mrs. Mason just wouldn't discuss it. On my birthday, Lois asked me to pick up a package at the airport. The package was the Poodle. Evidently, Lois was a lot more persuasive than I."

A puppy match where exhibitors bring their young stock to get experience, rarely causes too much excitement. But one held in Griffith Park in Los Angeles caused a traffic jam. Not only did it draw 160 pups but there were crowds at the ringside. For this was no ordinary match. Wilson was making his debut as a judge. At the end, when the star of the airways made his final decision, there was an ovation and a rush to get his autograph. That's dog biz and show biz.

To the one or two-dog owner who feels that he has little opportunity in the show ring, Chester Collier should be an inspiration. For the TV programming consultant has rarely owned more than two dogs at a time and only one would be being shown. However, the one he would have on the circuit invariably was a big winner.

Chet obtained his first Bouvier in 1964, a fawn bitch, from Ray and Marion Hubbard. He bought other dogs later but great success did not come fast.

As in his illustrious career in radio and television management (where he launched the Mike Douglas and the Steve Allen shows and brought David Frost to America) Chet was not one to be kept waiting.

With the help of Mrs. Hubbard, who took movies of good Bouviers in Belgium, he selected and imported Naris du Posty Arlequin who made history for the breed winning 10 best-in-show awards and 35 groups. Next, he imported Naris's grandson, Raby du Posty Arlequin. Raby didn't particularly like the show ring but he managed to win the silverware three times and had a dozen groups.

Then came — Ch. Taquin du Posty Arlequin, who set all records for the breed with 39 bests and 110 blue rosettes before being retired in 1976. Chet then decided it was time to stop showing and he obtained a judge's license.

Over the years, he also became involved in club work. He is chairman for Westminster, vice president of Westchester and a past president of the Dog Fanciers Club. A raconteur of wit, Chet is in demand as a speaker.

Once a star, always a star. When Lina Basquette gaited a dog across a ring, every onlooker could feel the spotlight stimulated by her superb interpretation of that dramatic moment.

A child star in California in 1916, Lina became a leading screen and stage performer and a noted dancer. "From 1923 to 1925, I studied ballet," she told me, "and I became the premiere ballerina in the *Ziegfeld Follies*. Then I returned to the films and had the leading role in Cecil B. DeMille's *The Godless Girl.*" Lina also appeared in pictures with such stars as Gary Cooper, Richard Barthelmess and Jean Hersholt.

The actress next organized her own stage company and played in South Africa, Australia, New Zealand and South America. She retired from the theater after World War II.

With her sense for the dramatic, she turned to a big animal, when she made her debut in the dog show world.

"I went to Westminster in 1948," she recalled. "While passing the Dane benches I noted a 'For Sale' sign and promptly bought a fawn bitch. I showed her a couple of times but she had too many faults and I realized she was going no place in the ring. I wanted a winner, so I went to William Gilbert, a leading Dane breeder. He sold me a fawn bitch pup, Gilbert-Duyster's Linda Mia, and she became my first champion."

Miss Basquette's Honey Hollow Kennel produced nearly 100 titleholders and fanciers from four continents bought its dogs. At times in her Bucks County establishments in Pennsylvania, she had from 100 to 150 of the big Danes. That meant feeding more than four tons of dogs. In 1978 Lina, who has had a handling license since 1950, moved to Wheeling, West Virginia, where she is semi-retired, showing a dog or two on occasion.

The sentimental favorite of all the dogs she owned, bred or handled was Gregory of Kent, a red golden brindle. "I found him in Virginia," she recalled, "where he had been hit by a truck. I took him to the University of Pennsylvania veterinary hospital, where they had to do a bone graft. It took two years before we had him together. Gregory proved a great sire in the fifties with 20 champions and of the right type."

In 1924, Isabella Hoopes walked into the ring at Westminster, then at the Madison Square Garden that was actually on Madison Square in New York, and showed a pair of Beagles. They both had the Saddlerock prefix, the Hoopes kennel name. Every year after, through 1978, she had an entry at the show.

"I have shown in all three Gardens," noted the octogenarian. The name Saddlerock has been seen in show catalogues more than 1,000 times. It has been carried by Beagles, Pointers, Whippets, English Setters, Cairn Terriers, Foxhounds and Dachshunds. Mrs. Hoopes was licensed as a professional handler by the AKC in 1929 and she holds the No. 9 ticket. Although today there are many women handlers, in the late '20s she was a bit of a rarity.

Mrs. Hoopes also had a successful stage and screen career. "In 1939, I was in a company at the Bucks County Playhouse, in New Hope," she reminisced. "I played in *They Knew What They Wanted*, with Richard Bennett, and in *The Man Who Came to Dinner*, with Moss Hart, George S. Kaufman and Harpo Marx." She made her Broadway debut in 1952 in *The High Ground*. Later she appeared with Rosalind Russell in *Wonderful Town*.

In 1964 I did a column about Mrs. Hoopes. She was a bit worried about it since casting directors would know her age. The story didn't hurt for she appeared afterward in the movie, *The Boston Strangler*. She phoned me to say, "I'm the first person he strangles, so be sure to get to the picture early." In a story I did for the *Times* about the 1978 Westminster, I mentioned the oldest owner-handler in the ring—Mrs. Hoopes. The next month she phoned to tell me she was back on Broadway, with a part in *The Effect of Gamma Rays on Man-in-the-Moon Marigolds*, starring Shelley Winters. Life begins at 85.

Jim and Helen Warwick are a husband-and-wife judging team. They have ruled in rings at the top shows in this country, as well as in England and Scotland. When they were active breeders and exhibitors, their Lockerbie Kennel at Little Silver, N.J., was one of the best. To an earlier generation, the Warwicks were known in the entertainment world. Jim was a successful stage and screen writer. Helen, a protégé of Anna Pavlova, danced with the Russian ballet and had her own company in Italy. Indeed, when she was showing the Lockerbie

Labs, as she would glide across the ring with a dog, many of the spectators would be entranced watching her and not the retriever.

It was the stage that led the Jerseyans to dog shows. Warwick, who came from Australia, wrote a psychological drama, *Blind Alley,* that was produced on Broadway in 1935 and enjoyed a long run. *"Blind Alley* gave me financial independence," he recalled. "I wanted a hobby and always liked having animals. I suggested to Helen we have dogs but neither of us had the slightest idea what kind. So we bought a dog book, thumbed through it, saw a picture of a Lab and agreed that was the breed." Their first three Labs were good pets but not show dogs. The Warwicks then decided it was time to get a good one. On the advice of a leading breeder they bought a black, Chidley Hocus Pocus, who, in 1951, became their first champion.

The next year they imported Ballyduff Candy, a yellow, from England. She became their foundation bitch. She gained her title in just six shows and was the dam of seven champions, exerting a great influence on the breed. Helen Warwick is the author of *The Complete Labrador Retriever.* She is particularly proud of the Labrador entry she drew at a specialty in Glasgow. There were 302 dogs, larger even than Crufts, a tribute to the esteem Britons held for the American breeder-author.

And the Band Plays on

Music, the theater and dogs have all played leading roles for Helga Tustin. "My husband, Whitney, was first oboe for the New York City Opera orchestra," she said, "so when I was groping for a kennel name, I hit on Kenobo."

Like so many others, Mrs. Tustin started with obedience. "In 1950, a neighbor had an English Cocker Spaniel. On occasions, I'd take care of it and I became so attached that I decided to buy one. Once I did, I had trouble trying to control him, so I enrolled in a training course. He earned a CD and was my constant companion."

A year later, Mrs. Tustin bought a bitch, On Time Michelle, from Maurie Prager, who had one of the top English Cocker kennels in the country. The pup went through to a CDX. "Since I had been going to shows, I decided it was time to get a show dog. Maurie sold me On Time Pamela and she became my first champion," said Helga. Pamela and Michelle were real show dogs. Pamela was used in the Pirandello play *Six Characters in Search of an Author,* and Michelle in Elmer Rice's *Street Scene.*

Having three dogs and living in New York proved a bit of a problem. "It was pretty hard walking my English Cockers on Broadway," added Mrs. Tustin, "so we bought a house in Massapequa (L.I.). I had been playing the harpsichord and gave it up for the dogs. I was far more nervous going into the ring than performing in a concert."

Importing a pair of English Cockers, Mrs. Tustin decided it was time to start her own breeding program. In 1965, she came up with her first homebred champion, Kenobo Blithe Spirit. Soon the kennel had outgrown the Massapequa quarters, and the Tustins moved to Muttontown. In just 10 years, Helga bred 35 champions, three of whom, Kenobo Constellation, Kenobo Rabbit of Nadou and Kenobo Capricorn, were best-in-show winners.

Music and dogs go hand-in-hand at the home of Captain and Mrs. Manuel Rodriguez. Mrs. Rodriguez, a former concert pianist, frequently either is at the keyboard or listening to concertos on her stereo record player. "My dogs have all been brought up on music," she said.

Mrs. Rodriguez gave her first concert in Boston, when she was 14 years old. Later she won a scholarship to the Music Conservatory in Paris. When the Nazis conquered the city, she returned to the United States to attend the University of South Carolina, where she received her doctorate and taught music.

Her dog show career didn't begin as auspiciously as did her musical. "I'd been breeding Chihuahuas as pets and ran an ad to sell some of the puppies. A woman came to the house and, after buying one, told me they were good enough to show. So in 1969, I took a bitch to the Bronx show. She promptly bit the judge, who told me to take her home and train her. That's what I did. We enrolled in an obedience course."

Ch. Scala's Blue Christina was seven months old when we bought her," said Mrs. Rodriguez. "She never had been on a lead, so I started to train her." Two months later, she took Crissy to Monmouth. "It was my first show since the biting incident," she said. "I was so nervous that Henry Stoecker, the judge, had to pick her up and put her on the table. He gave her a three-point major."

"My days as a concert pianist have helped me in the ring," said Mrs. Rodriguez. "When you are playing, you concentrate on the keyboard and aren't conscious of the audience. When I handle, now, it's the same. I never hear the crowd. However, in the old days, it was just me performing. Now there are the two of us."

Music and dogs have played leading roles in the lives of Bob and Joy Messinger, too. "We met in the entertainment world," said Bob. "I had a talent agency for jazz, blues and folk singers. In the late sixties, for four years, I was stage manager for the Newport Festival. I needed a Girl Friday, advertised, and along came Joy."

The latter had quite a backgound in the field herself. English, she had worked in London for the National Jazz Federation, which promoted concerts and tours. "I also managed a jazz band," she said. "I came to America in 1960, to listen to jazz. I intended to stay six months. But then I helped to compile *The Book of the Blues* and stayed on." The couple married and later decided they would have a dog.

"We went to Westminster," said Bob, "and I steered Joy over to the Northern breeds. You see, in World War II, I had been stationed in Labrador. I was a radio operator, but when it was learned I was fond of dogs, a team of 10 Greenland Huskies was assigned to me. The Greenland is leggier and heavier than the Siberian. The nearest town to our camp was 10 miles away and the hospital 50 miles. If a man was ill, we used the dog sled to get him to the hospital. During my tour of duty, we logged more than 1,000 miles."

So when a friend offered them a Siberian Husky pup, the Messingers quickly accepted. "The first time I showed her at Eastern, I fell flat on my face," recalled Bob. "The next day Joy took her in at Worcester and did much better. Although she never earned any points, we learned about showing." Next they bought a show dog, Sir Lancelot II and quickly put a few points on him. Then tragedy struck. Bob, on the way to lecture at the Philadelphia Folk Festival, took Lancelot along. The dog escaped from a hotel kennel run and later was found killed by a shotgun blast. To ease the loss, a friend gave them another Husky, Snoridge's Rusty Nail, and the couple decided to move from their New York apartment to the country.

They then bought a Siberian bitch, Misty Ahkee. "The first time I showed her, it was to a 4-point major," exalted Bob. "She finished in six weeks, beating specials, and she was our first champion." Rusty Nail, who later earned his title as well as a CD in obedience, became lead dog of an eight-dog team Bob races.

"Joy cannot stand the cold weather, so she never goes to any of the races," said Bob. "I race the Huskies to keep them in condition. I don't think a dog should be shown until he has proven himself a capable runner. He doesn't have to race, but he should demonstrate his ability to work. I take my vacations by the day and not the week, so I can go to 60 shows a year and drive the team in 10 races. On my eight-dog team, seven have points toward championships and the other has a CD. In training and competition, my dogs run at least 300 miles."

I was a witness to the start of what must have been the most bizarre race the Messinger dogs ran. It happened at Blydenburgh Park in Long Island. Sixty-one teams from five states were competing. There was no snow, so heavy gigs were used. The two big races were in the morning, when it was cooler. The first event, the unlimited, was for teams of seven dogs and upward, and drew four starters. They were sent away at two-minute intervals for the 7.3-mile race.

Bob Messinger and his eight Siberian Huskies were first off. I was standing at the first turn, a half-mile from the start, and they flashed past me, taking the turn smartly as Bob shouted "Haw", commanding the team to swing left.

Thirty-six minutes later the race was over, but the Messinger team was not at the finish line. "We were about halfway when my team spotted a girl riding a horse," Bob told me. "Siberians love to run with horses, so I sensed trouble. The trail divided, with our course swinging to the right. However, my team wanted to follow the horsewoman. My leaders made the turn but the others didn't, resulting in a hopeless tangle.

"I called to a trail steward to hold my Siberians until I straightened things out. However, he was unable to control them and they took off."

Lynn Witkin, also a trail steward, saw what had happened and leaped into her car and was off in pursuit, only to find the road barred. Seeing a horseman, she explained the circumstances. He told her to jump up behind him and they were off, galloping to Jericho Turnpike, a main highway. "A motorist told us a dog team was running up the turnpike in all the traffic," she said. "We finally overtook the Siberians. I dismounted, turned them around and drove back. By the time we were in, they probably had covered 10 or 11 miles."

A week before, Bob had had his Siberians pulling 500 pounds as a tuneup for the race. "They certainly gave me much more excitement than I had anticipated," he said.

The Messingers are firm believers in obedience and hope to get obedience degrees on all of their Siberians. And are they good watchdogs? "No, they love everyone and are very quiet," said Bob. "We keep a Skye Terrier to sound an alarm."

Judging is sweet music for Nellie V. Anderson, an upstate New Yorker. "In my younger years," said the Schenectady soprano, "I had hopes of singing in the Metropolitan." So it is no surprise that she gave her dogs operatic names—Aida, Radames, Tonio and the Rhine Maidens—Flosshilde, Wellgunde and Woglinde. Mrs. Anderson started with Boxers in 1939 and unlike so many fanciers who become discouraged and leave the sport early, she refused to let adversity stop her. "It took me ten years before I had my first champion," she recalled. "My favorite of a couple of hundred I bred was Nutwood Schaunard, a flashy brindle son of the great Ch. Bang Away of Sirrah Crest, the Westminster winner in 1951."

Nellie has had her judge's license since 1940. However, she is so busy working with the aged that she was forced to curtail her judging activities. Mrs. Anderson is recreational director for a home which has 527 geriatric patients. In 1972 and 1973, she served as president of the New York State Geriatric Recreational Activities Association.

"I prefer judging to showing," she admitted, "for I feel one can help the novice. I'm proud of the fact that I chose Shirkhan of Grandeur over 19 other Afghan hounds in a match show and that later he went on to go best at Westminster. It's a great thrill to find a young dog in the classes and get him started on a winning career."

Look, Ma, I'm Dancin' —

Richard Thomas and his wife, known professionally as Barbara Fallis, were dancers with the New York City Ballet. When they would be on stage, they had a Great Dane as a baby-sitter. "Our son, Richard, received a Dane as a present for his second birthday," said Thomas. "During the performances, they would both be in our dressing room, with the dog watching the baby." The dancer, who also performed with the American and Ballet Russe de Monte Carlo, recalled how he started with dogs.

"My father was a Welsh coal miner in Kentucky. He liked to hunt and would take me along. He had a Foxhound." When I asked how he started in the show ring, Richard replied, "The breeder of the Dane asked us to show her. She was a very good pet and baby-sitter but not much in the ring. But she did introduce us to the shows. And we learned enough, so that when we went after another Dane, we turned to a top kennel and came up with a good one. She was Kolyer's Gretchen Go Lightly and I finished her."

But Great Danes and touring ballets proved a problem. Jerome Robbins, the noted choreographer and a friend of the Thomases, had a Brussels Griffon. "We decided it would be much easier for us to have a small dog," said the dancer. "We liked the Griff and bought one. So I've gone from hounds to Danes to Toys."

The dog show is a Thomas family project. I remember a Progressive Club event where in one class there were five entries, three carrying the Go Lightly suffix of the Thomas kennel. Thomas left the ring with the blue ribbon, his daughter, Bronwyn, also a ballet dancer, was second with her brother's dog and Mrs. Thomas danced in and out with another of her son's dogs but received no prize. Thomas, who was showing a homebred, went on to beat two champions and take the breed, the third year in a row a Thomas Griff had accomplished the feat at Progressive.

When I asked Thomas, who had danced before many thousands, whether it bothered him when he walked into a ring with a dog, he replied, "Yes, I still get butterflies. When you perform on the stage you are separated from the audience. In the ring, the spectators are practically next to you. On stage, we deal with a script and steps. You have rehearsed and know exactly what you are supposed to do. When you show, you always have the unknown quantity—your dog."

Incidentally, the two-year-old boy whose Dane started the Thomas family show-ward now is a TV (The Waltons) and screen star. At a Saw Mill River show I covered, he and not his dogs was the attraction. The crowd was three deep around the ring, waiting to get his autograph.

A dancing instructor ("I taught the cha-cha to a football team"), a private detective, a professional handler, the owner of a boarding kennel, chairman of a humane society, a former president of a kennel club and a refinisher of antiques. That's Ann Hoffman of Waverly, N.Y. "I started much the same as so many other youngsters," she recalled. "I was in high school and by baby-sitting, saved $50 and bought a German Shepherd as a pet." But it wasn't until 1958, when Mrs. Hoffman, then a detective, really started. Said she: "I was driving past a Dachshund kennel, in Hector, N.Y. I stopped and learned none of the puppies was for sale. That whetted my appetite, so I did a little fast talking and left with a pup bitch."

Urged by the breeder to show Hectoria, Ann and the Dachshund made their ring debuts. They weren't a howling success, for Hectoria never earned a point. Ann then bought some more Dachshunds and began to breed them. "Although I learned the difference between a purebred mutt and a good conformation dog," she laughed, "I never finished a Dachshund."

Mrs. Hoffman decided it was time to turn to another breed—the Lhasa Apso. She bought a pair from Keke Blumberg and showed both to their championships. In 1970, Mrs. Hoffman saw an ad for a Lhasa bitch in Oklahoma and wrote to inquire about it. On the stationery she received from the breeder was an imprint of a Skye Terrier. "I wrote and told her I no longer was interested in the Lhasa but would like a good cream-colored Skye bitch. She shipped me Quizas Pippin Popsiepetal." Mrs. Hoffman finished her quickly and in 1971, Pippin was the top-winning Skye bitch in America.

Ann later applied for a handler's license "to help pay for the dogs." She also opened a boarding kennel. In club work, she was president and show chairman of Elmira for two years, and treasurer of the New Penn Kennel Clubs Association, consisting of a dozen clubs in New York and Pennsylvania. When I asked about her dancing, she replied, "I had been an Arthur Murray instructor and then opened my own studio. A Troy high school team was in the midst of a losing streak and the coach came to me and said he thought many of the players lacked coordination. Could I teach them something with a fast and broken rhythm? So I taught them the cha-cha. It must have done the trick for the losing streak ended."

To go to the shows, she has a truck with a large chassis-mounted camper, fitted with eight dog pens. "When people ask me about my occupation," laughed Ann, "I tell them I'm a truck driver." So go the *Tales of Hoffman*— from dancing to dogs.

Dorothy Bonner was doing a special dance number in Earl Carroll's Vanities, when she saw her first Pomeranian. "One of the girls in the cast had a Pom and I was so taken with it that I vowed I would get one," she recalled. Then her husband, an electrical engineer, was transferred to San Antonio. "When a vaudeville act came to town, I was asked to put on a production in conjunction with it," she said. "I worked up a dancing routine for 100 youngsters. The vaudeville group wanted to give me a gift and I asked for a Pomeranian. I called her Pitti Sing, after a character in Mikado. She was my pet for 14 years." When Pitti Sing died, Dorothy bought a good bitch from a breeder. That was in 1942 and Bonner's Honey Chile was to be the start of her kennel.

A Honey Chile pup, Bonner's Adorable Nip, was the first dog she ever walked into a ring. "I didn't know what I was doing but I learned, so that when I showed a Honey Chile granddaughter, Bonner's Sunny Cherub, I finished my first champion. Cherub had two pups, and one, Ch. Bonner's Tiny Showstopper, a clear orange, was the start of a line whose bloodlines are carried by some of the top Poms in the country today." Mrs. Bonner was the breeder of three best-in-show performers, Ch. Bonner's Peppersweet Red Pod and Ch. Prettytune Petit, both of whom she sold, and Ch. Bonner's Stylepepper Preshus. Red Pod was a multi best-in-show winner in the East and Petit, on the West Coast. Preshus, an orange four-pounder, the first time he was in a ring, was best in show.

"Of the 60 champions I bred," said Mrs. Bonner, "Preshus was the greatest. I only had him out 13 times, and he was best five times. He sired some 25 champions. Preshus had everything, coat, conformation and he really could move. He had something of a hackney gait and looked like a drum major. A ham, the crowd loved him." Dorothy started to judge in 1970 and immediately began to curtail her showing and breeding. Three years later, she still had nine champions but they were all pensioners on her 10-acre ranch in Texas.

It was always a pleasure to watch Marco Leynor show a Saluki and now that he is judging the breed, I miss him as an exhibitor.

The sleek Saluki gives an impression of grace and symmetry — there's a spring to the breed's gait. And when Leynor was showing, the slight man moved with the same effortless spring and grace. Easily understandable, for back in the 1940s he was a member of the Ballet Russe and later did flamenco dancing in South America.

Leynor indeed has had a artistic career. At one time he had a three-year scholarship to the Art Students League in New York City and then he received an Edward A. MacDowell grant for a year's study in Europe. As an expressionist, he had several exhibitions. He lived in Greenwich Village, where he had a small apartment.

Then he bought an Italian Greyhound and this was to change his whole life. "My father, a Turk, had trained horses in Constantinople," said Marco. "He had IGs and Salukis, so I'm just following in his footsteps. My first dog I called Demetrius. That was after my mother's native country, Greece."

I remember the Rockland County show in 1959, when Leynor and Demetrius made their show debuts, and a spectacular one it was for the little IG came out with a five-point major. He quickly became a champion. "Now I wanted a Saluki," said Marco, "and I bought a Canadian champion, Kesari Baga Latyf. She became my foundation bitch." When he bred her she produced two American and two Spanish champions. But breeding created problems. "With grown dogs and pups, I suddenly had 17 in my little apartment," he said. "I looked for a house and found one on Staten Island." Marco imported a smooth in 1969, when there were only three others of this variety in America, and Marcoleyn Khalif became the first smooth male Saluki champion in this country.

That'll Teach You

The dog show world attracts many educators. One of my favorites was the late Dr. Hadley C. Stephenson, professor emeritus of veterinary therapeutics and small animal diseases at Cornell University and a consultant to the Cornell Research Laboratory for Diseases of Dogs. I wrote a column using the word *philotherian* and I received a letter from the good professor, saying I had sent him to three dictionaries before he could find its meaning. Every Christmas, I would get a card from Ithaca, N.Y., with the terse note, "I still qualify as a philotherian."

Years later, while I was covering the Finger Lakes show, an elderly gentleman came up to me as I typed and asked, "Are you Walter Fletcher of *The New York Times?*" When I replied yes, he said, "I'm the philotherian from Cornell." Although I was rushing to make an edition, we had a delightful few minutes. It felt like meeting an old friend and I'm sure it was mutual.

Dr. James A. Baker, who was then Professor of Virology and director of the Veterinary Virus Research Institute at Cornell, told me an amusing anecdote about his colleague. Dr. Baker and I were at a Gaines Dog Research Center breakfast to receive Fidos, he for being Dog Man of the Year and I for being the Dog Writer of the Year. I asked how Dr. Stephenson was faring. "Do you know," said Baker, "we have a bit of a problem with him. When he comes in to do a special lecture, he writes a word on the board and then faces the class and says, 'If you don't know the meaning of this word, you don't belong in this room' That word is philotherian." I shook my head, never blinking and answered, "Do you know, he is entirely right." Baker never did know who was the instigator.

An educator who always does his homework before he walks into a ring is Dr. Harry Smith, a former dean of the School of Management at Rensselaer Institute in Troy, N.Y., and chairman of the biostatistics department at Mt. Sinai School of Medicine in New York. "I'm a mathematician and statistician," the slender gray-haired bespectacled man told me. "The night previous to a show I always reread all of the standards of the breeds I'm to judge. A good judge must be gifted with an eye for an animal. Any intelligent human can memorize the standards but he or she cannot interpret them without having the eye."

Smith recalled how his wife originally had a Boxer. He always had wanted a Bulldog. So after going to a couple of shows and looking over the breeds, they settled on a Pug, as a compromise. "We bought a bitch for a pet, one we were told wasn't show quality," he laughingly recalled. "I decided to show her anyway. My wife also took her for obedience training. So Little Jumping Joan leaped to both a championship and earned a CD obedience degree." That was in 1957. For the next few years the Smiths bred and showed Pugs, most of whom were named after Robin Hood characters. When the educator started to judge, he stopped showing.

"As a teacher, one has to organize and to exercise patience," said Dr. William S. Houpt, vice president of Allan Hancock College, in Santa Maria, Calif. "They are both good qualities for a dog show judge and certainly have helped me when I'm working in a ring." The same qualities also paid off in his administrative role at the college. He arrived in Santa Maria in 1943, when Allan Hancock had 200 students and he was told to build it up. That he did, for in 1976, there were 10,000 undergraduates.

Houpt started his career in the world of dogs on a modest scale. "I bought a Cocker Spaniel pup and decided before I did any showing I'd go to a show or two and see what it was all about," said he. "I learned quickly enough that mine was no show dog. Meanwhile, I had become intrigued with Collies, so I bought a bitch. She probably set a record for reserve ribbons, but never did get a point." Next he acquired a Beagle. Since he was studying for his doctorate, he turned her over to a handler. "She was Round Table Blaze and became my first champion," said the educator. Her success encouraged Houpt to breed Beagles and he came up with five champions. "They no longer were a challenge, so I decided to turn to Poodles," he said. "I bred several litters of Toys and Miniatures and then discovered Whippets. They have a wonderful temperament and are very elegant."

Houpt has always been community-minded and played a leading role in raising funds and setting up a Visiting Nurse Service, for which he served two years as president. "We started with a $10,000 budget," he recalled. "In 1976, it was $500,000, with nurses and home-care workers to serve the entire Santa Barbara area." And what does a busy dog show judge and college administrator do in his spare time? "I raise cymbidiums, or baby orchids, as they are more commonly known," he replied. "They rather have run away with me. I started with a few pots. Now I have more than 100 five-gallon containers. In each, there are six or eight spikes, with up to 20 blooms on each." No, he's not competing with the commercial growers. Dr. Houpt gives them to his friends.

Another educator who went to the dogs was J. Donald Jones, dean of student activities at Emory University in Atlanta. "All week I deal with students and their problems," said Jones. "On weekends I face canine problems. It's a change of pace, when I'm in a ring, and although it calls for a great deal of concentration, I find it relaxing." Born on a farm in Georgia, Jones grew up intending to become a veterinarian. He studied animal husbandry for two years at Berry College. "As part of the program, we had to judge cattle, pigs and poultry," recalled the dean. "We also had to show livestock. The experience of showing and judging has been a great help to me in the dog ring."

When Jones decided the veterinary field wasn't his forte, he turned to English. After graduation he taught at a high school in Tennessee, and did graduate work at the university.

When he decided to get a show dog, his farming background steered him on an intelligent procedure. "It was in 1957," he recalled. "I wanted a German

Shepherd. I knew enough to go to a reputable breeder and I picked out a good one, who quickly won some blue ribbons." Jones added a Doberman and a Pembroke Welsh Corgi. The Corgi, Twin Mars Cholly of Donshaus, won a championship. Many people spend a fortune to finish a dog. It cost Jones exactly $40 for Cholly to gain his title. "I entered him from the puppy classes and he was never beaten. He finished when he was nine months old at Albany (Ga.). In 1965, he was best in show at Knoxville (Tenn)." Jones then retired Cholly. "My teaching and graduate work was just too demanding," he said. "I didn't have time to go to shows and I couldn't afford a handler."

In 1967, Jones decided he would like another show dog. He went to Houston Clark, a professional handler, and asked him to be on the lookout for one. Clark suggested a Schipperke. Jones bought the little black dog and never regretted it. He was Ch. Klinahof Marouf A. Draco and he set records for the breed, taking 12 bests, 50 groups and had 131 group placements. "To be a successful breeder and exhibitor," said the educator, "calls for intelligence, honesty, hard work and a love for the sport, which should be treated as a sport."

Then there's the judge I always called a young man in a hurry. He's Edd Bivin of Fort Worth and he's on the staff of the dean of students at Texas Christian University. When I retired, Bivin was 35 years old but he looked much younger. At the time he already had accomplished more than fanciers much older. He had bred champions, handled a best-in-show dog, been president of a major kennel club and judged at such key fixtures as Westminster, International and Beverly Hills. But he still said to me, "I know very little in comparison to the old timers and there's a great deal for me to learn. The sport has been so good to me, I feel I owe it much. I'm particularly concerned about the youngsters. I try to encourage them not only to show but to work up breeding programs."

"People started me in the sport when I was a kid," he said. "They taught me not only the mechanics but also the ethics. 'You must give as well as take,' they stressed." So involved is Bivin in the sport that before he took the post at TCU, he had to be assured he would be permitted to take a number of weekends away from the university so that he could judge.

Dr. Bernard E. McGivern is an assistant professor in oral surgery at New York University and attending oral surgeon at five hospitals. His wife, Dr. Diane McGivern, is associate dean in the School of Nursing at the University of Pennsylvania. Both have been prominent in the show world with their Vizslas. Bud, as he is known on the circuit, started as a student at Notre Dame. "The mascot of the football team was an Irish Terrier, Shannon View Rudy," he recalled. "I showed him at International in Chicago in 1958. He received a red ribbon, second in a class of two."

Not until he came to New York to intern at Bellevue Hospital did he seriously start with dogs. "Diane and I had married and she was studying for her master's at NYU," said he. "I was on call every second night at Bellevue and I wanted a dog to protect Diane and also one I could use for hunting,'' said McGivern. Their problem was solved when Bud's mother gave them a Vizsla as a Christmas present in 1962. When the pup, Diane's Golden Karratz, was eight months old, she scored the first of several firsts for the young couple.

Shown at the first match ever held by the Vizsla Club of America, she was best pup. Then the McGiverns, who have done so much to help popularize the Hungarian hunting breed, organized the Vizsla Club of Northern New Jersey, with Bud its first president. They also helped found the Vizsla Club of Greater New York. Karry gained her title in 1965 at the first parent club specialty. When she died at the age of 11, in 1973, she had produced a total of 18 puppies, with many of her descendants champions. There's a painting of her over the fireplace in the lovely McGivern home, itself a Staten Island historical landmark. When Bud was showing, he finished seven Vizsla bench champions and one German Shorthaired Pointer field champion.

The oral surgeon is a former president of Staten Island and he's a member of Westchester, Westminster, the Stewards Club of America and the national Vizsla club. McGivern received a judge's license in 1968 and since has been a busy arbiter. When I asked him the most exciting assignment he has had, he answered, ''The Irish Kennel Club's Golden Jubilee show in Dublin, in 1972. I drew 205 entries, of which 110 were Irish Setters, which they told me was the greatest turnout of the redcoats in 30 years.''

Bud's way with a dog once served him in a most unlikely circumstance. He was in an aisle seat at a concert of the New York Philharmonic in which the featured work was a hunting concerto. As a special effect, when the hunting horns of the concerto sounded, a real Beagle pack was to run across the stage. However, the last dog jumped off and started to run up the aisle. Bud reached out, scooped up the little hound and returned it to the stage. Flashlight bulbs went off and the next day the picture appeared on the second front page of the *Times*.

Dog show history was made at Greenville, S.C., in February 1972, when Ch. Szentivani Ingo was named for the top prize. It was the first time since dog shows have been held in America that a Komondor had been chosen as best. Derek Rayne, who made the decision, said, ''He's one of the soundest dogs of any breed I've ever judged.'' High praise indeed!

The Komondor, known as Duna (Hungarian for Danube) is owned by Dr. Marion J. Levy, Jr., and his wife, Joy. The professor, who is Director of the East Asian Studies Program at Princeton, is a well-known figure around the campus. Tall, bespectacled, he was wearing blue jeans long before they became internationally popular, and often he trudges across the campus carrying books in a canvas bag, slung over his shoulder. When he and his wife decided they wanted one of the big white dogs, whose coat hangs in coarse cords making him resemble a huge mop, they couldn't find one.

''We called the Hungarian consulate and even wrote to the Prime Minister,'' said the educator. ''Finally, we received a photo and an offer for two pups. Next we were greeting them at Kennedy Airport.'' At that time the Levys knew nothing about showing, and entered the pups at what they thought was a little local show. It was none other than Trenton, and the judge was the noted all-rounder, Bea Godsol. ''Mrs. Godsol gave us so much encouragement about Duna, we decided to show him,'' said the professor. ''We couldn't see traveling around the country, so we waited for another local show.'' That was Trenton the next year, and Duna won a 5-point major. Since Dr. Levy was extremely busy at the university, he turned Duna over to Bob Stebbins, a professional handler.

In April 1971, the big white dog won a Working group, the first Komondor to ever gain that achievement. A great crowd-pleaser, Duna went on to score 4 bests in show and 86 group placements—records that were to stand until 1979. But even more, he really introduced the breed to America.

When President Nixon was preparing to go to China, the State Department phoned Dr. Levy and asked that he come down and brief members who were making the trip about that country. The professor agreed, but only if they would permit him to bring Duna. So for a month the pair would drive to Washington. ''He learned to open the revolving door,'' said the professor. ''He would stand on his hind legs and push.'' Duna, ever the gentleman, curled up next to the professor and slept during his lecture on China.

By far, the majority of judges have just a breed or two. In this category is Dr. Alvin Novick, a batman and Shih Tzu man. The Yale professor, who teaches animal behavior, is a world authority on bats. In 1955, he spent a year in Ceylon, and then in the Belgian Congo collecting the nocturnal flying mammals. He recorded their sonar signals and studied how they use them. Since then he has made a series of field trips to Panama, Mexico and Jamaica to study bats. ''They measure distance, direction and target movement by analyzing the echoes they get back from their own signals,'' said the professor. He keeps a colony of bats at Yale. ''I have a simulated tropical cave, which is kept dark, at 80 degrees Fahrenheit and with high humidity. The bats are free to fly and there are six species, four of which have reproduced in captivity, a most rare event.''

Dr. Novick went to his first dog show, Elm City, in 1964 and was captivated by a pair of Shih Tzu, then being shown in the Miscellaneous Class. ''For two years I tried to buy one and then stumbled over one at a pet shop in New Haven,'' he recalled. ''She was such a pleasure that I decided to get a male pup, from the same pet shop, and breed. When eventually there were pups, I gave them to friends.'' While walking in the city with one of his pets, a passer-by said he knew the breed and offered to introduce Dr. Novick to other Shih Tzu owners. Shortly after, the professor was visited by Audrey Fowler and he persuaded her to sell him a bitch. Then he bred the bitch to Rover, his pet shop dog. ''My breeding may not have been too scientific,'' admitted the scientist, ''but it did rather well. One of the pups, Marlboro's Tawny Rock, I took to a match show. Neither of us had ever been in a ring but the Rock was best male pup over 24 others and I felt I really had accomplished something. His grandson, Marlboro's Ursus Teddyi, took the breed from the puppy class at the Canadian national specialty.''

Although the professor bred very sparingly, he managed to finish a half-dozen champions. He also became involved in club work and was president of the Elm City club. A charming, witty man I remember him at the microphone at an Elm City show, describing the breeds in the groups to a full house. His was not the stilted reading we hear at too many of the large shows; he ad libbed continually, throwing in some choice morsels about a dog's behavior and characteristics of the breed.

Dr. Gerda Kennedy, transplanted from Austria to Oklahoma, breeds Afghans and Lippizaners—and does great with both.

Using Horse Sense to Breed Dogs

Among the nicknames the Dalmatian has acquired over the years is that of "coach (or carriage) dog." So it was perfectly normal for William (Bill) Fetner and his wife Jean to have Dals for she is one of the most talented equestriennes in America. For years, Jean has ridden her mounts to world and national saddle horse championships. Since I covered many National Horse Shows at Madison Square Garden, it always was nice to see her triumph. It made for a good story, since I could allude to her winning Coachman Kennels' Dals, as well.

"Showing dogs is a great family sport," said Fetner. "All three of our sons joined us in the ring and all finished champions. When I started to judge in 1953, I stopped showing but the kennel name was kept in the ring by the boys. And they had problems, since they couldn't show if I happened to be judging at a particular event."

The Fetners never had a large kennel, although they bred 25 champions. "The secret of having a successful kennel is to have good bitches," said the St. Louis fancier. "They are the backbone. The same is true with a winning stable. You must have good brood mares. Of the Dals we had, I'm most proud of Ch. Coachman's Cake Walk. We showed her very sparingly, preferring she leave her mark on the breed and be a brood bitch. That she did, for six pups she whelped became champions."

Fetner said he prefers judging to showing. "When I received my license I said I wanted to judge for a specific reason," he explained, "to be absolutely impartial. It's a hobby with me, not a business, and I felt I had a good eye." Fetner, who is chairman of the board of one of the largest independent insurance agencies in America, maintains he has learned a great deal, as far as judging is concerned, from having owned horses.

"With saddle horses, movement is the key factor and my eyes are trained to watch for the good mover. In the dog show ring, I also demand movement, particularly in the Sporting and Hound breeds. They are supposed to be able to go."

During World War II, Fetner was an Air Force pilot. "I always liked to fly," he said. So it is no wonder that the Fetners enjoy birds as another hobby. They have ten big birds—four macaws and six cockatoos—as well as a collection of finches. "Our Hyacinth, the largest of all the macaws, is 40 inches in length and a lovely blue," said Bill, "but it is a Cataline—a cross between scarlet and blue and gold—who really gets things going. His name is Ralph. If we move him to a new cage, it calls for much conversation. 'Hey, Ralph, how ya doing?' say the others."

Walking in circles usually leads nowhere. But it has brought Mrs. Alan Robson of Glenmoore, Pa. fame in two sports—dogs and horses. In the canine rings, she has had more than 60 champions and her Basset, Ch. Slippery Hill

Westbury believes in getting next year's show underway fast. Manning the departure gate are Nan Goodman, Walter Goodman (no relative) and Mrs. Vana Mapplebeck. — *Spear.*

Two breeds we don't get to see very often. At left, Mrs. Floyd Mann with her Spinoni Italiani, which is not yet accepted for AKC registration but may compete in the Miscellaneous class at the shows. Right, Mrs. Herbert H. Miller with her Portugese Water Dog, one of about 350 of the breed believed to be in the world today.

Hudson, became the top winner in the history of the breed. In equestrian circles, year after year her open fine harness horses and harness ponies were among the best in the country. In 1975, she rode her homebred mare, Christmas Carol, to the world amateur three-gaited championship. At the National Horse Show, I had the pleasure of watching Mrs. Robson triumph with her horses as well as with her dogs.

"As long as I can remember, we had dogs," she said. "When I was only 10, I took an English Setter to Morris and Essex. I was also riding at the time, and I did better on the horses than in the dog ring."

In dogs, Dalmatians were her big breed, although she also had Shelties, all three varieties of Poodles, Dobermans, Schipperkes, Smooth Dachshunds and Pembroke Welsh Corgis. She has been a judge of Dals and Shelties for more than two decades.

What about Bassets? "Only Hudson," she replied. "Bobby Barlow, my handler, phoned one day and said he had seen a good one and would I like to buy it. I agreed but said he would have to do the showing, that I was too busy at the time with my horses. He certainly did well with him."

Mrs. Robson told me that it took 30 years before she had her first best in show in dogs. "That was in 1974, when a liver-spotted Dal, Ch. Coachkeeper's Blizzard of Q. A. finally made it. I wasn't there and the editor of a local paper phoned to give me the good news." Since then they've come a little more frequently, and at this writing her Dal, Ch. Green Starr's Colonel Joe, has 18 bests in show.

But the real silverware has been won by horses—over 1500 trophies!

It was a fall that sent Mrs. William Wimer to the dogs. Active in horse show circles, she was thrown by a hunter in 1927, and decided to switch her activities, so she bought some Airedales and Sealyhams. Although most modern day breeders associate Mrs. Wimer with Sealyhams (her Ch. Dersade Bobby's Girl culminated a tremendous career by taking Westminster in February 1977, and in the 1950s and '60s she had other great representatives of the breed) Mrs. Wimer also gained fame as a Beagler. It was while she was judging at Back Mountain, in 1946, that she bought a Beagle pup as a pet. That was Lord Brentwood, who became a champion on his first birthday. Her Brentcliffe Kennel soon became a top winner among the little hounds. Later she also had some Welsh, Wire and Smooth Fox Terriers, as well as some winning Harriers.

But by far the greatest little campaigner was Bobby's Girl, or Binny, as she was known. Haworth Hoch, who named her best at Westminster, said, "She is virtual perfection. She is probably the best specimen of a Sealyham I ever have had my hands on." Peter Green, her handler, in 1975 had flown the Sealy and several other dogs to the West Coast to compete at Santa Barbara. When the plane landed, two of the dogs were dead and Binny was in desperate shape. It took two months to bring her back, and a sensational comeback it was, for she gained the silverware at Mispillion her first time out. The next day I saw her at

Talbot, and quiet-spoken Howard Tyler, who did the final, enthusiastically told me, ''She is outstanding, showing all the time. Even in the thunderstorm we had today, she never let up.'' Then she made it three in a row in as many days, when she scored at Annapolis.

When Binny was retired after Westminster, she was the top-winning bitch in dog show history, with 51 bests. Her owner now is judging on a reduced scale. Ever the gracious lady, she lends her expertise to tell the exhibitor the good and bad of their dogs.

When I visited the kennel of Mrs. Willard K. Denton, it appropriately enough was on Succabone Road, in Mount Kisco, N.Y. That was in the early '60s and Mimi told me, ''I want a happy dog and that's what I seek, when I breed them. If you have a moody, vicious animal, he isn't good either as a show dog or pet.'' And her dogs were shining examples of what she preached. She had a tail-wagging group of dogs, from the star performer Ch. Gay Boy of Geddesburg, the top-winning Beagle in the country at the time, down to a litter of miniature Dachshund puppies, who just wanted to play and be petted.

Mrs. Denton had an interesting background, for she had been an accomplished equestrienne in the 1940s. She rode her jumpers to many trophies and blue ribbons at the National Horse Show in Madison Square Garden and won other major fixtures. After a bad spill she turned to saddle horses. Then she and her husband, who was president on the Manhattan Savings Bank, decided to show Morgan horses. They had a stable of 13 Morgans and won numerous honors with the American horse. When they turned to trotters and pacers, Mrs. Denton frequently curried and groomed their Ardencaple Stable harness horses.

In the forties, they bought a couple of Kerry Blue Terriers. Then came Pomeranians, Poodles, Shetland Sheepdogs, Miniature Schauzers and Keeshonds, and they had champions in all these breeds. In the kennel they had four large cartons brimming with ribbons won by their dogs and they had more than 300 trophies. When I visited they also had a fawn she had found wandering on the road, when it was just a couple of days old. There also were pheasants, geese, ducks and chickens.

Denton, with an eye to the future, said, ''Our economy is changing. People are interested in smaller homes and compact cars. And the smaller dog is going to have his place. It is much less expensive to feed him and it's easier to take him in the car for travel. As a result, we are breeding Miniature Dachshunds and Miniature Pinschers.''

The Dentons, living in Southbury, Conn., added Whippets to their Ardencaple Kennels and the little hounds added ribbons and trophies to the Denton collection. And in 1977, Mimi was showing a blue merle Sheltie. ''After 30 years, I'm back with the breed again,'' said she.

''My grandmother was three-quarters Mohegan,'' said Mrs. Ronald Thibault, ''so I give most of our homebreds Indian names. My kennel name, Nashau-

Auke, means between two rivers, and our town, Mansfield Center, Conn., is between two rivers.''

Long before Mrs. Thibault was winning with her Newfoundlands, she was taking home ribbons and championships with her Pompey Hollow Stable saddle horses. She did exceptionally well on the New England circuit in 1958, when she captured the saddle-seat and pleasure-horse titles, with Country Gentleman, which she had bought as a colt in a 4-H project. ''When my husband and I decided to have dogs, we wanted a big breed such as Great Danes or Great Pyrenees,'' recalled Mrs. Thibault. ''We went to Westminster but we didn't go near the rings to watch the judging. We spend our time at the benches. One look at a Newf and that settled it. We quickly forgot the Danes and Pyrenees.''

From the Little Bear Kennel of Mr. and Mrs. V. A. Chern, they bought Little Bear's Cinderella. The Connecticut fancier trained her in obedience and took her through to a CD. The Thibaults were so smitten with Cinderella, they decided to buy a male, so they could breed. They acquired Little Bear's Dauntless and in 1968, he became their first champion. Mrs. Thibault is particularly proud of a homebred, Koki De Nashau-Auke. ''Koki means 'little' in Mohegan,'' she said. ''Our Koki was the runt of the litter. But he was big in the ring for he won championships in both the United States and Canada.''

From the Thibaults' first two homebred champions—Ki Nunka (The Gay One) De Nashau-Auke and Koki Winnota (Little Woman) De Nashau-Auke, there was a litter of seven pups. Four gained their championships in this country, another was sold to a Mexican fancier and became a champion south of the border, and a bitch went to Canada, where she not only finished but became the first Newf in that land to earn a tracking degree. Ch. Da Cody De Nashau-Auke, a multiple best-in-show winner, was the top Newfoundland in America in 1976. The Indians are doing all right in the Nutmeg State.

When you speak of a man with a lot of drive, that's Harold Sydney. When he isn't judging on a weekend, he is probably driving a trotting pony. Then again, he's likely to be in Afghanistan, Africa or on the Amazon, for he's a great traveler. ''I like to get off the beaten paths and see the cultures of primitive people, living the way they did hundreds of years ago,'' he said. In his home atop Jacobs Hill, in Seekonk, Mass., are shelves filled with trophies won by his dogs and horses. On the walls are Sepik River artifacts from Papua, New Guinea ceremonial masks, wooden combs and tapa cloth from the South Pacific. On stands are wood, ivory and malachite carvings from other parts of the world.

''I was born into a household that always had dogs,'' Sydney recalled. ''I didn't actually buy a dog of my own until I was 19. It was an Irish Setter and we had little success in the breed ring. But my wife and I both like to hunt and I organized the first field trial to be held by the Irish Setter Club of New England.''

At Westminster, Sydney saw some Gordon Setters and decided it was time for a change. He did much better with the black and tan and in each year from 1950 to 1955, his dogs won the Gordon Setter Club of America award as the year's top

Gordon. In the late '50s, the Bay Stater acquired some Bedlington Terriers and he had a half-dozen to match his Gordon titleholders. He also had Salukis, Pointers and Cocker Spaniels. "The dogs led me to the ponies." he admitted. Clint Callahan and Charlie Palmer, professional handlers, owned some trotters and after watching them, Sydney decided he would take a fling. So he bought a pair and began to race them at nearby tracks. On his grounds, he has his own training track and on the walls of his stable are more than 225 ribbons the horses have won.

Sydney has had a license to judge dogs since 1951.

The first time I met Dr. Gerda Kennedy, there were tears streaming down her cheeks. For her pride and joy, Shangrila's Phaeahna Phaedra, had just won the national Afghan specialty. "She's a homebred," the former Viennese surgeon exalted, "the fourth generation of my breeding." And when I asked, "Were you nervous when you were in the ring?" she confessed, "More so than when I was operating in Vienna, with bombs falling all around the hospital."

On occasions, I would meet this charming, gracious woman, first when she was actively showing, then when she began to judge. In 1972, Gerda was judging International and I was there with Vera, covering. We were on our way to the Southwest and the transplanted Austrian, who was living in Broken Arrow, Okla., invited us to spend a day or two at her home, to break up the trip. There we learned her story.

She stopped practicing medicine after she married William Kennedy, a chemical engineer. They lived on 13 acres in a suburb of Tulsa, where Gerda, at the time, had 85 dogs (mostly Afghans), three Lippizaners, two cats, geese and ducks. The star of her kennel was Phaedra, for the black and silver, with a name from Greek mythology, held the national record for victories by an Afghan bitch.

Gerda's career in dogs started in 1961, when she acquired her first Afghan. "I heard there was a show, at Muskogee, not too far from home, so I entered my Afghan to see what we could do. We did terribly. I messed everything up." But this slight woman has an iron will. "I left determined to come up with a winner," she declared. "So I bought two champions from Cynthia Guzevich—Vishtah Joh-Cyn, who became my foundation bitch, and Swedveikas Joh-Cyn. Using my knowledge of genetics from my medical days, I have line-bred over the years. Phaedra is the culmination of my program."

Gerda was especially proud of her Lippizaners. It certainly was strange to see these beautiful white horses in Oklahoma, so far from the Vienna ring, where they have thrilled millions over the years.

Since 1969, Gerda has been judging extensively, both in this country and overseas. She is a busy business executive, too. When her husband died, this woman of determination stepped into the meeting of the board of directors and announced, "Gentlemen, you are looking at the new head of the company. All the final decisions will be mine." Which shouldn't be too difficult a role for her — she has been making final decisions in the rings for years.

From Near and Far

Whenever Veronica Tudor-Williams judges, she invariably draws a huge entry of Basenjis. And with good cause, for this is the intrepid woman who has done so much for the barkless breed.

When I was in London, in 1968, I invited her to luncheon and there heard a fascinating tale. During World War II, she had met Maj. George Richards and he told her he had seen some Basenjis where the Sudan adjoined the Belgian Congo. "We made plans to go into the bush country to try and bring out some dogs. But our trip never materialized, for he was killed in action," she recalled.

In 1959, Tudor-Williams met Michael Hughes-Hall and Col. John Rybot and with them made a historic safari into central Africa. "We sailed to Port Sudan," she said, "and flew to Juba. With a native as an interpreter, we set out in a Land Rover and trailer into the jungle. Exactly where Major Richards had told us, we saw our first Basenjis. Owned chiefly by members of the Zande tribe, the dogs ran the gamut, ranging from poor specimens to very good ones, which could have competed in any show ring. Then there were a few that were better than any we had in England at the time."

When the visitors tried to buy dogs, they found the natives weren't willing to sell. "I made a ghastly error," said Tudor-Williams. "I offered $50 for a beautiful Basenji, along with some costume jewelry. The owner turned her back, called the dog and walked away. What I didn't realize was that I had offered a sum big enough to buy the whole village. The owner apparently figured if the dog was worth that much, she should keep him." Tudor-Williams finally managed to buy a six-week-old pup for the equivalent of $8. The Englishwoman named her Fula of the Congo and Fula made Basenji history. Not in the ring, for she was never shown, but Fula's offspring won more than 50 championships since they first were shown at a specialty in London in 1962. Stanley Dangerfield, the English judge, told me, "Fula made a bigger contribution to her breed than any other animal." High praise indeed for an $8 purchase.

Basenjis with the "of the Congo" suffix have been sold to many parts of the world. "A couple knocked on my door and asked to see some Basenjis," reminisced the small Englishwoman. "The man said his mother had bought one from me and that he and his wife were enchanted with the breed. When they picked out a pair, I asked their names. 'I'm King Michael of Rumania,' he replied, 'and this is my wife, Queen Anne. We are so indebted to you for permitting us to buy these two.' "

As a boy in Wales, Denis Grivas was surrounded by Terriers—Scotties, Smooth and Wire Fox. "My father and all my uncles and aunts had Terriers," he recalled. So what did the slender, sandy-haired man breed when he came to this country? "My specialty was breeding and showing Boxers," said he. "I started before World War II and had them for 35 years."

The transplanted Welshman, a resident of New Orleans for almost three decades, started to handle professionally in 1952. He never had a large string, being content to show from six to eight dogs. "I didn't want to have more than I personally could take care of," said Denis. "We knew each other. It was almost as if they were my own dogs." In 1963, he stopped handling and began to judge.

In his quiet way, he will help the newcomer, offering encouragement, or if he sees an obvious pet, suggesting the owner stop showing the animal and try and acquire a dog with greater possibilities. "I've been in the sport for 55 years," he told me, "and can see quite a difference. In the early days, there were far fewer dogs but overall there was quality. Now there is quantity but except in the top dogs of a breed, much of the quality is missing."

Cynthia Guzevich is a woman of many talents. She, her husband and their dogs played a role in the space program and did research for the Atomic Energy Commission. As a breeder, she is well known for her Italian Greyhounds, Miniature Poodles, Pekingese and Afghans and as an international judge she has ruled in rings on four continents. Cynthia is the only American to be a member of the women's branch of The Kennel Club in London. In the art world, the New Mexican has gained fame for her oils and sculptures.

For six years Cynthia and John Guzevich and their dogs—six Weimaraners and six German Shorthaired Pointers—were engaged in the space-and-missile program. "The dogs had to recover instruments in the missiles that were dropped from jets," explained Cynthia. "Often the instruments would only be the size of a cigarette pack or even smaller, and would be buried in five or six feet of sand. We worked in the blazing heat of the desert and then in snow to our waists in the mountains. The instruments would have the scent of squelene on them and the odor would last for a year. Probably the most famous find our dogs made occurred when an instrument, worth $75,000, fell from a plane. All the Air Force could tell us was that it was within a 60-mile area. One of our Weimaraners located it in 38 mintues. In this phase of the work, we taught the dogs just three commands — Look, Find and Retrieve. However, when we were operating with high explosives, the orders were — Look, Find, Hold and Don't Touch. One of the astronauts was so impressed with their performances, he said, 'I hope they are assigned to our programs, so that in our return to Earth, should anything happen, the dogs will find us.'"

Mrs. Guzevich, who lives in Las Cruces, emigrated to the United States from her native Munich, Germany, in 1948. "I brought some Pekes with me," she recalled, "and later I added silver Miniature Poodles. Then I became interested in IGs and imported 18 from Sweden." She had great success with them. "The breed matures quite young," said the attractive blonde. "I finished 35 champions, when they were still puppies."

Her IGs gained such fame that the Maharajah of Mysore, who had been in this country, stopped at the Vatican on his way back to his state in India. There he saw some IGs and became intrigued with the breed. Told the best were in

America, and in New Mexico, his aides contacted the State Department. Washington called the Governor, and officials at the State Executive Mansion eventually phoned Cynthia. Thus, a pair of the Toy dogs were dispatched to New York. From there a private jet flew them to India.

And which IG was the greatest dog she ever owned? "None," was the reply. "It was an Afghan, whom I showed just enough to gain his championship in this country. He was Ch. Tanjores Domino and I have a framed certificate calling him at the time, 'the most titled dog in the world.' I bought him in the late fifties' in Sweden. He then held six championships acquired in Europe, so I made it seven with his American."

Long before I met Olga Smid, I heard about her. Stanley Dangerfield, the British arbiter, had judged a show in Brno, Czechslovakia in 1965, and reported that he had ruled on some of the best Skye Terriers he ever had seen and that they were owned by a Prague resident, Mrs. Smid. The Czechoslovak expatriate left her homeland in 1968. There she not only had been a famous breeder and judge but had played a leading role in the Czech Kennel Club. For six years she had been in charge of the stud book and signed all the pedigrees. She settled in Chickasha, Oklahoma, and is now judging in this country.

When I asked how she had become interested in Skye Terriers, certainly an unusual breed for Central Europe, she replied, "My husband's college roommate gave him a puppy in 1944. It happened to be a Skye, although neither my husband nor I ever had heard of the breed. After the war, I bought a bitch and started to breed. One of my dogs, Beauty of Scalpy, was the first Skye in Europe to win a hunting certificate. He was the Czechoslovak national Skye champion in 1951 and 1952." Mrs. Smid never had a large kennel, breeding only a litter or two a year. But her dogs became famous and she sold them to fanciers around the world. Two of which she is particularly proud went to the Isle of Skye—the breed's original homeland. When she was in Europe, she had six international champions and 34 titleholders, with certificates from eight other countries. She received her license as an international judge in 1954.

"Now I have to begin all over," she told me. "The AKC has approved me for a half-dozen Terrier breeds. It's not much, but it's a start."

When Leslie Benis first showed a corded Puli, in 1965, the judge gave his dog reserve, for the arbiter never had seen a corded dog. The same thing happened at the next two shows but then an Australian broke the ice. The Aussie had judged corded Pulis back home and chose Cinkotai Czibesz best of breed.

Czibesz had come to this country with impressive credentials for he was an international champion, with awards in Czechoslovakia, France, Belgium, and Mexico. "I'll never forget Pasadena," said Benis, an architect, who lives in Tarzana, Calif. "Bea Godsol gave him the group. I was so nervous that when I took him in for best in show, I goofed things up. But before I stopped showing him he was the top-winning Puli in America three years in a row."

101

Benis, who left Hungary during the revolution in 1956, recalled that "Back in my native country we always had dogs. My uncle, Dr. Erno Kubinszky, was a veterinarian and a judge. As the vet for the Hungarian police, he would select dogs for the department. As a result, he had some of the best German Shepherds in the country."

Benis imported his first Puli in 1964 and she quickly became a champion. His next import was best of breed from the classes at Santa Barbara the next year. "She arrived with a corded coat," he said, "and I quickly combed her out before taking her into the ring, for no corded Pulis were being shown."

Benis, who judges both here and abroad, when asked about the progress the breed has made in America, said, "In my early years here, the Puli had become long in body, the coat was silky and the muzzle too long. This has been largely corrected. In Hungary, they still come from working stock. At a show in Budapest I judged 160 Pulis. My best of breed belonged to a forest ranger, who used him as a working dog." Benis is a great believer in conditioning. "Each day I ride a bike for five miles and I have my Pulis run along beside me. It keeps us all in shape."

"Everything I have in the United States, I owe to the dog show sport," Pedro Rivero of West Palm Beach, Fla., told me. Rivero, now a judge, was president of the Cuban Kennel Club for 15 years. "I left Cuba shortly after the ill-fated Bay of Pigs invasion," he said. "My wife had been able to get out a couple of months earlier. We received a phone call that she was to be arrested, so we rushed to the airport, with one suitcase and two Cocker Spaniels. I was worried as to how she would fare when the plane landed in Miami. Then I remembered a Lubin family I had met at a show. I phoned them and they very kindly not only met her at the airport, but drove her to their home."

Meanwhile, Rivero was having his own troubles. "We owned the oldest newspaper in Cuba, *Diario de la Marina,* founded by my grandfather in 1832," he said. "After the Castro regime took over, the paper was shut down. I had to leave in even more of a hurry than my wife. A jeep pulled into my front driveway, with militiamen, who would have arrested me. I ran out the back door. A friend put me into the trunk of his car and drove me to a park. Then I went to a movie, where it was dark, phoned some friends I had made showing dogs, and they helped me escape to Miami. I arrived penniless, with only the clothes I was wearing, and phoned the Lubins. They again came to the rescue, taking me into their home." Two weeks later, Charles Davis, president of the West Palm Beach KC, found Rivero a job. Rivero, who in 1979 was 65 years old, recalled how his family always had dogs—German Shepherds,, German Shorthaired Pointers and Fox Terriers. However, it was principally Cocker Spaniels for which he was known.

"I imported a Cocker, South Florida Showgirl, from the United States, when I was 20," he said. "She took best in show at the second dog show ever held in Cuba." She was the first of a dozen Cocker champions Rivero owned. The fancier showed one of his Cockers, Cuban Latest Edition, to titles in Cuba, the United States, Mexico and Venezuela, going best in show in Havana, Mexico City and Caracas. "In 1946, I received an AKC license to judge," recalled Pedro, "the only Latin at the time to be certified." Rivero accepts a limited number of judging assignments, and charges no fees, just expenses. "I judge for the love of the sport and what it has done for me," he said.

The Heskethane Yorkshire Terriers have been bred on three continents. Beryl Hesketh started with them in her native England, continued when her then husband, a geologist and exploration manager for an oil company, was transferred to Venezuela and since 1960, when the Heskeths moved to the United States, has bred them on both the East and West Coasts. "We had the only Yorkies in Venezuela," she recalled. "When we were living in the jungle, besides my little dogs, I had a wild pig and a jaguar for pets."

In addition to her activities with Yorkies, when she was in England, she played a good deal of field hockey. When she was in South America, a team arrived from the West Indies to play the Caracas Sports Club field hockey squad and Beryl promptly was drafted to play on the Caracas men's team.

"We returned to England, from South America," she recalled, "and I started to breed Yorkies earnestly. So when we came to America, I brought 17 with me. I was sure they all would become champions but it took me only a few trips into the ring to realize that I had good pets but not show dogs."

She learned quickly. Acquiring Bermyth Lad of Heskethane, she finished the three and a half pounder at Providence, in 1963. He became the kennel's basic stud dog. Two years later, Beryl showed Amanda of Heskethane to her title, the first homebred champion. At Saw Mill, in 1979, her Heskethane Tempaling became the 64th champion Beryl has bred or owned. Beryl also is prominent in clubwork, being a vice president of the Progressive Dog Club and a director of the Owner Handler Association of America.

The mystique surrounding Mrs. Geraldine Dodge, the lady of Giralda and sponsor of the matchless Morris & Essex shows, remains strong for the dog fancy. So strong, in fact, a public auction of her bronze statuary and some other possessions, conducted by Sotheby Parke Bernet, brought an astonishing $7,000,000.

Legendary judge and legendary dog—Alva Rosenberg awarding best in show to the Pekingese, Ch. Chik T'Sun of Caversham, the foremost best in show winner in AKC history. Chik, owned by Mr. and Mrs. Charles C. Venable and handled by Clara Alford, was retired following best in show at Westminster 1960 with a record of 126 all-breed bests. He won 169 Toy groups (including Westminster three times).
- *Ludwig*

Judges

$\mathbf{A}$ DOG JUDGE must rise to all occasions.

I remember Henry Stoecker doing a group, when a Great Dane messed in his ring. Now if there is anything that upsets that all-rounder it is a dog having an accident (Henry would use a much more graphic expression). Livid with rage, the judge stormed across the ring, placed a chair over the mound, and roared at his steward, "Call for a clean-up man." Minutes went by and no clean-up man. This time Henry grabbed the walkie-talkie and spluttering, demanded immediate attention. Looking up he saw a small Boy Scout walking into the ring. "What are you doing here?" demanded Henry, "Get out!" "But sir, I'm the clean-up man." "Well, clean it up," pointing to the chair. "Pardon me, sir," said a very astonished youngster, "but what dog did that?" Stoecker, in disgust, motioned to the big Dane. Looking left and right, a bewildered clean-up "man" inquired, "But sir, how did he get under the chair?"

Although there have been many changes in the half century since the *Times* sent me to the dogs, fanciers today have one complaint in common with their exhibitor cousins of yesteryear—the judges.

I was in a unique position in the dog world, for I was neither a judge, steward, exhibitor nor club official. Indeed, while I actually was covering the shows, I wasn't even a dog owner. To compare the show ring to the theater, I stood in the wings. I heard comment from all sides, often contradictory, frequently amusing and always I'd lend a sympathetic ear, for this was serious business for those involved.

At the show's end, the judges would tell me why they had made their selection. First there was the statement to be printed, then off-the-record remarks. Some of the stock phrases were so inane, I would use nothing. A favorite was, "He was asking for it all the time." Now I have seen thousands of dogs but I have yet to see one so articulate that he could talk to the judge. However, at one show, Ch. Marinebull's All The Way, the extroverted Bulldog owned by Karl and Joyce Dingman of Richfield, Minn., was just about to be given the blue rosette by the judge. Karl, believing the arbiter had pointed to the

Bulldog, released Goober from the lead and showman that he is, the red-and-white sourmug ran over to the No. 1 spot. Whereupon the judge bellowed, "Put him No. 4—no dog is going to tell me how to make my placements!"

Then we have the arbiters whose choice comment is, "He was in magnificent condition and had a beautiful coat." If Rover wasn't in condition and had a poor coat, he had no right being shown and something was amiss with the group judge who sent him into the final. On occasions, and rare ones, an arbiter would come up with a surprisingly illuminating observation. Years ago, when ocean travel still was the principal means of transportation between America and Europe, Len Carey, after picking his winner told me, "I can tell how long a Terrier has been off the boat from England. This one must have just come over, for he has a superb, hard coat. That English climate and the dogs getting plenty of outdoor exercise certainly do wonders with the coat."

Three times in succession, a well-known judge gave me the "He was asking for it" routine and three times I gave him no quote, the last time not even mentioning the arbiter's name. Whereupon, I received a letter from him asking if there was a misunderstanding between us. When I expressed my feelings about talking dogs, he changed his line. At his next best-in-show assignment, he proclaimed, "I gave it to Rover because he is an outstanding specimen of the breed." That put our official back in print, but I warned him he would have to think up something else the next time.

Several prominent judges have told me, "You write something. You can say it better than I." A sorry admission, I'm afraid.

After many a show, when the tents were coming down, I had to battle the chair concessionaires or superintendent's men so that I could have a table and something to sit on when I pounded out my story. At a Monmouth County fixture I called out to Dr. Ed McGough, the club president, "I'll have to miss the edition if I can't keep the chair, since I'm unable to type standing." The good psychiatrist rose to the occasion, buying it from the concessionaire. The next year when I arrived, there was a formal ceremony, with the chair being presented to me. On the back, in large black letters, was printed my name and *The New York Times*.

With shows running so late, invariably I was faced with the problem of typing my story hastily and then getting to a telephone. On a Saturday, the *Times* went to press on its first edition at 5:30 P.M. Very few shows ended early enough to make this deadline, for the story had to be typed, phoned to New York (where a tape recording was made of my voice) and then transcribed so it could be edited. Minutes, even seconds counted, for by making that first edition, some quarter of a million readers across the country would learn who had been best in show. The first edition was particularly important, since that was the one mailed to out-of-town subscribers.

Many judges are so eager to have their picture taken, which will appear in dog magazines and perhaps lead to more assignments, they give precedence to the show photographer, thinking the press coverage can wait. It can't. Speed is the decisive factor in having the show results printed in the next day's paper. Dog magazines, after all, will not carry the pictures until two or three months later.

Some Experiences as a Handicapper

Dr. Tom Davies, a research chemist, and president of Springfield, was among the first to put on his own show, without a superintendent. I had talked over the situation with him and he scheduled his groups early enough so that I had a fighting chance to make the first edition.

By the time the fifth group was over, I selected two of the group winners I felt might go all the way. Hastily I pounded out two stories, one for each dog winning. The moment Herb Roling, the best-in-show judge, made his decision—and fortunately it was one of my two choices—I raced to the table where he was signing his judge's book and asked for a sentence explaining his selection. I jotted down a few words on the catalogue, ran for the telephone and quickly dictated my story. By the time the picture of the best-in-show winner had been taken, my story already was in New York and we made the edition. The next day at Willimantic, Monroe Stebbins, the AKC field representative, asked, "What did you do, tell Roling who to pick?" The efficiency of the press apparently isn't always appreciated.

I didn't always guess right. At a Boardwalk show, the top-winning bitch in the East had won her group and I figured she would easily go all the way. I typed the story and phoned it to the paper. But Henry Stoecker, doing best in show, didn't agree with my choice. Hastily I ran to the telephone and killed what would have been my first-edition story.

In a little park in Memphis, there's a statue of W.C. Handy, composer of "St. Louis Blues" and other early jazz classics. In 1973, the 100th anniversary of his birth was observed in Tennessee's largest city.

A few months later there was another centennial. The Memphis Club celebrated 100 years of dog shows in America. It did it with a munificent flourish, with $2,000 for the top winner and $500 for each group victor. "As far as we can ascertain," Jim Vaughters, the show chairman, told me, "It's the richest award ever made in the United States for a best in show."

The judging took place at the Mid-South Fair Grounds, site of a show held on October 7, 1874. The Centennial drew 1,839 dogs from 40 states, Canada and even two from England. Helen Furber and Lynette Schelling from Australia and Ernest Chang, from Honolulu, were among the 44 arbiters. None of the group judges did any breeds and Stoecker had only the best-in-show assignment. So the six finalists had had to pass the scrutiny of three arbiters. It was a festive night. All the officials wore dinner jackets and women, dressed in crinolines, assisted with the trophy presentations. There was a huge ring—100 by 50 feet—and the wildly enthusiastic spectators, four deep, remained until the end. And they had something to cheer about for it was a brilliant final, all six dogs having been best-in-show performers.

Irene Nail (now Mrs. Edd Bivin) was the AKC field representative and as I sat to type my story, she stopped at the table. "Bet you a nickel I can pick the winner," said I. With the large entry, it was quite a boast. Irene, never one to pass up a bargain, quickly produced her five cents. At the end of the first group, I typed a couple of paragraphs and phoned them to the *Times*. Then came the second group and it went to Mrs. Robert V. Clark's Wire Fox Terrier, Ch. Sunnybrook Spot On. At that time, the little English import, handled by Peter Green, had been best 18 times, and he had been my choice with Irene.

Suddenly there was a fast meeting with Vaughters, C. W. Flowers, the club president, and several other Memphis officers. Stoecker was called over and asked, "What's this about the show being fixed? The reporter from the *Times* claims he knows who is going best." Stoecker laughed and responded, "Well, he knows more than I do. There are still four groups to be judged." Fortunately, Spot On wasn't Stoecker's choice. He picked Mrs. Randall Frech's orange four-pound Pomeranian, Ch. Randy's Jolly Wee Peppi, from Kenesaw, Ga., and handled by Mrs. Houston Clark, much to my relief, and I'm sure the Memphis club's as well. It taught me a lesson. Never, even as a joke, announce a winner.

Incidentally, when I would arrive at a show early in the morning, I'd invariably be bombarded by fanciers, who are great gossips, telling me who was going best in show. "You can write your story now," I'd be told. Rarely would their predictions come true. Indeed, my winning average was considerably better.

Judging the Judges

I have always felt the AKC permits arbiters to work long after they are capable of judging. There was one all-rounder who was extremely vain and refused to wear glasses. His eyesight was so poor, he couldn't read the signs on the rest rooms and had to be guided to the door marked "Men." Handlers knew he couldn't see or remember too well so they would strive to get at the end of the line, for he would forget those dogs he had gone over at the start.

Then there was an all-rounder who the AKC finally stopped. At his next-to-last show, he did the Terrier group. He was so befogged that the handlers helped to guide him through the proper procedures.

Another all-rounder's sight was so bad, his steward had to ask him for his placements and show him where to sign his book. Yet these men continued to draw good entries, so clubs were anxious to have them judge. I always felt that the exhibitor was being short-changed by these once-great arbiters.

I suppose it is human nature to occasionally favor a friend, but sometimes it can be almost ludicrous. One of our judges had a best-in-show assignment and the Terrier representative was being handled by his owner and breeder, unfortunately also a neighbor and good friend of the judge. It was foregone conclusion who was going to get the red, white and blue rosette and the five other handlers realized it. The only difficulty was that the Terrier wasn't making the judge's job easy. He refused to cooperate and kept acting up. He jumped around like a puppy when he was gaited, and didn't stand too well when the judge was going over him. Our arbiter sent him out a second time and the feisty little dog again leaped around. The judge had just about given up on him and started to walk to the table to sign her book, when she wheeled around and asked the owner to try once again. This time the Terrier decided to walk and to the relief of all, the judge was able to award him the silverware.

However, the record for long judging would have to go to a breeder judge at an Irish Setter specialty, who spent nearly two hours going over her champions. Exhibitors were so tired waiting, they brought chairs into the ring and sat while the judge went over the dogs. "It took you rather long to make your decision," I told her. "Yes, I was afraid I'd make a mistake." She did.

At the other extreme was Ed Pickhardt. At a Staten Island show on the old pier, which jutted into Lower New York Bay at Tompkinsville, Ed was doing best. Staten Island was a favorite for exhibitors. Not only was there a pleasant ferry boat ride, in those days still five cents, but one could sit on the wharf and watch the ocean liners sail by. Pickhardt always was so fast that I could never type the summaries of the last group, lest I miss the judging and fail to get a statement from him. On this day, and it was an extremely hot one, when the call came over the loudspeaker for best in show, only five dogs appeared. The Toy group winner's owner was out on the pier, on the shady side, keeping cool and enjoying the breeze. "Make one more call," said Ed to his steward, "and then I'll start judging." So for the only time in my career in the sport, I saw a final start with five dogs. Suddenly a red-faced owner appeared carrying a Chihuahua. Ed let him into the ring but was so angry, he was even more red-faced than the exhibitor. The Chihuahua didn't go best.

The late Joe Faigel was also a speedy judge. I was once sitting beside him as he waited to go into the ring to judge a Toy group. The show superintendent came over to him, and said some of the breed judges were running behind schedule, and could he possibly take an hour with the group. "I can do it only if you let me make a speech," quipped Joe.

As difficult as it is to get a good statement from a judge in English, think of the difficulties from an arbiter who doesn't speak the language. At a German Shepherd specialty on Long Island, the judge was a man considered by most fanciers at the time as the world authority of the breed, Dr. Werner Funk, president of the 40,000-member *Verein für Deutsche Schäferhundes*. He had been active with German Shepherds since 1922 and had owned and bred the Sieger (top male) or Siegerin (top female) at six national shows in his native land. John Ringwald, a noted obedience judge and a German teacher, who had done graduate work at the University of Heidelberg, served as steward for Dr. Funk and volunteered to act as interpreter for me. But this wasn't good enough for the Doctor. He had his own interpreter, who would listen to John's translation and repeat it to Herr Funk. The latter then would dispute with Ringwald, which made it all very jolly for me.

In all of Dr. Funk's judging, it was the first time he had ever been called upon to pick a best of breed. In Germany, he explained, only the best male and best bitch are chosen, with the sexes never competing against each other. "In Germany," he said, "we rate every dog (excellent, very good, good, sufficient or undesirable). In this country, you pick only four dogs in a class and the rest of the exhibitors do not know how their dogs rate. I think it is better to give each dog a classification." Herr Funk took notes on all the dogs he judged here and said he would write a critique for each of the 216 owners. When I was alone with Ringwald I asked what impressed him the most about the German. "He stood in the ring from 8 in the morning until 7:30 in the evening and, do you know, he never once went to the men's room," answered John.

As shows continue to get larger, competition gets ever keener. Still, there is only one best. The winning handler or owner beams. And five losers complete the occasion with a few choice words of their own.

I've always felt a great sympathy for the group judges. In the final, the judge has only six dogs in front of him, all presumably of the very top quality. But in the group, he may have up to 32 (as in the Working)—and so many times the judge has said to me, "I just wish I could have handed out a half-dozen rosettes, there were so many good dogs in there."

Unfortunately, we have some judges more interested in who is at the other end of the leash than in the dog they are supposed to be ruling on. We've already observed that some tend to favor a friend and give him (or her) an edge. I saw too much of this. Fanciers term it "political" judging.

Then we have another group of arbiters who are just ignorant of the breed. A judge must not only know the standard thoroughly, he must have a sharp eye. It is like a critic understanding a good painting. Exhibitors have told me they prefer showing under a "political" judge to competing under one who doesn't know what he is doing. For the "political" arbiter may well be knowledgeable, and if he has no friends in the ring that day he can do a good job.

A judge's selection should not be too predictable, nor should it be predetermined when he walks into the ring. Unfortunately, some of our arbiters are avid readers of the dog magazines and the well-publicized canines are the ones that wind up with their nod.

However, sometimes it's the dog that the judge *believes to be* the well-publicized canine that gets the decision. A prominent Eastern handler had been having great success with a Keeshond, taking several bests in show. Another client, also a Kees owner, kept badgering him as to why her dog, whom she was certain was as good as the big winner, was unable to achieve such a win. Finally, to appease her, the handler took her Kees to a show and sure enough, he went all the way. The owner, terrifically excited, ran up to the handler, kissed him and asked, "What do we do now?" The retort was fast—"Retire him immediately!"

Alva

In any gathering of dog people, a name comes up that is treated with unanimous reverence as to authority, knowledge and integrity. For some 60 years it was known across the country and whenever Alva Rosenberg was mentioned, there was attention. For his opinions were heeded as much as appreciated.

I wanted to have a quiet chat with Alva, when he was already an octogenarian. So one autumn day I drove to his home in a lovely Connecticut valley. Above a swift-flowing brook, shaded by tall trees, on a terraced garden was a small house with a very "lived-in" atmosphere. Books and objects of art were everywhere, suggesting their constant use as part of the life and soul of this home and explaining that it was primarily a love for beauty that led Rosenberg into the antique business. The shop was in another building on the property. As I browsed through the china, lamps, pictures and figurines, Alva had an interesting story to tell about each. Perhaps it was the same understanding of form, purpose and harmony that made this man a connoisseur of dogs.

When we finally sat down in front of the fireplace under the portait of a youthful Franz Joseph, the man and living room blended into one gentle individuality. For the most striking first impression was that of great kindness and humility. A couple of stray cats curled gracefully on the sofa as the famous dog authority stroked their backs and answered my questions, clearly and knowledgeably. His only request was that he not be praised.

Rosenberg drew his first judging assignment when William Howard Taft was president. That was in 1910 and Rosenberg was 18 years old. "I judged Pomeranians at the old Red Bank Kennel Club, which has long since departed," he recalled. Later on he was to rule at more than 1,000 shows, including almost every major one in the United States. He also presided in rings in Canada, Puerto Rico and Cuba. In 1969, he did all the groups and chose the best in show at Windsor, in England. For some reason, he was never asked to pick the top winner at Westminster. His judging was so sought after and his opinion so valued that clubs often burdened him with the maximum amount of dogs—175. And this fragile, little man, quite stooped in later life, always did a remarkable job.

Alva was born in Brooklyn and went to his first show—Westminster—when he was eight years old. "My mother liked dog shows and she would take me," he reminisced. "But she was a little apprehensive, because I was so young, and said if I became tired to tell her and we would leave. Late in the day, she had a hard time getting me out of Madison Square Garden."

It was a dentist, Dr. Edward Berendson, and his wife—both judges, who started young Alva on his doggy career. "They had Bulldogs, Japanese Spaniels and English Toy Spaniels," said Rosenberg. "After school I would run to their house on Eighth Avenue, in the Park Slope section of Brooklyn, and help around the kennel. They were members of the Long Island Kennel Club and when I was a teenager they proposed me for membership. They introduced me to Dr. John deMund, who later was to become president of the AKC. Whereas most people start with a poor specimen, my first dog was a winner. Dr. deMund noticed how enthusiastic I was around the Berendsons and one day he brought a dog over to their kennel and said it was mine. It was a Russian Wolfhound, Novosti, and already was a champion. Novosti means 'news' in Russian and it was good news for me. I was just 16.''

Rosenberg had the good fortune to meet other leading figures in the dog show world of the day. He credited James Mortimer, the superintendent of Westminster from 1885 until 1915 and one of the great judges of that era, for giving him much of his knowledge. ''I'd steward for him and after judging a class, he frequently would come over and ask my opinion of the dogs we had just seen,'' he recalled. ''Then he would tell me their good and bad points, what I should be looking for when I would be judging. He stressed soundness and movement. Harry Peters was another really great judge of that period and he, too, would always tell me why he had chosen one dog over another.''

When Rosenberg started to show, in 1915, his breed was the Boston Terrier. Although he did very well, finishing a dozen, he modestly disclaimed any credit for his achievements. However, he was proud of just one, Ravenroyd Rockefeller, whom he sold to a breeder in the Midwest. ''Almost all the good Bostons at any of the shows out there today,'' he said, ''go back to my Rockefeller.''

With Alva's first best-in-show assignment came a singular honor, for he became an all-rounder. ''At the time I was licensed to do all the groups, except Sporting,'' he recalled. ''I gave best to Dr. A. A. Mitten's Irish Setter, Ch. Delaware Kate. Dr. deMund was watching the judging and came over to me and said, 'If you can pick out such a good Sporting dog, it's time you should have the group,' so I became an all-rounder.''

Rosenberg didn't belong to the school that constantly complained that shows were becoming too large and should be limited. ''As long as there is room, I feel the more dogs the better. We are striving to improve the breeds and if someone breeds a dog, he should have the opportunity to show him. Over the years I've seen a tremendous growth in entries, with more and bigger shows. I'm all in favor of this trend. Under the able supervision of the AKC, they are beautifully run.''

When I asked Alva the greatest thrill he had experienced in the sport, he promptly answered, ''Finding a good dog and starting him or her on a career. I've never hesitated to take a good one out of the classes and put it over champions. It's been my good fortune to have given some really great dogs their first best in show.''

Probably the most difficult story I ever was called upon to write was the obit for this great man. It was written from the heart and the *Times* gave it a good display.

How proud exhibitors were to say, ''My dog won under Alva Rosenberg.'' That was the seal of approval. The octogenarian was to have judged at Bronx in 1973, but he died two weeks earlier. The show was dedicated to him and I had the honor to be quoted in the catalogue, under his picture, where I said, ''I never saw him put a bad dog up, or turn a good one down.''

Some "Never-to-be-Forgottens"

Two old-time judges that stand out in my memory are Vinton Breese and Billy Lang.

Billy came up from the show world, starting as a drummer in a band and for three decades played on all of the big vaudeville circuits. He also was a theater manager and a song writer. When he retired from show biz in 1927, he entered another show biz, as a professional handler.

While beating the drums, he had become an avid fancier, attending shows and breeding dogs. Over the years, Lang handled many famous dogs, being especially successful with English Springer Spaniels. Lang never had too big a string of dogs, but those he showed invariably were good ones. In 1946, he turned in his license and was made an all-round judge.

A great raconteur, he always was popular on the circuit. He told the story of how he was driving to judge a show in Florida. Being a little late, he was moving along rather briskly. Stopped by a state trooper, Lang was asked to produce his license. The officer noted that under occupation it said AKC Judge. "What does AKC stand for?" asked the trooper. "American Kriminal Court," replied Lang. "You may go, your honor, but please drive a bit slower."

In 1953, Billy became an AKC field representative. He did such a good job he was chosen "Dog Man of the Year" in the Gaines competition.

Breese was a newspaperman, writing the dog column for *The New York Sun* for 18 years, then moving on to become dog editor for *Town and Country* and *Country Life* magazines. I often saw him judge in the late 1920s and '30s and he always put on a show. Although born in New Jersey and living there until his death in 1940, he was invariably taken for a Briton, perhaps because of his tweeds, ascot tie, white vest with stripes and pince-nez.

What a show he would put on for the gallery! He would get down on all fours, even stretch out full length, to get a better view of the dogs. Everything he did was with a flourish. Three times he judged best in show at Westminster and each time he gave it to a Terrier.

It was a poignant moment at the Vineland show in New Jersey in October 1976. For just as the leaves were turning color and falling to the ground, the career of a grand old figure in the sport was tumbling down. It was the last show Louis Murr, then 82 years old, was to judge. It ended 56 years in the sport for the stocky little man, whose once black hair then was streaked with silver. Murr had gained fame as a breeder, exhibitor and judge. His Romanoff Kennels—he once had as many as 90 Borzois—was one of the best known in America. His most famous dog was Ch. Vigow of Romanoff, considered by most authorities as the greatest Borzoi ever bred in the United States.

Murr, who came from the Basque country, shortly after completing service with the United States Army in World War I opened an antique shop on West Fourth Street in New York City. In 1920, a friend persuaded him to go to

Westminster, then held in Grand Central Palace. "It was my first show and I was entranced," he recalled. "Soon I was showing."

Murr and Westminster were synonymous. In one span, he judged at America's most prestigious show for 21 years in a row and in 1969, he had the best-in-show assignment.

Murr would put up a class dog as quickly as a champion. "I judge them according to the standard and not for their pictures in dog magazines," he maintained. He ran a tight ring for steward and exhibitor. He wouldn't tolerate a steward chatting idly with spectators. He was tolerant of amateurs but a professional handler had to follow his direction to a T, or take a verbal lashing.

In his prime, Murr judged from 50 to 60 shows a year. Was Westminster his most exciting assignment? "No," said the octogenerian, "it was in Colombia, when I judged the first show ever held in that country. There were soldiers, with fixed bayonets, standing between the ring and the spectators to make certain there would be no trouble. The next day I held a clinic and explained to each exhibitor how to show his dog and discussed the good and bad points of each animal." That was typical of the little man. He did the same thing in Hawaii and had more dogs for the clinic than were at the show.

Certainly one of the greatest all-rounders was Percy Roberts, who died in 1977. The English squire, as he was known, was 86. He had retired from judging just a couple of years earlier, because of failing eyesight.

Percy had learned his trade the hard way, starting as a kennel boy at the age of 16 for J. J. Holgate, a noted terrier breeder in Doncaster. In 1913, he was sent to this country with a shipment of Poodles Holgate had sold to an American. That started his long career in the United States.

Percy managed to get a job with the Vickery Kennels in Barrington, Ill., where Walter Reeves was manager, and he remained there for a couple of years. Shortly after World War I, he decided to branch out on his own and set up his Reverly Kennels at Noroton, Conn. It was as a handler for Stanley Halle that Percy really gained fame. In 1926, he scored a sweep at Westminster, showing Halle's Fox Terrier, Ch. Signal Circuit of Halleston to best in show, Ch. Halleston Deykin Surprise and Ch. Wyche Wondrous to best brace, and then taking the same pair, along with Ch. Signal Circuit and Ch. Signal Crusader of Halleston, to the team title.

The next year, at my first Westminster, I watched Roberts gait Ch. Pinegrade Perfection to the top award. He was back in 1934 with Halle's Ch. Flornell Spicy Bit of Halleston and in 1938 with Ch. Flornell Spicy Piece of Halleston to gain his third and fourth best in shows at the Garden. No other handler ever has guided four dogs to the premier prize.

When I was interviewing Halle, I asked him who was the greatest dog he ever owned and he promptly replied, "Spicy Piece. She was best in show every time Roberts handled her, except in 1939, when she was beaten at Westminster, after she took the group." When I expressed a little concern about the Wire's record, he said, "Well, check it with Percy." Now this was 30 years later. Yet when I called Percy, he rattled out the shows the dog had taken as though it had been the previous weeks.

In 1948, Roberts retired as a handler and applied for a judging license. Because of his wide experience, he was made an all-rounder. Roberts, who considered Westminster the greatest show in the land, judged best there in 1968.

When they were judging, Major and Bea Godsol were two of the most sought-after arbiters in the country. They both were all-rounders and were active judges for 25 years. Bea was only the second woman ever to name the best in show at Westminster. It was in 1957 and I remember her doing the unexpected; she put up an Afghan, Ch. Shirkhan of Grandeur, the first time an Afghan had taken that exalted show.

During World War II, Godsol, was in charge of the War Dog Center at Fort Robinson. "We had 1,200 dog houses and an occupant for each," he told me. Bea had a rather amusing story about her husband's unusual first name. "Major was a family name," she said. "When he joined the service, before he went to Officers' Training School, he was the most saluted private in the Army."

When they were living in Dixon, Calif., the Godsol "pack" was a topic of conversation for their neighbors. "When we were married, I had 25 dogs— Newfoundlands, Sealyhams and Beagles," recalled Bea. "Major had the same number of German Shepherds. We had 20 unfenced acres. The Beagles would take off, followed by the Terriers, Shepherds, with the Big Newfs bringing up the rear. When they started to roam off our land, the neighbors were a little startled. So we put up a fence."

The Godsols were pioneers in obedience training. The first class to be held in California was on their ranch and the first obedience match also took place there. It was a real loss to the fancy, when Major died in 1970 and Bea in 1978.

"My greatest pleasure in judging is not to find one, but not to lose one," said Joe Faigel, the short, balding, all-rounder who was one of the happiest-natured of the arbiters. Faigel, who although in his late seventies judged about 75 shows a year, died of a heart attack en route to an assignment in early 1979.

Faigel started in 1916, when he bought a Boston Terrier pup. He took the dog to a match show in Lawrence, Mass., where he met the great Alva Rosenberg. "That was to influence my whole life," said Joe. "He taught me so much. Later, when I moved to Detroit, Alva would frequently stay at my home and we would discuss dogs for long hours. I started to judge in 1932 and Alva, when he was at the same show, would try and spend some time at my ring, watching, and then tell me about my mistakes."

Before he began to judge, Faigel had been an exceedingly astute breeder. In Bostons, he bred 19 champions and sold another 20 who became titleholders. With a breed that requires so many Caesarian sections, Faigel had eight generations of free whelpers.

The Detroiter always had the habit of removing his judge's badge, even before he left the ring, when he was through with his assignments or going to lunch. When I remarked about it to him one day, he answered, "I'm a little guy. When some of these exhibitors come rushing over looking for me to find out why I didn't put up their dog, if they don't see the badge, they forget who I am. I remember one man saying, 'You look just like Joe Faigel,' and I quickly replied, 'That's what everyone tells me.' One wild-eyed exhibitor angrily told me, 'I've forgotten more about this breed than you'll ever know.' I quickly replied, 'That's the trouble, you've forgotten.'"

Faigel, in addition to breeding dogs in his early years, also raised and raced homing pigeons. Some of his birds were used by the Army Signal Corps to carry messages in World War I.

The Top Circles of Judging
The All-Rounders

Max Riddle

Max Riddle is an old friend and we've spent many hours together in this country, in the Caribbean and in Mexico. Both being newspapermen, we had a common bond. Then he has a wit and charm much too rare among the arbiters. Not only is Max licensed to judge all breeds but the Ohioan has also been a field trial judge. Indeed, he judged in the field before the ring and he was instrumental in staging the first English Springer and retriever trials in Ohio. Riddle also was chairman for both the first Brittany field trial and championship show ever held in America, both taking place in November 1943 at Ravenna, Ohio.

Ravenna and Riddle are synonymous, for he was the founder of the club and he has been its show chairman for 38 years.

A staff member of *The Cleveland Press* for three decades, when he retired in 1968, a Max Riddle Day was declared in the city, with 265 persons gathering to honor him at a dinner. It was held on a bitterly cold night and the Mayor, Carl Stokes, in his speech said, "Only Max Riddle could get me out on a night like this. When I was a law student, he helped me. Again, when I was a State Senator, he helped me. And when I became mayor, any time there were any problems with dogs, I always could call upon him to help solve them."

Riddle has judged on six continents and has flown more than a half-million miles. He has ruled in rings 28 times in South America. Three times he has been the Pooh-Bah at Japanese shows, twice each in South Africa, Hong Kong and Australia. He did Crufts in 1967. Twice at the big Richmond fixture in England, Max judged all the groups and best in show.

When the Western Reserve Club found itself deep in debt, it called upon him to help bail it out. "We opened the show with just 50 cents in the treasury," he chuckled. "In three years, the club paid off all its debts, tripling the entry."

Riddle and I met several times in Puerto Rico, when the show was at the Dorado Beach Hotel. One early morning, while splashing around in the blue Caribbean, I asked Max how he started in the sport.

"Actually it was my rabbits, that got me into it." he replied. "I had 40 or 50 and my mother decided I had to get rid of them. So I traded the entire lot for two American Foxhounds. My mother threw up her hands in despair."

Max showed his business acumen a year later, when at the age of 14 he put on a dog show. Not only did he obtain benching and serve as superintendent, but he was the watchman, as well. "I brought a cot and slept with the dogs that night to make sure they were all right," he recalled. "Best in show was a Chow Chow. I'm sure it was the first anyone had seen in Ravenna."

But then Riddle suffered a serious leg infection that required two operations. In the hospital for three months, he read every dog book he could get. He also kept busy making bamboo casting rods. "I made some money selling the rods to fishermen," said Max, "so as soon as I was discharged from the hospital, I took the money, hobbled into Cleveland on crutches and bought a Great Dane pup."

Riddle showed her at Akron and she was best of winners. The youngster, up in the clouds, took the ribbons home and framed them. Three weeks later, to his dismay, he was told he had to return them, the AKC ruling he had made a mistake on his entry blank. "I felt it was the end," said Max.

As we all know, it was far from it. Riddle now judges some 50 shows a year. Not only is he a familiar figure ruling in rings in this country, but he is the best known American arbiter overseas.

He is also perhaps the most prolific writer on dogs in history. The author of at least a dozen books, he contributed more than half the articles in *The International Encyclopedia of Dogs,* and he has won every award offered by The Dog Writers Association of America—some of them several times.

Vince Perry

The face of Vince Perry is a familiar one to millions of TV viewers. In the Perry Mason series, he was the tall, gray-haired man, who as the judge added luster to every closing scene. In films, he was the school principal in *Good Morning, Miss Dove,* with Jennifer Jones; the bishop in *Lady Godiva* and an undertaker in *The Bounty Hunter,* with Randolph Scott.

Then for more than four decades, he's been licensed to judge all the dog breeds in the United States. In his native Canada, it's been nearly a half-century.

"At the end of a year in which I had judged 60 shows, which took me into three countries," he chuckled, "I tried out for a part as a dog show judge in a movie based on the life of Albert Payson Terhune. The writer-producer looked me over and with a shake of her head, said, 'He just isn't the type for a judge.'

Fortunately, the casting director chose me for the role of a show official. It didn't bother me for the pay was just as good.''

"I've been doggy all my life. My mother said that as soon as I could crawl, I would nestle between the paws of a giant St. Bernard, who was the family pet, and go to sleep.''

Although Perry's father bred Cocker Spaniels, young Vince had a friend in every dog in the neighborhood. He especially liked the short-nosed breeds. "When I was 11," he recalled, "I went to visit an uncle who I hoped would take me to the Canadian National Exposition. But I never got there. He had a Boston Terrier, the first I had ever seen, and all I wanted was to play with the dog. And I still like the Bostons. Ever since 1918, I've had a champion of the breed.''

Perry became a member of the Canadian Kennel Club as a teenager and later served on the board for several years.

Vince also had success in the theater. In 1935, he received the best actor award in the Western Ontario Drama Festival and for his work in the Dominion Drama Festival, he received a citation for distinguished acting from Lord Bessborough, then the Governor General of Canada.

For several years, Perry was a reporter on *The Toronto Globe*, so when he registered his kennel, he named it "Globe." "Ch. Globe Glowing Ember was the first Boston Terrier bitch to go best in show in the United States," he recalled. "She did it in New Orleans.''

Perry isn't doing much acting now but he still is active judging. "Between assignments and writing for dog magazines, I manage to keep busy," said the septuagenarian.

Jim Trullinger

The big, rather slow-moving man is a collector. In his apartment in Forest Hills, N.Y., is an eight-panel Chinese screen, soapstone Eskimo carvings, an unusual mounting of moths and butterflies, and any number of artifacts he has gathered on judging assignments, including Royal Copenhagen, Royal Doulton and Beswick porcelain dogs. He is James W. Trullinger, an all-rounder, who achieved that distinction in 1938 when he was 28 years old, one of the youngest in the history of the AKC.

Big Jim had his first judging assignment when he was a freshman at Penn State University in 1929. Since then he has been seen at every major fixture in this country as well as Canada, Cuba, Puerto Rico and South America. Trullinger, an extremely articulate man, always was a pleasure to interview after he had chosen best in show. Whereas so many arbiters would blurt out something inane, Jim would ask for a few minutes to compose a statement and then it would be meaningful and succinct. It probably was part of his long training in public relations, for he was a PR director with the Statler hotel organization for more than 30 years.

Trullinger had a rather unusual start in the sport. "A magistrate in my home town of Harrisburg (Pa.) sold me a Dachshund puppy, when I was 10 years old,''

118

he told me. "By the time I was in high school, I had bought several other Dachshunds and I had the good fortune of winning championships with two dogs of my own breeding. I began to think I was pretty good. Then, I showed under Col. Robert M. Guggenheim and he straightened me out. I was 16 and showing a Saluki. There weren't too many of the breed competing at the time and mine was winning consistently. I took him to Syracuse and he was the only Saluki in the ring. Colonel Guggenheim was the judge. He went over my dog and instead of giving me a blue ribbon, handed me a red. I promptly put it on the table and started to walk out. The colonel called me back and laced me out. He told me to take the ribbon and walk out like a gentleman. I learned a lesson in sportsmanship and politeness that has served me well in life." Years later, when Trullinger became president of the Harrisburg, the first person he invited to judge at its show was Colonel Guggenheim.

Shortly after Jim was graduated from Penn State, he began to breed Dachshunds on a really big scale. He had from 35 to 50 of the badger dogs, including any number of champions. He has owned some top dogs of other breeds, particularly Pugs, for which he was well known and is the author of an important book about the breed, *The Complete Pug*.

Bill Kendrick

When William Kendrick is in the middle of the ring, you can look for surprises and he won't disappoint you. For the silver-haired judge isn't swayed by dog ads or the animal's standing in any of a half-dozen rating systems. The Philadelphian calls them as he sees them and frequently in his group placements, "Wild Bill"—as he is affectionately called—will come up with a breed that too long has been overlooked.

The nephew of W. Freeland Kendrick, a Bull Terrier enthusiast who was Mayor of Philadelphia in the mid-1920s, started to judge when he was a 20-year-old junior at Princeton, in 1924. Asked about changes over the years, Kendrick bemoaned rating systems and overhandling. "The rating system depreciates the value of best in show," said the septuagenarian. "It places too much emphasis on people with money, who can send a handler all over the country, weekend after weekend. Some of the top-ranking dogs leave very much to be desired. I feel all rating systems should be confined to the ash can. As to handling, the best handling is the least. And along those lines, I feel junior handling has done much to encourage overhandling. The whole premise of junior handling is wrong. We should be judging dogs, not kids. As long as I'm president of Philadelphia, we never will have junior handling."

Kendrick was scornful of foreign judges. "After looking at them work for 50 years in our rings, there are only two I respected and admired, Walter Glyn and Mae Pacy," he said. The Philadelphian praised the AKC for ceasing to license handlers but he said he thought the club was in error when it decided to have the.selection of best of winners follow selection of best of breed. The judge also felt that the AKC should permit other breeds, as well as Toys, to be placed as twosomes on a table. "It would be helpful if a judge could put two of the short-legged Terriers on a table together, so he could compare them."

Kendrick did a bit of reminiscing. "The AKC show, put on in Philadelphia in 1926 to celebrate the Sesquicentennial, was the first event of any consequence where there were groups. There were five judges to do best in show. Morris and Essex, which I judged many times, was the greatest show in the country. Mrs. [Geraldine Rockefeller] Dodge was conscious of the exhibitor, who today is the forgotten person. Judges invariably are provided with luncheon, but the exhibitor is lucky to be able to buy a hot dog."

Derek Rayne

The six-foot-six-inch dark-bearded Derek Rayne is an imposing figure in the ring. Opera-going fanciers agree he could be cast as Mephistopheles in *Faust*, especially after he has failed to give their entries a placement. In picturesque Carmel, Calif., where Derek has one of the better men's and women's boutiques, the well-built, slender man commands attention as he strides down the street, tourists invariably asking whether he is an actor or perhaps the mayor of the city. For many years he took pride in that he was the tallest of the AKC judges and he was rather put out when Alvin Maurer, the Pennsylvania lawyer, came along at six-feet-seven. "Well, he's not an all-rounder," laughed Rayne, "so I'm the biggest of the all-rounders." When he was made an all-rounder at just 35 years old, he was, at the time, the youngest in America.

Rayne was born in London and started showing dogs for his grandfather. "I have a card from England dated 1923," he said, "giving an Airedale I had shown a third place. I was eight years old, so that means I've been in the sport for more than a half-century." As a youngster, Derek attended many small British shows and he would listen to the old timers discuss such basics as correct ear placement, coat, shoulders, fore and hind quarters. "I learned what every judge should know—breed type," he said. "Each breed has a characteristic expression. If you see a dog looking over a fence, from its head and expression you should be able to identify the breed, without seeing the rest of the body.

Rayne is particularly proud of his library, which includes more than a thousand dog books. He also has a collection of Terrier prints. "It's a great relaxation to sit here after a busy day," said Derek. "There's always a dog story to read." To which his tall and blonde German wife, Gerda, added, "Yes, and it means a great deal more housecleaning, dusting all those volumes."

Len Carey

A wordly man known on five continents is Len Carey. A judge since 1939, his assignments have taken him around the world. "The only continents I've missed are Africa and Antarctica," he notes. "I've done Westminster 25 times, including best in show in 1964 and 1974."

Two decades earlier, his own great Doberman, Ch. Rancho Dobe's Storm, twice took the top award at Westminster, in 1952 and 1953. "I was living in New

York City at the time," recalled Len, now a resident of Solana Beach, Calif., "and as a real New Yorker, I used to run him in Central Park." Stormy sired a litter that long was the talk of Dobe breeders. Six of the seven pups became best-in-show winners.

Carey has very strong feelings on a judge not showing. "When Stormy was being campaigned," he said, "I stopped all judging. I always have maintained you shouldn't carry water on both shoulders. Speaking of judging, and I've judged in so many countries, I'd say the American exhibitor gets the best deal of all. Much as we hear our judges criticized, I feel overall they do a very good job, much better than their counterparts overseas."

Peter Knoop

Peter Knoop is one of the select group of all-rounders and he's another of that rare breed, a native New Yorker. Peter was born in Brooklyn, where he spent his early years, and grew up in Lynbrook, L.I. Knoop had a rather unusual career as a judge. Approved by the AKC in 1938 to judge Doberman Pinschers, he turned in his license after he had served three years with the Marines in the War Dogs Detachment and became a professional handler. Then in 1960, when he began to be very busy with a career on Wall Street—he was just handling weekends—he retired from walking dogs into the ring and again received a license to judge.

Since then, he has become active in club work. Shortly after he stopped handling, he was invited to join Westchester and for seven years was its bench show chairman. Peter became president of that prestigious club in 1970, and was still in that position when I stepped down from the *Times*. He's also a member of Westminster.

It was while he was a schoolboy in Lynbrook that Knoop met the son of Ellie Buckley, a partner of F. D. H. Fleitmann, whose Westphalia Kennels was one of the pioneer Doberman kennels in America. Peter, as a youngster, worked in the kennels and went to dog shows with its owners. Some years later, he acquired his first Dobe, a brown bitch, Orissa of Westphalia, who hated to show. "It took me two years and some 25 shows but I finally made her a champion," he recalled. Orissa did all right for Knoop as a brood bitch. Bred twice, she produced eight champions.

Meanwhile, Peter was handling Dobes and other breeds for friends as a non-professional. When World War II ended, Knoop returned to the brokerage business on Wall Street. He also began to handle professionally and I remember watching him guide Len Carey's Dobe, Ch. Rancho Dobe's Storm, to best in show at Westminster in 1952 and 1953.

Peter is in great demand as a judge. The debonair silver-haired Wall Streeter, who dances a tango as smoothly as a professional, is also in demand as a speaker. "My career in the dog show world was greatly influenced by such friends as Fleitmann and the dean of judges, Alva Rosenberg. As I recall the late thirties, I feel that the dogs of the seventies overall are better; the judges more capable and the AKC more open-minded, progressive and understanding."

Mel Downing

Melbourne Downing is the only all-round judge in the history of the AKC whose father was also an all-rounder. "My father judged from the late 1920s until the 1950s," said Mel, as he is known in the dog show world. A labor lawyer, Downing not only followed in the footsteps of his father, Frank Downing, as a dog judge, but also took over as president of a contracting company his father founded in 1912.

"I learned a great deal about judging from my father and Alva Rosenberg," said Downing. "I frequently served as a steward for them and when a class was over they would discuss their choices with me and explain how they had decided on them."

Dogs have played a part in the Towson, Md., resident's life from the start. "When I was born my parents were breeding Poodles," he said. "Then my father turned to German Shepherds and my mother to Pekingese. From the time I was 10 years old, I was showing both breeds."

When Mel was 17, he visited his grandmother in England and he returned with a Pug, Rufus of Ellerslie of Holly Lodge. "I showed him to best at the Progressive show, took the breed at Westminster and had some group placements," he recalled. Downing, who judges some 60 shows a year, started in the center of the ring in 1938, when he was licensed for seven breeds. He's been an all-rounder since 1969.

"It is a pity we don't have a good apprentice system for judges," said the Marylander. "It would be very good to have someone just starting steward for older judges. He should also read books about the various breeds and attend seminars. As great a judge as Alva would read the standards a night or two before a show. I follow the same policy."

The lawyer goes a step further. When he is judging, he makes notations, using symbols to designate the faults and the good points of each animal, particularly when they are not readily apparent. "Very early in my judging career, I was doing Dalmatians. One dog was stunning looking and moved well. But he had an atrocious bite. I completely forgot about the fault and when I had them all in front of me I gave him the breed. Later, an old-time handler, for whom I had great respect, came over and said, 'Your judging was good until you chose best. How in the world could you give a dog with such a bite the breed?' He was right, of course. Now I make notations, so I cannot forget. My system makes judging much more objective."

Herman Cox

At Fort Worth, a tall, lean gray-haired Texan is known as "Mr. Dog Show." He is Herman Cox and he was president of the Fort Worth KC in 1937, 1938, 1947, 1948, 1973, 1974 and 1975. "When I started," he recalled, "we had an entry of 250. Handlers would come down to us with their second-rate dogs, so they could make them champions." That's all past history. Now the Texas circuit is a major one and it draws the top dogs in the country, with more than 2,000 entries.

The Texan, a structural engineer and a fellow in the American Institute of Architects, the highest honor the membership can bestow, is also an all-round judge. He doesn't tarry in the ring for he makes up his mind quickly.

Cox was well known for his Dachshunds when he was an exhibitor. At one time he had as many as 60 brood bitches and 10 champion studs, a total that included dogs of all three varieties.

His Ch. Brentwald Joshua, a salt-and-pepper, did much to popularize the wire-haired variety. Buzz, as Cox called him, took the variety at Westminster three years in a row, starting in 1948, and was the top-winning hound in America. "Buzz was best in show 20 times," said Herman, "and took more than 80 groups. He was best of variety 165 times and was defeated in the breed only once in his entire career—and then by his dam. He invariably would bring down the house when I would gait him, with his piston action. There were so few Dachshunds being shown in our part of the country, I had to win groups so he could finish. There are few pedigrees that don't go back to him. He sired more than 45 champions."

Cox is one of the school who believes the mini Dachshund should be shown in the Toy group, and not in the Hound. "Some exhibitors are overly sensitive on the subject," he admitted, "and insist the Dachshund is a Hound and not a Toy. But remember, Poodles are shown in both the Non-Sporting and Toy groups, Schnauzers in the Working and Terrier, and Manchesters in the Terrier and Toy, so we have precedents. The mini is pretty much lost with the big hounds. In the Toy group, he would be meeting dogs more compatible in size. The way it is now, it is terribly expensive to finish a mini."

He is one of the most active of the all-rounders, judging about 70 shows a year. Ahead of him at this writing was the best in show assignment at Westchester 1979 and the working group at Westminster 1980.

"Winnie" Heckmann

The death of Winifred Heckmann (I never knew her as anything but "Winnie") in 1979 robbed the fancy of one who was truly an all-rounder. Breeder, exhibitor, professional handler and judge - she had mastered it all.

Down-to-earth Winnie (there were always traces of the Western twang of her native Iowa) came up the hard way. Her father had Airedales and Dalmatians. When she was 10 years old, she finished her first dog, an Airedale. "I learned how to pluck," she once recalled, "and even as a child I did a lot of grooming. Then, when I was a teenager, a woman gave me a Standard Schnauzer to show, and I made that one a champion."

A few years passed and Winnie married. By now, she was a professional handler. When her husband died, leaving her with two small boys, she bought a home in Towson, Md., and built a big boarding kennel, which was her main source of income. She also turned to breeding Irish Wolfhounds. "Many of the pedigrees today trace back to my Wyndale line," she told me.

During World War II, Winnie married Col. Heckmann, closed her kennel, stopped handling, and applied for a judging license. She was given two groups—Hounds and Sporting—and breeds in several others. After her divorce from Heckmann in 1945, it was back to handling for Winnie. She sold the Towson property and bought a kennel on the Baltimore National Pike. She added to it, so she had boarding accommodations for 300. Meanwhile, she was in great demand as a handler and was on the road every weekend.

It was getting increasingly difficult to get kennel help, so Mrs. Heckmann felt it was time for a change. She rented the kennel, bought another house, and once again applied for a judging license. "It was rough going at the start," she said. "I really was depending on my fees for judging and the AKC merely reinstated me for the breeds they had given me some years before. Assignments weren't too plentiful. But within a couple of years, I was an all-rounder."

As a result, until her health forced a change, she became a very busy judge. "I enjoy it," she once told me, "You forget about everything else when you are in the ring. All you are doing is concentrating and trying to find the best dog."

The tradition is being carried on by her daugher, Susan Fisher, who with her husband Bob makes up one of the handsomest and most successful handling teams today.

Ramona Jones

One of the most respected judges is Mrs. John Marshall Jones, better known as Ramona. An all-rounder, this commanding arbiter from Palm Beach, Fla., reigns supreme in her ring.

I aroused her ire at a Devon dog show that ended in darkness. Five of the finalists had dark coats with only a Siberian Husky having white hair. When it came to gait the dogs, all except the Husky disappeared from view into the blackness, until they were brought back to Ramona. So when she gave best to the Siberian, I wrote it was the only dog visible to the judge and ringsiders. For months afterwards, every time we met, I was assured by her, in no uncertain terms, she had seen them all.

For years, Ramona ran the Beverly Hills show on the Coast and Westbury on Long Island.

Since she is a well-organized person, everything ran very smoothly. Some of the fanciers quipped there was no need to worry about the weather, Mrs. Jones wouldn't permit rain. Ramona would get very upset if spectators littered the grounds and she could be seen picking up paper, scowling and muttering dire threats. Every ring had flowers on the tables, pennants flying from the tents and at one time there was real china, with silverware, for the judges' luncheon.

As an exhibitor, she was best known for her Dachshunds. Her smooth standard, Ch. Aristo v. Marienlust accounted for 10 bests, 47 groups and 118 varieties. Then she did well with one of his sons, Ch. White Gables Ristocrat, getting a best, 10 blue rosettes and a specialty.

When judging, she punished herself, as well as the exhibitors. I remember a show where there was a cloudburst while she was doing a group. Whereas, the other arbiters judged the dogs under the tent, not Ramona. Each animal, with its handler, was sent out into the pelting rain, where Mrs. Jones stood spartanlike, doing her judging.

Mrs. Riggs

Few judges have been ruling in rings in America longer than Mrs. Augustus Riggs 4th. "My first assignment was in 1929, at Rhinebeck (N.Y.)," she recalled, "when I did Smooth and Wire Fox Terriers." Forty-nine years later, she was named an all-breed arbiter by the AKC. Mrs. Riggs was the first woman ever to judge a Terrier group at Westminster, and only the fourth woman to select best in show at the blue-ribbon classic, handling the assignment in 1973.

Mrs. Riggs registered her Hillwood Kennels in the 1920s. Her daughter, Ellen Iverson, still uses the kennel name. Ellen shows Pulis, Bichons and Tibetan Terriers, whereas her mother bred, among others, Fox Terriers, Standard Schnauzers and Great Danes.

Mrs. Riggs deplores the move by so many specialty clubs to change the standards. "Although some standards are rather ambiguous and could stand overhauling," she admits, "I feel in most cases it is unnecessary. There also seems to be a tendency toward exaggeration in the breeds, rather than moderation."

Mrs. Riggs, a daughter of the late Marjorie Merriweather Post and a sister of screen star Dina Merrill, accepts only about a dozen assignments a year. "I have so many other activities," she said, "I just haven't time to judge any more than that."

Langdon Skarda

In 1940, Langdon Skarda of Clovis, N.M., married and bought his bride a German Shepherd. "I finished her as a puppy," he recalled. She was the first of more than 40 titleholders the New Mexican was to breed or own. Indeed, in the early 1960s, Skarda had five all-breed best-in-show Shepherds at one time and all had won specialities. "It is unfortunate," he said, "but many Shepherd people only show at specialties. They have a number of good dogs that would do well at all-breed events."

Discussing the breed as it was in 1978, he said, "The German Shepherd has much more rear angulation than in the past. Some of the dogs are overangulated, as breeders go to extremes. Many of the handlers want the owners to be at ringside, to double handle. I'm one of those nasty judges who demands the handlers show a Shepherd on a loose lead. They much prefer to show them on a tight leash, so that a saggy topline can be straightened out. The handlers also like to speed the dogs around the ring."

Skarda, who practiced law for a few years before he went into banking, has a

52,000-acre ranch, on which he raises Herefords. He's been a judge since 1947 and an all-rounder since 1970. "Much of what I know about judging," said he, "I learned from Alva Rosenberg." He's one of many taught by that great master.

Henry Stoecker

As you drive to his home in Holmdel, N.J., a house dating to the Revolution, you pass Stoecker Road. "I owned much of the land around here," said Henry Stoecker, "and when I decided to sell some of it, the township put in a street. So long after I'm gone, my name will be known in Holmdel." And if the house remains, visitors will see the Stoecker touch, for Henry is as adept with carpenters' tools as he is in a show ring.

"I guess I've been judging all of my life," he said. "In Nordenham, Germany, my father was a judge, as well as a breeder of Airedales, Smooth Fox Terriers and Boxers. He'd take me to match shows in a beer garden and I'd hear the men discuss the good and bad points of the animals. The day I was born, a Fox Terrier had a litter under our kitchen table. One of the pups was given to me. In 1910, when we were both seven years old, I showed my dog."

After coming to this country, however, it was Boxers and Doberman Pinschers that made the Stoeckersburg Kennel famous. "At one time I had from 50 to 60 dogs," he recalled. "Ch. Dodi von der Stoeckersburg was the first American-born Boxer to become a champion. I bred another dozen champions." Stoecker's first judging assignment was in 1934, when he did Boxers and Dobes.

Stoecker next began to handle for Mrs. Milton Erlanger and he and the Erlanger Poodles were to play a big role in obedience training once the activity was recognized by the AKC. "Ch. Cadeau Pillicoc Noel won the first trial ever held under AKC rules, in 1936," he recalled. "We had eight Standard Poodles who earned CDs. I showed Ch. Pillicoc Rumpelstilskin to a best in show and he scored a perfect 200 points in obedience the same day. He was the dog of the year in 1937."

During World War II, Stoecker was busy in the United States Army training dogs. "I wrote the program for scout dogs in the Army manual," he said, "At Fort Robinson in Nebraska, I was the director of training dogs for all the armed forces."

Stoecker really started his judging career in 1950, when he stopped handling. One of the busiest arbiters in the country, he has judged as many as 67 shows in a year. With all his judging, Stoecker doesn't rely on his memory, but reads and rereads the breed standards. And when the deceptively impish-looking man goes into a ring, he carries little cards, listing the faults and desirable points of each breed. "If I am in doubt, I can whip them out and refresh my memory," he said.

Rutledge Gilliland

In 1978, Rutledge Gilliland of Siloam Springs, Ark. was 77, so as a concession to his age, he started to refuse assignments. "I'll only do 40 this year,'' said he. Not bad for a man who three years earlier had fallen and fractured his pelvis.

The Arkansan has been judging since 1928, but not continuously. In 1939, he became a sales manager for a dog food company and turned in his license. Retiring from the company 24 years later, he started once again as an arbiter. "The AKC gave me all the Sporting and Hound breeds," he recalled, "and four years later made me an all-rounder. In 1976, I judged in Hawaii and that gave me all 50 states. I've done Alaska four times and in 1977 had a dozen assignments in Canada." Gilliland also has judged field trials.

"As a kid, I had several of the hunting breeds—Foxhounds, Beagles and Coonhounds," he said. "Then I began to breed German Shepherds, English Setters, Pointers and Dachshunds. When I look back over the half-century I've been in the game, I'd say there has been an overall improvement in the breeds."

Maurice Baker

Whereas most arbiters get a breed or two when they are licensed by the AKC, Maurice Baker started with two full groups. "I had been one of the founders of the Minneapolis club," he recalled. "That was in 1932. A couple of years later I spoke to the AKC representative about getting a judge's license. The next thing I knew he called me to say I had the Sporting and Hound groups and that I was to do the Sporting breeds at a show in Mankato and the hounds at Rochester. When I protested, saying that I only had bred and shown Irish, English, and Gordon Setters and Pointers, he replied, 'You can do it.' ''

But it took another 25 years before the Minnesotan had the four other groups and became an all-breed judge. Although Baker now is curtailing his activities, he still does 15 to 20 shows annually. In the Midwest he long was known for his Irish Setters, having bred the redcoats for 35 years, including a pair of best-in-show performers.

"Dogs shows were pretty rough when I started," said Baker. "There's been a big change over the years and for the better, both in show management and supervision by the AKC. You can speak of the good old days but overall the quality of dogs and their presentation today is much better than when I started."

Arthur Zane

In Hawaii, Arthur Zane is Mr. Dog Show. A founder of the Hawaiian KC in 1935, he has served it continuously, being president from 1946 until 1977, when he decided it was time for someone else to take over. The Honolulu exhibitor, breeder and judge started with German Shepherds in 1931 and four years later imported the first Poodle and first Afghan to the islands. Later he added Great Danes, Boxers and Fox Terriers to his Kuliouou Kennels. He helped to organize the local German Shepherd and Great Dane specialty clubs in the 1930s.

On the mainland we know the gentleman, and that he is, as an arbiter, for he has ruled in all the big ones—Morris and Essex, Westminster, International. He also has judged in South America, Australia, Tokyo, Manila and Hong Kong.

Speaking at a Dog Fanciers Club luncheon, Arthur told how his father and uncle sailed from China looking for a new homeland and riches. Suddenly Tahiti loomed on the horizon. His uncle whipping out a spyglass took one look and said, "Keep sailing, no business here for a laundry." It was the hit story of the day.

Izzy Schoenberg

If you walk into a dog show and see a judge wearing a wild outfit, you probably are seeing Isidore Schoenberg. During the nation's bicentennial, he appeared in a red jacket with white pockets and blue slacks with a white stripe. Then he wears red slacks with alligator shoes; green slacks with matching green suede loafers and jackets with custom-made linings depicting bullfight scenes and golden horses.

Izzy, who has been an all-rounder for 25 years, was one of the greatest Pomeranian breeders of his day. He established the Aristic line, which many of the top-winning Poms today have in their pedigrees.

"I judged my first show at Fayetteville (N.C.), in 1927," he remembered. "I had to do Beagles and Foxhounds. There were more Foxhounds in that ring than I ever have seen in a ring since. When I finished, they presented me with a red coat, for excellent judging of the breed. I didn't tell them it was the first time I ever had seen a Foxhound."

In past years, Schoenberg was a busy arbiter, doing from 60 to 70 shows. In the mid-seventies, he reduced this to 20. One of the leading art dealers in the country, he hasn't the time to spare from his Oklahoma City gallery. "We have more than 3,000 original oils," he said. "If they were measured, end to end, they would stretch for five miles. I've discovered some unknown artists and made them well known." Then Izzy is proud of his collection of ceramic and bronze dogs. "I have more than 1,200, including some 40 pugs from China and Germany," he said.

Bob Waters

The only Canadian licensed to judge all breeds in the United States is Bob Waters of Vancouver, British Columbia, and he's been an all-rounder since 1949. A former police officer, he retired from the Vancouver force at the age of 51 in 1962, and since then he has spent much of his time in the air. "In 1977, I flew more than 100,000 miles, running up air fares of $20,000," he said. "My sixth trip to Australia was in August 1978, and I've done all the big shows there."

Waters started in the late 1920s and over the years bred Dobermans, Keeshonds, Boxers, Scotties and Miniature Pinschers. "Bill Pym, who represented British Columbia at the Canadian KC and was a vice president, started me judging. I showed under him any number of times and he liked my style. "It's time you moved from showing to judging," he said. Although Waters doesn't accept any assignments in July and August, he manages to keep busy. "I judge about 50 shows a year," he said, "mostly in the United States."

Gordon Parham

For 39 years, Gordon Parham was connected with the Detroit public school system as a teacher, guidance counselor or administrator. During World War II, the educator was gunnery officer on a large naval vessel in the Pacific. Then he has played an active role in the dog show world. As a breeder, he raised and showed English and Irish Setters, German Shepherds, Cocker Spaniels, Beagles, Dobes and Coonhounds.

Parham started to handle in 1933 and had marked success. In 1941, he stopped handling and began to judge. Quickly he received the Sporting and Hound breeds. Then came the war.

With the cessation of hostilities, he began looking ahead to where he might become an all-rounder and decided the best way to learn the breeds was to go back to handling. So in 1948 he turned in his judge's license and started to show dogs again. Probably the most famous dog he has handled was Fred Jackson's English Springer, Ch. Frejax Royal Salute. "I had six straight best in shows with him," he recalled. "Jackson refused $25,000 for that dog."

By 1952, Parham felt he had a good enough background with the breeds and stopped handling, returning as a judge. His dream of being an all-rounder was realized in 1970. Discussing the Sporting dogs, Gordon bemoaned the fact that breeders have been working to get the dogs ever taller. "They have opened the angle from 90 degrees at the shoulder to get a taller dog, with a high sloping topline. As a result, the animal must be high stepping in front, to get the feet out of the way for the hind legs. This hackney gait in front looks attractive to ringsiders but it is extremely tiring and no good in the field."

Parham likes to judge. "I don't know anything else I could do with the same enjoyment and be paid for it," he said.

Phil Marsh

It was a catalogue that was to start Phil Marsh off on a career as a handler and eventually an all-round judge. "I went to work for George Foley, as a teenager," he recalled. "Ben Lewis, a top handler, came over and asked me for a catalogue. They were locked in a small cabinet. I yanked the lock off and gave him one. The next day Foley fired me and Lewis hired me. I learned all about Sporting breeds from him. Then I joined Dick Davis, an all-breed handler and was taught how to pluck Terriers."

In 1937, Phil opened his own kennel. He acquired his greatest fame as a Working dog man, particularly with Boxers and Dobermans. In 1949, he gaited Ch. Mazelaine Zazarac Brandy, a Boxer, to best in show at Westminster.

"It's a whole new ball game today," said the Floridian. "In the old days we had bench shows where one could visit and learn. Now all the exhibitor wants to do is get into the ring, be judged and rush home. As to the handlers, I feel only a small number really know what they are doing." And Phil can speak with authority, for he was the nation's top handler in 1948, 1949 and 1951.

He has been an all-rounder since 1964, but he has been gradually cutting down on his assignments. "Whereas in the past, I would handle from 50 to 60 assignments, now I do no more than 35. I don't want to take them too far from Tampa. I like to judge and be home the same night."

Bob Braithwaite

In December of 1977, the AKC approved Robert Braithwaite for 13 Working breeds and the native-born Scot joined the exclusive coterie of all-round judges. It has been a fast climb to the top for the septuagenarian for he only started to rule on dogs in 1970.

"I never expected to make it," he admitted, with a Scottish burr still strong although he has been in this country for a half-century. But few judges came up with the credentials of the thin man from the Highlands. "I showed a Scottie when I was seven years old," he recalled. Eight years later, Braithwaite was in a much more serious business. Only 15, he enlisted and served from 1914 to 1918 with the Cameron Highlanders, seeing action in France and Palestine. A most modest man, when I asked if he suffered any injuries, he replied, "Nothing very serious. They had to take shrapnel out of me, now and again, and then I was gassed."

At the end of the hostilities, he found employment as a gamekeeper and he had Labradors, Springers and Scotties. He showed at Crufts in a special gamekeepers' class and had a second and third. Emigrating to this country in 1928, he worked for a year with the American Society for the Prevention of Cruelty to Animals in New York and then joined with Leonard Brumby, Sr., on Long Island, as a professional handler. Over the years he was manager for some of the major kennels and walked any number of winners into the ring. A quiet man, he has an excellent eye for a dog. His appointment as an all-rounder was hailed by the more knowledgeable exhibitors and handlers who appreciate good judging.

Howard Tyler

"The greatest change I've seen in the dog show world is the tremendous growth," said Howard Tyler, and he's seen a great deal in nearly a half-century with the sport. "When I was an assistant to Bob Braithwaite in 1931, a show with 250 or 300 dogs was a big one."

Tyler pointed out the difficulty in getting to shows in the early 1930s. "We brought a truck and converted it so that we could get crates into it, to transport the dogs. Now, of course, there are big vans and motor homes, making travel so much easier. And dogs are flown from coast to coast, all of which has contributed to the big shows today. A match today gets far more dogs than we had at the point shows. I also feel there isn't as much collusion now. In the so-called good old days, some of the very important and wealthy exhibitors would be on the phone early Monday morning, deciding who should go up the next weekend."

After working with Braithwaite, Tyler left in 1935 to manage the Saye and

Sele Kennel at Old Lyme, Conn. Then he started to show Standard Poodles for Mary McCreery, whose Blakeen Cyrano was his first best-in-show performer. After the war, Howard bought a place near New Fairfield, Conn., where he started a small kennel, keeping perhaps a dozen dogs for clients. He was best known as a handler of Poodles and Greyhounds. In 1968, Tyler became an all-breed judge. The tall, quiet man, now living on Cape Cod, is respected by both his fellow arbiters and exhibitors.

Ed Bracy

Ed Bracy is a stickler on movement in a dog. This shouldn't be too much of a surprise, since the judge from Memphis was running a dog in the field long before he took one into a ring. "I started with Pointers," he said, "and then did some hunting with a Cocker Spaniel. That little dog was a superb retriever, being especially good on pheasant. Then I decided to show him. I was so green I used a hitch lead from a horse as a leash."

Ed then went to work for Thelma Miller, who had Sealyhams and Scotties. "I learned how to pluck and put a dog down," he stated. In 1939, he started to handle and for the next 30 years he did his share, finishing dogs of 79 breeds. Probably the best known was Ch. Gerd von d. Lueg von Edelweiss, who had 21 bests and 47 groups, a record for St. Bernards. He traded his handler's license for a judge's in 1969 and four years later was an all-rounder. "I do about 65 shows a year," drawled Ed. "That gives me time to do a little gardening and some bird watching."

Dr. Booth

"There's a saying in Indiana that the first present a man gives to his son is a basketball," said Dr. Frank R. Booth. "In my case it was different. When I was eight years old, my dad gave me a piece of rope with a Beagle on the end."

Dr. Booth remained tied to dogs for the rest of his life. Even after two retirements — the first after 28 years as a veterinarian, and the second after nine years as Executive Secretary of the American Animal Hospital Association — he continued as an all-round judge until his death in 1979. His assignments took him all over the United States (including Alaska and Hawaii) and to such distant lands as India and Australia.

A Wire Fox Terrier breeder from 'way back—"we bred 100 litters"—he scoffed at the idea dogs dislike visits to the doctor. "I kept statistics," said he, "and found that 75 per cent were perfectly happy when they came to the office. Some of my best friends romped in on four feet to greet me."

The Man Who Played the Palace

It's been dogs and horses for most of his life for Bob Wills, who became an all-rounder judge in March, 1979. Conformation and movement are musts for the Ohioan, which is understandable since he has trained thoroughbred race horses for over 25 years.

131

With dogs, Bob received his first Collie when he was five years old, from Santa Claus. Four years later the dog was stolen and Wills' father bought him another Collie, Lad.

"That was a dog," he recalled. "I delivered newspapers and I trained Lad to take the paper in his mouth and drop it at the door. I also taught him 55 stage tricks and when I was 16 years old, he and I appeared with Johnson and Olson at the Palace, for a week. We often performed before church, club and school groups. He died when he was 20 years old, the day that I won a group with a sable-and-white Collie, Ch. Al-Lo-Way Assault, at Birmingham, Alabama." Assault was quite a dog, too. The first time Wills brought him out, as an eight-month-old pup, Assault won the breed over 147 Collies and then took second in the group. He was shown from 1948 to 1952.

Wills first judging assignment was at Westbury in 1940. He stopped showing in 1962, after long success as a Collie breeder, because he was getting many judging invitations and felt that a judge should not actively campaign a dog. Currently he handles close to 75 assignments a year.

The Two Newest

Many a judge bemoans that the AKC won't give additional breeds. "If I live long enough, I might some day get a group," is the usual plaint. Then we have the exceptions. Take Peter Thomson, an Australian who arrived in this country in 1968 as a representative for a company in his native land. Although he had been an all-rounder for 25 years Down Under, Peter had to start from the bottom here. But in a relatively short time he began to amass breeds, and now—within 11 years—is an AKC all-rounder.

In Australia, Thomson not only had been a busy judge, but he had done a great deal of breeding. He had Fox Terriers, Scotties, Dachshunds, Whippets, Pembroke Welsh Corgis, English Cockers and Labrador Retrievers, an impressive assortment.

"It's a judge's obligation to give every exhibitor an equal, adequate examination and with courtesy," said Ted Wurmser, who became an all-rounder in September 1979, the newest at this writing. This has been the credo for the Louisville, Ky., trial lawyer since he first became a dog show arbiter in 1950.

Ted and his wife, Ruth, who have been married for 46 years, have been prominently identified with the dog sport over many years. Their Terudon Kennels (an acronym of Ted, Ruth and Don—their son) sent out many a winning Boxer and Poodle, the best known of whom was the Boxer, Ch. Terudon's Kiss Me Kate, winner of 35 bests in show in the mid-50s. At one time, the kennel had as many as 60 dogs, but the Wurmsers are both busy judging now and haven't bred or exhibited since 1973.

Do dogs know when they have won? Skye Terrier Ch. Glamoor Gang Buster seems as happy over his best of breed win as does his owner Walter Goodman.

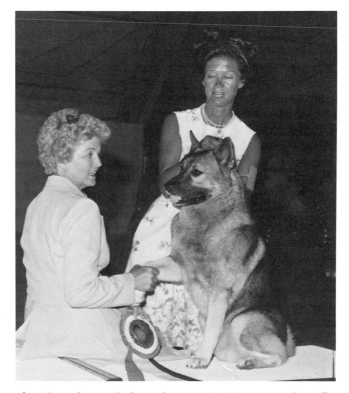

Ch. Vin-Melca's Nimbus, the top winning Norwegian Elkhound of all time appears as happily aware of winning best in show at Ventura County as does the judge, Mrs. E. C. Urban, or his handler, Pat Craige, who co-owns him with Dr. Harold Shuler.

The Virginian

Ask almost any Irish Setter fancier to name a leading kennel of redcoats, and invariably the reply will be Tirvelda Farms. Tirvelda (T for Ted, Irv for Irving and Eld for Eldredge) is owned by Mr. and Mrs. Irving (Ted) Eldredge of Middleburg, Va.

The tall country squire should know something about the breed. He's had Irish since he was 10 years old. "I was given a six-week old pup," he reminisced, "and we called him St. Patrick." Two years later the master and Saint made their debuts at three local shows. "We certainly weren't an overwhelming success," he chuckled. "We didn't bring a ribbon home, not even a fourth." However, it was a good learning experience. Now the Virginian has bred or owned nearly 100 champions.

It was a gift from his grandmother that started Ted on his winning career. Eldredge was at school, so Harold Correll showed the bitch, Kinvarra Mollie of Gadeland, for him. She was Tirvelda's foundation bitch and she's in the bloodlines of almost every leading Irish Setter kennel in America.

With all its success, Tirvelda isn't a particularly large kennel. There are never more than 20 of the redcoats at one time and usually it's about 15. The only time the Setters are kept in the kennel runs is at night or when it is excessively hot. Otherwise they all run together in three fenced enclosures, one of two acres, the others twice that size.

Eldredge has had many good Irish over the years. Two that stand out are Ch. Tirvelda Nutbrown Sherry, the top-producing bitch in the history of the breed, with 23 champions, and a son, Ch. Tirvelda Michaelson, the No. 1 sire of Irish Setters, with 46 titleholders. Sherry's second litter made Irish Setter history. Of 12 pups, 11 became champions.

The Virginian, born in 1922, had his first judging assignment when he was 21. He's a member of the AKC board of directors, having been elected in 1978. "When I was eight years old, I said I wanted to be a farmer," Eldredge recalled, "and that's what I am." He has won many prizes with his livestock. A homebred herd of Holsteins led the state for four years in milk production per cow. He also had Suffolk and Montadale sheep and for two years was president of the Montadale Sheepbreeders Association of America. "My knowledge of livestock has been a great help in my breeding dogs," he said.

As this is being prepared for press, we learn that Ted has been accorded the judging plum of the year—the assignment to select best in show at Westminster in 1980.

Chuck Hamilton

Back in the early '30s there was a young man working for the handler, Charlie Davis, at Syracuse, N.Y., and he learned enough about the business so that in 1933, he started to handle himself, taking over Charlie Palmer's kennel in Lakeport, N.Y. He was still another Charlie, more familiarly known as Chuck Hamilton, and he did very well. During World War II, he was in the K-9 Corps at

Fort Robinson and he took a platoon, with 27 dogs, to Italy. "The dogs were used extensively on night patrols," he recalled, "and they did an excellent job."

Hamilton received his judge's license in 1951 and by the '70s had five groups. In 1976, he was certainly one of the most active arbiters in America, judging at 82 shows. "One of those gave me more trouble than any I've ever experienced," he said. "I was scheduled to judge in Halifax but there was a strike in Canada. So I flew from Omaha to Chicago, changed planes and went on to Boston. Another took me to Portland. From there I sailed overnight to Yarmouth. I rented a car to drive to Halifax and nearly missed the show, after all. It was a two-lane road, with big lumber trucks. You would get behind one and be stuck for a half-hour before you were able to pass. I made the show with minutes to spare."

Elsworth (with one "l")

Where would all we dog enthusiasts be without Howell Book House? For that publishing concern covers every facet of the sport—training, grooming, judging . . . and so much else. Then there are all the individual breed tomes it turns out, as well as the AKC's official *The Complete Dog Book*—the best-selling dog book of all time.

The driving force behind all this, of course, is Elsworth S. Howell. A tall and slender man, quiet-spoken, polite, Howell's reserved manner belies his strong determination and accomplishment. Starting at early age as an assistant editor at the Grolier Society, publishers of *The Book of Knowledge* and other encyclopedias, he rose to become president and board chairman of their Grolier Enterprises division. He was also a director on the boards of other educational publishing projects.

In 1961, combining this publishing expertise with a lifelong devotion to the dog sport, he founded Howell Book House. In the years since, ten books published by the firm have won "Best Book of the Year" awards from the Dog Writers Association of America.

He is himself a writer of distinction. He has served as breed columnist and written many articles for the dog magazines, and is co-editor (with Stanley Dangerfield) of the award-winning *The International Encyclopedia of Dogs*, and with the late Davis Tuck of *The New Complete English Setter*.

"I've had dogs all my life," he told me. "My father (Clarence S. Howell) had a kennel of Schipperkes. He bred, exhibited and judged, and inoculated me with the disease."

His father, who was also a chess master and at one time New York State champion, judged Schipperkes at Westminster in the early 1930s. A decade later, Elsworth had the same assignment at the Garden.

As a boy he also had a field-bred English Setter. "I won what was only the second children's handling class ever held," he chucklingly remembered. "There were just two of us in the ring. I was scared to death, but my father came over and said, 'Never be afraid of competition.' That advice has served me in good stead over many years."

He began his judging career in 1938, when he was 22 years old, doing the Schipperke specialty at Morris and Essex. In the more than four decades since, he has ruled at most of the important all-breed fixtures and is regarded as one of the most knowledgeable of our arbiters. Licensed to pass upon all Sporting and some Hound breeds, he was the Sporting Group judge at Westminster 1979 and chose the Irish Water Spaniel that went on to best in show.

Many associate him primarily with the English Setter. "I bought my first in 1949," he recalled, "and during the '50s and '60s had some very good ones." He has been the English Setter Association of America's delegate to the AKC since 1958. But he has also bred, owned or shown Cocker Spaniels, Dachshunds, West Highland White Terriers, Bassets and Whippets. And he is currently president of the Dog Fanciers Club, an organization made up of owners of many breeds, which meets at a monthly luncheon at Sardi's in New York City.

So, when Elsworth Howell reads a manuscript about dogs, he doesn't have to go far beyond himself for an authoritative opinion.

Ellsworth (with two "l"s)

Lieut. Ellsworth Gamble, in 1942, was so severely injured in a jeep accident that he was given a medical discharge and told that he had no more than six months to live. When I retired, 34 years later, the gentleman from Fremont, Calif., was still going strong. A well-known dog show judge, he had five groups and needed only some working breeds to become an all-rounder.

"When the Army doctors told me I had but a short time left on this good Earth, I decided I needed company and that a dog would help me in my last days," he recalled. "As soon as I could travel, I went to visit Dr. Leonard Goss, dean of the veterinary school at Ohio State, where I had been a student before entering the service. He gave me an Irish Terrier. To the surprise of the medical profession, I was not only still alive after six months, but a year later I had improved so much I was taking long walks with my dog. I was so proud of my Irishman, a friend suggested I show him. That's how we both landed at Golden Gate. It was the first time for either of us in a ring and we walked out with the best-of-breed ribbon."

Two years later, Gamble decided that he would become a professional handler. After all, he had been beating the pros consistently with his Irish Terrier and since his days were supposed to be numbered, this was as good a way to earn a living as any. Gamble's gamble paid off. The next year he became kennel manager for Mrs. W. B. Reis and he did well with her Smooth and Wire Fox Terriers. Then he became an all-breed handler and showed for some of the leading fanciers on the coast, including Kay Finch of Afghan fame.

In 1963, Gamble, still very much alive, decided to give up handling and apply for a judge's license. He was given nine breeds. In his work in the ring he has the reputation of being an exacting judge. If he doesn't think a dog worthy he will withhold the ribbon. "It's better for the breed," said the Californian. "That's what the sport is supposed to be all about."

I'd Rather Judge than Handle . . .

Jerry Weiss is much happier judging than when he was showing. "Let's face it, I was a lousy handler," he admitted. "I have five daughters and every one of them is better at showing a dog than I am." And the girls are active in the sport. At a regional specialty of the Labrador Retriever club in Virginia, in 1975, it was quite a sight to see them, ranging in age from eight to 18, all handling.

"Bill Metz gave my daughter Lisa, then 12 years old, our first Lab showdog," said Weiss. "Gunslinger's Tawny Boy was just a pup but Lisa worked with him and put the first points on Boy. He finished when he was 17 months old with three majors." Metz then arranged to get them a bitch, Spenrock's Cognac. When Boy and Cognac were bred, Jerry kept one pup from the litter, Lobuff's Dandy Lion, who became the first Weiss homebred titleholder.

"We have a small kennel," said the Huntingdon, L.I. fancier, "over the years breeding some half-dozen litters." Weiss was a Marine aviation cadet during World War II. After graduating from law school, he was recalled into service and sent to Korea, where he served as a company commander, putting in six years on active duty. He stayed in the Reserves and is now a colonel in charge of Marine reserve recruiting on Long Island. Jerry is also president of a legal and financial printing company. He is one of the guiding spirits of Riverhead and is show chairman.

Frank Oberstar is a man of determination. "When I started in dogs," he recalled, "I owned a cocktail lounge and restaurant in Cleveland. My partner, Larry Ward, had returned from the Coast where he had seen a Maltese. Since I had a small house in the city, he thought it would be an ideal dog for me." But when Oberstar tried to buy a dog in the area, he couldn't get any breeder to sell. So he imported Vicbrida Clare from England and she was to be his foundation bitch. "A group from Cleveland was going to Westminster in 1960," he said, "and I piled in with them bringing the bitch, whom I had owned for only three months. She earned two points. Larry and I did a little breeding and I finished four homebreds, but mostly we sold to people in Cleveland, who wanted pets."

But then they acquired Aennchen's Poona Dancer and this was to change Oberstar's life. From 1964 until 1968, he was constantly on the road with the white six-and-a-half pounder. Poona was sensational, the owner-handled Toy winning 131 groups and 38 times going on to best. "But it was a grueling experience," shuddered Oberstar. "I would work late at the restaurant, and then travel the rest of the night to a show. I might sleep a couple of hours at the side of the road, pull into a service station, wash, shave and appear fresh when I went into the ring. In 1966, I went to 80 shows. That was the year Poona won 67 groups, including Westminster."

In 1970, Frank received a judge's license. "I'll never show again," he said. "That was real work. Judging is most enjoyable. It satisfies the ego." Oberstar must be satisfying the exhibitors too. He is one of the busiest arbiters of Toys and Non-Sporting.

"Do You Take This Judge to be
Your Lawfully Wedded Mate?"

The Hartleys

Heywood and Inez Hartley have been a well-known Virginian judging team for more than three decades. And their Woodhart Kennel (a play on his name) is an establishment that long has been familiar to the Scottish Terrier cognoscenti. Although the Hartleys never were big breeders, with only a litter a year, they succeeded in finishing 20 Scotties—all since 1946, when they were successful with two in one weekend. But it didn't come easy for it was ten years before Woodhart had its first.

"When I started to show in 1936," recalled the Richmond fancier, "I didn't do too well. I rationalized by saying that the handlers always had an edge and were favored by the judges. I was getting nothing but reserve ribbons, if I was fortunate enough to even get those. Suddenly I realized I was at fault, that I was presenting the dogs very poorly. I began to watch the professionals closely and to ask questions. Eventually I learned to groom and show properly and then I began to do some winning with our Scotties. I'm firmly convinced that an amateur can do as well as a pro, if he will apply himself. But it takes work."

Heywood did work. He would gait a dog in front of a full-length mirror, so he could see the animal and himself and observe the presentation. Then he would set the dog up and watch carefully. Meanwhile, Inez would act as judge and criticize. Heywood is an all-rounder and Inez has four groups. They usually judge together and do about 40 shows a year. They have ruled in rings at most of the major shows in this country as well as at shows in Canada, Puerto Rico, South America and England.

When the slight, little man isn't at a dog show, he is likely to be on a golf course. Although in his mid-seventies, he manages to get in three or four rounds a week and shoots in the 88-90 range. "Now that I'm retired from my printing business in Richmond, we have a place for the winter in West Palm Beach and we are right along a golf course," said Hartley. "The 10th green is my front yard." Inez added, "When we joined the club, Heywood started to play with a 70-year-old-and-up group. He stopped very quickly, complaining there were too many old duffers."

The Clarks

Anne Rogers Clark has the distinction of being the only member of her sex to have shown dogs to best in show three times at Westminster. Then she was the first woman professional handler to gait a dog to the silverware at America's most prestigious fixture and when she took Ch. Wilber White Swan to the top prize in 1956, it was the first time a Toy Poodle had accomplished the feat at Madison Square Garden.

In 1978, she selected best in show, only the fifth woman ever designated to make the final Westminster award. And she did it with a regal flair befitting a woman who stands six-feet-two-inches tall. "Dogs are my life," said Anne, "and I've always considered Westminster my personal show." And well could she say it, for her 1978 appearance was her eighth as an arbiter at the classic. As a spectator, she saw it for the first time when she was 12 years old.

Poodles have played a large role in Anne's life. Her mother, Olga Hone Rogers, bred them and both of the daughter's other Garden victories were scored with Poodles—with a black Miniature, Ch. Fontclair Festoon, in 1959, and two years later with a black Toy, Ch. Cappoquin Little Sister. When Anne was 21, she started to handle professionally and she kept her license until she married Jim Clark, in 1964.

Clark had been showing dogs for the Puttencove Kennels and later managed Mrs. Clarkson Earl's kennels. Upon his marriage to Anne, he too, gave up his license and they moved to Cecilton, Md., where he is in the real estate business, and as an avocation does some judging. He's the Maryland delegate to the AKC and serves as show chairman.

"We are probably the only married couple with two kennel names," said Anne. "Our Miniature Poodles and English Cockers are under my Surrey name, while the Whippets, Greyhounds and Standard Poodles have Jim's Rimskittle prefix. We've bred five best-in-show Poodles and eight English Cocker champions over the last dozen years." Anne isn't superstitious. But she wears a good-luck charm into the ring—a tiny gold ladybug that she pins to her judge's badge.

The Stevensons

Tom and Ann Stevenson of Santa Barbara are probably the busiest husband-and-wife judging team in the nation. "By the end of the year (1978) we will have done 67 shows," said Ann. That included a month in Europe, when they ruled in rings in the Netherlands, England and Ireland.

Britain is an old story for the Californians. They judged there for the first time in 1965 and have been back every two years.

Tom has had a diversified career. He started as an anthropologist and received his master's degree at the University of Washington. But then he turned from this science dealing with man's origin, development and culture to another culture—that of the theatre.

Stevenson crossed the country to New York and had a few bit parts on Broadway. "I wasn't there too long and didn't have any great success," he recalls. So it was back to the West Coast, where he became an associate director of the California Playhouse in Pasadena. As a director, Tom fulfilled an ambition but didn't fill his pockets. To supplement his income, he went to Hollywood. He was in more than 40 films and late TV viewers still can see him with Bette Davis in "Mrs. Skeffington," with Charles Boyer and Ingrid Bergman in "Gaslight" and with Humphrey Bogart in "Across the Pacific."

Then came World War II. He joined the Navy and was at sea from 1942 until 1956, winding up as Lieutenant Commander.

As a boy, Tom had shown Bulldogs, finishing one while still a teenager. So it was from the sea to the show ring, Stevenson handling. In 1964, he traded his handler's license for a judge's, and by 1978 was approved for all the Hound, Working, Toy and Non-Sporting groups.

Ann had come to California in 1948 and taken a job in a kennel, and it was here she first met Tom. Ernie Ferguson gave Ann her first Poodle and Tom showed him. After their marriage, they bred and showed some good Poodles.

Ann started to judge in 1965 and she's been busy ever since. "Our most in-depth experience was at the Royal Melbourne in 1975," she said. "The show ran for 11 days and we averaged 300 dogs a day. One day Tom was down for 255 Irish Setters. And as if that wasn't enough, they added 50 Terriers. We both were exhausted by the time Melbourne was over, but for experience—it was the best we ever had."

Ann judges all Sporting, Terrier and Toys, so between them the couple do all the breeds.

The Marvins

I sat down one day with that husband-and-wife judging team, John and Bea Marvin, and we started to talk about the old days—the 1930s and '40s. "We were living in Cleveland, at the time," said the tall, silver-haired man, "and it was a big show that drew 350 or 400 dogs. They all were benched and lasted from two to four days." "There were no shows in December, January, July or August," added Bea. "We all traveled by train, with the dogs in a baggage car. Railway Express would take them right from the train to the show."

It was a doggie—a Wire Fox Terrier—in a pet shop window who started the Marvins in the sport. "We thought we had the world's best," chuckled John, "but when we went to breed her, the people with the stud dog told us in no uncertain terms she was all right for a pet but not for showing. Then we began to go to shows." Becoming more knowledgeable, after a couple of years, they bought an English import, Adastra Argonne, sired by the great Talavera Simon. Now that they had a good dog—and during the depression years he proved a big help with his stud fees—they bought a brood bitch, and began to breed.

But success wasn't to come too quickly to the Ohioans. "We must have had reserve winners at least 100 times with the Wires we bred," Marvin recalled. In 1941, the couple turned to West Highland White Terriers. "Just to show how one has to be lucky," said John, "the first Westie litter we bred produced Ch. Cranbourne Arial, who won four best in shows, 25 groups and two specialties. Shown 58 times, he had 54 breeds and 52 placements and Bea did all the handling. Arial also sired two best-in-show Westies."

Once the Marvins started to breed champions, they did very well, finishing 20 Highlanders and two Wire Fox Terriers, all from 1945 to 1966. That was the year they dispersed their kennel. Marvin had retired, after being a patent attorney 30 years for General Motors, and the couple returned East, settling in Doylestown, Pa. Now both are judging. They agree the biggest change over the years has been the proliferation of dog shows. "It's a whole new world, since we started," reflected Bea.

The Felltons

It took Herman and Judy Fellton 15 years to breed their first champion. Then 15 years later, they had the top-winning hound in America, an Afghan, Ch. Dahnwood Gabriel.

Perhaps it was fitting that the black-masked golden dog should have climbed to the top, for the Felltons had bought Gabby so he would have a home where he could run. A veterinarian had been boarding the Afghan for a couple who found they could not afford to keep the dog and the Felltons purchased him. "Judy thought Gabby might do something as a show dog," recalled Fellton. "To get him into Westminster, he had to have a blue ribbon, so we sent him to Logansport, Ind. It was Gabby's first time in a ring and we just hoped he would take a class for that blue. He not only took the blue but the breed, the group and best in show. What a start!"

The Felltons have been in dogs seriously since 1935, when they bought a Doberman Pinscher. "He managed to get a blue or two but usually he was second, third or out of the ribbons," said Herman. "We realized we had a good pet but no show dog. I was with the Public Health Service and when I was transferred to Georgia in 1950, we went out and bought a really good Dobe. She was Storm Crest Allure and became our first champion."

When they were showing, the Felltons would bring each dog into the house from the kennel, one at a time, every night, and give it a biscuit. "They slept in the kennel but that way felt they were part of the family," said Judy.

Now the Felltons are busy judging, another husband-and-wife team. Mr. Fellton served as president of the Doberman Pinscher Club of America from 1976 to 1978.

The Thompsons

Clark C. Thompson long was known for his Cocker Spaniels. His wife, Arlene, did much to bring the Irish Water Spaniel to the fore. So what did they have in their home in Freeport, L.I. when I visited there—a houseful of Chihuahuas. The Thompsons, both of whom were born in New York City but are now retired in Texas, are one of our better-known husband-and-wife judging teams. Clark has been ruling in rings since 1944, Arlene since 1968.

Clark still chuckles about his start in the sport. "I bought a Cocker Spaniel in 1935," he said. "He was cowhocked and everything about him was wrong. But to me, he was a beauty. At the breeder's urging I showed him, starting at Westminster, no less." It was quite a start. There were some dog buscuits under the judge's table. When the arbiter went to look at the Spaniel, the dog broke

141

away from Thompson and made a bee line for the goodies. "My show career almost ended right there," said he.

But by 1940, Thompson had learned a bit and he showed a homebred bitch, Coggeshall Dulcinia, to her championship. Thompson has been continuously active in the American Spaniel Club and has twice headed the 1,000-member organization.

And what does the "C" stand for in his name? "For Coggeshall," replied Clark, "it's a family name. I used it for my kennel name when I was showing. John Coggeshall, an ancestor, was the first governor of the Newport Province in Rhode Island in the early 17th century."

Arlene played a leading role in the Bronx club, where for years she was show chairman, and then moved on to do a great deal of judging. As an exhibitor, she started with Irish Setters, then Scotties, but it was the Irish Water Spaniel that really caught her eye and heart. Arlene's Kalibank's Mister Fitz-Gee, better known as Jiggs, finished quickly and left his stamp on the breed, siring 15 champions.

Arlene always has been one to speak her mind. "Judges often are accused of favoring professional handlers," she said. "Actually the pro is a boon to the owner-handler. Watch him, ask questions, learn from him, steal his thunder. His dog is trained, in good condition and expertly groomed. I can't tell you how many times I've examined a long-coated dog the owner is handling and the animal has been groomed only on the surface. When you get into the furnishings under the forelegs or chest, frequently you find clumps of matted hair."

The Seaver Smiths

In 1963, rangers in Estes National Park in Colorado received a battery of phone calls from startled visitors, who insisted they had seen a polar bear ambling over the countryside. Needless to say, it wasn't a white bear from the Arctic. It was a 140-pound Great Pyrenees, Ch. Quibbletown Beau Olard. Rocky, as he was known, was found two days later and returned to a very worried Seaver and Edith Smith, from Taunton, Mass.

The Smiths, another husband-and-wife judging team, have come a long way since, for they have bred or owned more than 100 champions. In the late sixties, when Quibbletown was at its height, the Smiths had as many as 50 of the massive dogs. When Rocky was around, he was the only Pyr permitted the luxury of the house, which he shared with a tiny Yorkie, two cats and nine tropical birds.

In 1971, the couple acquired Ch. Karolaska Glacier from Rick and Carol Kentopp of Anchorage, Alaska. Glacier had already taken a best in show at Anchorage, but the Kentopps wanted him campaigned and realizing there are so few shows in Alaska, let him go to the Smiths. Glacier was shown 194 times, winning the breed every time, with 56 groups and 10 top awards. He was quite a traveler, covering 65,000 miles during the three years he was shown.

The Smith saga had its start in 1945 at Radcliffe College. Cote de Neige Guerrier, owned by Edith, an art major, was a familiar figure on the campus. She and the Pyr shared her dormitory room. Two years later she married Seaver and they decided to show Guerrier, who became their first champion. Between 1951 and 1955, they acquired all of the best stock owned by Marjorie Butcher.

When I asked Seaver why the unusual kennel name, he chuckled. "We lived at New Market (N.J.), when we started. There was a marker in the town explaining that in colonial days it had been called Quibbletown, since the farmers would bring their produce to the square and then quibble with buyers over the prices. The name was so unusual we decided to adopt it." There is no quibbling about the quality of the Great Pyrenees that have come out of the Quibbletown Kennel, for it is the top winner of the breed in America.

The Starkweathers

Don and Pat Starkweather are a husband-and-wife judging team who not only have judged extensively in this country but overseas, as well. Starkweather is teaching in Birmingham, at the first public diabetes hospital in the United States. "If it wasn't for the dog-show sport, the hospital still wouldn't be built," he told me, while the three of us had lunch in the Alabama city. "The hospital, opened in 1973, was largely financed by contributions from fanciers and two of them are on the board—Jud Streicher and Dan Hamilburg, Boxer breeders. Our director is Dr. Buris Boshell, who for years bred and showed top Boxers and Miniature Pinschers and is a judge."

I remember Starkweather from when he had Great Danes before World War II. He sold his dogs when he went into the service and in 1944 he was severely wounded during the fighting in New Guinea. Sent back to this country to recuperate, he was at a hospital in Battle Creek, Mich., where he was given two Boxer bitches. So successful was Don with the breed that he won the American Boxer Club's breeder-of-the-year award five years in a row. "I probably bred 50 to 60 champions," he said. "My Ch. Rainey Lane's Elixie was a really great sire and his bloodlines today are on four continents."

Mrs. Starkweather's Glen Hill has been a famous name in Collies since 1951 and sent out more than 50 champions. "My Glen Hill Dreamer's Nobleman gained his championship in the early 1960s," she recalled. "Everything we've finished traces to him. To help the breed in Japan, I sold Nobleman to a breeder there. I've also sold dogs to Germany, Italy, Brazil, Colombia, Mexico, the Dominican Republic and Canada. Most have become champions in those countries."

Mrs. Starkweather also has had some good Shelties. It was while judging in Bath, England, that she saw one she liked, Lonesome of Nutbury, and bought him. "I liked the type of Sheltie I saw in England better than those back home," she said. "They had better temperaments, heads, and were more refined."

Asked to compare today's Collies with those when she started, Mrs. Starkweather said, "Overall the present Collies are of a higher level but there were more outstanding individuals in the past." Don then had his say about the Boxer situation. "I believe those 20 years ago were generally superior to the current crop. However, there are exceptions. The very good ones today are as good as those in the past.''

The Meyers
Wilton and Mary Meyer comprise another of the husband-and-wife judging teams. ''We try to do the same shows, whenever possible,'' said the Orange, Calif., fancier. ''We both enjoy traveling and meeting people. At almost any show in the country, we can walk in and shake hands with at least 20 people. It's a nice feeling. Then judging is an ego trip. You are the boss and no one can talk back.''

Meyer is well known on the Coast not only for his dogs but also for his Volkswagens. ''I was the first dealer in California,'' he said. ''I started in March 1953. The VWs were such a novelty that when two of the Beetles would approach each other, the drivers would honk their horns. There was real cameraderie.''

In the dog show world, the big man has played several roles. In addition to judging, he has hunted, exhibited, bred, helped to organize the Harbor Cities KC, and has served as a delegate to the AKC.

It was in 1934 that he had his first judging assignment. ''I did Pointers and English Springers,'' he recalled. ''I knew both breeds well for I had been hunting with them since I was a boy.'' But it was to be neither a Pointer nor a Springer that was to be his first champion. ''I bought an English Setter, Shiplake Major, from a miner in Canada for $35,'' said Meyer. ''One day I showed Major and he took the breed. Before he was through he had won a group at Palm Springs.'' Since then the Meyers have had many titleholders—Bassets, Clumber Spaniels, Springers, Pointers and Chihuahuas.

In 1961, Meyer went to England and brought back four Clumber Spaniels, two of whom were English champions. ''As far as I know, they were the first Clumbers on the West Coast,'' he added. ''The next year we bought our first Chihuahua. It was a birthday present for our son, who complained all we had were big dogs and that he would like a Toy.'' The Californians had great success with the Chihuahuas. ''Wilton showed Ch. Kapen's Sugarcreek Kid to second in the group at International in Chicago in 1967,'' said Mrs. Meyer. ''They made quite a picture in the ring. Wilton was 225 pounds and the Kid five. It was his finest hour as a handler. The Kid was top Chihuahua in America in 1966 and 1967.''

The Landgrafs
Frank and Mildred Landgraf have been familiar figures at dog shows for more than three decades. Whenever Frank is judging, Mildred serves as his steward. In 1978, they celebrated their golden wedding anniversary. I remember them in the early 1950s, when my wife was showing our Dalmatian bitch and Frank was showing a dog. Many years later, Landgraf always mentioned our bitch, Rundy, saying how one never forgets a good one.

The Landgrafs started with a really good bitch, Sinful of Tomalyn Hill, Frank showing her for the first time at Morris and Essex in 1940, when she was nine months old. It was quite a debut, for she took winners for five points. The following Sunday, at Northern New Jersey, she won the breed, beating three champions and was second in the group. "Those are days one never forgets; she was the best we ever had," said the Jerseyite.

Frank stopped showing in 1964. "I was doing so much judging I felt it wasn't a healthy situation, judging one day and then taking a dog into the ring the next. There is always the suspicion the judge is going to favor you." Landgraf admits he also prefers the judging. "You meet more people, not just the ones in your breed," said he, "and you see people from different parts of the country you never would ordinarily meet. I would like a judge to have more time in going over the dogs. Frequently, I feel the exhibitor doesn't get a fair shake. As to the dogs today, I feel they are superior to those when I was showing. To me it is a great thrill to be able to put my hands on a super dog. My day is made when I have a really good one."

The Schwartzes

Mr. and Mrs. Alexander C. Schwartz, Jr. are another husband-and-wife team seen almost every weekend on the show circuit. Sandy now is busy judging and rarely takes a dog into the ring. Glorvina, on the other hand, makes a striking picture as she gaits one of their Afghans. Many times I've heard ringsiders comment when Glorvina is showing an Afghan, "I don't know whom I prefer seeing, the handler or the dog." Certainly she doesn't detract from the hound's efforts for she is a superb handler as well as being extremely attractive.

Both Schwartzes were brought up with animals. Among the neighbors of Glorvina, when she was a child at Tuxedo Park, N.Y., where Mrs. George B. St. George, Priscilla St. George Ryan, Adele Colgate and Mr. and Mrs. David Wagstaff, whose dogs were all big winners from the 1930s to the '50s. Gerald M. Livingston, president of Westminster from 1937 to 1942, was her uncle. It was Mrs. Livingston who gave Glorvina her first dog, a Labrador Retriever. Glorvina's aunt was also a noted Miniature Pinscher and Pug owner. Indeed, Glorvina's first show dogs were Pugs and by 1954, she had a champion. Before she turned to Afghans, she had bred or owned five more.

Although Sandy and Glorvina—their kennel name is Sandina—never had a large establishment, breeding a litter or two a year, they have been singularly successful. Their Ch. Sandina Starstream was the top winning Afghan in America in 1975, and Ch. Sandina Sparkling Champagne, a champion in the United States and Canada in 1976 and 1977. But Glorvina hailed Ch. Sandina Spellbound, a blue homebred she was campaigning in 1978 and 1979, as "the greatest Afghan I've ever owned."

Sandy, in addition to judging, is a busy clubman. He helped to reactivate the Tuxedo Park KC in 1971, after it had been dormant for 18 years, and became president. He's also an officer of Westchester.

Portias of the Sport

When Anna Katherine Nicholas pointed to the best in show at Westminster in 1970, it was only the third time in the 94 years of that classic a woman had judged the final. Cool and unruffled by the crowd's applause, the small, slender woman was a picture of concentration as she studied the six dogs, finally making her selection after 17 minutes. "I could hear the noise in the background," she told me, "but I was concentrating so hard on the job at hand, I couldn't tell you who the crowd liked."

Although so many judges have been long time breeders, have shown frequently or have come up from the professional handler ranks, the demure Miss Nicholas walked a dog into a ring on only three occasions.

"In the 1940s, I was at the Greenwich show, when a friend, with a couple of Scottish Deerhounds, asked if I would take one in," she recalled. "I beat him for best of breed and did the same thing the next day at Longshore."

Perhaps, she should have stopped right there. For in the '70s, she returned with a champion Beagle at Westchester, and this time her dog did nothing. However, she drew one of the largest crowds at any of the breed rings, the fanciers wanting to see a famous judge in action as an exhibitor.

Although there always were dogs in the Nicholas household when Anna was growing up, she never was interested in showing them. "As long as I can remember, all I wanted to do was judge," she told me. It was as a teenager that Miss Nicholas made her judging debut. At 16, she was invited to rule on Pekingese at Hartford. In a show that only had a total entry of some 300, the girl drew 31.

Her first best-in-show assignment was at Old Dominion in 1942, and she put up a Borzoi owned by the late Louis Murr, who as it turned out made the final decision at Westminster just a year before Anna.

In 1978, she was the owner of two champion Beagles, one of which, Ch. Rockaplenty's Wild Oats, had sired 23 champions, with at least another dozen well on their way to titles.

"One of the great satisfactions in judging," said the petite arbiter, "is finding and starting dogs on their winning careers. I've had the good fortune to have had that privilege many times."

Since 1957, Thelma Brown has been one of our busiest judges on the Coast. The AKC had been very slow giving judges multiple breeds in the Far West, the vast majority having merely one breed. So Thelma, with several groups, constantly was being called upon to accept assignments. Much of her success in the ring she attributes to her husband, Curtis, a civil engineer and a former president of the American Congress of Surveying and Mapping. "We have applied Curtis's knowledge of structure and movement to dogs," said the attractive arbiter. So something now has been added to the show world—a dog engineer.

Thelma, whose vocation is health-agency management, and Curtis had an unusual start in the sport. "I had never been allowed to have a dog as a child," said the La Mesa, Calif., fancier. "So when Curtis and I were married, I suggested we should get the dog of the day—a Cocker Spaniel. Now Curtis had been saving for weeks to buy tickets for the 1937 Rose Bowl football game but his goal was never achieved. He took the Rose Bowl money and we bought a little red Cocker bitch instead. The first time we showed her was in a novice class and she won a silver bowl. That did it. We were hooked." The Browns, after breeding Cockers for a number of years, decided it would be much less work with a smooth-coated dog and that a Beagle would be just right. Then came World War II. They sold their dogs and moved to a small apartment. "But we put the money into a special 'dog account' at the bank," said Thelma.

During the war, she kept careful statistics on all the winning Beagles, even writing to owners for the pedigrees of the little hounds. In 1946, when the Browns decided to get back into the sport, Thelma consulted her files and the Californians bought a 15-month-old tri-colored Beagle bitch, Culver's Carol. "The file system really paid off," recalled Thelma. "Carol was never beaten in the breed." The system kept paying dividends. The Browns bred 19 Beagle champions, three group winners and a best-in-show bitch.

Again they had a system when it came to breeding. "We kept only bitches," recalled Thelma. "The males we either sold or put out with other exhibitors as co-owners. That way we could keep an extensive breeding program, without having a great many dogs around the house. When we wanted to breed, we had the whole country from which to choose a sire."

"The accent is on the first syllable of my last name, when I'm judging," said Edith Nash Hellerman, who has been active in the sport for four decades. Although best known as a judge, she has been a successful breeder, exhibitor, club official and a leader in the steward ranks. "I have no sympathy for the owner or handler who does a sloppy job in presenting a dog," she said. "As to the stewards who complain, after working an hour or two, I tell them that we each have a job to do. If they get the dogs into the ring, I'll get them out. The professional handlers should be good enough to try and hide the faults of their dogs but the judges should know the standard well enough and be sufficiently sharp so as to detect the faults. I've shown too many dogs myself and the handlers know they cannot come into my ring and do a sloppy job, even for a reserve ribbon."

Mrs. Hellerman, long before the AKC let it be known it approved of withholding blue ribbons for dogs not sufficiently worthy, would do it on her own volition. She would give a red ribbon. "The only reason for a dog show is to improve the breed," she declared. "I can't see them automatically handing out blues." However, on many an occasion I've seen Edith help a novice by setting up the dog herself. She has also taken some inexperienced ring stewards in tow and guided them through the routine so that by the end of the day they were performing like old-timers.

In the days she showed, Mrs. Hellerman was best known for her Brussels Griffons, having bred a dozen champions. But at one time or another she also had English Setters, Cocker Spaniels, German Wirehaired Pointers, Dachshunds and Shelties. Before her retirement, she had been the Registered Record Administrator for a psychiatric hospital in Maryland and this experience should help her in dealing with some of the slightly neurotic exhibitors in the show ring.

I interviewed Mrs. Maynard (Kitty) Drury for a column in *The New York Times* in 1960. For years I had watched her show Newfoundlands. Indeed, she had gaited a Newf at Westminster as far back as 1932. We laughed many times when she told me about my phone call to her home in Locust Valley, L.I. A busy mother, she was caring for five children and eight of the big black dogs. She said when she announced at the dinner table that I had called, one of the children, a real doubting Thomas, said, "Mother, it really couldn't have been *The New York Times*; probably it is someone trying to pull your leg." So when I arrived at their home on Long Island, I was introduced to all the youngsters to prove it really had been *The New York Times*.

The children and Newfs made me think of the Darlings in Peter Pan. When I tried to get the book in the library, I was sent to the children's section and sat on a low stool, the kind used in kindergartens. I wrote how the Drurys had two more children then the Darlings and whereas the latter family had engaged one Newf, Nana, to take care of the Darling trio, the Drurys had eight, plus a dozen pups. For generations the Newfoundland had been known as a traditional protector and playmate of children. Unlike a smaller dog, a 180-pounder isn't easily hurt by small tugging fingers.

My story must have gained attention for when Peter Pan was being produced on Broadway, Kitty received a phone call, asking for a Newf to play the role of Nana. "I never kept more than eight adult dogs," she recalled, "so I could give each individual attention. Only one was permitted to be the housedog, but we kept rotating them, bringing a different one in each day. The others stayed in the kennel. No need to coddle them and they developed good coats. In the winter, they frequently slept in the snow. When I would open the door to feed them, a mound of snow would turn into a Newf."

Mrs. Drury began to judge in 1937. She was the arbiter at the first Newfoundland specialty ever held in the land where the breed originated, at St. John's and she put up a dog bred and raised in Newfoundland. "The most beautiful black I saw overseas was in Denmark," she said, "and the most striking Landseer was at the golden jubilee show of the Irish Kennel Club at Dublin, in 1972."

Kitty was particularly proud of the Newfoundland national specialty in 1977, at Rockton, Ill. "Of the 200 dogs, 99 percent went back to two of my dogs—Ch. Dryad's Sea Rover and Dryad's Goliath of Gath—within a 10-year span."

Few judges have had a better background for work in the middle of the ring than Iris de la Torre Bueno. All her life she has been associated closely with the sport, so it is little wonder that she constantly is being called upon to rule on dogs.

It was on February 19, 1917, that her mother, Cecilia de la Torre Bueno, received a certificate from the AKC, then at 1 Liberty Street, signed by the secretary, A. P. Vredenburgh, saying that the All Celia's kennel name had been duly granted. Although All Celia's is almost synonymous in this era with Brussels Griffons, Mrs. de la Torre Bueno had started with Bulldogs. Then she turned to Pekingese and it wasn't until the 1920s that she bought her first little Belgian Toy dog. In 1927, when I first started to cover dog shows, All Celia's Mademoiselle became the kennel's first Brussels Griffon champion. A half-century later, the number of Griff titleholders had increased to nearly a hundred.

"Ch. Beau Brummel was the greatest we owned," said Iris. "I believe a real champion should be a stayer. I showed Beau for five years. The first time I took him into a ring he was beaten for best of breed by a kennelmate. In the next 62 shows in the United States, Beau always was best Griff and 57 times he placed in the Toy group, of which 22 were firsts. He was also a Canadian champion, winning the group all three times I showed him."

What advice would Iris give to a beginner? "Don't show a dog too young," she replied. "I think it is to a dog's advantage if it isn't brought out until it is two or three years old. This is particularly true of the short-faced and thick-set breeds, since they tend to mature later. When a judge looks over the finished product, he can compare the animal to the breed standard more effectively."

One of those memorable moments in the dog world occurred at Riverhead, L.I., in 1969, when Dona Hausman showed her Shetland Sheepdog, Ch. Sutter's Golden Masquerade, to the top prize. Owners, handlers and ringsiders rushed to congratulate the Stamford, Conn., fancier for after 32 years of taking dogs into the ring, Dona finally had her first best in show.

Mrs. Hausman comes from a family long prominent in the dog world. Her grandfather imported from Switzerland one of the first St. Bernards to be seen in the East and her father's Airedale, Ch. Red Raven, three years in a row was best of breed at Westminster. The Raven was a big winner early in the century and many of the modern-day Airedales trace to him.

"My first dog was a Scottie, a present on my 11th birthday," recalled Dona. In 1937, she showed My Own of Meadow Ridge, a Cocker Spaniel, to his championship. It was this dog (bought from Herman Mellenthin, the owner of Ch. My Own Brucie, twice best at the Garden) who was the foundation stud for her Meadow Ridge Kennel. Before she stopped breeding Cockers, she had three other champions of the breed, as well as finishing a Springer import. In 1950, Dona's husband, Jim, bought a Brittany Spaniel for hunting. Mrs. Hausman promptly took the Brit, Meadow Ridge Trash Man, into the ring and made a champion of him. Two years later, she repeated the feat with a Gordon Setter her husband had bought to shoot over.

But it was with the Sheltie that the Connecticut fancier was to attain her greatest success. "I always wanted a Collie," Dona told me, "but I felt it was just a little too big for me, so I turned to the Collie's little brother, the Sheltie." That was Meadow Ridge Golden Dawn, who went on to become a champion and the foundation bitch for the kennel. The golden sable bore five champions.

A visit to the Pixie Dell Kennel of Mr. and Mrs. Ray Miller, and Dona came away with a four-month-old puppy, who was to become Ch. Pixie Dell Bright Vision, the only Sheltie to go best of breed at Westminster three times. "I guess I followed in the footsteps of my father's Airedale, with his three Westminster wins," she said. Vision, who also took the national specialty three times, was a great sire, with 18 champions, including Masquerade, "the greatest showman I ever owned."

Back in 1942, Dona, long an obedience enthusiast, began to judge the educated set. Seven years later, she gave up her obedience license and started to judge in the breed ring. Since 1950, Dona has been show chairman for Ox Ridge. "I've seen it go up from 500 to more than 2,000 dogs," she said proudly.

More than 500 oils, water colors and etchings done by Mary Nelson Stephenson are in private collections around the United States. Now that the tall, silver-haired woman has moved to a little white house in Centerville, on Cape Cod, she's painting seascapes. Around the cottage are any number of dogs but they make nary a sound. For Mary's dogs are china, porcelain, or in her collection of engravings, etchings, Oriental silk scrolls and wood block prints. For the first time in three decades there isn't a live dog about.

It's quite a departure from her days as a breeder and exhibitor, when she had almost a dozen breeds. The last dog she bred, she fittingly called Finale—Ch. Nebshire's Drum Hill Finale—and he was the Dandie Dinmont of the Year in 1976.

Mrs. Stephenson's first show dog was a Standard Schnauzer, Major Pfeffer. Not only did he finish quickly but he won the breed at Westminster in 1951 and 1952, took three national specialties and was best in show four times. He sired many champions, including Coterne Pfeffer's Trudi, who was sold to Britain, where she became an English titleholder. "Many years later, when I went to Crufts," beamed Mary, "it was so thrilling to see a great-grandson of Trudi's take the challenge certificate."

When Pfeffer died, Mrs. Stephenson bought a magnificent Afghan, Ch. Crown Crest Kabul. But then Mary was severely injured in a near-fatal auto accident. For months she was confined to a wheelchair, and was away from the rings. There were cheers for both the owner and dog when Mrs. Stephenson, recovered, showed him to best in show at Beverly-Riviera.

"When I judged my first Afghan specialty in California," said Mary, "it was a great satisfaction to learn that more than a third of the entries were Kabby's grandchildren. That's what makes breeding so exciting and worthwile."

Mrs. Stephenson had a variety of breeds, including Greyhounds, Irish

150

Wolfhounds, Salukis, Scottish Deerhounds, English Springers, Miniature Schnauzers and Dandie Dinmonts.

Now she has stopped all breeding and showing and does nothing but judge. She was one of the relatively few arbiters who would give me good, intelligent statements after she chose her best. "Learning a breed standard just isn't enough," she said. "Understanding a breed is something else. I believe that painting gives me a more discerning eye and helps me with my judging."

Show chairmen frequently have a rather difficult time getting arbiters to judge junior handling. Grace Brewin thrives on the assignments. At Springfield, Mass., she drew an entry of 125 in 1973, a year in which she judged the young fry 19 times. "I'm pleased when parents and children come up to thank me after the classes," said the Agawam, Mass., judge. "When I was a nurse, I always enjoyed caring for children."

Not only was Grace a registered nurse but she also earned her bachelor's and master's degrees at Columbia. She taught anatomy and physiology to other nurses, became public health supervisor for the New London area and then moved on to become state consultant in public health in Hartford, a post she held for a decade.

In the dog show world she gained fame with her Bedlington Terriers. "I bought a liver-colored bitch, Center Ridge Terry Cloth, in 1959," recalled Grace. "To put it mildly, we weren't a great team and after showing for eight months, Terry still didn't have a point. One day my son, Peter, then 15, said, 'Mother, you are doing such a bum job, let me try.' The first time he went into the ring, Terry was winners bitch for one point. Then my husband, Vel, took over and she quickly finished." Terry became the Brewin foundation bitch and two of her puppies gained titles when they were seven months old.

The Bay Staters also did well with Lakelands, Welsh and Fox Terriers, having group and best-in-show winners. When brace competition was popular, the Brewins excelled. Grace handled the Bedlingtons, Ch. Petercrest Spitfire and Ch. Petercrest Blue Painted Doll, to three best brace-in-show awards. She also handled a pair of Lakelands, Ch. Petercrest Bold and Brassy and Ch. Petercrest Black-Eyed Susan, to three top prizes, including Westminster in 1970, the next to last competition ever held by the Garden classic for twosomes.

Wilt Chamberlain with his Great Danes, Thor (black) and Careem and Odin (harlequins). Note the uncropped ears.

Familiar Faces from
Other Places

AS THE REPORTER on dogs for the *New York Times,* it became my lot to interview some owners whose activities were more often reported upon in other sections of the newspaper. There were political figures, society page headliners, show personalities, athletes—and even some other newspapermen. I found most of them more than eager to tell of the joys their dogs have afforded them.

A Tall Tale

The shortest interview I ever conducted was with one of the biggest men in sports and fortunately an extremely articulate one. It was with Wilt Chamberlain, who had come into New York to receive an automobile as the most valuable player in the National Basketball Association. The interview, in a taxi, lasted from Mama Leone's restaurant on 48th street to Madison Square Garden, a distance of 15 blocks, and I kept praying for red lights. When I asked the 7–foot–1–inch ace of the Los Angeles Lakers for the interview, he thought it was going to be about basketball and promptly declined. But when he heard it concerned his dogs, he agreed.

''I'm going to the Garden to pick up my bag and then go to the airport. Why don't you ride to the Garden with me and we can talk?'' In the cab, he said, ''I'm a big man and I like big dogs, so I have Great Danes. Years ago, when I decided to buy one, I read the ads and called a breeder. He said he had three pups—a fawn and two blacks. I drove to his kennel with the intention of buying the fawn. But those blacks were beautiful. I couldn't stand separating a pair of brothers, so I wound up with a pair of 6–week–old puppies. I named them after the Norse gods—Odin and Thor.''

Nine years later, when Odin died, Wilt sought a replacement so Thor would have a playmate. Again the big man couldn't think of separating litter brothers, so he drove home with two pups.

''This time I bought harlequins,'' he said. ''I now knew more about the breed

153

and I'd been told it was extremely hard to raise a good harlequin. That was a challenge. All my Danes have the drop ear. I've always felt it was cruel to crop them. It may look strange to some people but to me it doesn't detract from their looks. To me the breed combines beauty, grace and strength. You know the Dane is called the Apollo of dogs. I named the pups Odin (after the dog I lost) and Careem. He's not a black and white but a cream and white. That's how I hit on the name.'' Basketball fans suspect that the big man named the pup after Kareem Abdul-Jabbar, another giant basketball star.

Wilt does all his own training and his Danes obey the basic obedience commands—heel, sit, down and come. "I guess I must be a pretty good trainer," laughed Wilt. "One night after I had scored 73 points, one of the best performances I ever had in pro ball, I returned to the apartment feeling mighty happy. About 3 A.M., I took the pups for a walk. Suddenly a big car stopped and a man called out to me. 'I've been watching you with those Danes and you do a good job. You must be a professional trainer. I'm having trouble with my dog and would like to have you work with him.' Back came the answer, "Sorry, but I'm all booked up."

"Those pups caused me to be evicted from the apartment on Central Park West," he recalled. "They kept growing until finally only the three of us could get into the elevator. Some of the other tenants complained. I was told to either get rid of the dogs or the apartment. In California I have a house with three acres and there are no problems." Chamberlain even considered his dogs when he came East to receive the car. He asked for a station wagon. "That way my Danes can be with me when I go for a drive," he explained.

Governor and Mrs. Lehman

Certainly one of the most gracious couples I had the good fortune to interview was the former Governor of New York State, and United States Senator, Herbert H. Lehman, and his wife. In 1960, I went to the "kennel" in their duplex Park Avenue apartment and I wrote that although they had more than 150 Boxers, there were no complaints from the neighbors. For all the dogs were ceramic. "It wasn't always this way," he said. "From 1912 until 1928, when I left the city for Albany, to become Lieutenant Governor, I bred more live ones than we have in the 'kennel.' The eight-foot-long shelf was located in his dressing room. A *Times* photographer, who accompanied me on the interview, took a picture of the couple standing in front of the "display," over which was a sign, "Lehman's Boxers."

Mrs. Lehman had the "kennel" built for him, when the Senator was in Washington. A carpenter constructed the long shelf, with a number of dog runs, and it was installed atop a fireplace in Mr. Lehman's quarters in the Senate Office Building. In each run there were several ceramic Boxers, largely the gift of his children, grandchildren and other members of the family. "Every birthday, anniversary or other special occasion, they would send some Boxers to E (Edith Lehman, his wife) and me," he said. "We have them from England, Germany, Switzerland, Denmark and even a white one from Venezuela."

154

The Lehmans were among the first to recognize the Boxer's potentialities and in 1912 bought one in Switzerland for a house pet. Two years later, when they moved to Meadow Farm in Purchase, N.Y., they decided they would like some more Boxers and imported several. One was the Sieger, Dampf von Dom. "He was the best we ever owned," said Mrs. Lehman, who campaigned him extensively. "I think he was one of the greatest Boxers that ever lived and that includes the modern generation. He had everything—a magnificent head, he moved beautifully and was a real showman." Dampf made Boxer history. Shown by Mrs. Lehman at Westminster in 1914, he took the breed and the following April became the first Boxer in America to become a champion.

The Governor told me an amazing story about a bitch, Cilly von Neapel, whom they called Molly, and was winners bitch at the Garden in 1915. "Molly had her first litter—there were two pups—at an animal hospital," said the statesman. "A few days later we received a phone call that there was a fire in the building and Molly's quarters had been flooded by water from the hoses. We rushed down and were told by the firemen that when they sloshed through the water, they found Molly standing on her hind legs with one pup in her mouth and the other on a narrow ledge, where she had placed him above the water. She saved both of her puppies."

The Lehmans had a large framed picture of the former Governor with two Boxer pups on his lap, while their mother affectionately licks his hands. "In 1935, when I was Governor," he explained, "we were having budget troubles and the subject was so very much on my mind that I named a Boxer, Budget. At a press conference, I mentioned this to some 40 reporters. One asked to see her. I opened the door and in came Budget, followed by her two puppies. The amused newsmen immediately named the little ones, Surplus and Deficit. Fortunately, Surplus grew to be the larger."

The Engelhards and their Goldens

In 1967, I was driven to Cragwood, a 160-acre estate in Far Hills, N.J., owned by Charles W. Engelhard, and his wife, both of whom liked animals. Mrs. Engelhard at the time owned the top-winning Golden Retriever kennel in America. Her husband's racing stable had won its share of stakes in this country and even more abroad. The St. Leger, run in England since 1776, had been won by only one living owner twice. That was Engelhard, his Indiana taking the classic in 1964 and his Ribocco in 1967. As Mrs. Engelhard put it, "My husband's main hobby is horses, which are not very good house pets."

Cragwood never failed to welcome an animal. When a decrepit blue-ticked hound showed up one day, he took his place with the prize-winning retrievers. In the living room at Cragwood was a large silver bowl. It was the perpetual challenge trophy for the top-winning Golden Retriever in the United States. The bowl originally arrived at Cragwood in 1963, when Ch. Cragmount's Peter was named the No. 1 Golden for 1962. It returned to Far Hills in 1966, when Ch. Cragmount's Hi-Lo took the honors for the previous year. When Hi-Lo repeated, the trophy remained in its niche. The achievements of the dogs were indeed spectacular, since Mrs. Engelhard didn't show her retrievers in the hot summer months. She sent them to her fishing camp in Canada.

Cragmount wasn't a particularly large kennel. "A friend, George Murnane, gave us our first Golden in 1949," recalled Mrs. Engelhard, "but Bobby was strictly a pet. Several times a week, he'd run eight miles to Peapack to visit his friends. When people would call us to say they had seen Bobby, we would ask them to send him home by cab. He became so accustomed to riding in a taxi, whenever he went visiting, he'd automatically trot over to the cab office. At the end of the month, we'd get a bill, with a Bobby notation on it some half-dozen times."

Mrs. Engelhard didn't start to breed and show Goldens until 1957. Harold Correll, who became her kennel manager, helped her to find two good show dogs—Finderne Gold Cloud of Kent (Sonny) and Rozzy Duchess. They were Cragmount's foundation stock. "Both Peter and Hi-Lo were homebreds, of which I'm particulary proud," said Cragwood's mistress. "Hi-Lo is the sixth generation of our breeding. The greatest thrills I've had in the sport was the first time we had a best of breed at Westminster—Sonny in 1959—and 1967 when Hi-Lo won the breed at the Garden. Hi-Lo is the most beautiful Golden I've ever seen and I've seen a great many in America and overseas. My great ambition was to breed a great Golden. I've succeeded with Hi-Lo."

The Cragmount retrievers were housed in a kennel that formerly was a stable for the Engelhard jumpers and hunters. In a trophy room were the best-of-breed, group and best-in-show rosettes, together with some of the major silverware acquired by the dogs' victories. Hi-Lo, in 1967, retired the Eastern Regional Trophy, when he won it for the third successive time, beating a total of 604 Goldens in the three shows. Framed on a wall of the trophy room was a letter to Mrs. Engelhard, which read in part: "Knowing your fondness for those beautiful puppies you and Charlie brought us, I thought you'd like to see how they are progressing. These pictures . . . Sincerely, LYNDON B. JOHNSON."

Mrs. Engelhard, who several times was selected as one of the world's best-dressed women, told me how her eldest daughter had pondered what to give her father for his birthday. Knowing that he loved animals, she gave him a lion cub. The cub was leash-trained and ran and played with the retrievers. But as he grew, there constantly was a need for a larger collar and stronger leash. When he was 10 months old, the Engelhard veterinarian said he had to be declawed, if he remained. Mrs. Engelhard objected, feeling it was cruel. So the lion was given to the Toronto Zoo. When the industrialist, who had grown very fond of his cub, Charlie, would visit the Canadian city, he would take time out to "talk" with his pet.

In the dining room of the Engelhard house, where we had a delightful lunch, was Jacob, a 90-year-old parrot, who had been with the family for 43 years and was able to imitate most of their voices. Next to the awards that her Goldens had won, Mrs. Engelhard's most prized trophy was a gold pin she received in 1966 for having landed the largest salmon on the Atlantic seaboard for the year—a 42-pounder she hooked on a 13-ounce rod.

Presidents and Their Dogs

It seems as if the Presidency always has had its dogs—the four-legged variety, of course. The Marquis de Lafayette, who gained fame as a general on Washington's staff and served with distinction in the Continental Army, also had the distinction of having a good eye for a dog. The French nobleman sent hounds to our first President, shepherds to Thomas Jefferson and two of the first Great Pyrenees to arrive in America, to a J. C. Skinner. Walter M. Jeffords, Jr., of New York City, owns the Jeffords Pack of English Foxhounds, which he says are descended from the hounds behind which Washington rode in pursuit of the fox.

When I was covering a dog show in Charlottesville, Va., I visited Monticello, the home of Jefferson. Having heard that the author of the Declaration of Independence had been a longtime fancier, I brought up the subject with James A. Bear, resident director and curator of Monticello. He was extremely helpful and compiled a list of references for me from manuscripts at the historic estate.

Jefferson believed in dogs for their utilitarian value. Having imported sheep—he thought the then young nation could be a sheep-herding country—he wanted guardians for the flock. So he turned to Lafayette and the Frenchman had two dogs shipped to Monticello. In a letter dated August 22, 1809, Jefferson wrote to his cousin, George Jefferson, who handled some of his accounts in Richmond, "The Marquis Fayette has sent me a pair of shepherds . . ." A friend, William Thornton, hearing of Jefferson's success in raising sheep and of the dogs guarding them, wrote to Monticello, "If hereafter you could favor me with the breed, I should be thankful, for I am very sheepishly inclined." Jefferson answered, "I have reserved the pair of dogs for yourself and Mr. (George) Dougherty . . . besides their wonderful sagacity and never-ceasing attention to what they are taught to do, they appear to have more courage than I had supposed . . . They make the best farm dogs or house dogs I have ever seen . . ."

Writing to Judge Harry Todd on September 18, 1813, Jefferson said, ". . . . we possess here the genuine race of Shepherd dogs. I imported them from France about four years ago. They were selected for me by the Marquis Fayette and I have endeavored to secure their preservation by giving them in pairs, to those who wished for them . . . There are so many applications for them that there are never any on hand, unless kept on purpose. Their extraordinary sagacity renders them extremely valuable, capable of being taught almost any duty that may be required of them, and they are most anxious in their performance of that duty, the most watchful and faithful of all servants."

However, Jefferson, aware of damage that can be caused by dogs, in a letter to Peter Minor, a neighbor, on September 24, 1811, suggested "making the owner of a dog liable for all the mischief done by him and requiring that every dog should wear a collar with the name of the person inscribed who shall be security for his honest demeanor." At Monticello, a dog collar was found with the name "Trench" on it and it is thought to have been one of the shepherds sent by Lafayette. There were two other dogs whose names were known at the Virginia home, Bergere and Grizzle, bought when the Jeffersons were preparing to leave for France in 1789.

I had an amusing interview with Traphes Bryant, kennelman at the White House from 1960 until he retired 12 years later. "King Timahoe, Pasha and Vicky are probably the least publicized residents of the White House," he told me, "but they are among the most popular." Tim, an Irish Setter, was a gift to President Richard Nixon from the White House staff; Vicky, a miniature Poodle, was Julie's pet, and Pasha, a Yorkie, was Tricia's. Bryant said that the President was a little shy with the pup at the start, so he helped them get acquainted. "I'd take the King to the President and give Mr. Nixon goodies to keep in his desk for the dog," he said. "Then I'd tell him what new things I'd taught Tim and he would put him through his paces, with a suitable reward."

Bryant said that President Johnson was especially fond of his dogs—Yuki, a mixed breed; the Beagles, Him and Her; and a white Collie, Blanco. Yuki was the favorite. "I'd get a call to bring Yuki to the second-floor family quarters," recalled Bryant. "The little dog would see the President, make a leap for the foot of the bed, curl up and go right to sleep. At Lynda Byrd's wedding, President Johnson took a few turns around the dance floor with Yuki. It's probably the only time a dog ever danced at the White House. Probably every world leader met the dogs. It was a common sight to see President Johnson and his dogs walking with a foreign visitor."

President John F. Kennedy, he said, would swim in the nude in the White House pool, with Charlie, his Welsh terrier, "splashing around him." He added that the President and Mrs. Kennedy would stroll on the sidewalk outside the White House fence at night, accompanied by a German Shepherd Dog, Clipper, and few passers-by would recognize them.

The most photographed of the Presidential dogs during my tenure as a newspaperman was Fala, the Scottish Terrier, who accompanied Franklin D. Roosevelt on international conferences and was ever a good-will ambassador. I'll never forget the furor created by the photograph of Johnson picking up one of his Beagles by the ears. Dwight D. Eisenhower had a Weimaraner, Heidi, who he would feed himself. Calvin Coolidge's Peter Pan had to be banished to Never Never Land, the country farm, because the Wire Fox Terrier persisted in nipping at the heels of White House employees. He was replaced by Prudence Prim, a white Collie, who was so gentle that she was allowed to attend garden parties. The Trumans had an Irish Setter, Mike; the Fords, a Golden Retriever, Liberty; while the only dog in the Carter household was a mixed breed, Grits, a gift to Amy from her teacher.

The Greatest Show of
Them All

Mention Morris and Essex to an old timer and it will bring a gleam to his eye. Immediately, he will regale you with stories about the most lavish dog shows ever held in America and about Mrs. Geraldine Rockefeller Dodge, the mistress of Giralda Farms in Madison, N.J., where the extravaganzas were held.

Once a year, she threw open the gates of the estate and crowds of up to 50,000 flocked to the polo field, on whose velvety-green turf the dogs vied for ribbons. Barnum and Bailey, Ringling Bros. Circus billed itself as the "Greatest Show on Earth," but it was dwarfed by the 1939 M&E, which drew 4,456 dogs, still the greatest entry in the history of shows in this country at this writing. Whereas the circus in 1939 used 70,000 square feet of canvas for its tenting, the "Greatest Dog Show" had 160,000.

It was a kaleidoscope of color, with a bright umbrella over each judge's table in the 57 rings. Flying from the six huge group tents were pennants, whipped by the breeze. There was no silver shortage when it came to the trophy table, for 383 pieces of sterling were offered outright. Mrs. Dodge arranged with a famous caterer to provide 4,600 luncheons for the exhibitors, judges and other officials. Then there was a huge cafeteria, so the visitors would have food. To keep the traffic flowing, 90 officers and special police patroled the roads and manned the gates. It was estimated that it cost around $70,000 to stage this "Show of Shows."

Morris and Essex started very modestly. Its first show was held on May 28, 1927, with only 17 breeds represented. There were no Toys or Hounds. Of the 504 dogs on the benches, German Shepherds predominated, with 120. But a Shepherd could do no better than third in the group. There were five judges to select best in show and it proved to be William W. Higgins' American-bred Irish Setter, Ch. Higgins' Red Pat. Fanciers left with wondrous tales about Giralda, how there had been 15 large rings, four big tents, ample chairs and even pipelines to bring water to where the dogs were benched. All this and box luncheons, too, in a magnificently landscaped sylvan setting. The night before the show, there was a dinner and dance for the judges and club members, and handsome, expensive gifts for the arbiters.

Presiding over it all was the Empress of Giralda, the niece of John D. Rockefeller and the wife of Marcellus Hartley Dodge, grandson of the founder of Remington Arms Company. She had dogs all her life. In the Dodge collection of bronzes, there was a study of Bayard, a St. Bernard pet she had as a schoolgirl, which had been imported by her father, William G. Rockefeller, from the famous hospice of St. Gotthard.

Mrs. Dodge never showed until she had German Shepherds, in 1923, but she then did much to popularize that breed. "It is my earnest wish," she said, "that dog lovers become interested in the German Shepherd. I'm only too glad, at all times, to let go even my best puppies to further the interest of the breed." Giralda had some of the great Shepherds in the 1920s and '30s. There was the 1926 Siegerin of Germany, Arna aus der Ehrenzelle; the Austrian Siegerin, Pia von Haus Schutting, and a stud dog, Ch. Giralda's Iso von Doernerhof, a prepotent black. Ch. Dewet von der Starrenburg had an impressive record. Shown 18 times, he won 16 breeds, took 12 groups and was best three times.

Mrs. Dodge never succeeded in winning Westminster with a German Shepherd. However, two of her other dogs did romp off with the best-in-show trophy at the Garden. A Pointer, Ch. Nancolleth Markable, accomplished the feat in 1932 and seven years later a Doberman Pinscher, Ferry von Rauhfelsen, led a field of 3,069. So the mistress of Giralda became the only owner to have two Westminster top winners with two different breeds.

There was a bit of talk about the Dobe's triumph. He made his American debut at the Garden, after having been off the boat for only three weeks. The five other finalists had a total of 65 best-in-show awards among them and they included two of the leading winners in America—the Cocker Spaniel, Ch. My Own Brucie, and a Smooth Fox Terrier, Ch. Nornay Saddler. George Thomas, who judged, was criticized, since to all appearances he didn't lay a hand on Ferry.

Mrs. Dodge made further history at Westminster when, in 1933, she became the first woman to judge its best in show.

M&E was held annually, except for the war years, through 1957. Then Mrs. Dodge became embroiled with the AKC over the show date and when her choice was denied, that was the end.

She owned more than 80 breeds and did some big winning with Bloodhounds, Beagles and Cocker Spaniels. It was largely through her efforts that the English Cocker Spaniel was recognized as a separate breed in the United States.

Although tremendous crowds flocked to Morris and Essex, few persons ever entered her Tudor manor house. All her life, Mrs. Dodge had been an avid collector and there were more than 5,000 pieces of art in the mansion when she died in 1973 at the age of 91. Every table was laden with bronzes, every wall covered with oils, water colors, etchings and lithographs. Glass cabinets were filled with porcelains. It took the auction firm of Sotheby, Parke-Bernet a year and a half to sort, appraise and catalogue everything.

Following the sale of the largest private collection of dog art in the world, part of the proceeds were given to an animal shelter Mrs. Dodge had established on the property. She had named it St. Hubert's Giralda, after the patron of the hunt. The shelter, which sits on six acres of the former Dodge estate, is under the direction of Edward Sayres, a former kennel manager for Mrs. Dodge. It handles more than 3,000 dogs, cats, and other small animals, serving more than 90 square miles in eight communities. A gallery has been constructed in a renovated barn to house the paintings, sculptures and books not included in the sale.

The 17 Chairmen

Westchester has long been one of the top outdoor events in the country and two of the pioneers who did much to bring the show to its eminence were Stanley J. Halle and O. Carley Harriman. Both men joined Westchester in 1922, at the suggestion of J. W. Harriman, Carley's father, who then was president of the club. Halle had some of the greatest Wire Fox Terriers in the country in the 1920s and 1930s. He and Winthrop Rutherford were the only two fanciers whose dogs were three-time winners at Westminster.

Stanley did it with a comparatively small kennel, for he averaged no more than 20 dogs, including puppies. The Wall Streeter stopped showing in 1940. "I felt my dogs had done sufficient winning," he explained to me, "and that I'd concentrate on judging." Halle had his first judging assignment in 1919 and he was to rule at almost every major show in this country, as well as at Crufts. At Westminster, in 1939, I watched him judge 146 Fox Terriers, a record entry for that event.

When he had been in the sport for 50 years, I asked him what was the greatest change he had seen. After reflecting, he replied, "The emphasis today, unfortunately, is on developing group and best-in-show winners. Now I had my share but from a breeder's viewpoint—and I had top Airedales and Welsh, as well as Wires—I always felt pride when one of my Terriers came through a strong class of eight or 10. I was interested in improving the breed and let best in show take care of itself."

Harriman moved to the West Coast and did quite a bit of judging out there. I had a pleasant afternoon with him in 1971, the last time he ever judged Westminster. He reminisced about his youth, the way he would roller skate in the Murray Hill area. "I did my first judging in 1915 and I started at Westminster, of all places, doing Great Danes." He held short shrift for judges who "grandstand" while doing best in show. It took him exactly 12 minutes to choose his Westminster winner.

Westchester for many years had exactly 17 members. Rumor had it that the table in Halle's dining room had eight chairs on each side. Halle presided at one end, the other was left vacant.

Fifteen of the 17 members of the Westchester club in the "uniforms" with which they made themselves readily identifiable to exhibitors at the 1978 show. Front row, l. to r.: A. Wallace Owen, Alexander C. Schwartz, A. Peter Knoop, Judson L. Streicher, Dr. Bernard E. McGivern, Roger Martin and Philip R. Toohey. Back row, l. to r.: John J. Archibald, Jack L. Taylor, Dr. Samuel Draper, Robert A. Hetherington, Philip A. Cleland, William A. Metz, Gilbert H. Wehmann and Chester F. Collier.

By the Sea

Among the members of Boardwalk, the earthy John Berry is known as the Godfather. Devotedly helped by Peggy Lee, Emma Pepe, Joan Cianchettu and the two dozen other members of the Atlantic City club, John, who has been Boardwalk's president since it was founded in 1965, said, "We are a big happy family."

Berry, an innovator, has built the show into one of the major fixtures in America. At the beginning, although indoors, it was held on grass. However, the evening before the 1975 event, someone forgot to turn off the water used to nourish the sod. So the going was muddy and there was an odor of rotting grass. That was the end of the turf. Now the dogs perform on cement.

For years, Berry strove to induce Philadelphia to join forces with Boardwalk by changing its date for the same weekend. But Philadelphia rejected the proposition. In 1977, Camden found itself without a show site and teamed up with Boardwalk, holding its fixture in Convention Hall, the day before Berry's extravaganza. Then, when it looked as if John finally would achieve his goal of staging America's biggest show, he was thwarted, for a national convention had already been booked into the big hall. As a result, Boardwalk had to limit its entry to 3,000. "If we had our usual space and not been limited, we easily could have gone over 4,000," moaned Berry. But ever the optimist, he predicted that with the advent of gambling casinos, top entertainment and more hotels and motels in Atlantic City, Boardwalk would reach its goal of being No. 1.

The first show held in 1967 drew 1,580 entries. Six years later, even though there was an acute gasoline shortage, Boardwalk soared to 3,709, to be the second largest show in the United States, surpassed only by Santa Barbara.

Berry has been with the Atlantic City police force since 1940 and been head of its K-9 unit since it was organized in 1970. You can expect Berry to do the unusual and perhaps that is one of the reasons for the show's success. Years ago, he and his wife, Evelyn, taught their German Shepherds to ride a surfboard behind a speedboat.

He is always open to suggestions. He would corner me and ask if I had any ideas for improving the show. "I intend to not only make us the biggest, but also the best," he would say. John received a license to judge in 1974. "I prefer judging to showing," he told me, "but best of all I enjoy putting on Boardwalk."

Closing Up Those Golden Gates

Golden Gate and Stanley Hanson are synonomous. For a quarter of a century, the retired business executive has been chairman of the two-day benched show in the Cow Palace. "We limit our entry to 2,200," he told me, "and over the years we have turned back an additional 400-to-700 dogs. Being one of a handful of benched shows left in the country, we want to keep it a blue-ribbon event. We strive to make it comfortable for both the exhibitor and spectator. To encourage

In this strong Working group at Westbury, note that every handler's attention is riveted on his or her dog, rather than on the one gaiting for the judge.

Not so, however, in this view of the 6-9 months puppy judging at the 1974 American Spaniel Club specialty at the Statler-Hilton in New York City.

people to attend, Golden Gate has special family admission rates. As a result we have crowds up to 30,000, over the two days, for our winter show.''

Hanson started with Dachshunds in 1943—five years later he was judging the breed. He's a member of the school that favors moving the Miniature Dachshunds from the Hound to the Toy group. ''The Minis are lost with the big hounds and they certainly would do more winning if they competed against dogs closer to their size,'' said he. Although Hanson accepts only 25 assignments a year, he has ruled at most of the big ones—Westminster, International, Beverly Hills and Westchester. He also has judged extensively overseas.

Show Pilot

A fifth-generation Sandy Hook pilot, Robert J. McCarthy showed he could steer a dog show committee as well as an ocean liner, when he was chairman of the Staten Island show in 1975. It was one of the most successful events ever held by the club on the historic grounds of Fort Wadsworth, the oldest continuously manned Army post in the United States, dating to the 17th century.

''I first went to sea in 1933,'' recalled McCarthy. ''Shipped aboard the American-South African Line. Took 31 days from New York to Cape Town. Later I started my apprenticeship on the pilot boat. Began as an ordinary seaman and wound up, eight years later, as captain. My brother, two cousins and a nephew all are pilots. We belong to the New Jersey-New York Pilots Association, which has 148 members. Since it was founded in 1694, there never has been a day a pilot boat hasn't been on station off New York harbor.''

In the show world, McCarthy is little more than an apprentice. For although the family has had dogs since World War I, the Staten Islander started seriously only in 1969, when he bought a Weimaraner. ''The breeder suggested we show the dog and my son-in-law managed to put a few points on him,'' said McCarthy. Four years later, McCarthy bought a German Shorthaired Pointer. ''We called her Pepper, and she was a champion when it came to reserve ribbons,'' laughed the big, ruddy-complexioned pilot. ''She must have had almost two dozen.''

The family bought another Shorthair, Winterwind's Amboy Man, who promptly was given the call name of Pilot. The pilot showed Pilot a half-dozen times at shows in the area but never to a blue. However, he had better luck in 1973, in Bermuda. ''I managed to show him to a couple of points,'' recalled Bob, ''and a friend took him in and won the group, so he became a Bermudian champion. Then the breeder took him to Canada and finished him up there.'' The McCarthys next acquired a German Wirehaired Pointer, Marbern Abbey Road. The captain showed her and she earned her title at Sand and Sea in 1974. ''It is the greatest thrill I've experienced in the sport,'' he said. Since then the McCarthys have had four more Wirehaired champions.

In their home are 47 lithographs by the marine artist, John A. Noble, whose works also hang in the Library of Congress, Lloyds of London and the Metropolitan Museum of Art. ''As long as I can remember, we had dogs,'' said

Bob. "My father, a pilot, was taking out the giant Leviathan, when she was a troop ship during World War I. Off Ambrose Light, a dog, mascot of the First Marine Division, was discovered on the ship and the MPs threw it overboard. My father, on the yawl going back to the pilot ship, picked the dog out of the ocean. The animal was in poor shape when they got it aboard and they gave it some brandy. The dog was wearing a collar with a Marine insignia and 13 stars riveted on it, for the 13 original states. Father brought him home and we had Splinters for a dozen years. We've had dogs ever since."

Alexander Feldman, former chairman of the board of directors of the American Kennel Club, shows a disdain for rain that is part of every serious dog fancier's makeup. — *Spear*.

When The Rains Reigned

THE DOG SHOW EXHIBITOR is a hardy breed. Few sports are more demanding. Should he or she own a longhaired breed, many hours are spent during the week brushing and combing Rover. And on Friday, should it be an Old English Sheepdog, an Afghan or a Poodle, our exhibitor spends the day bathing, drying and preparing his pride and joy for the ring. No Hollywood star is more beautified than one of these canine prima donnas. First comes the bath. After oils and lotions comes a hefty session with combs, brushes, a manicure, plastic curlers on the ears. There are drops to clear the eyes and eyebrows are trimmed. However, false eyelashes still are not being used. Then comes a downpour and it's all for nought. Our perfectly groomed star looks like any other naked pooch.

Which brings to mind some memorable shows as to weather. There are some one never forgets. The Trenton, New Jersey, show has had more than its share of rain. The last year the club was at the armory, there was a torrential downpour. With the high winds, there actually was a horizontal rain. The cars tore up the grounds and the club had to pay $5,000 to repair the damage. Twice when the show was at Washington Crossing State Park, the rains came and tow trucks worked overtime to get autos out. The second time both the best-in-show judge and the handler were in bare feet and the official photographer took his picture of the finale from the waist up.

It was Friday, the 13th of April, in 1979, that dog show history was made weatherwise at the Macon fixture; a tornado swept across that Georgia city and for the first time in the memory of the oldest of the old timers, a show was started but not completed.

Of the 109 breeds, 73 had been judged when the twister put an end to the proceedings. Actually it passed 50 feet over the park but the accompanying winds were strong enough to bend a 4-inch metal pole holding the tent into a crescent and the canvas was ripped in three places. Fortunately, none of the 3,000 persons at the show or any of the 1,546 dogs were injured. A police car had rolled onto the grounds shortly after noon and the officer, over a loud speaker, told the people of the approaching storms, urging them to take cover. Then the Civil Defense sirens sounded a tornado warning and Ruben Reynolds, the chairman, called the show off.

The winds blew down the tents at Old Dominion in Virginia, with exhibitors and dogs pelted in the rain. At another Old Dominion, the heat was so oppressive that many exhibitors dropped their dogs into a shallow brook on the show site, lest the animals suffer heat prostration. There was a Westbury, Long Island, fixture, where it rained the previous night and continued unabated until late afternoon. Everyone moaned except Mrs. William H. Long, Jr., who was judging best in show. She assured me the wind would shift and the rain stop. Just as the dogs were called in for the final judging, the rain suddenly ended. I was one of the few remaining onlookers. Mrs. Long came striding across the ring and said triumphantly, "Didn't I tell you it would stop?" Maybe she ordered it.

There was a Montgomery County, Pa., show I'll never forget. It was pouring so hard, everything was flooded. A bitter wind howled. "Stay on the paved road," said a state trooper. "They'll have to tow the cars out." With a sense of duty, I slogged through the mud. Miserable, soaked and shivering, when the show finally ended, came the problem of finding a phone to dictate my story. Eventually I reached a half-deserted gas station and called the paper only to be told, "We're tight for space. Can't use your story."

With rain I always felt a sympathy for the obedience judges. Whereas the breed arbiters could judge under tents, the obedience officials had to stand in the open and take it. From my point of view there was another difficulty; the judges' sheets, on which they write the scores after each dog's exercise, on more than one occasion couldn't be read, the rain fading the pencil marks.

There was a memorable Hartford show. I was staying at a hotel with a room overlooking the Connecticut River. Before retiring on Friday night, I looked out the window and it was a stunning view, with the lights reflected on the water. What a shock when I awoke in the morning to find the city hit by a blizzard. Dressing quickly, I hurried to the bell captain—it was 7:30—and asked him to get a taxi, saying it was urgent to get to the armory. Some two-and-a-half hours later, a cab arrived and managed to get me to the show. Major George Ford, the chairman, greeted me. "Our luck finally ran out," said he. "For 25 years we had good weather." Of the 1,200 entries, a third failed to show. For the first edition, I had to have a story phoned to the paper by 2 P.M. In order to get the results, I would go from ring to ring and speak to the owner or handler of the breed winner. By one o'clock, at the latest, I'd start writing. When I walked into the armory, the Great Dane judging had just ended, with a harlequin bitch, Ch. Harldane's Kitty K., best of breed. The owner told me all about her and she was the lead for my story. Since many sports events had been canceled, the story led a page and had an 8-column streamer.

The following week was Providence and once again there was a knee-deep snowfall. The show was held in the clubhouse of the Lincoln Downs race track and was marked by absentees. So I was delighted when the Danes ended early and Kitty K. won the purple-and-gold rosette. In my notebook, I had plenty of material on her, so I again used the Dane for the lead and she received another big play. Now the first edition goes all over the country, so out-of-town dog readers learned of what must have seemed like a new sensation on the circuit. The big play proved a boon to Kitty. For the next half-dozen shows she swept the breed and had some group placements. Her owner came over, shook my hand, and said, "You brought us luck."

There's No Business Like Snow Business

But the show that really tested the exhibitors' fortitude was Westminster in 1969. Snow started to fall throughout the East the day before the Garden event. I was covering the Associated Terrier Clubs' specialties in an armory at 168th Street, off Broadway. It was snowing lightly when I arrived early in the morning. By late afternoon, when the specialties were over, the storm had reached blizzard proportions. Many of the handlers and exhibitors, unable to move their automobiles, took the subway. I was in a subway car with at least 15 terriers. Other fanciers, bound for Westminster, used bus, taxi and truck. They walked, trotted and ran. They came by every form of transportation except dog sled, which would have been most appropriate in snowbound New York. I stood at the foot of the ramp at the Garden and interviewed people as they arrived with their dogs. Some of the stories were incredible.

Bob Sharp, then a professional handler, had been driving to New York from Norwalk, Conn., to show Marvin Frank's top-winning Lhasa Apso, Ch. Kyi-Chu Friar Tuck. With Sharp was Mrs. Ruth Smith, Tuck's breeder, who had flown to New York from Saudi Arabia to see the dog perform. She never did.

"We left Norwalk a little after 2 o'clock Sunday afternoon, with four other dogs for the Monday showing," Sharp told me. "We soon were snowbound on the Connecticut Turnpike and had to spend the night in the truck. At 5 A.M., Mrs. Smith insisted I leave with Tuck so the Lhasa could be shown, while she remained with the other dogs, until a snowplow would open the road." With the 20-pound dog under his arm, Sharp trudged more than six miles through the snow until he reached the Pelham Bay line of the subway. "It was 9:30," said Bob. "Tuck didn't like the ride but he sure had a lot of attention from the other passengers." Unfortunately, the walk was in vain. Tuck didn't take the breed, having to settle for best of opposite.

Mr. and Mrs. Leo Farrell of Norwood, Mass., were lavish in their praise of New York hospitality. "We left Boston at 9 o'clock Sunday morning so we could show our 180-pound Great Dane, Ch. Jupiter's Apollo," they told me. "Twelve hours later we were in a snowbank in the Bronx. We asked a passerby how to get to Madison Square Garden and he suggested the subway. But the subway attendant refused to let us go through, saying it was against the law to take a dog on the train. A man on the station saw our plight, told us he was a social worker and had worked with the police. He volunteered to go to the precinct house and get us a note so we could get Apollo aboard. He accompanied us all the way to our hotel. We had heard how cold and heartless New Yorkers were but we certainly have changed our opinion.''

Gayle Bontecou pulled away from her Millbrook, N.Y., home with her Scottish Deerhound, Ch. Gayleward's Timber, at noon on Sunday. ''Ordinarily, it takes me two hours to drive the 89 miles,'' she told me. ''We moved right along on Taconic State Parkway until we ran into a snowbank at Yorktown Heights. That was 3:30. There was nothing I could do, so I curled up with Timber and tried to sleep. We used his blankets, my mink coat and some clothes that I had brought along. Even so, with no heat, it was cold. Four good Samaritans came along at 8:30 A.M. and dug us out. We had nothing in the car to eat, so Timber and I shared a can of dog food. It didn't taste too bad as long as you held your nose and didn't get the odor. We reached the Garden at 2 P.M., which was 26 hours after leaving home.''

Mrs. Clayton Thomas and Mrs. Caroline Kierstead, who were showing a Pembroke Welsh Corgi, left Northampton, Mass., at 9 A.M. on Sunday. ''We had a rough trip but finally reached the Bronx at 3 A.M.,'' they said. ''We saw some lights and it was a bowling alley. They let us come inside and we stayed until 6:30. Then it took us another three hours to reach the Garden.''

Walter Goodman carried his Skye Terrier, Ch. Glamoor's Good News across Seventh Avenue in knee-high snow. Plowing along in his wake was his octogenarian mother, co-owner of the bitch. When another exhibitor inquired, ''Why aren't you carrying Mama?,'' Goodman snapped back, ''I'm not showing her.'' He had a point. His Skye made it to the very top—best in show. Mother was thrilled.

Then there was a show in New Haven, the day after a snowstorm. Bill Ernst pulled up to the front of the armory, where it was very icy, to unload, only to be told by a policeman to move on. Remonstrating, Bill asked where he could park to get his 19 crates into the building. ''That's your problem, not mine, but you can't block traffic,'' was the curt reply. When Ernst decided to take matters into his own hands and started to unload, he promptly was arrested. ''What about my dogs?,'' pleaded Bill. ''We'll impound them,'' said the officer. Someone rushed inside to tell Barbara Fournier, the club president, who immediately phoned a police captain and was told to send someone in authority and Ernst would be released. Alan Winks, then with Foley, drove to the station and came back with an extremely irate handler. ''Where do you think they had him?'' asked an incredulous Winks. ''Locked in a cell.''

Ernst had a propensity for getting into trouble. At Providence, the first year it was held in the Civic Center, Bill arrived the night before and asked an officer if he could park his van at the show site. Assured it was all right, Bill left the vehicle and checked into the Holiday Inn, a block away. Early the next morning, when Ernst went to exercise his dogs, there was no van. Rushing to a policeman, he reported the theft. ''Your van wasn't stolen, just towed away. It was in a no-parking zone.''

Jim McTernan, show chairman for New Brunswick, ran askew of the county police, who, seeking a pay rise, were stopping all cars entering the grounds and demanding to see license and registration papers. With traffic backed up for miles and exhibitors unable to reach the rings, McTernan literally took things into his own hands. He removed part of the fencing and waved cars in before they reached the main gate. "I was able to get 4,500 cars into the grounds before the police discovered what I had done and arrested me." The case was dismissed.

Training for Raining

When kennel clubs in the Maryland area want to know what the weather forecast will be for their shows, they phone Kenneth M. Nagler, a member of the Rock Creek KC and the Hyattsville Dog Training Club. A Dalmatian breeder, Nagler is also Chief of Space Operations Support Division, National Weather Service. He headed the meteorological team that worked on the Mercury, Gemini, Apollo and Skylab missions for the National Aeronautics and Space Administration.

When it comes to dogs, it was complaints from neighbors that turned Nagler and his wife, Ann, into fanciers. "We bought a Dalmatian in 1956," said Nagler. "He was a collector. He'd collect the neighbors' doormats, mops, garden tools and anything else he could find and bring them home. In defense, we started him in obedience training. He was a headstrong dog but by persevering we took him all the way through to a CD, a CDX and a UD."

Princess Lois of Loki, a third-generation Dal bred by the Naglers, was their first show champion, gaining her majors when she still was a pup. Lois's obedience training was a family affair. Mrs. Nagler took her through to her CD; a daughter, Betty, handled her to a CDX and Nagler to her UD. Both Ann and Ken have been instructors at the suburban Washington Canine Training Association for more than a decade. They have trained hundreds of dogs and their owners. It is strictly a hobby with the Naglers, for they accept no pay.

"We try to get to the school four nights during the week to see if we can help," said Ken. "It's a nice change of pace from my weather service work." Perhaps the training organization will give him a citation to go with the gold medal he received in 1973 from the United States Department of Commerce, of which the Weather Bureau is a part, "for organizing and managing the weather support to the manned-space flight programs."

All the glamor — and beautiful trophies — of a best in show win at the nation's most prestigious dog fixture, the Westminster Kennel Club show at Madison Square Garden in New York City, is caught here. Pictured is the 1973 winner, Ch. Acadia Command Performance, Standard Poodle owned by Edward B. Jenner and Jo Ann Sering, and handled by Frank T. Sabella—now a much-respected judge.

Garden Roses

OVER THE YEARS, I had the privilege of seeing many very good dogs, some I would even call great. They were the big winners of their day and were outstanding showmen. Unfortunately, some actually harmed their breeds. Because of their records, there was a rush to breed to them and they passed on conformation and temperament faults. But in the ring, they all had a presence that brought them fame and ribbons. Because of space limitations I only can cover a relatively few but these are names that long will be remembered for their feats.

John G. Bates's Wire Fox Terrier, Ch. Pendley Calling of Blarney, was Best in Show at Westminster in 1930 and 1931, the first dog to score a double at America's most prestigious fixture in 15 years. She practically stepped off the boat from England to take the breed at the American Fox Terrier Club specialty in 1930 and then three days later Bates showed her to the red, white and blue rosette at Westminster. In taking the breed, she defeated Ch. Talavera Margaret, who had been best at the Garden in 1928. Pendley's main opposition in the final was from Mrs. Geraldine Rockefeller Dodge's German Shepherd, Ch. Giralda's Lola, who drew cheers after the group judging, when she took the blue rosette in her mouth and trotted off to give it to her mistress at ringside.

The 1931 show is one I'll never forget. The Wire really was not in top condition and I felt she was fortunate to take the breed and group. Whereas the previous year, she was hailed by the crowd, in 1931 the cheers were for a flashy blue-ticked English Setter, Dr. A.A. Mitten's Ch. Blue Dan of Happy Valley. When Tyler Morse pointed to Pendley Calling, there was prolonged booing. "I did not like the way the Setter moved toward me," explained Morse. "I tried him out several times but he never seemed to improve." Much criticism was heard for Bates was show chairman and Westminster's vice president and Morse was a member of the board.

Speaking of booing, another occasion comes to mind. In 1969 Percy Roberts was judging best in show at International in Chicago. Just before the big final, he had to pick the best brace. Now the spectators in Chicago are among the most vocal in the United States and their choice was a pair of perky Maltese. When Mr. Roberts instead pointed to a Miniature Poodle twosome, not only were there boos and loud whistling but the onlookers began to stamp on the wooden bleachers and the place was a bedlam. There were many calls for quiet over the loud speaker but they went unheeded. An angry red-faced Mr. Roberts—and you always could tell when he was annoyed because he would twitch his upper lip and his waxed moustache would go in all directions—stood waiting for the best-in-show dogs to come in but the crowd refused to give up. Every time the noise began to lessen, there was someone to rouse the gallery again. Eventually, of course, a very irate Englishman was able to resume his judging.

Back to the great performers of yesteryear. Mrs. Cheever Porter's Ch. Milson O'Boy was the greatest Irish Setter I ever saw. Handled by Harry Hartnett, the redcoat earned his first points at Boston in 1933, when he went from the puppy class to best of winners. Retired after Westminster, five years later, a month before his fifth birthday, O'Boy had been best Irish 103 times, taken 46 groups and 11 bests. His most memorable victory was at Morris and Essex in 1935 when, before 35,000 aficionados on the polo field of Giralda Farms, in Madison, N.J., O'Boy was chosen by G.V. Glebe as best of 2,784 dogs. Like a celebrity the handsome redcoat had a Pinkerton detective who guarded the dog when he was on the bench and walked with him to and from the ring.

It was also in 1935 that an elegant white standard poodle, Ch. Nunsoe Duc de la Terrace of Blakeen had his greatest hour, when he was proclaimed best at Westminster. That was quite a day, for this dignified dog had caught the imagination of the crowd when he was singled out as best in the Non-Sporting group by William McCandlish, the noted British judge. Shown magnificently by his chic, slender owner, Mrs. Sherman R. Hoyt, the Poodle swept around the ring in the final to the cheers of the crowd. When Alfred B. Maclay pointed to him there was a tremendous ovation.

The Duc, a champion in France, Switzerland and England, was purchased as a gift for Mrs. Hoyt by her mother, Mrs. Whitney Blake. Shown 18 times in the United States, the Poodle was undefeated in the breed, took 16 groups and nine bests. He also proved a great sire, his Ch. Blakeen Jung Frau capturing the silverware 19 times and his Ch. Blakeen Eiger, 17.

Ch. Vigow of Romanoff stands out as the top Borzoi in many a year. This white dog. owned and handled by Louis Murr, made a spectacular debut when he was just a little over a year old by going from the novice class to best in show at the 1934 National Capital. For the next two years, Vigow gained the AKC award as best American-bred competing at all-breed events. From 1934 until 1938, the Borzoi took groups four of five times at Morris and Essex. The elegant dog never was beaten in the breed in 77 outings, during which he won 67 groups and was best 21 times.

The best American-bred for 1937 was a black Standard Poodle, Ch. Pillicoc Rumpelstilskin, CD, owned by Mrs. Milton Erlanger. Curly, as he was called, was a big, powerful dog, 24½ inches at the shoulder, weighed 65 pounds and had a perfectly magnificent coat. He was Henry Stoecker's pride and joy, for that now eminent judge then was a handler. Mrs. Erlanger once said, "Curly's triumphs are 50 percent Rumpelstilskin and 50 percent Henry Stoecker." When Curly was retired his owner gave him to Stoecker. "He lived to be 17," said Henry, "and slept in my bedroom."

Also in 1937, a white Wire Fox Terrier, Ch. Flornell Spicypiece of Halleston, was imported from Britain by Stanley J. Halle. In her first appearance in a show ring in America, she was gaited to the breed honors at the specialty just before Westminster. Three days later, George West made her best of 3,146 dogs in the Garden. Roberts, who had handled so many good dogs over the years, told me she was the best he ever took into a ring. After Westminster, Spicypiece wasn't out again until Ox Ridge, in the fall, when Carley Harriman chose her best. The white bitch took the specialty once more in 1938 and then was back for the Garden. The Fox Terrier won her group but in the final John G. Bates selected an English Setter puppy, Daro of Maridor, bred and owned by Dwight Ellis. Daro was six days under 11 months and was one of two pups ever to go best at Westminster. (The other was Florence B. Ilch's Rough Collie, Laund Loyalty of Bellhaven, who was a day over 9 months when chosen in 1929.) Incidentally, Halle never showed the Wire again.

The year 1937 was an eventful one, for in that same year James Austin imported an 11-month-old Fox Terrier, Ch. Nornay Saddler, the greatest smooth I ever saw. This little dog's career really didn't start until 1939, when he was gaited to best at Morris and Essex by Leonard Brumby, father of the current AKC senior vice president. The Brumby-Saddler team went on to take 54 more top awards. Saddler made it No. 56, again at M & E, the greatest of outdoor shows, in 1941, but this time Austin was handling. Saddler was to win three more major awards before he was retired. He also did his bit for the British war effort. In 1940, a magazine in England was conducting a drive to raise money for the Air Fighter Fund. The periodical received a cable, "I sink my teeth into Adolf Hitler with this draft of $1,200. I earned it all by myself in stud fees. Signed Ch. Nornay Saddler, New York."

A black Cocker Spaniel, Ch. My Own Brucie, was to make history in 1940 and 1941, when he was shown by his owner and breeder, Herman Mellenthin, to best at Westminster, the first double winner since Pendley Calling. Mellenthin, who raised peonies and roses in addition to Cocker Spaniels—and in the thirties he had as many as 75 at his kennel in Poughkeepsie, N.Y.—was such an astute breeder that many fanciers would go to him for advice.

Brucie, whelped May 5, 1935, won the AKC award as best American-bred of 1938. Still it wasn't until 1939 that he scored his first really big victory, at M&E, when he led a field of 4,456 representing 82 breeds, in the largest show ever held in America up to this writing. So keen was the competition, that in 20 breeds there were dogs that had been best-in-show performers. William H. Pym of Vancouver, British Columbia, judged the final and at the end he had it down to the Cocker Spaniel and the Fox Terrier, Nornay Saddler, and then chose Brucie. When the Cocker died, he had become such a national figure that *The New York Sun* ran his obituary on Page 1.

The Bedlington Terrier looks like a lamb but then looks are deceiving, for he can be a tiger should the occasion arise. One Bedlington stands out over the years and he was a tiger in the ring. That was Ch. Rock Ridge Night Rocket, owned by Mr. and Mrs. William A. Rockefeller, whose son William is now president of the Westminster Kennel Club and is chairman of the board of the Metropolitan Opera. The little terrier was handled by Anthony Neary, who came from Bedlington, that mining county in England from which the breed takes its name.

In 1947, the blue 14-month-old came out of the classes, beating his sire to take the breed and went all the way to triumph at M&E. The following February, Dr. Samuel Milbank chose the Rocket in a particularly strong final at Westminster, in which he defeated three group winners of the previous year, including the great Boston Terrier bitch, Ch. Might Sweet Regardless, with 28 best-in-show awards. The Bedlington wasn't shown again for three months but returned to successfully defend his M&E laurels, where he became the first dog to ever take that "show of shows" two years in a row. The great arbiter, Alva Rosenberg, who gave him the decision, was lavish in his praise: "I'd say, without reservation, that he is one of the best I've seen in 38 years of judging. He beat a grand lot of dogs but he won quite easily."

More history was made in 1951, for when Dr. and Mrs. R. C. Harris' Boxer, Ch. Bang Away of Sirrah Crest, from Santa Ana, Calif., went to the top at Westminster, it was the first time in the classic's long history that a dog from west of the Mississippi took the silver bowl. Bangy, who was just four days from being 2 years old, was truly a Harris creation, for he was the fourth generation on his sire's side and the fifth on the dam. "He's the result of 10 years of consistent breeding," said Dr. Harris. When Nate Levine walked the flashy fawn Boxer into the Garden ring, the experts made him an odds-on favorite for he had won the silverware 15 times, far more than any of his rivals. At the end it was between the Boxer, a superb showman, and a white-and-liver ticked Pointer, Ch. Captain Speck, owned and handled by Charlie Palmer. The judge, William Ross Proctor, a former Westminster president and show chairman, pulled out the two for a final swing around the floor and then motioned to Bangy. "The Boxer is an extremely stylish dog and magnificent when he is moving," commented Proctor.

Ch. Rancho Dobe's Storm was bought by Len Carey, when the pup was 3 months old. He had a rather brief show career, for he was retired when he was 38 months old. Peter Knoop, now an all-round judge, handled the black and tan and walked him into the ring 25 times. A great showman with a wonderful disposition, Stormy was undefeated in the breed, took 22 working groups and was best 17 times.

Twice he went all the way at Westminster, in 1952 and 1953, and his first victory in the Garden was one I'll never forget. For Stormy beat Bang Away in the group and then he disproved the 13 superstition. It was Stormy's 13th show and his catalogue number was 13. Also, it was 13 years since a Dobe had gone best at the classic and Stormy was the 13th Dobe Knoop had gaited to a best in show. Joseph Sims, who judged the final, said of his choice, "The Dobe is in pluperfect condition."

A 2½-year-old Afghan, the only member of his breed to take Westminster in my 50 years with the sport, was Ch. Shirkhan of Grandeur, owned by the late Sunny Shay and Dorothy Chenade, and bred and handled by the former. It was in 1957 and of the six finalists that Bea Godsol was judging, the silver-blue Afghan was the least known. But he was a picture of gaiety, when Mrs. Godsol, only the second woman to have judged Westminster up to that time, sent him down the ring. "He is a beautifully balanced hound, with the correct lean head and expression," she told reporters. "He was the soundest moving of the six and he's a showman, a really great hound." It was the 65-pounder's first all-breed victory.

Sunny brought him back in 1963, when Mrs. Godsol was judging the Afghans in the Garden. The gray-muzzled Shirkhan, stepping out like a youngster, had to compete against a huge number of specials and Bea kept them in the ring for an unusually long time, as she went over each dog carefully. Finally, she gave Shirkhan, now much darker than when he triumphed six years before, the breed. "I did everything I could to put him down," she told me, "but there was nothing in there that could do it." Shirkhan is the top Afghan sire in the history of the breed, with 43 champions to his credit.

Then we come to the greatest winning dog this country has seen and the only Pekingese to ever take Westminster. It was Mr. and Mrs. C. C. Venable's Pekingese, Ch. Chik T'Sun of Caversham, an English import, handled by Clara Alford. In three years of campaigning, the little dog with a rich red coat that trailed to the floor ran up 127 best-in-show awards and 169 groups in the United States and 11 bests and 26 blue rosettes in Canada. At one stretch Chik took 14 top prizes in 46 days.

Still he had a hard time to triumph at Westminster. He won the groups there in 1957 and 1959 but was beaten for the big prize. The next year, however, he went all the way, although he was pushed by a Pembroke Welsh Corgi, Mrs. William B. Long's Ch. Cote de Neige Sundew. At the end George H. Hartman, after sending the two out a final time, pointed to the little Toy. "The Peke was in gorgeous bloom," he said. "I make him one of the few great dogs—great I said—that I have ever seen. The Corgi also is as sound as they come." The Venables retired Chik immediately after the Garden. "He will come home and live with us in Atlanta," they said. Up to that time, he had been living with his handler.

The year before Chik bowed out, another great dog started his career. He was Ch. Rebel Roc's Casanova von Kurt, a Miniature Pinscher better known as Little Daddy. A deep red, this little dog was shown 165 times and his owner, E. W. Tipton, now a well-known judge, handled him all but twice. The six-pounder captured the top prize at 75 all-breed shows and was best Toy on 143 occasions. He was best for the first time at Jacksonville, Fla., when Alva Rosenberg put him up at the age of 7 months. By the time he was a year old, Little Daddy had added four more pieces of silverware and had taken 10 groups. He was a showman and I always enjoyed watching him in the final. The little dog would keep his eyes on the judge. When the arbiter pointed to him, the Minpin would let out a bark and run to the center of the ring.

We had some very good terriers in the sixties. Barbara Keenan's West Highland White, Ch. Elfinbrook Simon won the silverware for his mistress 26 times, including Westminster in 1962, and did much to gain popularity for the breed. But his great contribution was as a sire, for he left behind him 58 champions, a record for a Highlander.

Mr. and Mrs. James A. Farrell Jr. had the great Lakeland, Ch. Stingray of Derryabah, whom the late shipping magnate imported from England after he had been best in show at Crufts in 1967. When Major B. Godsol chose the Lakie at Westminster, the next year, he became the first member of his breed ever to take that blue-ribbon event. He also was the only dog to capture the two top shows in England and America. Said Godsol, ''The Lakeland is in perfect condition, clad in a jacket that fitted him exactly.'' An exuberant Mr. Farrell declared, ''I've wanted this for 40 years.''

Then in 1969, a slickly groomed Skye, with silver-colored hair trailing to the floor, was the choice of Louis Murr. She was Ch. Glamoor Good News, a homebred owned by Walter F. Goodman and his mother, Mrs. Adele Goodman. Murr paid tribute to the Skye's type, balance and condition. ''She practically knew what she was in there for,'' said the judge. Goodman did the handling and was the only amateur in the ring. ''I did it for Mother,'' said Walter. He had his Skye groomed to the last shimmering inch, the hair parted down the middle of her back as if it had been done by a master barber.

A great English Springer Spaniel came on the scene in 1971, when he was the top-winning dog in America. He was Ch. Chinoe's Adamant James, owned by Dr. Milton E. Prickett. That year the Springer was shown 97 times, winning the breed 94, the group 86 and adding 48 pieces of silverware to the veterinarian's collection. He kept right on winning the next year and by the time he ended his career, the Spaniel had been best in show 60 times, including Westminster in 1971 and 1972—the first time it had been accomplished since Dobe's Storm in 1952 and 1953.

Called DJ, an abbreviation for Diamond Jim (a name given to the liver and white because of a little diamond-shaped white mark on his back) the Spaniel was a real crowd pleaser and was the favorite of the Garden crowd both years.

It took Carley Harriman just 12 minutes to make his decision in 1971. ''The Springer was a superlatively good dog, practically faultless, and a most sensational mover,'' said Harriman. When I asked Carley about the relatively short time it took to pick his winner, he responded, ''I find a fast decision is generally right, otherwise you tend to be confused.'' Dr. Prickett was at the time a pathologist at the University of Kentucky, where he specialized in equine research.

The second year it was a very strong final, with the dogs having a total of 100 best in shows among them. But again DJ, handled as usual by Clint Harris, stood out. ''This dog is most nearly perfect in structure and conformation to accomplish the purpose of the breed,'' said William Brainard. ''He is sound and demonstrates a practical elegance and quality.''

Said Prickett, ''DJ is a great favorite at the university, where I teach. He sleeps through all my lectures. He was a gift to me on my birthday and I never intended to show him.''

The only German Shorthaired Pointer to go best at Westminster was a California dog, Ch. Gretchenhof Columbia River in 1974. The 4-year-old, who led a field of 3,146, was owned by Dr. Richard Smith, an anesthesiologist from Hayward, who called him Traveler, ''because he travels so much.''

Handled by Jo Shellenberger, the liver-and-white ticked Pointer won 60 groups in 1973, more than any other dog in America. The Garden victory was particularly satisfying for his owner, since the dog had been beaten in the breed at Westminster the previous year, one of the few times that happened. Traveler traveled East the September before the Garden and showed he was ready when he took both Somerset Hills and Westchester.

When the Shorthair triumphed at Westminster, it was his 29th best-in-show award and his 102d group. Len Carey, whose Dobe had taken the top award two decades earlier, was the judge and said, ''I've never seen the dog better and I gave him his first group, three years ago. He never put a foot down wrong. Wouldn't you like to shoot over him? I would.'' That may have been wishful thinking, since Traveler never had hunted or run in the field. ''I don't even own a gun,'' said his owner.

At the festive Westminster centennial (1976), the winner was (in horse-racing parlance) a 1-to-4 shot. He was Ch. Jo-Ni's Red Baron of Crofton, a Lakeland Terrier, owned by Virginia Dickson of La Habra, Calif. The Baron came into the Garden with a record of 74 top awards, more than four times the combined number of the other five finalists. At the time, he was the top-winning Terrier in the history of dog shows in America.

William Brainard, who had his third major Westminster assignment, took exactly 14 minutes to name the red dog best. ''I've judged the Lakeland before but never sent him to the top,'' he said. ''He was all confidence and quality, a truly outstanding dog.'' Ric Chashoudian, the Baron's handler, was tremendously elated: he had been going to the Garden for 27 years before hitting the jackpot. In 1975, Chashoudian had brought the Baron to New York as the top-winning dog of the previous year, only to finish second in the group. ''The Baron's a great showman,'' said Ric. ''Sometimes he's a little too spirited for the judges but that's probably because he has a redhead's temperament.''

More recently, we have Dorothy Wimer's Sealyham, Ch. Dersade Bobby's Girl, and a Yorkshire Terrier, Ch. Cede Higgins, owned by Charles and Barbara Switzer. Both ended sensational careers at Westminster, the feisty white coat in 1977, and the 5½-pound Toy the next year — the first Yorkie ever to take the classic.

Binny, as the Sealy was called, went out as the top-winning bitch of all breeds, with 51 top awards. Just four and a half months after she had whelped three pups, she was brought back to score her largest and last victory. Peter Green, who handled her, literally stumbled into the Sealy on a street of Neath, Wales, his native town, and managed to buy her for Mrs. Wimer.

The Cede Higgins triumphs were amateur-achieved all the way. "I showed him to a 4-point major his first time out when he was 9 months old," said Mrs. Switzer. Then her daughter, Marlene Lutovsky, took over and she handled the Yorkie to 33 bests. She was known as the "lady in red" for she always wore a red dress and sandals and the little dog sported a red polka dot tie in his topknot. The day after Westminster, Anne Clark, who gave him the decision, her eyes moist with tears, said, "I can't look at the Yorkie without getting choked up."

Between Toronto and Montreal, the Canadian capital of Ottawa is known not only for its government buildings, all in the Italian Gothic style, but also for Anne Snelling's kennel. Since 1938 she has had Cairn, Irish Setter, Boxer and English Springer champions. But now she is best known for an Irish Water Spaniel—Canadian, American and Bermudian Ch. Oaktree's Irishtocrat.

"When I married Lee in 1938," reminisced Anne, "he had an Irish Water Spaniel, Flanagan. Now you know the Irish always is known as the clown of the dog world. Flanagan lived up to the breed's reputation. He didn't get to our wedding service but he broke away from the maid and was right there for the reception."

For five years Mrs. Snelling had looked for an Irish Water Spaniel and she finally located one on Long Island—Naptandy Annie Oaktrees. When Annie was bred, she had a dozen pups. Mrs. Snelling kept only one—Dugan.

Her choice certainly was a good one. Shown by Bill Trainor, the liver-colored dog, who loves to clown in the ring with his handler, gained his Canadian title when he was only 11 months old. There were so few Irish Water Spaniels north of the border that he had to win groups to finish and he took four of them. He had the same problem in the United States and captured three blue rosettes on his way to his championship, which he earned when he was 14 months old. The next month, at Newtown, Conn., he was best in show for the first time.

The pattern was set, and was climaxed at the 1979 Garden when Dugan won the group under Elsworth Howell and went on to best in show under Henry Stoecker. In a heart-warming show of appreciation for what his handling had meant for the dog, Mrs. Snelling rewarded Bill Trainor with half-ownership of "Dugan" after the show.

The liver-colored dog has a wonderful temperament, exudes personality and is a real fun dog.

What now? "I'm anxious to have Dugan trained for the field," said Mrs. Snelling. "We have ten acres on the Rideau River and all my dogs love to swim." Meanwhile, a best in show Pekingese, Ch. St. Aubrey Dragonora of Elsdon, ("Lee-Lee") had opened up a new chapter for the kennels.

180

The only repeat winner of best in show at Westminster over the last 25 years has been the English Springer Spaniel, Ch. Chinoe's Adamant James, owned by Dr. Milton E. Prickett and handled by Clint Harris. "D-J" took top honors in 1971 and 1972.

An informal shot of Ch. Dersade Bobby's Girl, Sealyham Terrier, best in show at Westminster in 1977. "Binny" retired as the top winning bitch in AKC history with 61 bests in show. Owned by Mrs. William W. Wimer III, she was handled by Peter J. Green.

Liz Clark's unbounded love for dogs seems well reciprocated.

Breeders and Exhibitors

IN FEW ACTIVITIES can one become so involved in such a short time as in the sport of dogs. A little here, a little there, and first thing you know . . .

Take Tom and Korky Quimby of Charlottesville, Virginia. In 1969 they drove to Staunton to visit an aunt. When they left they had a smooth Dachshund pup as a gift from their hostess.

After starting in obedience, they decided to try the breed ring. ''I took her to a match show,'' said Korky, ''and she finished second in a class of two. I still have the ribbon.'' Next they bought Kudach's Mark of Lancelot and he became their first champion. ''We took turns showing him,'' said Tom, an insurance agent.

Meanwhile the young couple were meeting oldtime breeders. ''When they saw we were serious,'' said Korky, a junior high school teacher, ''they took us under their wings. They gave us some bitches on breeding terms, whereby we would give them a pup from the breeding. Before long we had 25 Dachshunds and had to move to the country.'' By 1976, they had bred or owned 11 champions.

The Quimbys became active in clubwork. Tom was chairman for Skyline KC's first point show and Korky is a former secretary of the Virginia Federation of Dog Clubs and Breeders. Tom was particularly proud of the Skyline Club. ''We are a community-minded group,'' he told me, ''and put on demonstrations at schools and shopping centers. Our greatest effort, so far, was for the Augusta County sheriff's department. A German Shepherd had been shot and killed while apprehending a criminal. Our club located a Shepherd in Boston that had been trained for police work. We raised $2,000 to buy the dog and pay for a three-week training course there for the officer.''

Liz Clark

The most diversified kennel in America is in Middleburg, Va. Owned by Mrs. Robert V. Clark, Jr., better known as Liz, on the farm are 70 dogs representing 12 breeds. Labrador Retrievers dominate with 45. There's a noisy welcome for a visitor to the Clark home for there are a dozen dogs romping around the living room. Just a purr or two away are a dozen or so cats, ranging from unknown ancestry to royally bred Abyssinians.

"Just think, it all started with one pet," said Liz. "In 1962, before my husband died, we decided to have a Lab. We just wanted one around the house as a pet, never dreaming of showing. Connie Barton, later to become my kennel manager, said she had a nice dog for us and brought her over. She was Kim Valley Cinderella. She was yellow and my husband didn't like the color. But Connie and I argued in her favor and he finally relented." The unwanted yellow was a real Cinderella Lab in the Clark household. "Barkie, as we called her because she barked a lot," added Liz, "was the foundation bitch for Springfield Farms. Right after we bought her, we added an Irish Wolfhound and a St. Bernard. We showed all three at Westminster in 1965. Barkie was winners bitch, to finish; the Wolfhound also was winners bitch, and the Saint, best of winners. Pretty good for three housepets.'

Mrs. Clark has bred any number of champions, but while she lived, Barkie was the queen of the kennel. Bred three times, she produced a champion in each litter. Liz took her every place with her. "When she actually wasn't in the car with me, I could see her anyway," said the Virginian. "I had a bronze hood ornament of her cast. I also have oil and pastel paintings of her." Barkie always was head dog in the house.

At present, Liz has eight housepets—three Labs, a Shorthair, two Newfoundlands ("my second favorite breed"), a Flat-Coated Retriever and a Pug. However, the show dogs are house guests on a rotating basis. Whereas some authorities maintain a dog's domain is the floor, this is not so in the Clark living room. They share sofas and chairs with any visitors.

Liz has a collection of paintings and sculpture featuring, what else, horses and dogs. If it is animals, she has them, for in addition to her two major interests, plus cats, there is a herd of Black Angus cattle, with a few ducks and geese for good measure. "It's quite a sight when my dogs charge out of the kennel in the morning," she told me. "We have 500 acres and suddenly there are 40 to 70 of them racing over the fields."

Julie

For years, Julie Gasow has been "Mrs: English Springer," From her Salilyn Kennel (a combination of her two daughters' names—Sally and Linda) have come many a champion, since her first in the early 1940s, Sir Lancelot of Salilyn. Her greatest was Ch. Salilyn Aristocrat, who not only was almost unbeatable when he was being shown, but produced 172 titleholders, making him the sire of more champions than any dog of any breed. Included were 12 BIS winners.

"All of my dogs are related," said the Michigan breeder and judge. "I divided my dogs into two families and criss-crossed the breeding. And it has been most successful. The dogs are distinctly different types, one being a long-legged variety and the other short. When I crossed the two, invariably I've had the good luck to come up with something good. There is no doubt that luck plays a big part. I hit upon a good cross and kept repeating it. I've used the same cross for 20 years."

184

It is a far cry since she attended her first show in Detroit in 1936. "It was love at first sight, when I saw the English Springers on the bench," Julie recalled. "Fred Hunt had the best of breed and I ran over to him and asked if I could buy the dog. Fred just looked at me and laughed. Billy Lang sold me a lovely bitch and he finished her for me. But I knew nothing about breeding and did everything wrong."

Julie is a firm believer in a handler. "A good handler is half the battle," she said. "I was so fortunate to have had Lang and Dick Cooper. Dick has handled for me for 25 years and five times we have won the Quaker Oats award for the Sporting dog with the most group victories, each time with a different dog."

Mrs. Gasow started to judge in the late 1950s. "I've always preferred breeding to judging," she said, "but every time I judge I learn something to help me with my breeding program. When you get your hands on a dog, it helps. But I could never have stayed in the sport if my husband wasn't a veterinarian. It is just too expensive."

Dual Capacity

Sixty years ago, Fred Hunt was given a Beagle. It started him on a career in the dog show world in which he still was active in 1979. "I haven't bred a dog for a dozen years," he told me, "but I keep busy judging. I accept 20 shows a year and turn down more than twice as many."

Hunt, who lives in Richmond, Ind., and is a retired Chrysler executive, has been an avid hunter. It was his interest in shooting over a dog that led him to become an authority on the Sporting breeds. "In 1919," Fred recalled, "I did quite a bit of quail hunting and found Pointers very satisfactory. When it came to pheasants, I found I wasn't having too much success. So I bought a pair of English Springers. A friend suggested I show them. I went to a local show. The one did nothing, the other took a fourth. However, I wasn't too happy. This was a challenge. I decided I'd do something about it and come up with a winner."

Doing some research, Hunt learned the best Springer of that era was in England—Ch. Rufton Recorder. "I wrote to Robert Cornthwaite, the owner, offering to buy the dog," said Hunt. "He wouldn't sell but agreed to send me a bitch in whelp to Recorder." That was in 1932 and the bitch was Rufton Rosita. She produced a litter of five, three of whom became champions. In 1934, Cornthwaite offered to sell Recorder, then seven years old, for $1,500. "It was the best buy I ever made," said Hunt. "He was the foundation stud for my Green Valley Kennel. From 1936 through 1941, I bred 53 English Springer champions and they all went back to Recorder. One of his sons, Green Valley Punch, I handled to both bench and field titles. He was the last American-bred Springer in the United States to become a dual champion."

"I don't think we ever will see another Springer dual champion," declared the tall, gray-haired sportsman, as he pulled pensively on his pipe. "There are almost two different breeds. The average bench winner weighs 50 pounds, which is 15 more than the field dog. The showdog has beautiful conformation and makes a satisfactory gentleman's hunting dog. But he has only half the speed and drive of a field dog and he couldn't win at a trial. The field worker hasn't the good looks. But he has speed, lots of stamina and a good nose.''

When Dr. L. William Goodman, Jr. and his wife bought their first English Springer Spaniel in 1954, they named her Lauranan's Project. "Our project was to develop a dual-purpose champion Springer," said the veterinarian. "I guess we were rather naive. After a dozen years I became convinced that it is practically impossible to produce a dual-purpose strain in the breed." And he could speak with authority for he had been active in both bench and field trial competition. Then, too, he is a third-generation veterinarian. In 1966, when I interviewed him, no less than seven members of the family were practicing vets.

"A breeder can stamp the characteristics of what he desires in a dog fairly accurately in three generations, certainly in five," said Goodman. "By putting into practice some of the genetics I had studied, we came up with a Springer bench champion, Ginger's Angus of Lauranan, in three generations." Mrs. Goodman, or Nan as she is known to the fancy, showed Angus to his title. Not that it was any surprise, for she had started handling dogs in junior showmanship classes. She had proven so adept, that she had finished several Collies for her mother, Mrs. W. Henry Gray.

"There hasn't been a dual Springer champion in years," said Goodman, "and I'm convinced there never will be another unless the two camps—bench and field—cease seeking exaggerations. The bench people are just interested in a pretty dog. The field man doesn't care how a dog looks. All he is interested in is the performance—how many birds his Springer will flush. For the bench you breed for conformation. Certain physical characteristics have been arbitrarily selected as a standard for the breed and the judge looks for them. For field work, native abilities, which have nothing to do with physical characteristics, must be inherent. The hunting dog must have the nose to find game, be intelligent, have stamina, courage, willingness and the ability to retrieve. Without any one of these qualities, the hunting dog is useless.''

Discussing the physical differences in the field and show Springer, the veterinarian said the muscle mass was virtually identical but the difference was in angulation. "The best comparison would be the skier," explained Goodman. "The field dog is always in the position of the skier going downhill, with his weight thrust forward. The showdog stands upright like the skier waiting for the chair lift. As a result of the angulation, the field dog covers ground with much less effort.''

The Versatile Breed

The Brittany is a dog of paradoxes. He's a Spaniel, but looks like a small Setter. He's the only member of the Spaniel family that doesn't flush his game—he points it. An excellent upland hunter, he also is a natural retriever. But unlike so many breeds, where there is a show dog, bred for conformation,

186

and a field type, bred for stamina and nose, the Brit remains a dual worker. Take Ch. Sequani's Dana Macduff. When the flashy, well-balanced orange-and-white dog was retired from the ring on June 10,1973 at the Longshore-Southport show, he went out on a high note, for three days short of his seventh birthday, he had won his 14th group, and he stood as the top winning Brittany of all time with a record of having defeated more than 6,000 dogs in the Sporting group during the six years he had been campaigned. Then in July 1976, the 10-year-old dog gained his amateur field title to become a dual champion.

"The American Brittany Club is dedicated to keeping the Brit a dual dog, forever," said Mrs. Frederick H. Murphy of Far Hills, N.J., who with her husband and Mrs. David Rigoulet of Livonia, Mich., owned Macduff.

"Duffy was the last of a litter of nine owned by Mrs. Rigoulet," said Mrs. Murphy. "When we bought him, she said she wanted to be a co-owner of the ugly duckling." Like so many fanciers the Murphys had no intention of showing, when they obtained their first dog. "Before moving to New Jersey, we lived at Grosse Pointe, Mich.," siad Mrs. Murphy. "Both my husband and I were avid hunters and frequently were in the field using Labradors and Setters. One day we hunted with our veterinarian. He had a Brit and we liked what we saw. The dog worked close in heavy cover and ranged in open country. So we bought a seven-months-old Brit bitch, Samantha de Bar Fleur. I must confess she proved no hunter and having been a kennel dog, was a terror in the house. However, Sam started us off on a show career, although we didn't realize it at the time. So she would learn manners, we entered her in an obedience training course. The pup took to the training beautifully. We had heard about obedience trials, while taking the course, so we entered her at a show."

Sam quickly earned her CD in both the United States and Canada. Meanwhile the Murphys saw the breed rings and decided to see what Sam could do. She did poorly. The couple bought Alf's Queen, excellent conformationwise but too old to start a show career. Bred, she produced Bonnie Kay's Duke of Sequani, who became the first Murphy champion.

Field and Bench

Bob Friedman is a field dog man; his wife, Jane, prefers the show ring. So it was natural for them to choose a Sporting dog. "We visited a friend who had a Gordon Setter and quickly made up our minds that we had found the breed just right for us," said Mr. Friedman. "Bob could run the Setter at trials. I would show and we would wind up with a dual champion. At least, that's what we hoped." So they acquired Lady Jane of Markham, named after Edwin Markham, the poet, who had written about the black-and-tan dog. Jane took the Gordon to a couple of shows "but we did so badly I was on the verge of giving up." However, she stayed with it and put a 3-point major on the bitch. "I always felt we had a good Setter and that confirmed it," said Mrs. Friedman. The Gordon eventually finished, after having had three litters.

Meanwhile, Bob had one of her pups, Markham Rhum Reuben, and was running him in the field. At the time Friedman was living in Freeport and twice a week, from October to May, he would drive far out on Long Island to work the Gordon. "We would cover five or six miles, each time," said Bob. Reuben proved so adept that he won a derby stake at a Northeast regional trial of the Gordon Setter Club of America. "The rest of the year, I was able to take Reuben to shows," said Jane. "I would have to work up his coat again. I also had to build him up, as far as weight was concerned, for in the field he would run it all off." Reuben never was too happy in the show ring. He much preferred running and was a different dog the minute he hit the field.

At a trial, Bob saw a Brittany Spaniel and his bold manner of going attracted the sportsman. "I went to the owner and said I would like a pup sired by the Brit," recalled Bob. In due time he had Markham Sampson. This is a real driving dog, and in 1976 Sam was Long Island derby dog of the year.

Bob and Jane since have bought a house in Jersey, deep in field trial country. Sam has been turned over to a professional and is being campaigned.

Bob is in charge of all the restaurants and bars at the Metropolitan Opera House. "I get my exercise running up and down the 54 steps of the main stairway of the Met," he said. "Keeps me in shape for running Sam."

Out of curiosity, John and Rita Remondi, driving back from Canada, stopped at a roadside kennel. There was a German Shorthaired pup for sale and they ended by bringing it home to Armonk, N.Y. The pup turned out to be Montreal Belle, who was to become the foundation bitch for their Robin Crest Kennel, which has sent out so many winners in both the show ring and field. When Belle was three years old, she was bred to Ch. Alnor's Brown Mike, a big winner at the time. From her litter came Robin Crest Chip, one of the really great representatives of his breed. Chip became a dual champion in the United States, scoring in the ring and at the trials, and he also was a Canadian show champion. He was best of breed more than 200 times and a multi best-in-show performer.

It was a pleasure to watch Remondi show the Shorthair, for he would take the lead off him and Chip would stand like a statue. "I had hunted with him but I didn't start him in field trials until he was seven years old," said the Westchesterite. A month after gaining his title in the field, Chip tore a ligament in his front leg, while competing at Watertown, N.Y. He finished on three legs to lead a field of 19. A week later, at Medford, N.J., still favoring the leg, the German Shorthaired won at the American Pointer Club trial over an entry of 24.

In 1976, John said he had another good one coming up, Ch. Robin Crest Achilles. Sure enough, the next February, the two-year-old was best of breed in a field of 56, including 19 other champions, at Westminster. Wearing his green Tyrolean hat, with a feather jauntily stuck in the band, as usual, was Remondi.

Growth potential is the key to the program at the Hilltop Farm of Charles and Betty Stroh. "That goes not only for our kennel," said Stroh, a lawyer and a gentleman farmer, "but for all our livestock. Give the best care right from the start and the animal will progress.'' Betty handles the kennel of German Wirehaired Pointers. Her husband oversees the 500-acre farm, with its prize herd of Holsteins, Black Angus cattle, a half-dozen brood mares and 5,000 chickens.

The mistress of Hilltop Farm is a strong advocate of early training. When a Wirehaired is only three weeks old, before the food pan is put down, a gun is fired over the pup. ''The Wirehaired was bred to hunt,'' said Betty. ''In Germany, he's one of the top shooting dogs. So by firing over the pup and then feeding him, he associates the noise with the food and never is gunshy. I put a lead on a pup when he's four weeks old and start to show him at six months, just as soon as he is permitted in the ring.''

Stroh, whose Ivanhoe strain of Holsteins has brought him fame not only in this country but overseas, where he has sold cows, said, ''There should be a law against anyone giving a pup as a present. I made the mistake of giving a friend a Wirehaired. Six months later the pup was back with us.''

Leonard Greenwald, a Spaniel judge and a neighbor of the Strohs, was so taken with the pup he suggested they show her. The pup was Hilltop Tina's Honey and shown six times in the puppy class, she took five best of breeds and a third in the Sporting group. Honey had a litter and from it came three champions, one of whom, Hilltop's Sugar and Spice, when only six months old, joined with her mother to form the winning brace at Detroit in 1967. The next year, they were the best Sporting brace at Westminster.

Sugar and Spice, bred to the Stroh stud, Ch. Hilltop Harvey's Beau Brummel, produced Ch. Hilltop's Cheese Cake, who was acquired by Patricia Laurans. ''Cheese Cake barked so much I urged Betty to get rid of her. We called her Racket,'' said Charlie. The barking dog certainly was heard on the circuit. She proved to be the top-winning German Wirehaired Pointer bitch in the history of the breed, with 156 group placements, of which 25 were firsts and one best in show.

''I started as a carpenter,'' said Max Holland, ''later became a contractor, following in the footsteps of my father, who had been a contractor for 25 years—and now I've gone to the dogs.''

That he has and in a big way. Not only is he active with the Vizsla in all three phases of the sport—showing, obedience and field trials—but also has a large boarding kennel in Burnt Hills, N.Y., which accommodates up to 150 dogs and cats. Holland began with the Vizsla, also known as the Hungarian Pointer, in 1953, which was eight years before the breed was registered by the AKC.

It wasn't until 1964 that the upstater became seriously involved with the breed in the ring. He bought a two-year-old, Caesar, and showed him to his championship. In 1976, Caesar, 14 years old, had sired seven show titleholders and one field. The Vizsla also had been worked in the field by Holland. ''However, you can't run a dog one day and show him the next,'' said Max. ''When he is working in the field, he is too lean for the breed ring.''

Holland had one of the largest Vizsla kennels in the East, with 16 of the rusty-gold dogs, five of whom were champions. He considers Szekeres Magyl the best he ever owned. She gained titles in the United States, Canada and Bermuda. "The Vizsla is an excellent bird dog who wants to please," said Max. "He will work close or, should you want, will range as far as you desire. He has power, drive, a superior nose and is good in both upland hunting and waterfowl retrieving."

Something Different

Milt and Eunice Geis are Shakespearean buffs and Anglophiles. When it comes to dogs, they like the unusual. So they took two breeds that are far down the popularity scale on the AKC registration list—the Clumber and Sussex Spaniels—and proceeded to play a missionary role in acquainting fanciers with them. Week after week, the couple from upstate New York, would show the dogs up and down the East Coast. Frequently they would have the only entries but ringsiders would see them and become interested. I remember Westminster in 1969. Three large white dogs on the spaniel benches attracted the attention not only of the casual spectator but also of the fancier. They were Clumbers. The breed at the time was so rare that only 10 had been registered with the AKC the previous year and of the 115 breeds then recognized, the Clumber stood No. 112. "We are making progress," insisted Eunice. "Last year my Alansmere Bess was the only Clumber in the Garden."

The Geis dogs all are named after Shakespearean characters or places of interest in England. The couple had started conventionally enough with English Springers in 1957. "Both of us like to hunt and we wanted good gun dogs," said Mrs. Geis. "Our Springers were trained to hunt as well as to show. Five of our breeding had working certificates and we had three show champions. When we began to think of a name for the kennel, we turned to Shakespeare. Along with others, we always have thought his first work was *Titus Andronicus*. This being our start with dogs, we decided the kennel should be Andronicus. Our first champion was Andronicus Hero of Messina."

Then Milt, attending Westminster, saw two Clumbers and immediately was smitten. "We couldn't find any in this country for sale, so we imported two 13-week-old sisters from the Alansmere Kennel in England—Alansmere Bess and Alansmere Ann," he said.

When the Geises obtained the Clumbers, they also bought 140 acres in Voorheesville with a lake on the grounds, so the dogs would have ample room to run and hunt. The area gets plenty of snow, which the Clumbers thoroughly enjoy. "Although we have a heated kennel," said Eunice, "they prefer to sleep outdoors. During one storm there were six to eight foot drifts and we had to go around on snowshoes. In the morning, we would go out and see mounds of snow near the kennel. We'd call, 'Gillingham, Garrick, Winchester, Lyndhurst, Portia, Dorchester Abbey,' and the mounds would turn into Clumbers as they shook off the snow. Sort of like Birnam Wood coming to high Dunsinane Hill.''

In January of 1971, two golden liver dogs were paraded across a ring at the American Spaniel Club's specialty in the Statler Hilton Hotel in New York and there was a stir from the spectators. Most were seeing their first Sussex Spaniels. So rare was the Sussex at the time that only three had been registered with the AKC in the previous decade. Of the 116 breeds in the studbook, the Sussex stood at the very bottom. Both Spaniels were English imports. Sharland Sussex Mayfly, an eight-month-old pup owned by Margaret Reid of Attleboro, Mass., had been in the country only three months and was in a ring for the first time. The winner, making his second appearance, was Sedora Quettadene Damon, a two-year-old owned by none other than Milt and Eunice.

I always had known Mrs. Reid as a Beagle and Cocker Spaniel breeder and was surprised when she showed up with the Sussex. When I questioned her, I learned that she had a Sussex who died in 1957. "For 13 years I tried to get another," she told me. "In the summer of 1970, a friend wrote to tell me he had found a breeder in Scotland willing to sell a couple of pups. That's how come I have Mayfly and Sussex Gold, who is seven months old."

On January 7, 1973, history was made at the ASC specialty when Damon became the first Sussex in more than four decades to become a champion. Damon was best of breed at the specialty for the third year in a row. "As far as I can determine," said Mrs. Geis, at the time, "there are approximately 25 Sussex in the United States. Only five were registered with the AKC last year. England isn't much better off. In 1971, the Kennel Club in London registered nine." Eunice, who teaches mathematics, English and social studies at the Adult Learning Center in Albany, said she and her husband frequently hunt with the Sussex. "They have excellent noses, retrieve well and give tongue, like a hound, when on the scent of game," she said.

Although the Welsh Springer Spaniel had been known in his native Wales for hundreds of years, he long was a comparative unknown in the United States. When one appeared at a show, ringsiders frequently mistook him for a Brittany. In 1966, I drove to Amityville, L.I., to interview D. Lawrence (Laddie) Carswell. At the time, there were only 10 Welsh Springer champions in America and three of them were owned by Laddie. A professional handler since 1938, Carswell long had been associated with Spaniels, particularly English Cockers. Over the years he had finished more than 500 dogs.

How did Laddie become interested in the Welsh? "A Long Islander, who had three Welsh, asked me to trim them," he replied. "That was in 1961 and I became intrigued with the breed. When I saw an ad in a British dog magazine for one, I answered it and soon I was the owner of Trigger of Tregwillyn, an English champion. I showed him for the first time at Suffolk County and he created a sensation. Although he was the only Welsh entered, the ring was crowded with Spaniel people. Most never had seen a Welshman." Carswell showed Trigger extensively and the pair invariably attracted attention. The Welsh won 53 consecutive breeds and had eight group placements. Trigger's first loss was his last, for Laddie immediately retired him. He was beaten by a grandson, Ch. Felicia's Dylan, a Carswell homebred.

Plymmon Carl Tuttle started to judge in the mid-sixties. At the time he was better known for having shown German Shorthaired Pointers and over the years he had a a dozen champions of the breed. Perhaps his most famous was Gun Hill's Mesa Maverick, who was best of breed 175 times and had 98 group placements. Four times Ricky, as Tuttle called him, was best in show and he took a dozen specialties, including the national on two occasions. At Boardwalk in 1970, it was a real thrill to see the old fellow—he was 10—come out of retirement and go best of breed over an entry of 35.

Then Tuttle worked hard to bring the Field Spaniel, one of the world's rare breeds, to the fore. Said he, "When I imported my first from England, Brigadier of Mittina, in June of 1967, there were only 19 others in England. I wanted to do some breeding but I had to wait two years to get a bitch." When he mated them, they had two litters, two pups in the first and four in the second. The breed is still an extrememly rare one here. Now Tuttle is kept busy ruling on other fanciers' dogs. When I asked him which role was the more demanding—judging or showing—he replied without any hesitation, "Showing. When you judge, you win all the time."

Behind the Names

Dream Ridge is a name known to Cocker Spaniel enthusiasts on four continents. Owned by Thomas O'Neal of Woodstock, Ill., who was president of the American Spaniel Club in 1977, the kennel has bred more than 50 champions in this country alone—all parti-colors. Dream Ridge Cockers also have won titles in England, Venezuela, Brazil and Japan. "I do the breeding and grooming," said O'Neal, an administrator for five nursing homes, "and Ron Fabis does the showing."

O'Neal started with Cockers when he was a student at the University of Wisconsin, when he bred a bitch to Ch. Scioto Sinbad, the top Cocker sire of all time, with 118 champions. From the breeding, O'Neal had two titleholders, both finishing as puppies.

Since then, there have been any number of famous Dream Ridge performers. A nine-year-old black and white, Ch. Dinner Date, known as Cassie, took a best in show at Caracas, Venezuela. After being bred to Sinbad, she produced three puppies and all became champions. One was sent to England and in 1972 won the gun-dog group at Crufts. "We were told he was the first American-bred to take a group there," said O'Neal. A second puppy, Ch. Dream Ridge Dance Step, was flown to Japan and was the top-winning Cocker Spaniel there in 1969. The other, Ch. Dream Ridge Domino, is the top sire in O'Neal's kennel. Indeed, he was the top-producing Cocker Spaniel sire of 1971, 1972 and 1973, with a total of 69 champions. After a repeat breeding with Sinbad, Cassie had four red-and-white pups and all became titleholders. One, Decorator, is an international champion, taking best-in-show awards in Venezuela and Brazil. "The greatest thrill I've had in the sport," said O'Neal, "was when Cassie had that third litter. The pups were only two weeks old and darned if she didn't take the breed. Domino was winners dog and Dance Step winners bitch.'

In the 1975 American Spaniel Club specialty in New York, the biggest show of the year for the 13 breeds of Spaniels, the winner was 13-month-old Dream Ridge Dandiman.

In addition to the 20 parti-colors at the kennel, O'Neal has nearly 100 dogs of all breeds. "You never hear a bark out of them," he laughed. "You see they all are porcelain figurines, including a half-dozen Boehms.'

(An interesting added note—the late Edward Marshall Boehm, whose figurines of birds and animals are treasured throughout the world, was the owner of Ch. Fraclin Colonel Caridas, the Parti Cocker that won the Sporting group at Westminster in 1961.)

What is an H Dog? To a Spaniel aficionado it's a Cocker from the kennels of Dr. and Mrs. Clarence Smith of Chapel Hill, N.C. For all the Smith homebreds have a name starting with H—Henrietta, Handy Man, Hobbit—and the kennel name is Heyday. But it wasn't an H dog who brought fame and silver to the establishment owned by the former Minneapolis public health commissioner. It was a black, Ch. Shardeloes Selena, the top-winning black Cocker in 1973 and 1974. Both years Selena also was the American Spaniel Club winner, the first time in 15 years that a Cocker had scored successive victories. She was also the first bitch to take the specialty in three decades. When she was retired in 1975, Selena had been best at all-breed shows 20 times, taken 20 specialties and had won 89 Sporting groups.

The Smiths began to show in the mid-1940s, when a friend gave them a buff Cocker, Ch. High Hampton Jessamine. "We especially enjoyed showing at specialties," said Mrs. Smith, "and with six dogs, we have had the good fortune to have won more than 40 of them." She had particularly warm words for their Ch. Nob Hill's Tribute, an outstanding sire who has had a tremendous influence on the breed. Selena is a granddaughter.

A leading English Cocker Spaniel Kennel is the On Time Farm in Califon, N.J. It is owned by Seymour Prager, who started the kennel with his wife, Maurie, in 1948, when they bought Prager's On Time Susie. Maurie, who died in 1975, decided on the kennel name. "We bought Susie on time, so what could have been more appropriate,"she told me. The kennel had its start only two years after the AKC recognized the English as a separate breed from the American Cocker. Since then, dogs with the On Time prefix have been seen from coast to coast and in South America.

The first homebred champion was On Time Susie Belle in July 1952. Her sire was Ch. Surrey On Time Morse Code, known to the fanciers as "Johnny". Maurie was extremely proud of him. In 1966 she told me, "He's the finest dog we ever owned. He sired 19 champions. We whelped, trained and showed him ourselves. He became a champion when he was only 17 months old. There are very few of our dogs who aren't descended from him." Susie Belle produced eight champions and for years this was a record for English Cockers.

When Maurie was alive, the Pragers kept some 20 adult dogs in the kennel. "That way we can give each individual attention, stressing their feeding program, general health and exercise," she said. The Pragers set up a ring on the farm and encouraged new owners to bring their dogs and get some advice on handling. They also showed them how to groom. "We were helped a great deal at the beginning," said Seymour, "so we decided that we would do everything we could to give the novice a hand. Maurie and I always showed our own dogs. We could have turned our dogs over to a handler, but we felt we were getting much more out of the sport by winning or losing on our own." Prager still is showing, but on a much lower scale. When he finished On Time Misty's Susie in 1977, it was the 88th champion to have been bred by On Time.

Lambert Labs

In 1963, I drove to Princeton, N.J., to interview Grace L. Lambert, who in the comparatively short time of nine years had developed the top-winning Labrador Retriever kennel in America. She was the wife of Gerald Lambert, whom I knew from when I had covered yachting. He was the owner of *Vanitie,* an unsuccessful candidate for the right to defend the America's Cup in 1934. In the living room were some striking nautical paintings and at luncheon we had a pleasant time discussing international yacht racing. With Mrs. Lambert was a yellow Labrador. "He's Rupert Channel Point, my first Lab," she said. "I bought him from Dorothy Howe."

The greatest Lab Mrs. Lambert has owned was Sam of Blaircourt, a champion in the United States, England and Canada. He stands as the top-winning Lab in history and the sire of 30 champions. Shown by Ken Golden, Sam was best Lab 261 times, captured 53 Sporting groups and nine bests in show at all-breed events. And he did all this in six years.

Sam closed his career at the age of eight on a high note, when the black dog won the national specialty for the third year in a row. A student of genetics, Mrs. Lambert had bought Sam from a kennel in England without ever having seen him. "I studied his bloodlines," she said.

In 1961, the mistress of the Harrowby Kennels decided she wanted some Labs of the Loughderg strain. "I wound up by buying the entire kennel of 16 dogs, sight unseen," she recalled. Mrs. Lambert said she maintained two kennels, her show dogs at Hopewell, N.J., with Golden, and the field trialers with William Wunderlich, near St. Paul. "When there are puppies, I'll have as many as 80 Labs between the two kennels," said Mrs. Lambert. When the 16 Loughderg dogs arrived in this country, she proved to be a good judge of dogs, for eight became champions and all earned working certificates, which meant they had to make dual retrieves, under fire, of both ducks and pheasants.

Visiting the Olin kennel in Illinois, she bought a Lab, who occasioned a massive hunt. Bolting from his crate, on his arrival at Princeton, the Lab ran away. State troopers, a helicopter and appeals over the air failed to locate him. One month later, on Christmas Eve, the pup was found 20 miles from Princeton. "He was one of the nicest Christmas presents I ever received," said Mrs. Lambert. "His registered name was Nilo's Timmy Buck and he became a champion in only eight shows."

Mrs. Lambert could pick a field trial winner as well as the show variety. She refused an offer of $20,000 for Fld. Ch. Ace High of Windsweep. Then at the national championship, Ace High went all the way to the final, only to be beaten in a run-off. When I asked her what she looks for in a Lab, she replied, "The dog should be strongly built and short coupled. There are too many Labs that are too leggy, too tall, lightboned and with poor tails. I want to get the Lab back to the standard and keep him a dual-purpose dog."

Man on the Move

Waldschluss, which in German means Castle in the Woods, is the site of one of the top Pointer kennels in America. The 70-acre estate in New City, N.Y. is owned by William A. Metz, a noted corporation lawyer. Metz, who flies over much of the world in his professional capacity—in 1968, he logged 155,000 miles—turned to the sport "because it is one activity in which the entire family can participate. Since I'm away so much, on a weekend I like to be with Anna May (the vivacious Mrs. Metz) and the children. This way we go to a show and we either are handling dogs or cheering for them from the ringside." When the children were small—there are six boys and two girls—they always were dressed in red, so they could easily be spotted.

Until the attorney bought a Pointer champion in 1965, a blue ribbon was hailed at the Waldschluss Kennel. But with the purchase of Ch. Silver Ridge Crackerjack, group and best-in-show rosettes began to trickle in. Then Metz added another Pointer, Ch. Counterpoint's Lord Ashley; a Labrador Retriever, Ch. Lewisfield Gunslinger, and a Golden Retriever, Ch. Ironstream's Sir Launcelot, and the trophies began to pour into the house. Over the years, Metz dogs have won so much silverware that only the more important pieces and best-in-show rosettes are on display in a trophy room. A red-letter day for the family was on April 29, 1968, when the two Pointers each were named best in show on the two coasts—Cracker at Carroll County, N.H., and Ashley in Yakima, Wash.

Four years later, I was in Atlantic City to cover the Boardwalk fixture. The morning of the event, when I was dressing to go to Convention Hall, my wife, Vera, related how during the night she had been awakened by a helicopter, which had landed momentarily on the beach in front of the hotel. She related how a man climbed out, hurriedly departed and the helicopter took off. Vera was certain they were smuggling diamonds or narcotics. (I was inclined to shrug it off and asked if she was certain she hadn't been dreaming, but she assured me she had seen it.)

Later at the show I ran into Metz and related the story to him. He laughed and said, "That was me." Then he related how a client phoned from the Bahamas saying he needed his counsel, the day before the show. The lawyer said it was impossible for he had to be at Atlantic City. The client assured Bill, he would have him back for Boardwalk. Accordingly, he sent a private jet for Metz. The Nassau conference concluded, the lawyer was flown back to Teterboro Airport in New Jersey, arriving at 1:30 A.M. Sunday. Metz had arranged for a helicopter to fly him to Atlantic City but the resort's heliport was closed at that hour. So the pilot, inquiring where Bill had reservations, landed in the sand in front of the Holiday Inn at 2 A.M. Seven hours later, the attorney showed his Pointer, Waldschloss Athena, to best of winners.

A Better Way To Start

Most often, when I interviewed an owner, I would hear the same story. "Our first dog, whom we thought was the greatest, never could make it in the show ring. We soon learned he was just a good pet." With time and patience, after a few years, perhaps the same owner would come up with a champion.

However, others, with no more experience but just good luck, had a titleholder almost before they realized it.

Take Earl Laue, a computer programmer, whom I met when I covered the Colorado Centennial Canine Circuit in Denver. He was treasurer of that impressive-sounding organization. Earl told me how on Easter Sunday in 1964, he and his wife, Diane, drove to a Basenji kennel. The breeder had two pups for sale. One, she assured the couple, was of show quality, the other a pet. The Laues had no interest in dog shows, so they chose the pet. Besides, he was cheaper.

"We took the pup to a vet for a check-up," said Laue. "In the waiting room, we struck up a conversation with another man there with his dog. He told us about match shows and said our dog looked so good, we should enter him in one. So we went to one, our pup took second in the group and we were hooked." The pet was Bwana Akers Solemn Promise and he became a champion. What about the other pup, the one who was supposed to be show quality? "Oh, he was shown," answered the Coloradan, "but he never even earned a point."

Next, the Laues decided it was time to make a big step and import a dog. So they obtained Snuff of Horsley from England. "He had been in a kennel for 11 months and was badly in need of exercise to strengthen his shoulders," recalled Laue. "He kept me in shape. I ran a mile every day with him." The workouts paid off. Snuff became a champion and was the Littleton couple's basic stud dog. The Laues then purchased a puppy bitch. Diane, who had been timid about handling, walked her into a ring and finished her in just a dozen shows.

It was the start of a career for Mrs. Laue. In 1970, she received a license as a professional handler and now is showing dogs at some 110 events yearly. "When Diane began consistently to beat me in the ring, I decided it was time for me to retire," said Laue, "so I turned to club work." He has served on the board of the Colorado KC and as its president. Diane has finished more than 40 Basenjis for the Laues. "We have trophies all over the house, including the attic and the garage," said Earl. "And to think it all started with what we thought was a plain pet."

Unlike so many fanciers whose first dog invariably is a good pet but certainly not of show quality, Erwin Hutzmann's first Irish Water Spaniel was the best he ever owned. The liver-colored spaniel was Ch. Shillalah Napper Tandy, CD, who 85 times was best of breed, twice won groups and had seven other placements. He also took a national specialty in which he defeated 13 other champions.

The Irish is an outstanding retriever and he has a good sense of humor. These were the two qualities that appealed to the Medford Station, L.I., breeder when he was looking for a dog.

"I had some friends whose Standard Poodle was a complete clown," he recalled. "I would have brought one but I was looking for a hunting dog. I saw a picture of an Irish Water Spaniel, heard it was a good duck retriever and decided that would be my dog." Hutzmann went to Dorothy Goodnow, who at the time had the largest kennel of the breed in the country, and asked her for a good one. That's how he got Napper Tandy, then three months old. The pup not only was a big winner in the ring but proved an outstanding sire.

Bassets, Bloodhounds and Banks

The Basset has a rich melodious baritone bark, a deep resonant voice. So when a litter was whelped at the Lime Tree Kennel of Robert and Nancy Lindsay, the Long Island couple from Syosset decided on musical names. The five puppies were named Conductor, Calypso, Music Box, Paradiddle and Descant. But then Lime Tree dogs have always been known for their distinctive appellations, being named for trees, birds and flowers. But they all had one name in common—Lime Tree.

"Originally the family came from France," explained Mrs. Lindsay. "The name was de Lindsée. Following the Norman invasion, in 1066, some members crossed to England and the name was Anglicized. After intermarriages to Scots, it was changed to Lindsay."

Of the Bassets, Ch. Lime Tree Micawber, or Mickey, as he was known around the Lindsay household, was not only a good stud dog, but also a goodwill ambassador for the breed. He appeared on several TV programs and was the model for magazine covers and pictures for articles. The Lindsays also achieved success with Bloodhounds. "We bought our first, Missy of Panther Ledge, when she was just six weeks old," reminisced Nancy. "She had an excellent nose and

I worked her in the field once a week for a year. She received the American Bloodhound Club working certificate and an AKC tracking degree, the only Bloodhound to be awarded both in 1957.''

The Lindsays call the den of their home ''The Dog Room.'' On a wall are the framed championship certificates won by their hounds and tucked away among them, almost inconspicuously, a Phi Beta Kappa diploma from Yale to Robert V. Lindsay. There are also trophies, and a collection of carvings and drawings. There is a Bloodhound of Hungarian lead, a couple of bronze Bloodhounds from Austria and another in china. Lindsay, a brother of the former mayor of New York, John, is senior vice president of the Morgan Guaranty Trust Company. He had been active in club work and was president of Westminster from 1969 till 1972. Nancy is now busy judging, and on occasions her steward is none other than her husband.

Probably the best known Basset fancier in the United States in the years from the forties through the early seventies was Peg Walton. Over this span, her Lyn-Mar Acres Kennel bred more than 75 champions. She attributed much of her success to her background with animals. ''My grandfather bred coach and hackney horses,'' she told me. ''Then my father raised standardbreds and had a herd of registered Jersey cows. When I married, my husband had a pack of Beagles, so I became a Beagler. However, he always had wanted a Basset. In 1943, I bought him one as a surprise.'' Unlike so many novices, whose first dogs invariably are pets, Mrs. Walton went to Westminster and picked out a really good one. She was Duchess of Greenly Hall and she became the foundation bitch for Lyn-Mar Acres. Duchess in her first litter produced a champion. Bred again, Duchess had four bitches and all became titleholders.

When I was in Italy, a leading judge asked me to recommend a Basset kennel for a big breeder there. He said they weren't too happy with dogs they had been importing from England, recommended by a well-known British judge, and were anxious to introduce some new bloodlines. I told him about Peg and she sold him a tri-color she had finished from the puppy classes. His first time out in Italy, the tri went best in show.

''I've consistently followed a policy propounded by my father,'' she said. ''He insisted on buying the best animal available, saying it costs just as much to feed a poor one, as a winner.'' As a judge, she is particularly proud of an entry she drew in London, where she did 196 Bassets in nine hours.

For nine years in a row, Peg was show chairman at Trenton. When she started that Jersey fixture had an entry of 2,060. At her last show as chairman in 1971, Trenton had moved up to 3,750, at the time the largest entry in this country in 30 years.

''In our household, it's dogs and tennis,'' said Patricia Fellman. ''We have a tennis court next to the kennels, so our Bassets can watch us play. We have named them all for tennis players.''

It was a lost dog that started the family in the canine sport. "My husband (Dr. Philip Fellman) and I were driving from our home in Harrington Park to New York to go to the theater," recalled Mrs. Fellman. "We had just reached a toll booth at the Lincoln Tunnel, when we saw a Basset running loose. I jumped out of the car, called to him, and he came over immediately. The next day we phoned the police and reported we had a Basset with no identification. We had fallen in love with him and hoped no one would claim him. But the police reported a woman had already called and she turned out to be the owner."

The Jerseyans were now intent on getting another. And they went about it intelligently, attending Westminster, meeting breeders and going to kennels to see dogs. They finally bought Lime Tree Iris and from her first litter came Courtside Gorgeous Gussie. "She became a champion in the United States, Canada and Bermuda," said Mrs. Fellman. "In Bermuda, it was amusing because my husband was showing her. He was playing in the over-35 tennis tournament and would rush from the court to the ring." Gussie produced four gorgeous champions, including Courtside Peaches, who gained her title from the puppy class at Philadelphia. "Before we retired her, she had been best Basset 17 times," said Mrs. Fellman.

The couple had one best-in-show performer. He was a tri-color, Webbridge Banner Bound, and he captured the silverware in Bermuda. "Since I now have my license to judge, our showing days are over," said Mrs. Fellman. She has long been active in club work, having been president of The Kennel Club of Northern New Jersey. This was the club that held the first show ever staged at Meadowlands, the huge sports complex in New Jersey, just across from the Hudson River from midtown New York.

On a trip to the Southwest, Vera and I met Bob Wilson, an American Airlines pilot, who also is a judge. He was wearing an attractive doggy tie and told us it came from a boutique in the Vieux Carre in New Orleans. When we reached that city, I was anxious to do a story about its kennel club activities and phoned Vance Evans, the president. Unfortunately I was unable to reach him. A few days later, when we were preparing to leave, Vera suggested we walk to the shop and buy the tie. When I inquired about it, the salesgirl asked if I was interested in dog shows. When I said yes, she replied, "You must know my boss—Vance Evans." Unfortunately, he had left earlier in the morning on a trip, so I didn't meet him until we ran into each other at a show he was judging.

Evans and his wife always have enjoyed dog shows. "We treated them as fun and not a serious business," said the Louisianan. "We looked forward to the weekends, going to shows, meeting other exhibitors and walking our Bassets into the ring. Whenever there was a brace, we would enter a pair of hounds. That way you had two chances to handle your dogs. If you were beaten in a class, you'd be back later with the brace. It's too bad more clubs don't have that type of competition. At the Louisiana Club's 50th anniversary show, my Bassets took best brace. We also won at Baton Rouge and other events on the Deep South circuit."

When Evans was approved as a judge in 1967, he stopped showing. He's a great believer in a prospective judge stewarding and then judging as many matches as possible. "You get good experience and have fun at the same time." That fits into the Evans formula for the sport—participate and enjoy it.

Judge in the Pulpit

Every morning for more than a quarter of a century the voice of the Rev. Dr. Braxton Sawyer has been heard on the Radio Pulpit program from Fort Smith, Ark., where it is beamed to four neighboring states. Two days a week it is frequently heard in a dog show ring somewhere in the United States, for the Baptist minister is in great demand as a judge. The Southerner is an authority on hounds, particularly the Foxhound. His Ch. Kentucky Lake Mike became the first American Foxhound to be named best in show in the United States, that landmark victory taking place in Baton Rouge, La., on April 8, 1963.

The cleric considers Kentucky Lake Big Red the greatest Foxhound he ever bred. "Big Red is the only Foxhound to become a duel champion in this country," Braxton told me. "He earned his field title before his breed championship. Most of the Foxhounds winning today go back to him. Big Red really introduced me to the dog world. He's buried in my backyard."

In addition to a doctorate in theology, the Reverend has a master's degree in genetics. And he has applied this knowledge very successfully in his breeding program. "It takes about three generations to know whether or not you are on the right track breeding genetically," he said. "I have bred champions in 14 breeds. The last litter was Miniature Pinschers. Of seven puppies, five became champions, one winning the national specialty in 1975."

The Arkansan maintains that experimenting with his genetic theories also has been a great aid to his judging. "When you raise a litter, care for the pups every day, and then campaign them, even if they fail to become champions you know much more about the breed than if you have gained all your knowledge from a book," he asserted.

Dr. Sawyer has conducted many seminars on genetics before kennel club groups. When he was judging in Australia, in 1975, he lectured on the subject at the University of Melbourne.

Perseverance and devotion are cornerstones in the credo of the Rev. Raymond Kelly, Jr., a determined and busy man. An Afghan breeder, exhibitor and judge, Kelly also served two terms as president of a specialty club and helped to organize another. He has master's degrees from Loyola and Howard Universities in education and religion. As a Baptist minister he organized a mission in Baltimore. He and his wife, Barbara, are junior high school teachers.

When the six-foot-one-inch cleric walked into a ring in Baltimore in 1954 with an Afghan, it caused a sensation. "It wasn't my Barza of Grandeur, for he was no great dog," said Kelly. "But it was the first time many ringsiders had ever seen a black exhibitor. It was too bad that judges or other exhibitors didn't tell me the truth, that my Afghan just wasn't good enough to finish. Instead, they kept saying I had a dog worthy of becoming a champion. After three or four years, all Barza had was one point and it had cost me a lot of hard-earned money. However, I did learn a lot and I met some beautiful people. It also taught me a lesson not to praise a mediocre dog.''

It wasn't until 1961, after Kelly had finished his military service, that he bought his second Afghan. "She was the runt of the litter, all I could afford," he recalled. With patience and loving care, he brought the black and tan along and she finally became a champion. Meanwhile, he was visiting Afghan kennels, and asking questions. "I read every Afghan book I could find to learn about the breed," he said. "Then to learn more, I would steward, whenever I could find the time." Soon, he had other champions and having such a good eye for a dog, fanciers urged him to judge. In 1974, he finished his provisionals and was approved as an arbiter. And a good one he has proven to be. "My only difficulty is time," he said. The cleric is an assistant at one of the largest churches in Baltimore and he organized and raised funds for the People's Community Mission. Whether he's in the pulpit or judging at a dog show, the Reverend is an impressive figure.

"Mrs. Afghan"

A fancier whose Afghans have had a tremendous influence on the breed was Kay Finch, an artist and sculptress from Corona del Mar, Calif., who started with the exotic hounds in 1940. Many of the younger enthusiasts perhaps won't remember that Kay also was a force in the Yorkshire Terrier world. She started to breed Yorkies only a year after Afghans and was the first president of the Yorkshire Terrier Club of America.

But it is Afghans with whom "Auntie Kay" is invariably associated. A silver anniversary present from her husband, Braden, in 1947, pushed the Californian into the Afghan limelight. Within a year, Felt's Thief of Bagdad, a silver-blue, became Kay's first Afghan best-in-show winner and he started the Finch dynasty.

Then came a succession of top winners, headed by Taejon of Crown Crest, a bright silver with black trim, and Ch. Crown Crest Mr. Universe, a golden, who owed his name to the fact that he was whelped while the Miss Universe pageant was on TV. Taejon, known as Johnnie, had won the silverware 19 times when he was retired in 1955. He and Kay made a striking picture in the ring and won many converts to the breed. Mr. U. ran up an even more impressive record, with 28 top awards and 96 groups. "They were 'great dogs,' " said Kay, "and a great dog is only as good as those he sires. They both were proven sires, producing many champions." Kay, for years, has been a leading judge.

Joan Brearley is the first to admit that animals in general, and dogs in particular, are a most important part of her life. "Since I was a child there has been a steady stream of dogs, cats, birds, fish, rabbits and snakes for my own private menagerie," said she. "Over the years I've owned 30 breeds of purebred dogs, as well as countless mixtures, since my door never was closed to a needy or homeless animal.''

A graduate of the American Academy of Dramatic Arts, Joan started her career in the arts. Later she studied journalism at Columbia and worked for a TV network.

Joan began to breed dogs in 1959 and her Sahadi Kennels gained fame with Afghans. She bred Ch. Sahadi Shikari, a cross of the Shirkhan and Crown Crest lines, and at one time he was the top-producing Afghan in the country. Joan has been a judge since 1961.

She is just as active in the cat fancy and constantly was after me to cover cat shows. The year Shikari won the Ken-L Ration award as top hound of the year, one of her Siamese cats won a comparable award. Then Joan is active in club work, being a director of the Dog Fanciers Club, the Afghan Hound Club of America and the Stewards Club of America.

Cowboy Beagler

For more than four decades J. Ralph Alderfer has had Beagles. ''I was four years old when my father gave me my first dog,'' he recalled. ''By the time I was 12, I had three and was running them in sanctioned trials against professional handlers. I have had some good hounds but my first really great one was Alderfer's Little Midget. When she worked a rabbit, she ran a close line. My other great field dog was Pin Oaks Cryline Cinder, who had eight generations of champions behind her.''

The sportsman from Souderton, Pa., told of how he always liked animals and rode horses for dude ranches in the area, took part in local rodeos, went on the circuit and wound up competing at the big one in Cheyenne, Wyoming. In 1962, after he married, Alderfer decided to turn from the field Beagle to the show dog. He had a good eye, bought a pair and quickly finished them. Pin Oaks Heidi, unbeaten in the classes, became his foundation bitch. Alderfer's Pin Oaks Kennel in a comparatively short time achieved real success in the ring.

''For years the owners of field dogs, who run at Beagle trials, and persons with show dogs, have been feuding,'' said Alderfer. ''As one who has had both, I contend that a show dog, if properly trained to work rabbits, can outrun a dog bred strictly for hunting. The show dog has conformation and will keep going. The field dog is bred strictly for nose. His legs frequently are bowed, his neck too thick and often he is sway-backed. The field man would do well to occasionally breed his dogs to show Beagles. He'd improve his stock. Every one of my show dogs hunts with me.''

The Barkless Dog

In the armed forces, reveille is the wake-up call sounded early in the morning. But at the dog show, when the call is for Basenjis, Reveille means Damara Bolte. ''My wake-up call is five in the morning, because I have to exercise and feed my hounds before leaving for work,'' said the Virginian. ''But then I'm an Army brat and accustomed to rising early. My grandfather was Maj. Gen. Benjamin A. Poore and my father, Gen. Charles L. Bolte, who when he retired in 1955 was the Army's Vice Chief of Staff.''

Five days a week Damara works as an animal husbandwoman at the National Institutes of Health in Bethesda, Md. That's an 84-mile round trip from the house and kennel she built in Leesburg, Va. The other two days she is showing dogs. The tall, attractive fancier has owned or bred 30 champions of the barkless breed, including Reveille Rifleman, Reveille Recruit, Reveille Re-Up and Reveille Ruffles of Rose Bay.

''Recruit did so much to gain recognition for the breed,'' she recalled. ''He had 63 group placements, including six firsts, and he was second in the group at Westminster in 1962. He was my foundation stud. Unfortunately, he was ahead of his time. Today, he would easily have been a best-in-show dog.'' Recruit is the sire of Re-Up, the top winner in the history of the breed. And Damara has done her winning with a small kennel. ''I never have more than one brood bitch,'' she said, ''and I have only a litter ever year or two.''

A graduate of Purdue, Damara later studied sculpture in Paris. In the ring, she wears a gold relief of a Basenji she sculptured. Although she invariably is associated with Basenjis, she has had Mastiffs for 20 years. ''I enjoy showing,'' said Miss Bolte. ''It's a great denominator. Anyone can have a dog. I was a nobody when I won my first group with Recruit.'' Since she has been so successful, I asked her what advice she would give a beginner. ''Stay with it,'' she responded. ''It took me 23 years, from the time I handled my first dog when I was still in high school, until I had my first best in show.''

I saw Damara at Boardwalk in 1977, when she had just returned from Brazil. ''It was a series of firsts,'' she said. ''It was my first vacation in 17 years. I brought down a smooth Fox Terrier, Ch. Waybroke Smooth Operator, Sergio Nogura had bought here and I showed him to his first best in show in Brazil. Then I handled a granddaughter of Re-Up I brought along for Sergio, and the first and only Basenji was best at Sao Poulo.''

The barkless dog, the Basenji, has intrigued many a showgoer. So when Shirley Chambers read about the breed, in 1956, she decided she had to have one. In response to an ad, she drove to a breeder and left with an eight-week-old red-and-white puppy, Khajan of Storybook. A year later the Altoona, Pa., fancier and Khajan made their show debuts at Harrisburg. The Basenji was winners dog and best of winners for 3 points. In just seven more shows, he became a champion, undefeated in the breed. ''I just couldn't believe it. I was walking on Cloud Nine,'' said Shirley. Now it's an old story. The Pennsylvanian has bred more than 75 titleholders.

''I was pretty busy in the early days,'' she told me, ''since I had a full-time position. I was job-estimating for an electrical contracting firm.'' So when Mrs. Chambers decided to breed Basenjis, she went at it just as systematically as at her job. She bought three brood bitches and not being too happy with the temperament and type of the dogs who were being shown, purchased a stud from Seattle. "We bred all three bitches to him," she recalled, "and had good luck. One of the pups, Indian River First Lady, finished in a half-dozen shows in 1961. When we bred her, a daughter was winners bitch at the national specialty. That started us off. For the next nine years we had the winning bitch at the national."

In 1962, Shirley bought a 10-month-old bitch, Fulaflashi of the Congo, from Veronica Tudor-Williams, the British woman who had brought the breed out of the Congo. Flash was the dam of 17 champions, including Khajah's Gay Flambeau of Ed-Jo, who in 1976 had sired 58 titleholders. However, it is Ch. Khajah's Gay Excalibur, who is the fancier's real pride. "I never campaigned a special until he came along," bragged Shirley. "I was more interested in breeding than winning. But Excalibur was what I had been striving for both in type and temperament. I showed him for just one year, retiring him at Cleveland in December 1975. He had been best Basenji 119 times, with 65 placements, including 20 firsts and three bests."

Going Doggy in a Big Way

For more than two decades, the Eagle Farm kennel of Irish Wolfhounds of Samuel Evans Ewing III and the Jacopa Kennels of Great Danes of J. Council Parker played a prominent part in the show world. Every 10 days a truck would pull into the establishment occupied by the two kennels and deposit a half-ton of dry food. And every two weeks, another truck would bring 600 pounds of ground beef. "We averaged from 30 to 40 permanent residents, plus puppies," explained Ewing. Since 1970, this has dropped to 25; Parker has stopped showing and turned to judging.

Ewing, a lawyer, was brought up with dogs but not with Wolfhounds. His father for years was Master of the Eagle Farm's Hunt, a pack of American Foxhounds. Sam wanted a big dog for the country that wouldn't require much grooming. He saw a picture of an Irish Wolfhound and decided that would be his breed. In 1953, he bought Ballymacad of Ambleside and both made their debuts at Devon. "Bally was the only Wolfhound at the show so we took the blue easily enough but when he also was placed third in the group, I really became enthused," recalled the lawyer. Ewing took the big gray brindle to the Westchester show in 1956 and Bally won the breed, beating a half-dozen champions, including a bitch with two best-in-show awards. "That was a tremendous thrill." said Ewing.

Since then there have been many victories for the lawyer, who has finished more than 30 of the big, shaggy dogs and has had multiple best-in-show winners. However, it was Ch. Hilloway's Padraic of Eagle who really brought fame to the kennel. He was the top-winning IW in 1965 and 1966, best of breed both years at Westminster, and in 1966, when six years old, took the national specialty from the veterans class. Ch. Broughshane of Eagle, a 175-pound black homebred who was a consistent winner for Ewing, in 1973 set a record of best-in-show awards by a Wolfhound when he ran his total to 15. The previous mark of 9 had been held by his grandsire, Ch. Sulhamstead Matador. Shane was the top-winning IW in 1971, 1972, and 1973.

It was from the links to the show ring for Dr. and Mrs. Thomas Powers. "We spent a good deal of our leisure time hitting a ball around the golf course," said Mrs. Powers, "but one day our son asked us to get him a dog. We looked in the paper, saw an ad for an Irish Wolfhound pup and bought it. Little did we realize we were buying the tallest of all breeds [the minimum height for a dog is 32 inches and he should weigh at least 120 pounds]. That was the beginning of the end for our golf. We began to spend our weekends at dog shows."

Dr. Powers, who is a dentist, after standing at ringside watching what was going up and speaking to fanciers, quickly came to the conclusion that their pup never was going to do too much winning. So he and his wife flew to Ireland and bought a pup, Ballykelly Ailbhe, who 15 months later became a champion. Determined to build a winning kennel, they bought Kilfineen of Killybracken from Mrs. C. Groverman Ellis, long an official with the Irish Wolfhound Club of America. Kilfineen was only 13 months old when she gained her title, remarkable for a breed which ordinarily matures rather slowly.

The Powerscourt Kennel has become a well-known name to fanciers. Their Ch. Ballykelly Powerscourt Tomas, a 175-pound Irish import, was a best-in-show and national specialty winner, and their Shanahan a multi-BIS performer. The dentist, meanwhile, was a driving force behind the Plainfield KC.

Going Doggy in a Miniature Way

Long a controversial woman in the sport but one who played a leading role as a Dachshund breeder was Mrs.William Burr Hill, better known as Gracie, who now lives in Florida.

Gracie was one of the organizers of the Dachshund Association of Long Island (DALI) in 1950 and was its president for 10 years. She also served the same period as secretary of the Dachshund Club of America. For two decades she was pretty much "Mrs. Dachshund" in the East. She was one of the leaders to champion the miniatures and was distressed that the AKC would not permit the standards and miniatures to be shown separately.

"We had our first litter of puppies in 1944," recalled Mrs. Hill. "Our three-room apartment in New York was getting crowded, so we moved to Hicksville, Long Island."

In 1952, Gracie helped to organize the National Miniature Dachshund Club and at various times she served as president, secretary and treasurer. In the early sixties she wanted me to do an article urging the two sizes be shown separately. "If the AKC would only do so, you would see the miniatures quickly outnumber their larger counterparts in entries," she said.

Mrs. Hill bought her first miniature in 1952 and was immediately smitten by the small Dachshunds. By 1963 her De Sangpur Kennels had finished titleholders in all three coats.

I covered several DALI specialties that were held on the front lawn of Mrs. Hill's home in Hicksville and in 1961 she triumphantly greeted me, saying, "We have 102 longhaired Dachshunds; that's a record for America."

Ever the champion of the miniature, in the early sixties Gracie, to prove their versatility, started to train them in obedience. Before long, three of the little De Sangpur representatives had CD degrees.

You name it and Gordon Carvill has done it, for the engineer from East Greenbush, N.Y., has engaged in almost every facet of the dog show sport. He's been a breeder and exhibitor of Dachshunds, has shot over dogs in the field, taught obedience, been the head of two kennel clubs, served as vice president of the Associated Dog Clubs of New York State and president of the American Dog Owners Association, and judged from coast to coast.

Carvill started in the sport in 1955, when he bought an English Springer to be used for hunting. Since a good hunting dog must obey orders, Carvill took his Spaniel for obedience training and before he was through, the dog had earned CD and CDX degrees. "I became so enthusiastic that I stayed with it and for five years was an obedience instructor for the Dutch Valley Dog Training Club," he said. "It's a tremendous satisfaction to see both dog and owner start with nothing and develop into a team." Meanwhile, Carvill and his wife, Jean, had bought a pair of Dachshunds. "Then we decided to show," he recalled, and they enjoyed remarkable success.

Carvill has been a leader in consulting with legislators in Albany on measures regarding the pet industry. He also has worked with the Civil Aeronautics Board to improve shipping conditions. To stress the magnitude of shipping problems, Carvill pointed out that 4,100 animals go through Kennedy Airport in New York each month.

Westphal Windfall

Few breeders have enjoyed the success of Peggy Westphal. Wire, Longhaired and Smooth Dachshunds that she has bred or owned have won more than 220 championships over a span of 25 years. Among the great badger dogs she owned and handled are the Wire, Ch. Vantabe's Draht Timothy, sire of 51 champions, and his grandson, Westphal's Shillalah,—the top-winning Dachshund of 1970, a best-in-show performer, victor of 46 hound groups, champion in this country and Canada (with a top award in Toronto) and the sire of 47 titleholders.

Peggy and her husband, Alan, started with a miniature Longhair, Westphal's Merry Mite. "She was eight-weeks-old when we bought her from a breeder living in a New York apartment, and our little Dachshund was causing havoc in a laundry basket," Peggy recalled.

But it was a silver buff Cocker Spaniel, Ch.Sagamore Toccoa, or Bunny as she was called, who was by far the most famous of the Westphal dogs. She took her first best in show at Worcester in December 1970 and for the next three years had a long string of successes. When Bunny finally was retired, she had won the silverware 40 times and captured 108 groups, including Westminster in 1973.

She stands as the foremost winning Cocker Spaniel of all time. I moaned and groaned when she would win because I had written so many times about her there was little else to say. Unlike so many top bitches who are failures when they are bred, Bunny had two litters and four of the pups became champions.

In 1975, Peggy was given an Airedale, whom she finished. "Then I was on a panel at a Bearded Collie symposium," said the fancier, "and I was given a Beardie, which I also showed to a championship. Linda Jordan gave me a Whippet, who always was getting into trouble leaping over fences, and I showed naughty Wilbur to his title. I've been showing dogs for friends for years. With the AKC no longer licensing handlers, now I'm going to do some handling."

A Real Exhibitor Judge

Judge William H. Timbers and the late United States Supreme Court Justice John M. Harlan had two things in common—a supreme respect for the law and a love for Norwegian Elkhounds. "When John, who was a great constitutional jurist, agreed to swear me in as a judge of the United States Court of Appeals for the Second Circuit," said the Darien, Conn., resident, "I told him I was planning a simple ceremony, with only the immediate family attending. Whereupon he said, 'If you don't bring the dogs, I'll declare the entire proceedings to be unconstitutional.' "

Judge Timbers has been an Elkhound enthusiast since 1958, when he and his wife, both skiers, took their children to Vermont to initiate them into the sport. A forest ranger in the village had an Elkhound, who made the rounds with his master. "The ranger, on his snowshoes, covered about 20 miles a day," recalled the jurist. "The dog, running back and forth, did at least twice the distance. Still, the Elkhound, on their return, would be so full of energy, he would play with my children. We all took such a fancy to him, I inquired where we could buy one and the ranger sent us to a kennel."

So it was that the Timbers obtained Leif, a pup, for a pet. The judge, realizing that the dog had to be trained, learned that the Ox Ridge Kennel Club had an obedience program. Leif earned his CD degree when he was only an 11-month-old pup and two months later he added his show championship. Then came his CDX and the judge worked with him until he had the Ph.D. of obedience degrees—tracking.

The Elkhound frequently accompanied his master to the courthouse, so it was no surprise when the pair arrived for the Second Circuit Judicial Conference. Attending as the Circuit Justice was Mr. Harlan. When Chief Judge (J. Edward) Lumbard made some reference to the numbers of reversals of the district courts by the Court of Appeals that year, the word reversals triggered a loud bark from Leif. Harlan laughed and never forgot the incident. For the entire week, Leif was always with the Justice. Judge Timbers told about how Harlan came to visit the family at its summer cottage in Maine. The cabin edged on a lake and Leif always stayed between the Justice, whose eyesight was failing, and the water.

In October 1974, I wrote a column about Judge Timbers and his dogs. I received a Christmas card from him. He wrote, "Two of my young colleagues (ages 70 and 68) on the Second Circuit (New York, Connecticut and Vermont) and I visited our senior colleague, Thomas W. Swan at his home in New Haven today, on his 97th birthday. First thing he said to me as I entered his study, 'Bill, where are your dogs?' I replied they were home and fine. He then remarked that he had read the piece in *The New York Times* about my dogs and Justice Harlan and he thought the article was excellent, especially since it reflected such credit on Harlan, whom Swan greatly admired."

The Timbers never have more than two Elkhounds at a time. The judge said, "I really enjoy handling but since I'm a director of the AKC, I feel it isn't proper. But I miss showing. It was always a perfect antidote for the tension of the courtroom. I'd always rule in its favor."

When you think of Norwegian Elkhounds, you think of Patricia Craige. The teacher from Monterey has bred more than 100 champions, even though she rarely keeps more than 17 Elkhounds at her kennel. It was indeed a surprise when I visited the Californian and her husband, Dr. John Craige, a veterinarian, for I had visions of a 50-or-60 dog kennel. Theirs is a very modest affair, typical of the small breeder. Yet Pat, as she is known on the circuit, has had a half-dozen best-in-show winners. They are names that every Elkhound fancier knows —Vicksen, Howdy Rowdy, Vagabond, Valley Forge, Homesteader and Nimbus—all carrying the Vin-Melca's prefix, Pat's kennel name.

Howdy Rowdy ranks as one of the greatest sires of any breed. When he died in 1975, he had sired 145 champions, with 10 best-in-show offspring. Pat always has been very proud of Vagabond. "It was a thrill to have him in the ring," she said. "He was the ideal type, powerful, moved beautifully, and he had the right temperament." Apparently the judges liked him too, for he was best in show 25 times and took 80 groups. Bond was the top-winning dog of all breeds in 1970.

In 1979, Pat won the Group at Westminster for the second time with Nimbus. Five months later she came East to visit with her mother, and guided Nimbus to BIS wins of the Rochester and Buffalo shows, bringing his total to 58—far and away the record for the breed.

Pat has long been a fancier. "When I was 13, I was given a 16-hour-old orphan pup," she recalled. "Every four hours I bottle-fed her. Three years later I showed her to her championship and a CD obedience degree, getting both the same weekend."

Pat also has some very decided opinions on breeding. "I never allow myself the luxury of keeping dogs that cannot contribute to my program." she admitted. "I try to not only keep the good points but strengthen the line where I find that it is weak. I breed outside when I feel it is necessary. I find breeding literature issued by the livestock industry to be very helpful. I always plan my breeding program a couple of generations ahead."

Pat is one of the most accomplished handlers on the scene and could give many a professional a lesson. She and her Elkhounds make a striking picture as they speed around a ring.

Deerhound Devotees

In August 1966, I was covering the Hunterdon Hills fixture in Flemington, N.J. When best in show was selected, there was a buzz of excitement. Many of the ringsiders didn't know the breed. One spectator called it an Irish Wolfhound. Actually it was a Scottish Deerhound and the owner was Gayle Bontecou, a slight woman, who also did the handling. The breed was a rarity. There were then 112 breeds in the AKC stud book, with the Scottish Deerhounds listed No. 106, only 19 having been recorded the previous year.

When the judge selected the Deerhound, he commented on its excellent condition and how well it moved. That was a tribute to his owner, for Gayle, who also owned a half-dozen hunters and rode with the Millbrook Foxhound Pack, constantly worked her own dogs.

''With my Deerhounds, I have my own pack,'' she said. ''When I ride cross-country, I take a dozen along. I ride at all gaits—walk, trot, canter and gallop—and the dogs keep pace. In cool weather, we cover as much as 30 miles. Every day they have a regular conditioning workout. I take them in a big trailer to where there is a four-mile dirt road. Then I drive a jeep at eight miles an hour and they trot along. I believe that's the best speed for developing their legs and backs. They work exactly eight miles. In the winter, I have a snowmobile and they trot along with me in the snow. They are tremendously fast. I've timed them at 42 miles an hour.''

Gayle's interest in the breed started in 1959, when she imported a four-month-old pup, Verona of Therwood, from England. ''Hoot, as I called her, did real missionary work for the breed. She was the first Scottish Deerhound many people had ever seen. I showed her more than 100 times trying to gain a championship. Invariably she was the only Deerhound, so we didn't get any points. Although I started to show her when she was six months old, she didn't finish until she was four-and-a-half years old.'' Since then the Royal Dog of Scotland, as the breed is called, has made real progress and there have been several best-in-show performances.

In 1975, Gayle received her license to judge. ''I look for conditioning and movement, when I'm judging,'' she said. Those are qualities she's always demanded in her own dogs.

Maurie Lewis is an artist. She also is a Scottish Deerhound breeder. In her studio at North Hills, L.I., one is likely to see a half-dozen canvases at various stages of development. And stretched out near their mistress, as she paints, invariably are a pair of the giant hounds, whose forebears once hunted in the Scottish Highlands.

209

Maurie has a couple of acres, between two of the busiest traffic arteries on Long Island—the Expressway and Northern State highway. Next to her are 60 undeveloped acres. So although she is within a couple of miles of New York City, one gets the feeling of blissful solitude. There are huge runs for the Deerhounds, described by Sir Walter Scott "as the most perfect creature of heaven." She usually has a dozen and each day two are permitted into the house.

"The Deerhound craves affection," she explained, "and they look forward to being with me." Maurie, who was born in England along the white cliffs of Dover, is one of the leading floral painters in America. "I have a love of flowers and animals," she confessed. "I paint to feed my Deerhounds. Since the breed is subject to bloat, instead of one big meal— I feed them twice a day. When they are puppies, they have five feedings daily. They weigh from a pound to a pound and a half at birth and within three months are up to 35. They almost seem to grow overnight. My dogs eat 50 pounds of high protein every two days and 100 pounds of dry food every two weeks."

It was the artist's son who started her with the breed. "In 1964, Peter said he would like a Scottish Deerhound as a birthday present," she recalled. "We went to Westminster and there was only one being shown, so I told him he would have to wait. The next year I flew to England, brought home Bellweather Ardkinglas, and Pete had his Deerhound." At the suggestion of Leslie Canavan, a Collie breeder, Mrs. Lewis showed the bitch at Plainfield. "She went best of winners and suddenly I had a hobby," said the artist.

Now her Highstone Kennel dogs are seen in many parts of this country and Canada. She named the kennel after her father, Capt. Julien Highstone, an ace with the Royal Canadian Air Force in World War I. "I think he would be proud if he could see the Deerhounds, who bear his name," said Maurie.

The artist maintained that her profession has helped her with her avocation—dogs. "When I look at a dog's head," she said, "I see the bone structure. If the dog has the proper bone structure, it means he will move well. Most people look, but they don't see. I see light and shadow. An artist has a discerning eye." That discerning eye has helped Maurie win prizes in the art gallery and ring.

When I retired, several clubs made me an honorary member, others gave me plaques. Westbury, of which the artist is a member, gave me a magnificent floral painting she did for the occasion, which Vera and I so much admire it hangs on our living-room wall.

CDs and Ph. Ds

Srinagar is in the Vale of Kashmir in India, a region famous for its lakes and towering mountain peaks. In the United States, Srinagar is a kennel in California, famous for its Salukis, Afghans, Scottish Deerhounds and Italian Greyhounds. When I interviewed Dr. Winafred Lucas and her daughter, Afton, in 1967 in Los Angeles, they had 92 hounds. Although they lived in a suburb of the city, they had an auxiliary of the kennel at Lake Arrowhead, where the hounds could run for miles through the forests.

210

Although Srinagar had champions in all four breeds at the time, it was the Saluki that reigned supreme. In the pedigrees of most of the top-winning dogs of this ancient breed, which appeared on carvings of the Sumerian empire of 6,000 years ago, invariably the Srinagar name appears. One of the truly great dogs from this famous kennel was Jen-Araby's Siva of Srinagar, a champion in the United States, Canada and Mexico. He also had a CD degree in both the United States and Mexico and was the first Saluki in America to complete his coursing championship. Siva and his half-brother, Ch. Abu's Krishna of Srinagar, CD, probably have been seen by more people than any other Salukis, for both performed in the film, "The Greatest Story Ever Told."

Dr. Lukas and her daughter helped to organize the American Saluki Association in 1963. It started with a dozen members. Four years later there were 138, from as far as Australia. "Half our members are either Ph.D's or physicians," said Dr. Lukas, a clinical psychologist. "We are exploring the latest canine research. I believe pups should be handled and socialized between 3 and 4 weeks of age. They must form permanent attachments before they are 16 weeks. Our group is doing a great deal of research in genetics, striving to improve the breed. We hope to be able to determine conformation characteristics."

The psychologist is a firm believer in obedience training. Every dog in the kennel has or is working to attain a CD degree. Dr. Lukas is an accomplished linguist, speaking 11 languages. She gave me a list of names in Sanskrit. "Perhaps there are some Saluki owners back East whom you know that might enjoy an unusual name for their dog," said she.

Borzoi Boosters

An outstanding kennel name in Borzois—they were called Russian Wolfhounds until 1936—is Tam-Boer, owned by Mr. and Mrs. Leonard Tamboer and their daughter, Lena, of Mahwah, New Jersey. The kennel had its start in 1952, when the Tamboers bought Snow Witch of Romanoff from Louis Murr. Their basic stud dog also was purchased from Louis. He was Vigow of Romanoff II. Mated to Lady Gretchen of Tam-Boer, he produced one of the greatest Borzoi litters of the 1950-60s. Of the five puppies, all bitches, four became champions.

Valia of Tam-Boer gained her title when she was a 10-month-old pup. Elena of Tam-Boer and Elizaveta of Tam-Boer, a pair of white and sables, took the trophy as best Hound brace at Westminster in 1959. Tamara, sold to a Nova Scotian, was best in show in Canada five times.

Ch. Ducies Wild of Tam-Boer, known as "Mr. T"., was shown by Lena to best of breed at Westminster four years in a row, starting in 1962. There was a real bond of affection between Mr. T. and Miss Tamboer. "We almost lost him," she said, "after a Caesarian, when he was whelped. It was touch-and-go for 48 hours. I fed him with an eyedropper, kept him under a heat lamp and massaged his heart. I was with him constantly." A brindle and white son of Mr. T., Ch. Tambo Makhayl of Tam-Boer, was another pride of the kennel. I remember at Mid-Hudson, in 1965, when he went from the classes to best in show.

It was a letter that started Lorraine Groshans in Borzois. "I couldn't decide whether I wanted Samoyeds, Salukis or Borzois," she told me, "so I wrote to breeders of all three. The most interesting response came from a Borzoi owner and I wound up buying a puppy bitch." The Center Valley, Pa., fancier is convinced that luck plays a big part in the sport. "That first Borzoi I had did nothing in the ring. I showed her four times and she didn't get a ribbon. But when she was bred, she produced one of the best litters I've ever seen. Unfortunately, I wasn't too knowledgeable at the time and I let most of the pups go as pets. Two I kept and both became champions. Since then I've bred or owned more than 50 champions."

But she hasn't confined her activities to the breed ring. She's also active in obedience, racing, judging and club work. "I believe we should encourage the dual-type dog," said Mrs. Groshans. "My Mudreigh earned his CD degree in obedience in three straight shows, after he had his championship." As a bit of advice to a newcomer, Mrs. Groshans said, "Have patience. Read, visit kennels and talk to breeders before you make the plunge. Luck is important but one also should have some background. The sport is so big, there's something for everyone."

Holding the Whippet Hand

"In 1956, I walked into a sea food store on a Saturday," reminisced Margaret Hodge. "The owner, a Whippet breeder, was to undergo surgery the next day and he was so sure he was going to die, he was offering all his customers dogs free, it they would just provide a good home. That's how I started with dogs. The Whippet he gave me was 17 months old and he lived to be 17 years, the longest living dog I ever owned." And that includes a lot of Whippets, for Peggy has bred 17 litters in the three-car garage she converted into a kennel in Bryn Mawr. Pa.

Her real start, as far as the dog show world was concerned, took place in 1960, when she bought Selbrook Highlight, whom Tony Rost had brought over from England. The blue, fawn and white, who had three bests, was the foundation bitch for the Hodge kennel. But it was another English dog, Ch. Greenbrae Barn Dancer, whom Rost sold her in 1963, that Mrs. Hodge rates her No. 1 Whippet "because he was such a great producer." The fawn, brindle and white, who died in 1976, sired 65 champions. He also was a triple best-in-show winner.

With all her breeding and having top Whippets, Peggy only once showed one of her dogs. "It was in Pittsburgh," she remembered. "I was so nervous I apologized to the judge, saying 'You have to forgive me, but I've never been in a ring,' whereupon he replied, 'You don't have to tell me.' I never returned."

All In The Family

Few sports give opportunity for family participation as much as showing dogs. Take the James Butts of Honey Brook, Pa. In 1979, they probably had the largest Whippet kennel in America, with 125 of these elegant Greyhounds in miniature. Whereas so many fanciers strive to finish a dog, no less than 60 of the Butt Whippets were champions. Each weekend, Butt, who owns the largest Ford agency in downtown Philadelphia, and his wife, would sit at the ringside and cheer their daughters—Debby, Jennifer and Melissa. "The kids do all the training, handle all phases of kennel care and do the handling," said Butt. "They are all good handlers and the dogs love them."

The Pennsylvanian started with Cocker Spaniels in 1945 and finished two. Then he turned to Poodles and enjoyed great success. "I began with a Standard, an imported silver, who was an English and American champion," said Butt, "but she was too big for the house. So I decided on Toys. At one time I had 50 of them."

Butt moved to Nevada in 1959, selling the kennel, and he was away from the sport for nine years. Returning to Pennsylvania, he bought a Whippet for his wife as an anniversary present. "That was the start of our Whippet program," he said. The eight-week-old pup was Sporting Fields Christobel and in 1970 became the first Butt Whippet titleholder.

Debby made her handling debut when she was nine years old and gaited Sporting Fields Charter Oaks to his championship. Melissa was only eight when she finished Ch. Sporting Fields Melia, and Jennifer, at 11, put the 15 points on Sporting Fields Midnite Lace. The family also is interested in coursing. Charter Oaks gained his coursing title in 1975, when he was the top Whippet racer in the East.

All the racing and show Whippets are exercised off the tailgate of their car. "We drive about a mile, at a speed of from 5 to 8 miles an hour," said Butt. "We want them to trot, for that develops a reach in the dogs. Our Whippets are in excellent condition. Time and again the judges comment about this." A dog's life is a pleasant one at the Butt 100-acre farm. There are 14 paddocks, ranging up to five acres, so there is plenty of running room. Then there are eight additional kennel runs.

Debby handled to her first best in show when she was 14. She took Ch. Winterfold's Bold Bid from the veterans' class all the way at Gainesville, Fla., in April 1976. "We retired Bold Bid right there," said Mrs. Butt. "It was her 11th best and she had taken 87 groups. She was the top-winning Whippet bitch in the history of the breed."

But it was another Butt Whippet that was to become the kennel's greatest, Ch. Sporting Fields Clansman, a red brindle and white, scored his 30th best in show at Susque-Nango in 1979 to break the record set by Ch. Courtenay Fleetfoot of Pennsyworth 15 years earlier.

Each of the girls has her own breed. Debby specializes in Scottish Deerhounds, Jennifer in English Cockers, and Melissa in English Setters.

Shepherd Pioneers

I was tremendously impressed the first time I saw Marie J. Leary at a show, for she arrived and led a dozen German Shepherds to the bench, all with no leads.

Miss Leary was a breeder, exhibitor and judge. Her Cosalta Kennels, in Greenwich, Connecticut for years produced some of the greatest Shepherds in America. At a New England specialty, she had 32 dogs and caused a stir when she took them all off the benches for exercise, without leads. At Westminster, Miss Leary would show a dozen Shepherds and leave them unchained on their large bench with no partitions. Then, when she would take them into the ring, she would show them without a lead.

She encouraged spectators at shows to pet her dogs and she did much to overcome a fear that many had of the breed.

"Because of their intense loyalty to their human family, Shepherds are eager to please and are completely unselfish," she said. "The more an owner trains and educates his dog, the more the Shepherd's personality and lovableness will develop." One of the pioneer advocates of obedience training, Miss Leary first would have her Shepherds win their breed championships and then get their obedience degrees. She trained nine of her titleholders to work in unison. They learned to do many of the exercises—stay, come, recall, high jump—and the exhibition always won acclaim from the spectators.

"The true breeder," maintained Miss Leary, "has only one goal—to improve the breed by planned mating to elevate the quality, type and soundness of his stock." She stressed getting pups out early, too. "I put them on a lead when they are two months old," she said. "I take them in the car, walk them in and out of shops and on sidewalks with people as soon as they have received their inoculations."

Forty years ago Eleanor and the late James Cole applied for the kennel name of Thornwood, only to have the AKC turn down the request, saying there was a town in Westchester County with the same name and that it would be confusing. So the Coles translated Thornwood into German—Dornwald—and so began an establishment that was to gain fame for its German Shepherds. Seventy-five who became champions were bred on the 80-acre farm at Pound Ridge, N.Y.

"When we started, the breed was at a low ebb," said Mrs. Cole, "and we just couldn't find a good dog. Then, we met Reginald Cleveland, the dean of the breed, and months later he came up with Klodo of Stone-Home, who was to become our foundation stud. Klodo earned both his championship and a CD."

The Coles were to have any number of top Shepherds. Ch. Merrilea's Vetter of Dornwald, CD, sired a dozen titleholders; Ch. Merrilea's Rima, UDT, was such a good tracker, she was used by the sheriff of Dutchess County; and Ch. Firelei of Dornwald, whom Eleanor called "the greatest bitch I ever bred." However, it was Ch. Fels von der Rottumbrucke, a multi best-in-show dog, with more than 20 groups, who was the kennel's big winner.

Eleanor did much of the handling herself, ably assisted by her daughter, Pamela. Had Pam chosen, she would have made an exceptional professional handler, for she has a rare touch with the dogs. Pam was a real help to me at the shows, in gathering material for my stories. When two groups were judged at the same time, I always could count upon her to handle one, while I did the other, and I never had to worry about inaccuracies.

"We were very careful in our breeding program," said Mrs. Cole. "Our motto was 'Sound Minds in Sound Bodies.'"

Eleanor stopped showing in the 1960s and has judged extensively since. She isn't too happy with the Shepherds that have been shown since the mid-seventies. "I would like to see a return of the soundness we had years ago," she said. "Too many of the dogs are poor in the hocks, which is so evident when you watch them going away. Unsoundness in the old days, when I was showing, was the exception; now it's the rule."

In the Cole town house, in New York's fashionable East Side, there are only two old Shepherd pensioners. But there is a picture gallery of more than 150 photos of their predecessors. In the library, an entire section of the room is devoted to ceramic figurines and bronzes of Shepherds. It's a miniature museum.

Perseverance and patience, that has been the story of Harriet Pross of Colorado Springs. Here's a woman who refused to be discouraged, when most people would have stopped. She started in the sport in 1948, when she bought a German Shepherd. "I bought a book on obedience training," she recalled, "and in exactly seven months and five days, my dog had his CD." Then she bought a bitch for the show ring. "I went to the Colorado Springs show in 1949 and pestered everyone to show me how to handle," said Harriet. "I knew absolutely nothing but I watched the professionals and gradually learned. By the time my bitch was 11 months old, she had 11 points, including both majors. Two months later, she suddenly died."

Then, Mrs. Pross heard from a friend in the K-9 Corps, at Fort Carson, just outside Colorado Springs, that there was a German Shepherd who was pining away. The soldier with whom he had worked had been discharged and the dog was distraught. Harriet was able to buy the Shepherd for $18. "He had a beautiful temperament," she said, " and I took him through to a CDX." Now she bought a bitch, with the intention of breeding. Said Harriet: "First I had to have a kennel, so scraping together some money I'd saved, I bought a tiny piece of land. After work, and on weekends, I built the place myself. On Christmas morning, three months after I completed it, there was a phone call. There had been a fire and there was no kennel."

Undaunted, Mrs. Pross started all over, erecting a cinder block building and nine concrete runs. Then she bred the dog and bitch. From a litter of 14, she kept four. "I called one Shaun of Hap's Bluff, because I was operating on a shoestring, a real bluff," she said. When Bluff was three years old, Harriet finished her. "It was at Cheyenne," she remembered, "and I was so excited I threw my arms around the judge and kissed him."

That was in 1954, and three years later Mrs. Pross received her handling license. She worked up to a string of 18 and did very well on the Rocky Mountain and Southwest circuits. In the sixties, the Coloradan decided to show some of her own dogs and bought a Belgian Tervuren. "When my Ch. Columbine Nikit won a group at Albuquerque, I was told he was the first Terv to have done so in the United States," she said. Nikit was best of breed 112 times. The last time Mrs. Pross showed him was at the Colorado KC show, when he was 12 years old, and he not only took the breed but was second in the group. He has left his mark, for he sired three litters, from which came 17 champions.

Mrs. Pross received her judge's license in 1976.

Old English Enthusiasm

When Mona Berkowitz was nine years old, her father took her to the Danbury Fair in Connecticut. "They were holding a dog show and I saw my first Old English Sheepdog," she recalled. "We had German Shepherds and Dobermans, but nothing made the same impression as that first bobtail. For my 10th birthday, I had only one request—a sheepdog." A family friend bought a pup for her in England. "I called her Beau and we were inseparable." But when the pup was six months old the bubble burst. One day, when Mona was walking her pet, a man asked her what breed it was. When the youngster replied an Old English Sheepdog, he assured her it wasn't. Although the family had the papers, apparently they were for another pup.

The youngster was so crestfallen, her father bought her a two-year-old Sheepdog. "This time he was taking no chances with a puppy we had never seen," said Mona. "I was 11 and did everything wrong. I overbathed and overgroomed him. When I began to show him, I was a real pest. I would rush up and ask the judge what I had done wrong. Most would just ignore me. But I wouldn't give in. Finally, some owners and handlers began to give me some tips on showing and eventually I learned." She must have been a apt pupil for when she was 14, Mona was the junior handling champion at Westminster. Her Momarv Kennel, registered in 1949, gained fame for its bobtails and produced more than a score of champions. Mona, who now lives in Thousand Oaks, Calif., began her judging career at Great Barrington, Mass., at the age of 21. Recalling her childhood days when she had such difficulty, she has always been sympathetic toward inexperienced fanciers. Invariably after finishing an assignment, she will spend time with exhibitors who have been in her ring telling them what they have done wrong and giving them advice about their dogs.

"We always liked the Fezziwigs," said Serena Van Rensselaer, who with her husband, Hendrik, owns one of the top-winning Old English Sheepdog kennels in America, "so when we began to think of a name for our kennel, we decided on Fezziwig." In "A Christmas Carol," Dickens describes old Fezziwig as a jovial soul and his wife as "one vast substantial smile." Said Serena, "We felt the name would be particularly appropriate for we consider temperament the most important quality in a dog. What better disposition could we look for than the Fezziwigs themselves?"

The couple from Basking Ridge, N.J., started with the breed in 1932, when they received an Old English as a wedding gift. "We bought two more and the family grew up with them," said Serena. "We had three children and lived in Lake George (N.Y.). We never had any worries when the youngsters were out playing. The dogs took care of them as well as any nursemaid."

It wasn't until 1956 that the Van Rensselaers really became active in the sport. They had acquired a bitch, Gill, and were on their way home from South Africa, when they stopped off in England. There they visited several kennels, searching for a good stud. They found one, Farleydene Bartholomew, whom they purchased for $350, probably one of the best buys ever made by an Old English breeder. Barty swept to his championship in six shows and gained his Canadian title by going best at Montreal and Barrie. But it was as a stud he really gained fame, for Barty and Gill litters produced 11 champions, with the ace, Ch. Fezziwig Ceiling Zero. A big dog at 130 pounds, Ceily was retired in 1964 with a record of 15 top awards and 50 groups. "We only showed him eight months a year, never in the summer," explained Serena. "We have a place at the shore and he would go with us. He loved to swim and was in and out of the surf."

Ceily not only did much to bring the breed before the public but he was an outstanding sire, with 63 champions. Carrying on was his son, Ch. Fezziwig Raggedy Andy, a smaller dog. Although campaigned far less than his sire, Andy, during 1964, 1965 and 1966 had 18 bests and 75 groups.

A grandson of Andy's, Ch. Fezziwig Vice Versa, took over in the seventies. But whereas Ceily and Andy were handled by professionals, the tall, wiry, gray-haired Van Rensselaer piloted Vicey himself. He did it so well that the dog had best-in-show awards in this country and Canada.

Stocks and Boxers

Five days a week, Judson L. Streicher is busy on the floor of the New York Stock Exchange, a specialist handling Walt Disney Productions and 41 other securities. Weekends the Wall Streeter is hitting a golf ball, fishing (he's landed big ones off Florida, Mexico and India and 70-pound Nile perch in Kenya's Lake Rudolph) on a picture-taking safari in Africa or judging obedience classes at dog shows.

In September, Jud is especially busy in the dog world, for he's chairman of the Westchester KC fixture, considered by many fanciers as the most glamorous outdoor event in the East. It's the Wall Street club, with more than half of its 17 members connected with the financial district. "I've always had a dog," recalled Jud. "In fact, I've had 20 breeds." But he and his charming wife, Gale, are best known for their Poodles and Boxers. Their Galandjud's Kennel has had a half-dozen Boxer champions and one Poodle titleholder.

On his 50th birthday, Jud received a brindle Boxer pup, which he named Galandjud's Blue Chip. Three years later, in 1976, Chip led a field of 2,437 at Baltimore. "He's an easygoing fun dog and a pleasure to have around the house," Jud told me, "but he hasn't been home too much." In nine months' of campaigning, Chip had been best of breed 60 times, had 30 group placements, including six blue rosettes and taken five specialties.

Jud is an old hand with the educated set. The first Boxer he ever owned, Chardyth Pace Maker, he took all the way through to a UDT. "We worked before 60,000 in Yankee Stadium, when Blanche Saunders put on an obedience exhibition before a baseball game," he recalled. The native New Yorker, an obedience judge for 25 years, maintains that almost all dogs can be trained in basic obedience and earn a CD. "In nearly every case where a dog had been to training class and failed to get a degree, it was the fault of the handler," he said.

"At Westchester, we are very fortunate with our small membership who all are workers," said Jud. "Five of our 17 have been show chairmen with other clubs. With a group like that, how can you miss?"

French Touch

To most people the word Fido is synonymous with dog. To exhibitors on the circuit, Phydeaux is synonymous with Briard. "We gave a Gallic touch to the American version and came up with our kennel name, "said Mrs. Arthur Tingley of Mendham, N.J. She and her husband are two of the top Briard breeders and exhibitors in the East and have done much to make the French sheepdog known.

"It all started in 1957, "said Mary Lou. "We had cats but on our physician's orders, we had to get rid of them. Our daughter was suffering from asthma and our doctor felt some of the trouble was caused by the cats. He said dogs would be all right. We liked long-haired animals. We saw a Briard and decided that would be our breed. We called the AKC, were told of a nearby kennel, so we drove over and bought a pup."

The Tingleys never had been to a dog show and had no intention of showing but on the urging of the breeder agreed to exhibit their Briard. She didn't prove much in the breed ring but was an apt pupil in obedience. In just four trials, when she was only 15 months old, she had her CD. The Jersey couple next imported a dog from France. "We were such novices, we didn't realize we needed two majors. So we ran up 19 points, without any three-pointers. Then we joined the Briard Club of America and began to learn what it's all about;" said Mary Lou.

They learned so well that at Northern New Jersey, in March 1978, Art showed Mary Lou's Ch. Jennie del Pastre to best in show, the first time a Briard bitch ever had taken a top award in the United States.

The Jersey breeders are firm advocates of obedience, feeling all big dogs should be trained. "Our Pinot Noire des Coteaux was 6½ years old when we started her in obedience," said Mary Lou. "She was a show champion and we wanted her to have a dual title. In the minimum of three trials, she had a CD. Who said you can't teach an old dog new tricks?"

218

The breed name gave me a chuckle. According to the style at the *Times,* the only breed names capitalized were those denoting a country—Irish setter, Norwegian elkhound, Newfoundland. Some years ago, we received an indignant letter from a Briard owner, saying that the breed had originated in Brie, a province in France also famous for its cheese, so he asked that we capitalize Briard. The sports editor agreed the man had a point, so overnight briard became Briard.

Editor's note: The American Kennel Club capitalizes each word of the breed names such as Irish Setter, Norwegian Elkhound, etc.

He Doesn't Toe the Linebreeding

The iconoclast of the Collie fanciers is a New York lawyer, Kenneth Goldfarb. Whereas most owners are strong advocates of line breeding, he has his own opinions on the subject. Then he breeds across colors—blues to sables—and he has his own ideas when it comes to feeding. "I recognize that line breeding has become the panacea for the breeder," he told me, "but I feel frequently it is a great fallacy. It is justified when you have great or very good specimens and want to mold a line. But if you take average-to-good animals and breed them, you merely repeat the faults that existed in the bloodlines. There frequently is a loss of size, substance and vigor. One is likely to get homogeneous litters of only moderate quality. On the other hand, outcrossing even an average-to-good bitch to an outstanding stud will give a widely diversified litter as to quality and type that may include a very good or even great specimen. The pups will have a hybrid strength. Generally they will be active and bold in character, which makes for good show dogs."

In feeding, Goldfarb and his wife, Lynn, who not only does the handling but the breeding, whelping and grooming as well, firmly believe in a meat diet. "We give our 11 dogs 25 pounds of meat a day," he said. "In summer, when so many dogs have skin ailments, we never have any problems. I attribute it to the fat they are eating, along with the meat." In breeding across colors, the lawyer said the sable becomes an attractive light gold, the blue is cleaner and the tri-colors do not have a rusty color.

Goldfarb said there has been quite a change in the breed from the 1950s to the 1970s. The Collies have nicer heads, better temperament and now that the "Collie Eye" disease is recognized, it is being eliminated in breeding programs. He added that breeders in Collie clubs subscribe to a code of ethics, which requires eye checks for all dogs being offered for sale or for breeding.

"We have the only sport," observed Ken, "in which the entire family and household pets can be involved. In spring, summer and fall, more then 750,000 families travel to scenic areas, where there are lovely green lawns and shade trees, to watch beautiful dogs compete in a beauty pageant. Here's a sport where people can give vent to the Pygmalion instinct to create a more beautiful living creature while enjoying fresh air, exercise and competition for a uniquely satisfying change of pace."

Symposium Sponsor

An all-rounder is a judge eligible to rule on all the breeds registered in the AKC stud book. Muriel Freeman of Manhasset, L.I., doesn't qualify on that score. However, among fanciers she certainly is known for her all-around work as a Rottweiler breeder, exhibitor, club official and judge. An arbiter since 1967, she not only has had many assignments in this country but in 1971 judged Rottweilers in Germany, the first American afforded the honor. And currently she is at work on a book of the breed to be published by Howell Book House.

Although Mrs. Freeman invariably is associated with the powerful black dog with tan markings, her first breed was Great Danes. In 1930, she and her late husband moved to Manhasset and decided to have a dog. Since she was home alone, her husband felt it should be a big one. Meanwhile, the slight brunette was playing a lot of golf. Five times she won the Long Island championship. "My husband wanted a dog who could travel easily in the car with me when I would go to the golf tournaments," she said. "We heard of a Rottweiler litter and I chose a five-week-old pup." As it turned out she chose wisely. The pup, Gerhardt von Stahl, shown by Muriel, gained his championship at Westminster in 1960.

Mrs. Freeman has been extremely active in club work, serving as president of the Westbury and the Colonial Rottweiler Clubs, and as a member of Ladies, Long Island and the Doberman Pinscher Club of America. But what she is especially proud of is her work in staging symposiums.

In October 1976, Mrs. Freeman conducted what she said was "the first Rottweiler symposium ever held in the world." At it, she discussed the standard, and then had Catherine (Casey) Gardner hold a measuring clinic, where she measured a dog's muzzle, angles of pasterns, bones, so one could discern what was incorrect with the animal's conformation. Finally she had an evaluation session, where fanciers would bring their dogs and three or four would be invited from the audience to judge the animals. "I gave them cards," she said, "and they had to evaluate for size, head, neck, forequarters, torso, hindquarters, coat and color, character, temperament, gait and overall." The neophytes also wrote critiques. Mrs. Freeman then took over, discussing the critiques and giving her opinion. "I believe these symposiums are invaluable," she said. "We have more planned in various sections of the United States.

The Great Dane Club of America, in 1973, when it was headed by Rose Sabetti, instituted a series of educational symposiums that won it wide acclaim. Under the guidance of Nancy Carroll Draper, the meetings were held in various parts of the country—Cincinnati, Dallas, New York, Portland (Ore.). Veterinarians lectured on anatomy and genetics; there was a film on movement and gait and a panel of authorities explored such subjects as ethics, sportsmanship and attire in the ring. A judging clinic would be held with a half-dozen arbiters going over some Great Danes. The audience then was broken up into small groups, each under the tutelage of a judge, and the "students" given a chance to demonstrate what they had learned by acting in a judge's role.

The club made a wise choice in having Miss Draper run the program. She has had Danes since 1945 and has bred 16 champions. From 1953 to 1961, she served in the Connecticut legislature, representing Ridgefield. Not that this was an unfamiliar role, for Nancy had been brought up in politics. Eben Draper, her grandfather, twice was Governor of Massachusetts and her great-grandfather, Benjamin Bristow, was in President Grant's cabinet.

In the Great Dane world, she's as well known in Britain as in this country. "All the top-winning Danes in England are of my Danelagh breeding," she told me. "Two of my pups are in Sweden, where one is an international champion. I sent Danelagh's Quillan to England and he's the sire of Ch. Fergus of Clausentum, a best-in-show winner and Dane of the year in England in 1970. A son, Ch. Simba of Helmcake, a multiple best-in-show winner, was the 1972 Dane of the year."

Easy Sledding

Pioneer of the Siberian Husky breed in the United States was Eva Seeley. Called Short, because of her diminutive size, she started to drive a sled dog team in 1929 and few could match her ability on the trail. Her Chinook Kennel did much in pushing the Siberian Husky and Alaskan Malamute to the fore and helping to get the breeds registered by the AKC. A breeder, judge and honorary life president of the Siberian Husky Club of America, on her 80th birthday a dinner was held in 1971, with tributes from across the country, including President Nixon's.

It was Short's breeding that was to be the foundation stock for many of today's kennels. She always stressed the dual-purpose dog, who could pull a sled as well as win ribbons in the show ring, and she drove a team, with several champions in the harness. Her foundation bitch, Cheeak of Alyeska, is in the bloodlines of most of the great Siberians, including Cheenag of Alyeska, who, in 1938, became the first bitch to attain a title. A grandson of Cheeak's, Ch. Wonalancet's Baldy of Alyeska was the first Husky to win a group, in 1941. Baldy and a brother, Ch. Wonalancet's Disko of Alyeska, were a great twosome, taking best brace in show at Eastern. Dogs for two of the Byrd expeditions to the Antarctic were trained at Chinook, as well as many of the sled dogs used in World War II.

In 1976 Mrs. Seeley's book, *The Complete Alaskan Malamute,* co-authored with Maxwell Riddle, the noted all-breed judge, was named Best Breed Book of the Year by the Dog Writers' Association of America.

Sled-dog racing struck a blow for Women's Lib long before the movement became a cause célèbre. "This is one sport in which women can compete on an equal footing with men," said Laura Demidoff. And she should know, for she was a pioneer on the New England trails, driving Siberian

Huskies in 1931. She had the distinction of being the first woman to win an official New England Sled Dog Club race.

It was the warm weather that drove the Fitzwilliam, N.H., fancier to the show ring. "I wanted the dogs to have something to do when they weren't racing," she reminisced. "I started at the Middlesex show in Cambridge, Mass., in the thirties. I knew nothing about handling but it made no difference, since I had no opposition. Most of the ringsiders never had seen a Husky and apparently many of the judges hadn't either, for my dogs never were looked at in the groups."

In order to gain a championship for her lead dog, Togo of Alyeska, Mrs. Demidoff persuaded some of the other owners of racing dogs to enter the show ring. Togo finished and was second in a group. Panda of Monadnock was Laura's first homebred champion. That was in the early forties. Panda not only excelled in the ring but she was a great racing dog and led teams to several victories.

Mrs. Demidoff's Ch. Monadnock Pando made history for the breed, becoming the first Siberian to place in a Westminster group. Then along came one of his sons, Ch. Monadnock's King and he became the first Siberian, outside of Alaska, to take a best-in-show award, accomplishing the feat at Mohawk Valley. Father and son a half dozen times captured best-brace-in-show prizes, including International and Eastern.

A true breeder, Laura worries about the tremendous interest in the Husky, with more and more being shown. "I just hope the breed won't go the way of so many others that have gained sudden popularity," she said, "for it always seems to be downhill."

It was sled-dog racing that started Mrs. Marguerite Grant on her career with Siberian Huskies. For seven years, beginning in 1949, she and her husband, Lyle, trained and drove teams for Mrs. M. Lee Frothingham. Then in 1956, Mrs. Frothingham disposed of her kennel and gave the Grants first choice of any of the dogs. "I took what I considered to be the top five," said Peg. "They were too old to start showing but they gave me a strong nucleus for a racing team.

Mrs. Grant drove on the New England circuit and in Canada for four years. In 1958, her team won the 10-mile world championship. Rola, one of the original team, was the Grant foundation bitch. A granddaughter, Koonah's Red Kiska, became a champion when she was only nine months old. "We raced her, too," said the Carlisle, Mass., fancier, "but she became such a ham, from going to the shows, that she wanted to clown when she was in harness."

In the ring at the age of nine, when almost all show dogs have been retired, Kiska was best of opposite sex at Westminster, in 1973. She and a sister, Ch. Koonah's Red Gold, did much to make the Marlytuk Kennel famous for red Siberians. Mrs. Grant is particularly proud of Ch. Marlytuk's Red Sun of Kiska, a son of Red Kiska. Sunny, as he was called, finished in just five shows, with four 4-point majors. He was best of breed 55 times and won the national specialty in 1970 and 1971. Sunny and his mother were a tremendous brace, being best in show five times. In 1975, when Sunny was 9 and Red Kiska 12, they won all three national specialties as best brace. "I guess you can say we were seeing red all the time," quipped Peggy.

Showing Siberian Huskies is a family project for the Kanzlers. I remember covering a show in 1974 when Trish, who was 18 years old, handled the winners bitch; John, 16, the winning puppy dog; Mrs. Kathleen Kanzler took the blue with a bitch in the open class, and Sheila, 14, showed a champion. "That's the way it goes," said Kitty, "when I send the entries in, I try to figure who can show a particular Husky. My husband (Lieut. Col. Norbert Kanzler) doesn't do any showing but he designs and builds our kennels and gives us moral support."

Trish, who gaited a dog to a major when she was only 10, and a year later was best junior handler at Detroit, and Sheila were both active in 4-H. Both also showed horses, Trish a jumper and her sister in the saddle division. Between horses and dogs, Trish has won more than 100 trophies. In a six-week period in 1978, the University of Maryland senior had gaited the red Ch. Innisfree's Sierra Cinnar to five best-in-show awards. With his win of the group at Trenton in May, 1979, Cinnar's overall score stood at 17 bests in show, 57 groups and he was sire of 24 champions.

"Sheila's my puppy girl," said Mrs. Kanzler. "She's wonderful with the young stock. All three can whelp puppies." Although fanciers invariably associate the Innisfree kennel with Huskies, Kitty actually started with Collies when she was 14. She studied animal husbandry for two years at Michigan State and then married. When her husband was stationed in Aberdeen, Md., she met a Minature Schnauzer breeder. "She taught me about dogs, shows and gave me a Miniature," recalled Mrs. Kanzler. "Then Norb was transferred to Alaska and before we left, we bought Ch. Eleazar of Marienhof. There were only four shows in Alaska and our Schnauzer won a group every time we showed him." While in Alaska, the Kanzlers became interested in Siberians. "Their ability to work and race appealed to my husband," said Kitty. "We bought a couple, Tanio, who had raced on one of the top teams in Fairbanks, and Innisfree's Rashiri of A-Baska, who became our foundation bitch."

In 1961, Mrs. Kanzler, back in Michigan, walked Rashiri into a ring at Detroit, the only Siberian being shown there. "Alva Rosenberg was the judge," recalled Kitty. "He said the bitch had soundness and was typy. He advised us to choose a stud with 'show-dog prettiness,' when we bred her. We followed his advice and quickly finished several Huskies."

In 1968, the family moved to Addis Ababa, where Colonel Kanzler was an adviser to the Ethiopian Army. "We took Ch. Innisfree's Lobo, a big blue-eyed gray, along," said Kitty. "The Ethiopians apparently never had seen a blue-eyed dog and they would bow to him as we drove through little towns. They would surround the car to see him. We raised the first litter of Siberians in Africa, the military and embassy people taking the pups." When the family returned to Maryland, Mrs. Kanzler bred a couple of litters from which two of the pups, Ch.

Dudley's Tavar of Innisfree and Ch. Innisfree's O'Murtagh, both of whom were sold, became best-in-show performers.

Growing a Bearded

Research is the field of Dr. Thomas M. Davies, a chemist. It was a different kind of research that led him to, what was at the time, a relatively unknown breed in the United States–the Bearded Collie. ''I had a bit of a problem,'' the scientist explained. ''I came from a family which always had owned dogs and I wanted one. But my wife was terrified of them. She finally agreed to let me buy an Old English Sheepdog, which she said resembled a teddy bear.'' Davies showed the bobtail but never won with him. ''Then one day Barbara and I saw a Bearded Collie and we both decided it would be our next dog.''

That was in 1969, when there were very few Beardies in the country. Exploring the situation, the chemist finally located a breeder and obtained a bitch, Heathglen's Dearly Beloved. ''There were only two breeders in the United States—Lawrence Levy and Frank Morrison,'' he recalled. That year the Bearded Collie Club of America was organized. There were five members, with Levy the president. Within a year, it had 45, and Ian Morrison, the club registrar, reported 50 Beardies from seven states. Two years later the membership had doubled, with owners from 21 states and 165 dogs registered. In 1974 the AKC placed Beardies in the miscellaneous class.

''We were an active group,'' said Davies. ''Our members showed more Beardies than all the other seven breeds in miscellaneous put together. We had a specialty at Mt. Kisco, N.Y., in 1975, and had 85 dogs.'' By the first half of 1976, there were 836 Beardies listed from 39 states and Canada and on October 1 the AKC accepted the breed for registration in its own stud book, the 122nd to be listed.

Davies was show secretary for the Springfield KC fixture in 1974 and drew the attention of the show world when he staged the event without a superintendent. ''We worked 10 months preparing,'' said the physical research chemist. ''Just before the show, I took two weeks of my vacation to concentrate on it. Any club willing to put on its own show can make a substantial saving. With Springfield, it ran to $5,000. And it was a club effort and did a great deal to get people together. Many members never had done anything except pay dues. For the show, at least 80 shared in the work.''

The Pleasures of Owning Dogs

''To me, judging is much more enjoyment than work,'' said Willis Linn, a retired Corning Glass executive, who with his wife, Helena, have long had one of the top Newfoundland kennels in America. I had known Willis for many years and my interview was conducted in, of all places, London. He and I and our wives spent a charming evening at dinner in the Cheshire Cheese, where Samuel

Johnson and his literary cohorts held forth many years earlier. Willis told me how they had started serious breeding in the 1950s, when they bought two puppy bitches, Dryad's Christine and Dryad's Nancy of Glenora, and Helena showed both to their championships. The two pups became the foundation for the Edenglen Kennel, which up to 1976 had produced 55 titleholders. Edenglen Newfs are seen not only in this country but in Europe, the Philippines and Australia.

"Chrissy was the mother of our top-producing stud, Edenglen's Tucker, and of Ch. Edenglen's Banner, who twice took the national specialty," said Helena. "Three of her grandchildren have been best-in-show winners. One of Nancy's pups, Ch. Edenglen's Beau Geste, was the sire of 25 champions, so you can see our original Newfs have had a great effect on the breed." The Linns did not campaign their dogs very extensively and they don't keep too many at Edenglen, so most of the top-winning Newfs whelped in their kennel were owned by other fanciers. Of 99 breeders in a Newfoundland Club of America listing, 56 had Edenglen pedigrees within the last three generations.

Few kennels have as lovely a site. It is on the shores of Lake Seneca, in upstate New York, just south of Glenora. "There have been Newfs here since my grandmother's days in the 1890s," said Willis. The estate has been in the family since Dr. Fred Hovey Willis, a physician and a Unitarian minister, settled on the land in 1870.

"My dogs never are going to herd cattle," said Neil McLain of Ithaca, N.Y., "so I'm not too worried about their working abilities. I'm more concerned with good temperament. All the herding our Corgis do is right in our house. At night, when we give the word, they herd our youngsters up to bed."

McLain, a former vice president of the Pembroke Welsh Corgi Club of America, originally had Miniature Poodles. "We started in 1955 and joined the obedience set. My wife, Kathryn, took one of them, Nicole of Ferchenhain, through to a CDX in this country and to CDs in Canada and Bermuda." Kathryn is an instructor in the Ithaca Dog Training Club.

However, when it came to showing, McLain decided a Poodle was just too much trouble. "I enjoy taking a dog into the ring," he explained, "but dislike all the grooming. We wanted a small dog, but one that would be smooth-coated and require little work. A Corgi fills that bill. It takes 15 minutes, at the maximum, to prepare him for the ring. In 13 years, I have shown 11 of my dogs to championships."

The Ithacan was especially proud of Ch. Cote de Neige Rush Hour, five of whose puppies were titleholders. Rush Hour's dam and granddam both are on the top-producing list of the Pembroke club. To be named, a bitch must have at least six offspring champions. Only about 15 have been listed in the last three decades.

"The Corgi, in Wales, is used to herd cattle, nipping at their heels to move them along. I have sold two to farmers and they both have done a good job in moving the cows."

Best in Show at Westminster

The names of the late James A. Farrell, Jr., and his Foxden Kennel were synonymous with Smooth Fox Terriers over more than four decades. But it was a pair of Lakeland Terriers, the first two he ever owned, who were to bring the greatest glory to this dedicated breeder, exhibitor, club official and judge. They were Ch. Stingray of Derryabah, and his son, Ch. Special Edition.

I interviewed Mr. Farrell at a Bronx show. It had been a long day and he was quite exhausted, so we retired to his limousine and there we talked. He was enthusiastic about Stingray, telling me, "Last year when Mrs. Farrell and I were in England, we heard of a Lakeland who was causing quite a stir. We never had a Lakie and thought it might be nice to have a good one for a change. Stingray had won 12 challenge certificates and three bests in show. Then we heard he was for sale and immediately put a binder on him. The Postlewaites, who owned him, asked if they could keep him until after Crufts, since they felt he had a chance to take the group. I agreed. He not only won the group but was best of 6,845 dogs." The next year Stingray won the silverware at Westminster, in the last dog event held at the Garden on Eighth Avenue — best in show at Crufts and Westminster in successive years!

His son, Special Edition, a red-grizzle and tan, was another great one, some fanciers believing he was superior to his famous sire. I could never get the Farrells to tell me who they considered the better.

Mr. Farrell started his judging career in 1938, when he ruled on Smooth Fox Terriers at Westbury. He judged at most of the major events over the years, and in 1953 and 1966 chose the best at Westminster. He became a member of Westminster in 1944 and was president of that club from 1972 till 1975, when poor health forced him to step down. He died in 1978.

Of indomitable spirit, despite physical ailments, in his last years he was at ringsides in a wheelchair. Always a competitor, he would be cheering for his dog, but ever the sportsman, if his dog wasn't chosen, he usually would have a good word for the winner.

Having seen Walter F. Goodman show the Skye Terriers he owned with his mother, Mrs. Adele Goodman, so successfully for almost four decades, I particularly look forward to seeing him judge. Walter got his license in 1977.

The Goodmans bought their first Skye in 1935 but it wasn't until 1947, the year Walter graduated from Yale, that they had their first champion, High Time Testy. Walter had picked High Time Testy out of a litter when she was a three-month-old pup. She became the first American-bred Skye to take a best in show in the United States. Goodman then took her to France in 1952, and she was best of breed in Paris. She went on to win an international championship.

The Glamoor Kennel for years was the top-winning Skye establishment in America. It bred or owned 35 champions who captured best-in-show awards 95 times. First it was a French import, Ch. Evening Star, who held the record for triumphs by a Skye, with 21 top prizes. Then Ch. Jacinthe de Ricelaine became the record-holder, with 35. A homebred, Ch. Glamoor Good News hit the jackpot for the mother-son team, Walter gaiting her to best at Westminster in 1969, the first and only representative of her breed to take the classic. She captured the silverware 12 other times. "I have only one regret," said Walter, "I never saw Jackie or Suzie (Good News) from the side as a spectator." Goodman, who gained an award as the top owner-handler, was always handling, of course.

He maintained that an amateur, with perseverance, training and hard work, could compete successfully with the pro. "Before the exhibitor goes to a show, he should spend hours preparing and working his dog," said Walter. His Skyes were always meticulously groomed with not a hair out of line. Bob Forsyth, one of the leading professionals, admitted no handler could put a Skye down to match Goodman. "We just haven't the time to spend the hours grooming one dog," Bob explained.

Before he began to judge, Walter had some very decided views on arbiters. "Judges are just too nice and don't withhold ribbons," he said. "In an ordinary class, this may be all right. However, when you come to winners dog or winners bitch, where points are involved, there may be a rare occasion when a ribbon should be withheld if the animal isn't of real quality." Goodman also pleaded for smaller shows with more quality dogs. Instead of breeding on a big scale, he urged the breeder to strive to produce better puppies. "When he has a good pup to develop a winner, it means work, work, work," said Goodman.

There are few fanciers who know more about terriers than Barbara Keenan. She had her first champion, when she was 14 years old. By 1975, when she cut back in showing, she had owned or bred 100 titleholders, including 15 best-in-show Westies, more than any other Highlander breeder ever had accomplished in the United States.

When we started to reminisce at a luncheon in 1978, I asked her what she thought of the current crop of terriers. Barbara shook her head sadly and replied, "The terriers, overall, are at a low ebb in both America and Britain. There are a few good ones, of course, but we lack depth. It's not like the old days."

Mrs. Keenan also stressed that records mean very little. "They don't make a great dog," she maintained. "Many good dogs are wasted because they are owned by people who cannot afford to campaign them. It's a costly hobby today, if you are doing the showing, what with the high entry fees, gasoline, food and motels. It actually is cheaper to have a handler, which is a pity for you miss the sport of going to the shows, handling and the family doesn't have a chance to participate."

It was pure chance that started Barbara in West Highland White Terriers. "When I was 13 my mother promised to get me a Scottie, so we drove to Concord (N.H.) to Mrs. John Winant's kennel. She didn't have any Scottie pups but did have an 11-month-old Westie bitch and we left with her." The bitch,

Wishing Well Belinda, not only finished but she gave the kennel a great start, producing five champions.

But the future Mrs. Keenan wasn't satisfied. She wanted a really top Westie. So she and her mother went to England and came back with Ch. Cruben Melphis Chloe, who won the breed at Westminster and was the dam of the great Ch. Cruben Dextor. "I've always felt Dextor was my best Westie," she said. "He was so good that judges began to take a second look at the breed. Not only was he best in show three times but he sired 29 champions. Most of the Westies in New England today go back to him."

By the time Barbara was 26, she had added Kerry Blues and Wire Fox Terriers to Wishing Well, and she was so active in the sport that she had two handlers, Henry Sayres in the East and George Ward in the Midwest. She also already had 22 champions. It was Ward who gaited her Ch. Elfinbrook Simon to best at Westminster in 1962. "He wasn't even going to show Simon," she recalled. "But Ric Chashoudian was driving East from California, with a string, and stopped at Ward's in Michigan. He persuaded George to accompany him."

Taking in Borders

The Border Terrier, which originated in the north of England's Cheviot Hills border country, was bred to hunt the fox. In America, it is among the rarest of the terrier breeds. Mrs. George H. Seeman of South Norwalk, Conn., has been one of the most successful with the Border in this country.

"In the late forties, we used them for hunting woodchuck and fox," she recalled. Golden Fancy, whom the Connecticut breeder bought in Scotland, made history for the Borders in America. Bred four times, she produced a total of 15 puppies and five of them became champions. At the age of seven, Fancy was put in a class for the first time. "We had a pup for whom we were trying to get some points, so we felt Fancy was another body," recalled her mistress. Not only did the seven-year-old beat the pup but she was best of breed for 5 points. The next weekend, she had two more 5-pointers to finish. "Each year, I'd go to England and try and buy the best I could find," said Mrs. Seeman. "I imported a half-dozen champions and they all gained championships in this country, as well." Then at Elmira, 1977, Mrs. Seeman reached the pinnacle with Ch. Workman Waggoner, when he became the first Border to ever gain a BIS in the United States.

The top-winning dog the Seemans ever owned, however, wasn't a Border but a West Highland White Terrier. He was Ch. Braidholme White Tornado of Binate, better known as Nikki. The little white-coat, the first ever owned by the Seemans, was imported from England in 1973 after he had been best in show at Birmingham. Handled by Cliff Hallmark, he became an American title holder at Montgomery County, where he was chosen over 31 champions. Nikki gained his first best in show in the United States, when he led a field of 3,566 at Philadelphia. "We never in our wildest dreams ever expected to own a best-in-show dog," said Mrs. Seeman. "We were in the Bahamas when we heard the news. George ran up and down the pier, where we had our boat, bragging to anyone who would listen. He likes to hunt and never cared too much for show dogs until Nikki came along. Then, when we were fishing in the Bahamas, he would call home every Monday to find out what happened over the weekend. George couldn't wait until he could get the papers, so he could add Nikki's clippings to our scrap book."

Taking in Boarders

"There's nothing closer to the Garden of Eden than a yardful of Airedales," said Betty Hoisington of Cordova, Tenn., "so we named our kennel Eden. Since the garden had to have flowers, we named our dogs accordingly." So they have had Eden's Spring Gentian, Eden's Freesia, Eden's Flower of Stone Ridge, Eden's Philadelphus, Eden's Spring Hepatica. Ch. Bengal Springtime, whom the Hoisingtons imported from Britain, was the leading terrier in England, that land of terriers, in 1969, where she had won 15 challenge certificates and nine best in shows. She finished here in three shows.

Like so many others, the Tennesseans started in obedience and they still are active with the educated set. Terriers generally are considered a bit difficult to train for degrees but the first Airedale they acquired earned her CD in three straight shows and her CDX nine months later. Meanwhile, she also gained her show championship.

When I asked Bob, who has been active for two decades, to evaluate the breeds for their ability in obedience, he said, "The working and sporting dogs basically make the highest scores, which indicates a greater capacity for training. Hounds are too interested in what comes natural to them—sniffing. Terriers are inclined to be too curious and are more interested in what's going on around them. Toys are the most difficult, since owners tend to coddle them. In training there are exceptions in all breeds. I have found the Basenji one of the most difficult. He resents regimentation."

The Hoisingtons own a plush boarding kennel replete with air-conditioning, electronic filters, indoor carpeting, music. There's even closed-circuit TV, so the kennel can be monitored from the house. Each inside run is color coordinated, a different color with carpeting to match. "It's easier to remember the dogs when you associate the color runs in which you have placed them," said Hoisington.

"Frequently people leave elaborate instructions. We had a German Shepherd left with us, along with four pages of feeding instructions. The owners brought 10 pounds of raw liver, cans of sardines and tuna fish, and we were told to spoon feed him. We tried the goodies for two days and he refused them. Then we used the regular diet with the food all the other dogs were getting and he gobbled it. Frequently, people will leave a dog with us and worry about whether it is happy and eating. Then they come for the dog and are annoyed when it isn't anxious to go home."

229

Sealys of Approval

In the early seventies, a little Sealyham was sweeping much of the Eastern circuit. He was Ch. Jenmist Dougal, owned by Mrs. Henry Sutliff of Richmond, Va. When the white-coat was named best of 2,736 dogs at Harrisburg, Pa., I phoned to congratulate her. "That's the tenth time Dougal has been best and I have yet to see him do it," she admitted. Al Ayers, who was handling the Sealy, said, "This time I thought the Sutliffs would see us. They were at the show earlier, when Dougal won the national specialty, and left to attend the Sealyham Club meeting and dinner and never returned."

Mrs. Sutliff, describing her start in the sport, said, "As a child, in California, I had a Sealyham and he was a great pet. After I married, we had a succession of dogs—Collies, English Springers, Beagles and Dachshunds. In 1961, I told Hank I would like a Sealyham and that Christmas he gave me Rinkelstone Tam O'Shanter." Tammy quickly gained her title as did Robin Hill Brigette, who was bought the next year. They were the foundation bitches for this highly successful Sealy kennel. Brastedchart Seascourt, a champion in England and the United States, was best of breed at Westminster three years in a row, starting in 1965. Ch. Sutliff Mame of Mannin took the honors in 1968 and Dougal in 1970.

Asked if Dougal was the best dog she owned, Mrs. Sutliff replied, "He's the best anyone's ever owned."

The trophy room in the air-conditioned model kennel is overflowing. "We have seven coffee services and 17 water pitchers," said Mrs. Sutliff. And what was her greatest thrill in the sport, Dougal taking which best? "No, it wasn't a Dougal win; it was when Ch. Sutliff's Onondaga was best of breed and fourth in the group. You see, she was my own breeding."

From Down Under to On Top

The Australian Terrier wasn't listed in the AKC stud book until 1960 and it was largely through the efforts of Mrs. Nell Fox and her late husband, Milton, that the breed broke through then.

Mrs. Fox was given her first Aussie when she was 13. After coming to the United States and marrying, Nell and her husband decided they'd get an Australian Terrier. However, there were very few of the breed in the country and those they saw all were sandy colored. "Although I have no preference now," said Mrs. Fox, "I remembered the blue-tan pup I had when I was a child in Australia. In order to get one, we finally imported an Aussie from England. Then we went to the home base itself, and brought several from Australia."

Since the breed wasn't on the AKC championship list, it could only be shown in the miscellaneous class. However, it could be shown in obedience. So in order to gain as much exposure as possible for the Aussie, the Foxes turned to obedience. "Their twists and turns might not earn the highest scores but they certainly amused the ringsiders, who invariably would ask us about them," said Nell. Her Willelva Wanderer, in 1961 became the first Australian Terrier in the United States to win an obedience degree, getting a CD.

The Foxes traveled to many events in the East and as far west as Chicago, to give as much exposure to the breed as they could. Whenever they sold a dog, they would ask the purchaser to show it. They did such a good public relations job that there were 44 of the breed entered in the miscellaneous class at Westminster in 1959 and a whopping 58 the next year.

Mrs. Fox keeps an average of 50 dogs at her Pleasant Pasture Kennels in Point Pleasant, N.J. She has bred or owned more than 90 champions.

Star of the kennel was Tinee Town Talkbac, who was a champion in Australia, the United States, Colombia, Mexico, Canada, Bermuda and an FCI international titleholder. Before being imported from Australia, Joey, as he was called, was the top-winning terrier and greatest winning show dog of all Down Under breeds. He had been best in show 11 times in his native land, and he had taken 64 groups. Joey also had accumulated 97 challenge certificates. In this country, before he was retired in 1976, he had been best in show four times, had won 27 blue rosettes, as well as 46 other placements, and taken four specialties.

I well remember his first best. It was in February, 1973, at Providence, and was held in the clubhouse of a racetrack. The snow was a foot deep and it was a chore to drive to the show. Mrs. Fox was so excited, she had difficulty in giving me the little dog's record. "That did it," she said. "It is the first time an Aussie in the East has ever taken a best in the United States. It's a dream I've had since 1944, when I established Pleasant Pastures".

Wheatie Champion

It was while exercising her Old English Sheepdog that Ruth Stein first heard about the Soft Coated Wheaten Terrier. "I had been given the bobtail as a gift," said Ruth, "and I was rather fed up with the breed. Brush, brush and brush. Then a stranger, whom I met while I was walking with my Old English and who listened to my tale of woe about all the grooming, suggested I look at a Wheaten."

So the Steins bought a book describing the breed, saw an ad in *The New York Times* and wound up getting an eight-week-old bitch. "My little pup was no show dog but she proved to be a wonderful brood bitch," said Ruth. "As she developed, she had tremendous bone and the very dark eye so desirable in the breed."

Over the years, the bitch had five litters and from the second came Raclee's Serendipity, the first Stein homebred champion. Since the breed wasn't recognized by the AKC until October 1973, Serendipity, or Bridgett as she was known to the Steins, owners of the Raclee Kennel, at the beginning could only compete in the miscellaneous class. In 30 outings, she had 26 first places. "All we would get was a rose ribbon," said Ruth, "but we were doing the missionary work for the breed, giving it exposure, so it became known." Bridgett became the sixth Wheaten champion, finishing with four majors.

Bridgett produced four champions, including Raclee's Express West O'Andover, the winner of a dozen groups and the first national specialty. "That's a day I'll never forget," said Ruth. "The best, best of opposite and the best brood bitch were all Raclee breeding. That's a breeder's dream."

Mrs. Stein is a former president of the Soft Coated Wheaten Terrier Club of Metropolitan New York. Organized in 1971 by six fanciers, in 1978 it had 115 members. Grooming, handling and conditioning symposiums are held regularly and twice a year, there is a workshop for breeders, attendance at which is required in order to be on the club's list of breeders. After a litter has been whelped, one or more of the directors visit the owner and help to evaluate the pups.

Nine Crowns

Most fanciers are delighted if they have a champion in one breed. Allan Sheimo has titleholders in nine. "I guess I just like dogs," said the Chicagoan, "for with all of the dogs I've owned or bred, I've sold exactly one in 16 years. If I find I have too many, I'll give one or two to friends but only when I'm certain they are going to good homes." Sheimo is best known for his Bedlingtons, having had the first top-winning liver-colored Bedlington in the United States—Ch. Titica's Gay Cinnamon Cindy.

According to her owner, she not only was the leading liver bitch in 1972 but the No. 1 Bedlington bitch and in 1973 the top-winning of all terrier bitches. Shown 101 times, Cindy was best Bedlington on 94 occasions, had 78 group placements, including 28 firsts and twice captured the silverware. "Cindy did a great deal for the liver color," explained Sheimo. "She's the only liver ever to take a best in show in this country. In 1973, I traveled 60,000 miles with her, of which 45,000 were by car and I hate to drive. At show after show, she would be the only liver. All you saw were blues. I was breeding for 13 years before I came up with Cindy and both her sire and dam were blues."

Allan also is active in club work. He is a former board member of the Bedlington Terrier Club of America and a founder of the Bedlington Terrier Club of Greater Chicago. In 1975, he was campaigning dogs in six other breeds, as well—Dandie Dinmonts, Scottish and West Highland White Terriers, Miniature Schnauzers, Dalmatians and Papillons. As to preferences: "I like a bitch as a house dog, but it's easier to win with a dog," said the Chicago fancier.

Airedale Royalty

In a pre-Revolutionary War house, in which George Washington might have slept, lives Countess Ercilia LeNy. It is in Milford, N.J., in the Delaware Valley, and to reach the house you drive over a small bridge, spanning a stream that flows into the Delaware. Adjacent to the 200-year-old house is the Querencia Kennel. The Countess, who comes from New Orleans, and has a doctorate in philosophy, started her kennel in 1959.

"I went to Westminster, watched the Airedales being judged, and wound up buying Bengal Kresent Duchess of Harham, a champion in the United States and

England," she recalled. The Duchess became the Querencia foundation bitch. From her first litter of six puppies, four became champions and the fifth lacked only one point. "The trouble was that I kept breeding Airedales," said the Querencia mistress, "and I couldn't bear to sell the puppies. Before I knew it, I had 45 dogs."

In its heyday, the kennel had 15 champions. Ch. Querencia's Suerte Brava was the pacemaker. Lucky, as he was called, took the Montgomery County specialty in 1962, when he was only 13 months old. Four months later he won the terrier group at Westminster. The Airedale, a great showman, captured the silverware three times in 1963 and was retired the next year. Lucky was his owner's favorite and he lived to be 14 years old. In 1973, when he was almost 12, I remember seeing him roaming over the 60 acres, king of the kennel. "He thinks he's a fisherman," said the Countess. "He runs into the brook and tries to catch trout."

The same year, the kennel had its first best-in-show winner in a decade. This time it wasn't an Airedale but a Lakeland, Ch. Tarnbreck Cassius. It was not a lean and hungry Cassius but rather a gay and friendly little terrier whom the Countess bought at Crufts in 1972. Campaigned sparingly, he scored his greatest victory at Trenton, in 1975, when he led a field of 3,677.

The Countess, who hadn't shown an Airedale in years, showed she hadn't lost her touch, when she gaited Ch. Querencia's Rudolfo to second in the group in Mexico City at the opening show held in conjunction with the FCI meeting in 1978. Like all Querencia dogs, Rudy understands both Spanish and English. Called *guaps* (beautiful), he immediately prances and *vamanos* (let's go) sends him flying to the door.

Triumphant Terriers

In the summer of 1974, I was going to the Coast to cover Santa Barbara and Ventura. Since I never had been to the Northwest, I decided to visit that area and cover some kennels. James Trullinger told me he had just returned from Calgary, in Canada, where he had given a Dandie Dinmont from the United States a best in show. It was a lead for a story but first I had to find the owner.

Looking through old catalogues I was reminded of Jeannine Dowell and called her. She remembered me from a show in Memphis and I told her I was flying to Seattle. "Do you know the name of the owner of a Dandie who just took three bests in Calgary?" I asked. There was a silence, then she replied, "Are you serious or are you pulling my leg?" When I assured her I was serious, she burst into laughter, "It's me," she said. So, early in the summer, Vera and I flew to Seattle and Jeannine was at the airport to meet us. The next day, we visited Jeannine and her husband, Steve, and met Ch. Graymorn's Hoot O'Dowell, a mustard-colored dog who had finished the previous year at the national specialty, when he was 13 months old. The next March, Hootie was shown for the first time in Canada, where he had been whelped, and at Evergreen was named best Canadian-bred in show.

"Twenty days later," said Jeannine, "Steve and I were celebrating our wedding anniversary, when Hootie took best in show at Shoreline." After another top prize in British Columbia, the little dog rang up the consecutive triple that had led me to him.

The Dowells had been pioneers with the breed on the West Coast, having the first litter of Dandies ever whelped in Washington. When Mrs. Dowell began to judge, she started to phase out her kennel. "It was the hardest decision I've ever had to make," she admitted, "I love Dandies and enjoy breeding. However, I don't believe a judge should show. Hootie was my last showdog."

Patience Rewarded

To the fancier who takes a dog to a show, wins a ribbon or two but never enough for the animal to become a champion, Mrs. Harry Quick of Chicago Heights, Ill., should serve as an inspiration. For 17 years she struggled until she finally made it. "I bought a black Standard Poodle in 1950," she told me, "and she picked up a few points, enough to encourage me to continue. Then I bought some Toys and Miniatures. I enjoyed showing and I did some breeding but never had any real success." In 1967, she married Dr. Quick, a veterinarian in small-animal practice. "In no time at all, I had my first champion and this time it was the easy way," she said. "My husband bought me a best-in-show Miniature Schnauzer, Ch. Moore's Max Derkleiner."

With the veterinarian's knowledge of genetics, the couple then worked up a selective breeding program for their Valharra Kennel. "We decided to cross two California Miniature Schnauzer lines—Allaruth and Arador. So we bought Allaruth's Daniel and Ch. Faerwynd of Arador," said the attractive Illinois blonde. Daniel finished undefeated in the breed when he was only 13 months old. Faerwynd already was a proven brood bitch, with three champions from her first litter.

Bred to Daniel, Faerwynd produced Valharra's Dionysos. Brought out when he was seven months old, at the Indianapolis specialty in 1970, Dionysos took the sweepstakes. Since he did so well, the Quicks decided he should have a chance to compete at Westminster, but he needed a point. So they flew him to the Coast, where he was shown in a puppy class in Carbillo. And they received a pleasant surprise, for he went all the way from the puppy class to best of breed. At Riverside, Calif., he was best of winners and he finished at Milwaukee. The pup came on to Westminster and took the breed, beating 15 specials.

It was the famous American artist, Edward Marshall Boehm, who opened the door into the world of dogs for Ollie and Bill Moore. "He was a neighbor of ours," said Ollie. "I knew Bill liked dogs and Boehm had Miniature Schnauzers, so I bought one." Moore liked it so much that the couple quickly acquired a couple more of the bewhiskered dogs.

From that start came the Travelmor Kennel, which over the years has enjoyed so much success. Reminisced Bill, "Boehm kept after us and in November,

1959, I made my debut as an exhibitor with Yankee Southern Colonel. I was scared stiff. The Colonel wanted no part of the ring, and we didn't even get a fourth place." All the next spring, either Bill or Ollie was at a show with one of the pepper-and-salt dogs and always with the same result—another defeat.

"It got to be so discouraging we were just about ready to give up," said Ollie. "At Rose Tree, we had a talk with George Hartman, the great terrier judge. He looked at some of our dogs, assured us they were of show quality and encouraged us to keep on. That day, with Frank Foster Davis judging, our Yankee Pattern Maker went from the open to best of breed. We have done a lot of winning since then but nothing could equal that thrill. To add to the excitement, our Yankee Squadron Leader took the reserve ribbon. Boehm had given me Squadron Leader as a gift, saying, "I bet you can't make a champion of him." By the end of the summer, the artist had lost his bet. He was so impressed with the progress the Moores had made that when he decided to get out of the sport, he gave them his whole kennel.

In the '70s Ollie received her judge's license and Travelmor sharply curtailed its showing. Now it is Judgemor and Showless.

Manchester Enthusiast

For three decades Ruth Turner has been extolling the virtues of the Standard Manchester Terrier. And with good cause, for she has bred some great ones. It all started in 1946, when the resident of Newtown Square, Pa., bought what she thought was a Toy Manchester to cheer her ailing husband. The Toy grew to be a Standard and in time the Turners began to show her. "We went to shows for two years," recalled Ruth, "and she could never get any points for there was no competition. There just weren't any Standard Manchesters. Finally we bred her and kept three puppies. Then we bought some good stock from Fred McLean in Ottawa and from Rudolph Branley in Chicago. That gave us three different bloodlines." Now the Turners had enough Manchesters to begin making champions. They would enter Terriers from all three lines to see which the judges preferred.

The Turners were able to breed the black and tans judges liked but the standard Manchester never appealed too much to the public. As a result, Mrs. Turner began to breed the Toy variety. Although Mrs. Turner kept her show activities largely within a 150-mile radius of her home, occasionally she would travel so others could see the breed. I watched her show her Chatham's Mitzie, a multi best-in-show winner, to best Terrier at the Puerto Rico fixture in 1966. At the time, the Pennsylvanian had 70 Manchesters, the largest kennel of the breed in America.

Now Ruth is busy judging and does a minimum of breeding. "The Manchester is such a good watch dog, so intelligent, clean and easy to groom, I cannot understand why it never has been more popular," she said. Certainly she has done everything she can to make it so.

235

Kay Jeffords

When Walter M. Jeffords, Jr. gave his wife, Kay, a Boston Terrier as a birthday present in 1966, little did either think it would be the start of a kennel that 12 years later would have more than 100 dogs.

"My life was very simple until I joined show forces with Michael Wolf in 1972," Mrs. Jeffords told me. "At the time I had only one Pekingese and three or four Bostons."

The Jeffords-Wolf team came up with some very good dogs over the years. "The greatest thrills I had in the sport," Kay recalled, "was watching our Peke, Bernard (Ch. Yan Kee Bernard) take the Group at Westminster in 1976 and our Boston (Ch. Jeffords' Abigail) go best at Philadelphia the next year. It was the biggest win for a Boston in some time."

At their Fifth Avenue apartment in New York (which was previously owned by Bernard Baruch), the Jeffords keep only three Pekes. "When I take them for a walk," she said, "they attract so much attention it takes me as much as a half-hour just to go around the block."

Walter Jeffords, who has a winning stable of his own, is a nephew of Samuel Riddle, who owned the legendary Man O' War. Kay is a daughter of George McLaughlin, who was a key figure in New York banking circles and who served for a time as the city's police commissioner.

The Jeffords' sporting interests are reflected in the tasteful display of priceless racing trophies in the living room of their Manhattan apartment. There is also a collection of bronze horses, and a dozen bronzes of dogs. Among the paintings is an oil of an English Springer Spaniel by Philip Reinagle that had been exhibited at the British Royal Academy in 1845.

In 1979, Kay began reducing the number of dogs maintained at her kennels in Christiana, Pa. At the same time, she embarked on a new phase of participation in the sport. At the Penn Treaty show, she took a dog in the ring herself for the first time - and it was a successful debut for both handler and dog. "We had winners dog for a point," she proudly told me. And was she nervous competing against the professional handlers? "Not at all." she said, "I was in there to enjoy myself, and that's just what I did." Indeed, she enjoyed showing so much, she quickly was back at three more fixtures, each time gaiting her little dog to winners. "Most fun I've had since I've been going to shows," she laughingly reported.

The Gregorys

Mrs. Joseph Gregory, better known among the show set as Mamie, has had a variety of dogs over the years, of which many were champions. "I was brought up in a doggy family," she said. "My father [the late Senator Robert Rice Reynolds of North Carolina] had Doberman Pinschers and when we were in Washington bought me a Cocker Spaniel. I started to handle when I was eight years old. By the time I was 10, I had shown my Cocker to a championship." As a teenager, Mamie had a white Miniature Poodle. "If you didn't have a Poodle, you were a nobody,'' she laughingly recalled, ''but being away at school, I didn't have much chance to show her.''

The first big winner was a Chow Chow, Ch. Lakeview's Hansum. Shown by Gregory, he had 13 best-in-show trophies, 70 groups and three years in a row took the specialty. In 1968, Hansum won the ''Supreme Chow Chow'' award. The next year, a 15-inch Beagle, Ch. Jennie John's Jr., brought fame and silverware to his owner, taking best on 13 occasions. ''We then bought a Brussels Griffon, Gaystock Lemonseigner,'' recalled Mrs. Gregory, ''and Ziggy not only became a champion but he took over the household.'' Ziggy also became the official mascot for the Kentucky Colonels of the now-defunct American Basketball Association. Gregory owned the club and Ziggy had a uniform with No.1.

But it was another Toy, a Maltese—Ch. Joanne-Chen's Maya Dancer, who probably was the greatest dog owned by the couple. The six-pound white bitch was best in show more than 30 times and won almost 100 groups, twice receiving the Ken-L Ration award as top Toy of the year. I was covering International, in 1971, the show Mamie said gave her the greatest thrill she ever had in the sport. ''Maya had taken the group but neither Joe nor I thought she had a chance in the final. Our plane was leaving at 8:30 that evening, so we packed our bags and took them to the Amphitheater with us. We started to leave for the airport and were going down the stairs, when we heard over the public address system that Maya was best in show. We rushed back. Joe was so excited he had three suits over his arm and a bag. He put the bag down and someone stole it. They handed me the trophy. I put it down and it also disappeared, although it was sent to us a couple of months later.''

''The Twins''

For more than two decades if you asked a judge which was the top Yorkshire Terrier kennel in America, invariably you would get the same reply, ''The one owned by the twins in the Midwest.'' The twins are Janet Bennett and Mrs. Joan Gordon of Glenview, Ill. How much they dominated the Yorkie rings is evidenced in the AKC records. Their Wildweir Kennel, whose first champion finished in 1950, had at this writing in 1979 bred or owned 174 titleholders of which 36 had won 407 Toy groups and 15 captured a total of 64 best in shows. Their Ch. Wildweir Pomp 'n Circumstance sired 95 champions, including three best-in-show winners. Both Miss Bennett and her sister do all their own handling, refuting the charge so often made that it is necessary to have a professional handler.

When I asked how the twins started in the sport, they replied, ''We were still at school, when we went to the International show in Chicago. We saw some Yorkies and it was love at first sight. We bought what we thought was a showdog but we soon learned otherwise.'' That was in 1949, when the breed stood 96th on the AKC list. Unless an owner had a potential group winner, it was extremely difficult to run up enough points to become a champion. ''We wrote to a breeder we knew in England, in 1950, and he bought us our first really good Yorkie,'' said Mrs. Gordon. ''He was Little Sir Model and he not only was our first champion but the first Yorkie to win an all-breed best in show.'' Model did a great deal to make the breed known. The twins showed him extensively; he was best Yorkie 63 times and had three other top awards. They imported other good ones, set up a carefully studied breeding program and traveled from coast to coast, so the public could see Yorkies. They proved good missionaries, for by 1979 the breed ranked 14th of the 124 listed and was the most popular of the Toys.

They both had great affection for their Ch. Star Twilight of Clu-mor, an Irish bred. This little dog was best in show 26 times, won 81 Toy groups, was best Yorkie 104 times and took the breed at Westminster four years in a row, starting in 1953. He also captured blue rosettes in the Garden in 1954 and 1955. Twice he and Model took best brace at International.

The influence Wildweir has had on the breed is international for dogs of its breeding have won championships in Canada, Bermuda, Mexico, Argentina, Brazil and Colombia.

Mayfair

Two Gilbert and Sullivan enthusiasts, Ann Seranne and Barbara Wolferman, have the very model of a modern canine kennel in their Mayfair Yorkie House at Newton, N.J.

The 64-by-24 foot building has an eight-foot wide carpeted corridor running down the middle, which is used to exercise and train puppies. There are eight indoor carpeted stalls, with sliding glass doors, leading to 6-by-8 foot screened and roofed runs. Ultra-red lamps provide heat during the winter. ''With carpets, we have no fear of a pup slipping,'' said Ann. ''As a result, with all the running they do, their leg muscles are strengthened and there is freedom of motion. This, in turn, leads to a beautiful topline, when they mature.''

The kennel has a kitchen that would be the envy of any housewife. This isn't too strange, since Miss Seranne is the author of some two dozen cookbooks and during World War II she headed a plant that processed foods for the armed forces.

Ann started with Yorkies when she bought Ch. Topsy of Tolestar, who had been best of breed at Westminster in 1962. ''I was living in New York at the time,'' she recalled. ''I bought others, began to breed and one day realized I had 18. Meanwhile, I had met Barbara Wolferman, who for years had Yorkies as pets. I persuaded her to go to a dog show and she quickly became converted to the sport. We decided to move to Jersey, where we could buy some land and build a kennel.'' So what began as a one-dog establishment now has grown until there are more than 50 Mayfair-Barban representatives on their Newton estate high on a hill overlooking the Pocono Mountains.

There have been some great performers over the years, starting with Ch. Dandy Diamond of Mayfair, the kennel's first homebred titleholder. His son, Ch. Mayfair's Oddfella was a multi-group winner and Gaytonglen Teddy of

Mayfair, a champion in the United States and Canada, four times was best in show, as well as winning 26 groups, two national specialties and siring 22 champions. He was the grandsire of Ch. Mayfair Barban Loup de Mer, a six-pounder who was No. 1 Yorkie in 1974 and 1975, a multi best-in-show and group winner.

Yorkie House is a bit of a misnomer, since Mayfair-Barban had done some exceptional winning with Standard Poodles. Ch. Alekai Luau, before he was retired, had 15 best in shows, six specialties and 67 group victories. But it is Yorkies for which Ann and Barbara are known. A half-dozen other kennels have based their breeding on Mayfair-Barban bloodlines.

Some Turns to the East

For 800 years the Hatori family crest has been an oak leaf and saber. "I've seen it on tombstones over the graves of my ancestors in Tokyo," said Frank Hatori, a realtor and member of the Seattle planning commission. Now the symbol and the name is known not only in the city of seven hills in Washington but on the entire West Coast and Western Canada. For the Oaksaber Kennel has sent out some top Yorkshire Terriers. In a stretch of seven years, the Hatoris took six top championships in the United States and Canada.

"Although Frank and I were born in Washington," said Mrs. Hatori, "we turned to Japan for the name of one of our dogs. That's Oaksaber Invincia Yoko Zuna. This little dog has been the Yuko Zuna of Yorkies for us." The six-pounder was a mighty big little dog. It took him only two weeks to finish and he gained his Canadian championship, with four best of breeds. Ch. Oaksaber Executive Eagle, a littermate, the Satoris affectionately called Ozeki. "That's the title of the sumo junior grand champion, second only to Yoko Zuna," explained Mrs. Hatori.

However, the pride of the kennel was Ch. Oaksaber Double Eagle. "Agnes is Oaksaber," said Hatori. "She plans the breeding and showing. I'm just the chauffeur. Golf is my sport. Any duffer will tell you that an eagle (two under par) is pretty good golf. When it came time to name our pup, he looked so good, I suggested Double Eagle."

I covered the national specialty in 1973 when Dee, as he was called on the circuit, triumphed in an entry of 136. The breeder judge told me in 25 years he could count on the fingers of his two hands the Yorkies he had seen who were the true dark steel blue and the rich golden tan and that Dee really conformed to what was called for in the standard.

Agnes is one of the most gracious fanciers I've had the good fortune to meet. When I wrote about the Hatori success story, several jealous fanciers were unduly vicious about the Seattle breeder. In her gentle way she merely said, "The kennel is strictly a hobby with me. At one time I considered not showing, just breeding. Yorkies have given Frank and me so much pleasure. I thought I'd just raise pups and give them to friends so they, too, could share in the pleasure and love." We could use more Agnes Hatoris in the world of show dogs.

Ruth Aston is a woman with a mission. For almost two decades she has been doing research on the Chin breeds. "In this country," she said, "only the Japanese Chin really is known. However, it is but one of eight types of the breed called the Chin in the Orient. At present I have three Chinese Imperial Chin. They have short legs and duck feet. The Japanese consider this the most beautiful variety. They are very deliberate and slow-gaited." Another variety is the Chinese Temple Dog, extremely rare even in his homeland. According to Mrs. Aston, he's massive, heavy-boned, dignified, with an outsized head, tremendous chest and a white ruff that makes him resemble a lion.

It was in Taiwan the fancier obtained her first Chin. Her husband, Col. David Aston, was assistant military attache at the United States Embassy. "We had an all-black that was Mme. Chiang Kai-shek's breeding," she said. "An old Chinese scholar told us he had seen the Imperial Chin in the court of the Dowager Empress, Tsu Hsi. She had 50 of them. They were trained so when she appeared, they would divide into two groups to form a lane, stand on their hind legs and kow-tow to her until she reached her throne."

Before the Astons were sent to Taiwan, they attended the United States Army Language School at the Presidio in Monterey, Calif. "I was the first woman to be accepted in the Far Eastern language section," said Ruth. In 1962, the Colonel was transferred to Greece. "Our Imperial Chin escaped from our walled yard and was killed by an automobile," said Mrs. Aston. Reassigned to Taiwan, the couple came up with one—a black-and-white brocade, with black mask.

The Colonel, now retired, and Ruth live in Gouldsborough, Me., where they have developed a kennel of Oriental dogs. Among them is a Japanese Chin sleeve bitch, which is one of the smallest dogs in this country. She is six inches high and weighs two pounds. "We feed her six times a day. She gets a teaspoon of chopped liver and a teaspoon of Koolianh wine," said her mistress. "I have bred 14 Chinese Temple Dogs, and I hope to establish the breed in America. Perhaps we even will get one with a black dot on its head. That's called the thumbprint of Buddha and an old-fashioned Oriental will bow to the sacred dog."

Best in Show for Openers

The Oriental is known for his patience. So also is his dog. For a decade the Shih Tzu was barking at the door of the AKC but it was not until 1969 that he finally was heard and admitted as the 116th breed in the stud book. It was a long climb for the little dog, whose name in Chinese means lion, and a devoted flock of breeders led by an Episcopal cleric, the Rev. D. Allan Easton, then the rector of St. Paul's Church in Wood-Ridge, N.J., and his wife.

The clergyman, who retired in 1976 and moved to Gardiner, N.Y., was serving a parish in Peking in 1947 when he saw his first Shih Tzu, the pet of the Chinese Imperial Court of another age. He tried to buy one but was unsuccessful. Reverend Easton returned to Scotland in the fifties and decided that he would get a breed that had originated in the East. "Actually, I wound up with two breeds, with a pair of Tibetan Terriers and a pair of Pekingese."

240

In 1961, he accepted a call from the parish in New Jersey. There he heard about a Pennsylvania breeder of the lion dog. "I had to come to America to get my first Shih Tzu," he recalled. Since then he has imported several and engaged in an extensive breeding program. One of his imports was Tangra v. Tschomoa-Lungma, a gold-and-white from West Germany who was a Swiss and Czechoslovak champion, when she arrived here. The clergyman, who has a summer home in Nova Scotia, showed her at St. John, N.B., where she not only was best of breed but took third in the group.

The star of the Easton kennel was Ch. Chumulari Ying Ying, a gold-and-white who lived up to his name. Chumulari is the name of a sacred Tibetan mountain, near Everest, and Ying-Ying is Chinese for brilliant. The little dog scaled the heights brilliantly, when he was named best in show at the New Brunswick, N.J. fixture, on September 1, 1969, *the first day the breed became eligible to be shown at a championship event in the United States.* He was at the time already a Canadian champion, for the Shih Tzu (pronounced "sheed zoo") had been shown there for some time.

To the Fore

Papillon, in French, means butterfly. The breed gets its name from its ears, which are fringed and carried high and wide apart, so they resemble the open wings of the butterfly. In this country, for years, Papillon meant Catherine Davis Gauss, who has the acronymically named Cadaga Kennel. Born in Texas, where her great-grandfather founded one of the first banks in the state, she is a resident of New Canaan, Conn., where she not only is known for her showdogs but also for her golf. She was president of the Westchester-Fairfield Golf Association for three years and twice was champion of Woodway. For 13 years she served as president of the Papillon Club of America and with the aid of her husband, a corporate lawyer, helped to write the by-laws for the organization.

Of the many Papillons Mrs. Gauss owned, she considers Ch. Cadaga's Deja the best. He won the breed 156 times and placed in the group on 91 occasions with 20 first places. The sable and white was retired when he was five and a half years old. When I asked Mrs. Gauss why she had retired the Toy dog just when he was dominating the competition, she replied, "I felt it would be good for the breed. When you win consistently with one dog, it discourages other owners from showing." The Connecticut fancier likes competition.

She also observed, "I'd rather train a pup at a show than at a match. At a match there isn't nearly the same discipline."

Toys by Design

An interior designer from Philadelphia became interested in Italian Greyhounds through having seen them depicted in old tapestries. He is Charles J. McManus, a former vice president of the National Society of Interior Designers, who was chosen to help restore the library in the mansion at Lyndhurst, a national landmark at Tarrytown, N.Y., where the Westchester and Tuxedo Kennel Clubs stage their shows.

241

"I had the good fortune to get a parti-color IG," said McManus. "Although the parti is not in favor in Italy, where they prefer solids, this was the type seen on most of the 17th century tapestries and the frescoes 300 years earlier. For example, there is a striking fresco by Andrea de Firenze in a chapel in Florence depicting parti-colored IGs."

In Italy, where the standard calls for a "model of grace and distinction," the maximum weight is 11 pounds. There is no weight limit in this country but they usually run from 6 to 10 pounds, with the ideal height from 13 to 15 inches at the shoulder." The small Toy, who was a favorite in the days of Pompeii and in the Middle Ages in Europe, is usually associated with salons. The McManus home has the appropriate setting. The house is the former French Consulate and with antiques collected by the designer, it is a veritable museum. In 1975, his Ch. Linsmoor Top Hat 'N Tails was a big winner. "He also proved an outstanding stud," said the Philadelphian. "He's chocolate and white and his distinctive coloring has carried over to his puppies." So perhaps the strikingly marked dog from the Quaker City may provide the neo-renaissance look in the breed.

From Show Room to Show Ring

Dogs, Tiffany's and the White House all played a part in Susan Clark Hutchins' life.

In 1974, Mrs. Hutchins practically was commuting between New York and Washington, where she served as a design consultant for White House state dinners. "Each dinner would have a theme," she explained, "such as Americana, where we would have antique Indian baskets and a silver clipper ship."

Susan also traveled throughout the country restoring mansions. "I worked for more than a year doing a house at Clairborne Farm for Mr. and Mrs. Seth Hancock," she said. Clairborne is the 6,000-acre estate in Paris, Ky., where Secretariat and Riva Ridge stand at stud. As for Tiffany's the famous store in 1975 had a show, presenting the room settings of eight young interior designers, one of whom was Mrs. Hutchins.

"As long as I can remember, I've been around dogs," said the New York interior designer. "As a youngster, I had a Norwich Terrier, a Pembroke Welsh Corgi, later three Samoyeds, all at the same time, incidentally, and then a Golden Retriever." Now her breeds are the Lhasa Apso and its little cousin, the Shih Tzu.

"I saw a Lhasa at a friend's house," said Susan, "and decided it was the perfect breed for a New York apartment. It's a small dog that acts like a big one. It's intelligent, clean and quiet." In 1970, she went to see Bob Sharp and picked out a pup, from ten that he had. It was a 16-week-old parti-color and a granddaughter of the great Friar Tuck. Then she acquired a second. "Although I swore I'd never show," said Mrs. Hutchins, "the more I was around the dogs, the more I wanted to breed them. I realized to be a successful breeder I would have to go to shows and look for some really top dogs. Once I had them, they would have to be shown. Then when I had a good breeding program under way, it would be essential to get the homebreds into the ring.''

In 1973, the designer bought Ch. Karmes Kee-O of Korky, a gold-colored-dog. Kee-O captured a half-dozen groups and had 40 placements. In 1974, he was best in show in Bermuda, gaining a championship there. The next year he won the silverware at Sudbury, Ontario, and gained a Canadian title. She also bought a bitch, Ch. Taboo Gold Galaxy, a red gold, and started an active breeding program. ''The most exciting part is to breed a good pup,'' said Susan.

She Helped Make It Number One—
And Now She's Sorry!

Mrs. Sherman Hoyt, who during her long career in dogs bred more than 100 Poodle champions, was extremely articulate and never loathe to give her opinion about the breed. ''The tremendous popularity the Poodle is enjoying in America today is lamentable, not commendable,'' she said. ''And I should take my share of the blame. For years I did my best to make the breed a favorite with the public. Once a breed has reached the top, various commercially-minded individuals, with no regard for the standard but whose one purpose is to make money, jump in. There is indiscriminate breeding and you get a poor dog. I've begun to notice some nervous, moody Poodles in the ring and that is so unlike the dogs we know. The reasons why the Poodle is so greatly loved are his wonderful, gay dispositon, his intelligence and his kindliness. I rate him the best all-round companion of any of the breeds.''

One of the most exciting moments I experienced in the sport was watching Mrs. Hoyt show her great white Standard, Ch. Nunsoe Duc de la Terrace of Blakeen, to best in show at Westminster in 1935. It was the first time a Poodle ever had gone to the top in America's classic. The Duc was really awe-inspiring and did much for the breed, siring nine champions, seven of whom were best-in-show winners. Mrs. Hoyt had so many famous Miniatures, it is almost impossible to enumerate them; it suffices to say a tremendous number of top Minis go back to Blakeen breeding. But not only Poodles came out of Blakeen; there were also many great Afghan and Gordon Setter champions. She also owned Irish, Scottish and Cairn Terriers, Borzois, Beagles, Dachshunds, Pekingese, Pomeranians, Irish Water Spaniels, Foxhounds and German Shepherds.

''I don't remember when I didn't have a dog,'' she said. ''I've also had some mixed breeds and loved them. It is better to have a parti-colored pet than a superb specimen that has to be given tranquilizers to be taken into the ring.'' Mrs. Hoyt also achieved fame as a judge, both here and abroad.

Round Table

South of Wilmington, on the flat lands near the Delaware River, I drove up to a tall, once-splendid Southern-style house, in a sylvan setting. Towering trees framed the entrance in a classical manner. Grazing in the pastures on the

1,000-acre farm of the Alden Keenes were 80 Holsteins, a Dorset ewe who answered to the name of Heloise, and a Tennessee walking horse with her foal. Waddling near a red barn were 13 honking geese. Then there were a few dogs of Mrs. Keene's Round Table Kennel—45 Miniature Poodles and eight shaggy Irish Wolfhounds, the giants of dogdom. With this menage, it is good that the Keenes have a son who is a veterinarian.

It is the Poodles that brought Round Table its greatest success. Whereas the ordinary fancier brags when he has one champion, Mrs. Keene had accomplished the feat 45 times. But it took patience and hard work. "I bred Poodles for 10 years before I had my first champion," said the Delaware fancier. "I get very provoked with people who go to a half-dozen shows with their dogs, are unable to get any points, and then give up."

Few people will remember that Mrs. Keene's original breed in the 1930s was the Old English Sheepdog. Just before World War II, with 40 bobtails lumbering around, Round Table Kennel was one of the largest for the breed in America. All the Old English were named after knights of the Round Table. There were Galahad, Launcelot, Gawaine, Gareth and others until Tennyson just didn't have any more. Perhaps it was just as well, since the meat shortage of World War II caused Mrs. Keene to sell them all.

But the Poodle dynasty was to have its start at the time. "One of my daughters pleaded for a Poodle, so to humor her we bought her one, but strictly as a pet," recalled the Delaware philotherian. But a died-in-the-wool breeder such as Mrs. Keene never would be content with just a pet. So in 1956, she acquired a white miniature, Cricket of the Valley, from a kennel in Oregon and he became a champion and the foundation stud. Two years later, Mrs. Keene imported Heather Maid of Fircot from England, who was Round Table's foundation bitch. "Bred to Cricket, she gave us Ch. Round Table Cloche de Neige," recalled the kennel's mistress. "He sired Ch. Round Table Conte Blanc, who sired my greatest homebred, Ch. Round Table Cognac. Charlie, as Cognac was called, had 24 bests, 76 groups, 12 specialties and 146 times was best of variety. He also was an outstanding sire."

The Delaware kennel not only was famous in America but made its mark behind the Iron Curtain. In 1966, the William Penn Poodle Club received a letter from the Poodle Breeders Club of Czechoslovakia, pleading for a white miniature that could be used at stud, in an effort to better the breed in that country. The William Penn organization went to Mrs. Keene and she promptly donated Round Table First Edition, a grandson of Conte Blanc. But how to get the dog to Prague? Louis (Satchmo) Armstrong, flying overseas on a concert tour, agreed to deliver the Poodle. In the summer of 1970, I was at a Poodle specialty in Czechoslovakia, held on the beautiful grounds of Konopiste Castle, once owned by Archduke Francis Ferdinand of the Hapsburgs. Six of the nine dogs competing in what would be our open class were First Edition sons. I sent the catalogue to Mrs. Keene.

Porter and Dicky

The Keeshond is the national dog of the Netherlands. But it is a kennel in California that has achieved the greatest success with the barge dog. For the Kees at Porter and Dicky Washington's Flakkee Kennel, on their magnificent estate in Beverly Hills, have won the silverware more than 200 times and have taken 1500 blue rosettes.

Although Dicky has had Kees since 1938, Flakkee started its string of ring victories 10 years later with a single pup. "We called him Riot," said Washington, "and I guess he was aptly named for we have been causing riots with the breed ever since." Shown by Porter, the pup, more formally known as Ch. Patriot Van Fitz, started the Californians on the victory trail when he triumphed at Los Angeles in May 1949.

"We have been extremely fortunate," said Washington, "for we established several firsts with the breed. We imported two champion bitches from England, Whimsey and Rona of Wistonia. They were to become the only two Keeshond bitches to win best in shows in the United States until then. Whimsey was the first undefeated Kees in the history of the breed and the first to gain a group placement at Westminster."

The Washingtons have had four generations in a row of best-in-show dogs. It started with Wilco of Wistonia, an English and American champion. His son, Wrocky won 33 groups and had 18 best in shows. Wrocky produced Ch. Canada—and was the record-winning Kees until 1967. Shown here 36 times, Wrocky won 33 groups and had 18 best-in-shows. Wrocky produced Ch. Cornelius Wrocky Selznick, sire of Ch. Flakkee Sweepstakes, who broke the record of his grandsire, when he added 46 pieces of silverware to the Washington collection and captured 109 groups. Then in 1974, Porter campaigned Ch. Flakkee Instant Replay. Speedy, as Replay was known on the circuit, led the parade on 45 occasions, was best non-sporting dog 144 times, and had 226 Bests of Breed, a record for Kees.

Washington, originally an aeronautical engineer, in addition to his Kees, has had champions in many other breeds. "My father had Pointers in the Twenties," he recalled, "and I became interested in the breed." Porter became a professional handler after World War II. "My first real topper," he reminisced, "was a black Cocker Spaniel, Ch. Heather's Mister Chips, owned by Simie Ater of Denver." The Cocker was a big winner for three years and other owners, impressed with Washington's handling of the dog, came after him to show their prides.

Handling Miniature Pinschers for Mrs. E. L. Doheny 3d, he had tremendous success with Ch. Patzie v. Mill-Maas, who was the top-winning Toy of her day and was retired with 25 best-in-show awards and 100 groups. But it's a Pomeranian, Ch. Rider's Sparklin' Gold Nugget, who probably is the favorite of all the dogs the Washingtons have owned. Sparky was bought as a seven-month-old pup and won his championship within a month. Porter gaited the spunky little Pom to 41 top awards and 119 groups, a record for the breed. "He's

245

not only the greatest dog I've ever shown," said Porter, "but the greatest dog I've ever seen. As far as I'm concerned, there never will be another dog with the natural ability and guts this little dog possessed. The thought of him brings mist to these old eyes."

Porter has taken home 10 Ken-L Ration awards, more than any other handler. These prizes, often called the Oscars in the dog show world, go to the owners and handlers of the top-winning group performers.

Charlie Westfield

I walked into a Chinese restaurant with Charlie Westfield and was tremendously impressed when the big man began speaking in Chinese to the waiter. A few minutes later in came the chef and there was an animated conversation. We had a meal that would have rated four stars in *The New York Times* food guide.

And how did Mr. Westfield learn Chinese? "It would be more accurate," he replied, "to say that I can speak Mandarin, Cantonese and a Shanghai dialect. I was with the 14th Air Force, Chinese-American Wing, and I flew 100 missions over the hump. For three years, we had to live off the land and if you couldn't make yourself understood, you were in trouble." Whenever a Chinese restaurant opens, Charlie strives to be there. He can tell you every good place within a three-state area.

The Air Force led Westfield to the dogs. The family of one of the squadron members had Pekingese. "Julie French Williams lived on Cape Cod," recalled Westfield, "and she had 50 or 60 Pekes in her kennel. Every weekend I'd drive to the Cape and she always had a houseful of very knowledgeable fanciers." In 1955, Charlie and his wife, Eileen, saw Dr. John Saylor's Bulldog, Ch. Kippax Fearnought, go best in show at Westminster, and they decided that would be their breed. They had little success in the show ring until Ernie Hubbard, a longtime breeder, gave their then little daughter, Virginia, a six-month-old pup. In the mid-sixties, the pup, Brookhollow Ginger, became the first Westfield champion.

"She was our foundation bitch," said the Long Islander. Ginger was the dam of Ch. Westfield Flying Colors, who had 15 best-in-show awards, 78 group victories and 15 specialties. Wingie, as he was called, established the family in the sport. And a family sport it was, for all three of the Westfield children— Charles Jr., Barbara and Virginia,—along with their father, showed Wingie. Mrs. Westfield had all the work and none of the glory. She never showed but kept the kennel going and had words of encouragement when there were losses and not ribbons. Westfield also bred and showed Ch. Westfield Cunomorous Stone and she became the greatest winning Bulldog bitch in the breed's history, with 38 bests, 140 blue rosettes and 24 specialties.

Westfield has been extremely active in club work. In 1967 he was one of the 15 founders of the Owner Handler Association of America, serving as president from 1972 to 1974. He was re-elected for a two-year term in 1977.

Humane-itarians

"**M**AN'S BEST FRIEND" fortunately has many interested in returning the favor.

The American Society for the Prevention of Cruelty to Animals, which as early as 1867 sheltered animals, and the Bide-A-Wee Home Association are the two best known for their humane work in New York City. Then there is the American Humane Association, with headquarters in Englewood, Colo., organized in 1877, which a century later was serving as a federation for 1,500 groups. The Humane Society of the United States, incorporated in 1954, is headquartered in Washington, D.C. and has five regional offices that cover 23 states. But a much smaller non-profit shelter — the North Shore Animal League in Port Washington, L.I.—always intrigued me. And the story behind North Shore is Alexander Lewyt, a master salesman. That he literally is, for in "America's Twelve Master Salesmen," published by Forbes, Lewyt is one of the chosen dozen. He is also an inventor—the Lewyt vacuum cleaner—and a Chevalier of the French Legion of Honor. Then he is president of the animal league. "When I joined, I knew little about animals," he confessed to me, "but I had some experience in business. So I applied merchandising techniques to a humane association."

Super Salesman

It all started when this human dynamo, at the urging of his wife, attended a North Shore meeting in 1969. The shelter, organized in 1944, was foundering and in financial trouble. "A couple of little old ladies were trying to figure how $2,000 could be raised to keep the animal league alive," recalled Lewyt. "I suggested a drive to get contributing members and the job promptly was given to me."

Now Lewyt put his business acumen to work. He visited villages on Long Island's north shore and compiled a list of 28,000 dog owners. Perry Como, a neighbor of his at Sands Point, agreed to serve as honorary chairman. Letters, signed by Como, with an appealing photo of a dog and a cat, asking for "just $1 to save their lives" drew an 11 percent response. The 3,120 new North Shore members gave the league a treasury of $11,000. "We followed with a personalized New Year's card from Como to every donor thanking him or her for the contribution," said Lewyt. "Many answered by sending us another donation." In 1970, Lewyt was elected president of the league. In order to learn more about humane societies, he flew around the country, at his own expense, visiting 22 shelters.

Upon his return, strict rules were established. Every animal had to be immunized, unless it had been done within six months. Puppies or kittens were isolated for 24 hours. People bringing animals were interviewed to get the backgrounds on the pets they were surrendering. "We are not competing with kennels," the president maintained. "We don't breed dogs or cats to sell, we just arrange adoptions for unwanted animals. Before we let anyone adopt an animal, we make him fill out a questionnaire and then we interview him. We turn down at least one in five. When a dog is adopted, the new owner receives a starter kit, which includes some food and a booklet on animal care. A week or 10 days later, we phone to make certain everything is all right. If people complain, we suggest they return the pet. We are a busy place. In 1977, we handled 150,000 phone calls. On Sundays people come to visit the shelter and bring their children. In 1977, there were 28,000 visitors."

Among the merchandising techniques Lewyt introduced: a "pet of the week" photo that ran in five North•Shore newspapers; letters to school superintendents, clergymen and veterinarians offering them weekly photos of animals; posters in the Long Island Railroad and buses, depicting a dog and cat available for adoption, with free copies of the poster offered "for your playrooms," a women's auxiliary, with 35 volunteers, to speak to groups and stage exhibits.

The league, in 1978, had 413,000 contributing members from all over the world and whereas in 1969, when the humane entrepreneur stepped in, there had been only 127 pets adopted, in 1977, there were more than 7,000. Every animal adopted gets free spaying or neutering. The vaccinations also are free. "So that a dog will be a good citizen," said Lewyt, "we also enroll the animal and owner in an obedience training program. We have two trainers and the course lasts for 10 sessions. Again there is no charge." North Shore received a plaque from the American Humane Association, for its "significant contributions to the humane cause." When Nelson Rockefeller was New York Governor, he cited North Shore's efforts, writing, "The league's work represents the kind of humaneness that eloquently expresses the basic decency of man in a troubled world."

And Lewyt's know-how has crossed the ocean. "My wife is French," he told me, "and we also have a home in Chartres. We noticed three villagers who were taking care of stray animals in the area. So my wife and I have become 'godparents' to a little shelter. We had chain link fences erected, with a dozen runs, and a 500-gallon water tank installed. Our job is to help animals to the best of our ability, whether on the north shore of Long Island, or in a historic French community."

Save-A-Pet

In the Midwest, an inspiring story of the humane movement is that of Gertrude Maxwell, a retired school teacher in Highland Park, Ill. In 1972, she and 35 other persons met in her home and organized Save-A-Pet, Inc. "We are a pet adoption center," she told me, "which cares for lost and abandoned animals until the original or new owners can be found. Dogs and cats are taken directly from the pound to one of our cooperating veterinarians for a checkup and a distemper-plus shot. We board them in private kennels until good homes are found. We are a completely volunteer organization. Not one penny is spent on administration. Our greatest expenditures are board bills, veterinary care and advertising."

When dogs and cats reach Save-A-Pet, if lost-and-found ads or local animal wardens are unable to locate the owners, then ads are carried to locate new owners. In addition to Highland Park, the organization takes strays from the pounds of 13 nearby communities. The city was so impressed with the work the group was doing, it donated land and Save-A-Pet now has a shelter, built through contributions, named after Mrs. Maxwell and Hannah Goldman, a leading benefactor.

Then there is Gretchen Wyler.

Gretchen Wyler and the ASPCA

The first time I met Gretchen Wyler was at a Wallkill dog show. It was late in the afternoon, when a car drove up with a woman wearing heavy makeup. When I was introduced to her, she apologized for her appearance, saying she had raced from a matinee in a theater in the area, where she was performing, and she wanted to see her Great Dane, who had won the breed, compete in the group. I felt here was an actress looking for some publicity, with no real interest in the sport. How wrong I was.

The next time I heard her, she was the speaker at a Dog Fanciers Club luncheon. The advance publicity said she was interested in the humane movement. Again, I walked in with the feeling that here is a dilettante trying to capitalize on animal welfare, in order to further her theatrical career. Instead, she turned out to be a self-sacrifing, dedicated idealist and one of the most dynamic speakers I'd ever heard, and the Lord knows, over the years I had heard many. Within minutes she had the entire audience, me included, hanging on every word. She had been elected to the board of managers of the ASPCA, the first woman on the board in the organization's 106 years.

Since most of the listeners were breeders and exhibitors, she urged them to channel some of their efforts toward animal welfare work. "To me a shelter should be a haven from discomfort, fear and anxiety," said Gretchen. And she could speak with authority for she was the animal welfare chairman of the Orange County Suburban Humane Society. Largely through her efforts, an animal shelter had been built at Warwick, N.Y. "Although I had the good fortune of owning a best-in-show Great Dane," she said, "and showing a pup to his championship, I feel we have a responsibility to the stray, who needs help. In the comparatively short time our shelter has been open (three and a half years), we have had 3,000 dogs and cats." In an effort to control the animal population, the actress told of steps taken at Warwick. "Before we permit a person to adopt a bitch, we require a $10 deposit. If the bitch is spayed, we return the money."

Miss Wyler recalled as a child in Oklahoma, she never had a pet. "When I was appearing in *Bye Bye Birdie* in New York," she said, "I decided it was time to have a dog. On a Sunday in March, I went to my first dog show, Saw Mill in White Plains. I saw the Great Danes being judged and knew immediately that would be my breed. But getting the dog was a real chore. Being in show biz, I was suspect. I was screened thoroughly by a Dane breeder, before she would sell me a pup. The pup turned out to be Ch. Gretchen's Khan of Mountdania. He was best in show at Lancaster in 1964 and I wasn't able to see him do it. I was appearing three times a day in *Wonder World* at the World's Fair."

Her Eaglevally Jingerbread gained his title as an 11-month old pup. "For two years I was a standby in *Applause,* first for Lauren Becall and then for Anne Baxter," she said. "Jingerbread helped to keep me in shape. Every day we would walk 80 blocks." Miss Wyler later was forced to step down from the ASPCA board, when she tried to introduce reforms, but she did stir that extremely conservative organization into action. She did so at great personal expense. For example, I suggested her as a speaker at a dinner and the ad agency was enthusiastic. There would have been a substantial fee for her, but when they heard she was embroiled in a battle with the ASPCA board, they said she was too controversial and engaged someone else. When she was starring in *Sly Fox,* a hit show in 1976 and 1977, in her dressing room were pictures of Khan and two other Danes. "They are Nureyev and Baryshnikov. I named a whole litter after famous ballet dancers," explained Gretchen.

A Lady Who Cared

Each year approximately 4,500 dogs are brought to the New York hospital of the ASPCA, after they have been hit by motorists. "Many of the times, it is the owner who carries in the injured animal," said a spokesman for the organization. "I'm sorry to relate that frequently it's the owner's own fault, for he had been walking his dog without a leash, which is a violation in the city." The NYC Department of Sanitation reported the bodies of 2,500 dogs are picked up annually.

So I was glad to be able to write how Audrey Topping had been driving to New York City from her home in Scarsdale, N.Y., when she noticed a dog lying next to the wall on the Triborough Bridge. Unable to stop, she drove off the exit to Manhattan and parked behind a disabled truck. Telling the driver about the animal's plight, the two walked back for more than a mile while trucks and private cars whizzed past. When they reached the animal, the dog raised her head. Mrs. Topping, a well-known writer, picked her up while her companion tried vainly to stop motorists to obtain a lift for them and the dog. So with the stocky truck driver leading the way, Mrs. Topping, and when she tired, the driver, carried the 20-pound animal back to her car.

The tall, attractive blond then returned to Scarsdale. "By the time we reached home, Triboro Bridget had recovered from shock and was sitting close to me," Mrs. Topping said. "She had no identification and we advertised but there was no response." So Triboro Bridget, who her new mistress said looked like a Border Terrier, joined the Scarsdale household of a German Shepherd bitch, an Australian cockatoo, six cats and five children.

Two residents of Liz Clark's Springfield Farm evidently see things eye to eye.

Two out of the ordinary obedience stars—and both are conformation champions, too. At top, Ch. Sarokhazi Cukor CDX, Komondor bitch, owned by Mark J. Kamen (handler) and Marion J. Levy, Jr. Below, Ch. Hetherbull Arrogant Lazarus UD, first champion Bulldog ever to achieve a Utility degree, owned by Robert A. Hetherington, Jr.

Obedience

MୖORE THAN ONE letter separates a pet from a pest. Surely everybody has visited a household, where the owner bows to the whims of his dog. When a master opens the door, King Fido greets you with a snarl or is overfriendly and bowls you over. Held back, with due apologies from the host, he is let loose again, when the cocktails are being passed. Promptly Mr. Dog charges, hits your arm and spills your martini. Meanwhile, he's pouncing all over the furniture so there's no place to sit. Finally he monopolizes the conversation with his barking.

Good manners will get the dog and his master every place. Fido is a pragmatist. His one interest is getting the most out of life, with the least effort. So the initial move is up to the owner. That assures a lot of lively hours together. To reach the dog effectively, one must build confidence. The animal must have confidence in his master and the master in him.

The solution is obedience training. Among the hardest working people in the sport are those in obedience. There is no best-in-show trophy, and the people who work with the educated set are the second cousins among show folk. Only a handful of clubs deign to present the top obedience trophy in the big best-in-show ring. In 1977, the AKC began granting obedience championship titles.

There is a marked difference between fanciers competing in the show and obedience rings. In the show, the owner who loses is everyone's friend, for he is building the entries and helping to make major points. The moment he begins to win, however, some of the previous so-called friends cool off. But in obedience, it is quite different. Nastiness is a rarity. Each dog is judged by itself and strives for a qualifying score. And each owner has spent hours training and appreciates the effort that goes into it. So there is a great spirit of camaraderie. I always enjoyed being at ringside when the ribbons were handed out and the judge announced the dogs with qualifying scores. There was applause even from those whose dogs hadn't qualified. After all, there's another day. When a dog would fail an exercise during the trial, one could hear the moans and groans from the other owners, as they commiserated with the poor unfortunate.

Obedience had its start in this country in 1934. After a trip to England, where she saw some training, Mrs. Whitehouse Walker of Mount Kisco, N.Y., organized a class here. Today, it is the fastest-growing segment in dogs. In 1976, the year I retired, 86,989 dogs competed in 1,074 trials.

In the obedience honor roll of judges and teachers would be such names as Blanche Saunders, Milo and Margaret Pearsall, John Ringwald, Dick D'Ambrisi, Dorothy Bach, Diana Henley, James Dearinger, John S. Ward and Russ Klipple.

Few persons had a greater influence than Blanche Saunders, the daughter of a Baptist minister and a graduate of Massachusetts State College. She was actively engaged in dog pedagogy from 1934 until her death in 1968. "I feel I can do more good by conducting training clinics and that's where I'm going to concentrate my efforts," she told me. At the clinics, she would divide the dogs into two groups. The first was for untrained animals, who would engage in simple exercises. The other was for the so-called problem dogs. "The dog is either trained to do the right thing, by avoiding the wrong, or he is corrected of bad habits that already are part of his behavior pattern," she would preach. Then, while the owner would stand by, Miss Saunders, with a firm hand and voice, would put the dog through his paces.

For 16 years, she was training director for the American Society for the Prevention of Cruelty to Animals. In that capacity, she brought 17,000 owners and their dogs to "graduation." For 11 years she headed the program for the Boxer Obedience Training Club of Westchester and for ten directed at the Poodle Obedience Training Club of New York. A teacher of teachers, Miss Saunders conducted special courses, limited to training instructors.

The AKC recognized obedience training in 1936. The next year, Blanche and Mrs. Walker, with three Poodles, started on a transcontinental tour, which was to take them 10,000 miles. They were "traveling with Charley" long before John Steinbeck, spreading the obedience gospel. Whenever they heard a dog show was being held, the two missionaries appeared and staged an obedience exhibition, using their three Poodles. Blanche was on the road, right up to her death. She had attended a meeting of obedience clubs and judges at the Henry Hudson Hotel in New York, where she gave a demonstration and talk on training problems. As she was leaving the hotel, she had a fatal heart attack.

Crowds never fazed her. In her zeal to popularize obedience, she gave pregame demonstrations at Yankee Stadium before crowds of 60,000, and she had the baseball fans cheering each dog as it ran through its exercises. For years, she showed out-of-towners at Rockefeller Center Plaza what a well-behaved New York pup could do after some training. Miss Saunders welcomed the rambunctious pup and his beleaguered owner. In nine lessons, she would bring order to a household. In just 15 minutes a day, both would learn the basic rules. At the end of nine weeks, if the dog proved satisfactory, a diploma would be awarded at graduation.

"What breeds are the easiest to train?" I asked Blanche. "The Poodle is the quickest to learn," she replied, "but he's a clown and loves to play to the crowd. In a jumping exercise he will race for the bar but instead of leaping over it, will duck under, then look to see if he drew some laughs. The German Shepherd,

Doberman, Shetland Sheepdog and Golden Retriever are dependable, methodical and do an excellent job. Terriers are too busy, hounds too sniffy.''

The Poodle sense of humor notwithstanding, two of the top performers among the educated clan from 1965 through 1972 were representatives of the breed with the Gallic names of Cygnette and Claudine. Owned by Carlyle and Gabrielle Fabian, each Poodle carried the suffix des Fabian.

Cygnette, a white miniature, was the No. 1 scoring Poodle in America from 1969 to 1972. Mrs. Fabian began training Cygnette, when the pup was only three months old. By the time she was ten months old, the Poodle had her CD. Four months later, she had added a CDX and when she was 17 months old, a UD. She also earned all three degrees in Canada and Mexico. ''We took Claudine to Mexico at the same time,'' the little dark-haired woman, a native of Brussels, told me. ''Claudine was only 14 months old but she earned her CD, CDX and a leg on her UD. It was a hectic eight days. I handled the two dogs 34 times and was in the ring a total of six hours.'' Gabrielle does all the handling but her husband also is very much involved. He's an instructor and has taught more than 500 dogs and their owners.

I have found that almost everyone is obedience has his or her own system of training. Whereas Miss Saunders felt man and dog couldn't take more than 15 minutes of each other at a time, the Fabians worked on a different schedule.

''We start working from 20 minutes to a half-hour, with the basic training and strive to establish good habits right from the start,'' they said. ''With advanced work, the practice sessions are longer—a half hour each—but not every day, perhaps three times a week. We have a cardinal rule: Be patient and firm with the dog, but not cruel. It's a team operation.''

David Holzman had his own training techniques and they certainly were unorthodox. For he and his black miniature Poodle, Charlie, trained an average of three hours a day for 27 weeks. ''I guess that disproves the theory that a dog's attention span is relatively short and that an owner becomes impatient and cannot work,'' said the West Palm Beach, Fla., fancier. ''We had three hourly periods, starting at 6:30 in the morning, then 11:30 and finally at 5 in the afternoon. In addition, we went to obedience classes twice a week, from 9 to 10:30 at night.''

The team was a sensation in 1973. First it swept aside the opposition in Florida. ''I was told the competition would be much tougher in the East, so I thought we would give it a try,'' said David. ''We took part in 31 trials, competing in two classes each time. Of the 62 events, Charlie was first 31 times and in 14 was high scorer in trial.'' Charlie was another Cinderella dog. He was the last pup in a litter, the one nobody wanted. Holzman didn't start training the Poodle until Charlie was three-and-a-half years old. But the dog took to the work so well that in just 27 weeks, he had his CD, CDX and UD degrees.

Over the years, the German Shepherd has won more degrees than any other breed. But generalizations about the mentalities of the various breeds are often as dependable as those about nationalities.

Take Kathy Kirk's German Shepherd, Frau Kim of Weisshund. "When I was 15 years old," Kathy told me, "I was given Kim, who was seven weeks old. She was the worst behaved pup I've ever seen. She was hard to housebreak, wouldn't walk on a leash and when she ran and tripped my grandmother, that was it. I was told I either had to train Kim or get rid of her."

The youngster went to the public library at Spencerville, Md., and borrowed a manual on obedience training. "There was no demand for the book and I was able to keep renewing it for the summer," she recalled. Then began a battle of wills that lasted for three months. Morning, afternoon and evening, there were training periods of five minutes each, with the pup rebelling.

Suddenly there was a complete change. The pup began to enjoy the training. When she was nine months old, Kim and Kathy went to their first trial. The pup gained a leg on her CD and then went on to earn it in three straight shows. That Christmas, the teenager asked for just two presents—a solid high jump and a broad jump, so she could train Kim for a CDX. By March, the young Shepherd gained her first leg with a 190 and came back with a 185 and 193 to earn her second degree. The next Christmas, Kathy's requests were for a bar jump and the scent articles, for she was looking ahead to a UD for Kim. "Her first test in utility was a booboo," said Kathy, "and so were her second and third. She just couldn't seem to master scent discrimination. Meanwhile, we bred her. Once she handled the scent exercise, Kim gained her UD, with an average score of 195. She finished at Old Dominion, just two weeks before she had 13 pups."

In 1967, Kim was the fourth-ranking German Shepherd in obedience. Fifteen times she was top Shepherd in her class. "But she still, on occasions, would give me a hard time," said Kathy. "At one show she ran out of the ring and it took me 20 minutes to catch her, obedience training to the contrary." The next year, Kim reached the peak, finishing first of all breeds.

The Shepherd's greatest performance was at a specialty in Washington. Kim had won the utility class in the morning, with a 197, when it was comparatively cool. In the afternoon, the temperature soared to the high 90s. Kim was in the open class and was doing the long stay (in which all the handlers have to leave the ring and their dogs for five minutes). Suddenly there was a cloudburst, with thunder and lightning. The place was a bedlam. "When I returned to the ring," recalled Kathy, "only one dog had held the stay and it was Kim. I could have kissed her. Through thunder, lightning and rain, she remembered all the work we had done together and never moved. The judge gave her a 200."

Some dogs are just stubborn and it takes unremitting patience and persistence on the part of the owner. A shining example was provided by Mrs. Michael Caruso of Glens Falls, N.Y. She started with a German Shepherd bitch and the pup took to obedience beautifully. She earned a CD title in the minimum three shows, both in the United States and Canada, before she was 11 months old.

"While we were taking our Shepherd to trials, we watched Borzois being judged and I fell in love with the breed," said Mrs. Caruso, "so we bought a pair and they both became champions. We also started the bitch, Wililea Sweet Diana, in obedience. She had her CD and CDX quickly enough, but what a time we had in utility. Diana just wouldn't pick up the dumbbell. I was just as stubborn as she was and it turned out to be a contest. It took nine months, but I won. She finally picked up the dumbbell."

In 1970, Diana made Borzoi history. She was the only living Borzoi to be a breed champion and a UD.

The most unusual obedience training I ever encountered was worked up by Mrs. Herbert Terry of Springfield, Mass., who enlisted her entire family in a project to train their Chihuahuas.

Most people take their dogs to class and do the training in the relative quiet of their homes. At a show, the poor dog is confronted with crowds, strange noises, barking and many other distractions.

So Mrs. Terry and her husband took a cue from the space program practices and decided to train their Toy dogs under simulated dog show conditions.

They walked around the rings at shows, placing the microphone of a portable recorder, where there was a great deal of noise.

"Our next step," said Mrs. Terry, "was to record and dub in additional noises. We had children screaming (courtesy of our son and daughter), squeaky toys, slamming doors. That was the noisier side of the tape. The other side consisted of plain barking, contributed by our three Chihuahuas.

"When I worked in training the dogs, I turned on the barking side, keeping the volume low at the beginning and gradually increasing it as the dog became accustomed to the din.

"When the dog became steady with that side, I turned the tape. Again I started with low volume, gradually increasing as the dog progressed. On the sit-and-down exercise, I also had my children run around to provide even greater distraction."

Once the Terry Chihuahuas were entered at trials, they were just about the steadiest in the ring. At several trials, where there were unexpected noises, dogs would break, but not the Terry Toys. One, Farriston Little Busy Bee, who earned her CD, was a real attention-getter. A smooth black, with tan markings, she was only seven inches tall and weighed two-and-a-quarter pounds. She never did get a CDX. The 12-inch high jump she easily cleared but the two-foot broad jump was just too much.

Natalie and Bill Hutchins of Bryn Mawr, Pa., two of our better known judges, made history in their younger days with a young Weimaraner bitch, Ch. Mischievous Misty, who has a list of letters for degrees after her name longer than the most erudite college professor. She was listed as United States and Canadian CD, CDX, UDT; Bermuda CD; W.C.A.—RD.

At the time, Natalie told me, "She's the first and only bitch of any breed to hold United States and Canadian championships, as well as UDT's for both countries. She also has a Bermuda CD and a retrieving dog certificate from the Weimaraner Club of America for excellence in retrieving birds from the water and field, in competition."

And then there's John (Never Hit a Dog) Ringwald, whose judging antics always enliven the tense atmosphere of the ring. Often he seems to be going through the exercise with the dog. When an animal takes a jump, John applies a little body English, as if to help the animal over. And the spectators love it. They come to watch Ringwald as well as the contestants. For years John taught obedience and his class drew so many, he always had to have an assistant.

"I never have a problem with the dogs, it's their owners," he complained. "For the first lesson, I always tell them to leave the dogs home. After going over the basics of what I expect them to do, I add, 'You have two hands, one is to hold the leash, the other to pet your dog.' "

At one of those first lessons, with some 45 in the class, I heard a woman ask, "What can I do with my dog, she messes in the house when I'm away?" Answered John, "Do you work all day?" When the woman replied she did, Ringwald snapped back, "How many times did you go to the bathroom today?" The woman, embarrassed, replied, "Twice." Said a scornful John, "Well, how do you expect your poor animal to hold, when you can't?"

When a dog wins both a breed title and obedience degree, his master justifiably brags a bit. A strong advocate of the dual purpose dog is Samuel Gardner of Lakeland, Fla. An engineer, Sam is a Bulldogger from 'way back. He's also a breed and obedience judge, and an AKC delegate.

Sam and his wife, Margaret, trained the first U.D. Bulldog—Anglo Saxon Gaiety. Because of the breed's short flat nose, many experts maintained it would be impossible for a sourmug to pass the scent discrimination test. "I'd hate to tell you how many hours the two of us worked with Gaiety," recalled Gardner, "but it was all worthwhile when we did the 'impossible' with a Bulldog."

But then Sam has a way with Bulldogs. During World War II, when he was a Marine major, his Bulldog became the unofficial mascot of the 14th AntiAircraft Artillery, Fleet Marine Force.

"How did you manage to have a Bulldog in the fighting zone?" I asked him.

"It was just a week after our landing at Guam that I got Toughie," he replied. "The beach area had been secured, but the fighting was very intense inland. On a road leading to the beach, I saw a white Bulldog. I called to my men to grab him. We took him in my jeep. I made inquiries but no one knew from where he had come. He could have been owned by one of our Marines, who had been killed, or by one of the Japanese.

"Toughie was with me for the rest of the time I was on Guam and he then flew with me to Saipan and Tinian.

"At Guam, the men built him a dog house, with a porch, on the heights over Apra, the choicest spot on the island. Whereas we had a hard time getting mosquito netting, his house was completely screened."

After the war, the Gardners settled in California. There they were initiated into obedience.

"We went to a show in Los Angeles," recalled Sam, "and wandered over to the obedience ring. A judge was seated on a tall chair, similar to that used by tennis umpires. Over a loudspeaker, he described the exercises in which the dogs were participating. We felt here was something every dog should be taught."

The Gardners enrolled in a club and started to train a Bulldog. "She was fat, lazy and obstinate," said Sam. "I often wonder how we ever had the patience to take her through her CD and CDX. She never could master the scent discrimination and that kept her from a UD."

Sam has his own theories of training. Instead of starting with the usual heel, sit, down, come and stay, and working up to utility and in rare cases, tracking, he starts with tracking.

"I believe any dog can be taught to track," said Gardner, "if he responds to the sit-and-stay command. We start with them when they are puppies. We had a Standard Poodle and an English Springer Spaniel — both had their TD's by the time they were 18 months old.

"I'd like to see every dog, whether purebred or mixed breed have some obedience. It's a gospel I'm always preaching."

Diana Henley taught good manners to 13,000 dogs and their owners over an 18-year span. She headed the ASPCA obedience program in New York. In the large breeds, she accepted dogs as young as three months old. There was no age limit for the dog or owner. "As long as they can totter around a ring, we will work with them," she said. "We had a 78-year-old woman who trained an Irish Setter and they both did very well. If you think you can't teach an old dog new tricks, you are wrong. We had a nine-year-old Shepherd and he was one of the stars of his class. It's exciting to see the improvement as the weeks roll by. The noisy dogs quiet down, the shy ones blossom out and by the time they graduate, some of the so-called problem dogs are models of deportment."

Mrs. Betty McDonell, a petite brunette, is a busy housewife in Ridgewood, N.J., and heads a school for gymnasts. In between her chores, she trains Newfoundlands and she does it so well that her Dryad's Lord Nelson was the first champion Newf to become a UDT. The Lord, a 150-pounder, outweighed his owner by 30 pounds. Betty also trained another of her big black dogs to a UDT, the second to gain that distinction. "I enjoy disproving the theory that one cannot show in breed and obedience at the same time," she said. Then she added a third dimension, training her Newfs for water trials.

When Mrs. John E. McIntyre brought her Ch. Don Juan to a UD in Calabasas, Calif., it was the first time in 27 years a Rottweiler had gained the degree and only the second time since the breed was recognized by the AKC in 1935. The first had been Gero von Rabenhorst, who Mr. and Mrs. Arthur A. Eichler had trained in Milwaukee in 1941.

Fred Henry, an engineer with Xerox, enrolled his German Shepherd for a 10-week training course with a club in Rochester, N.Y. "They had a year-round program," he recalled, "and I was there, year-round, for the next 14 years. I became so interested, I finally was assisting the instructors." The long apprenticeship served him in good stead. He opened his own school and trained more than 300. Now he is also judging. "It's been a hard climb in our area," said Henry. "When we started, there were only 13 dogs competing at a trial. Now we get 75 just for a fun match. But few take their dogs through the advanced work."

Week after week I had to write about Russell H. Klipple and his Golden Retriever, Moreland's Golden Tonka. For the Golden was the top obedience dog in the United States in 1974, 1975, 1976 and 1978 and was the first dog in the nation to become an obedience champion.

Tonka, who was whelped June 2, 1972, made her debut at Wilmington, Delaware, the next April. In three straight shows, she had her CD, added her CDX in another three and her UD at three trials, with the final leg on October 13.

During 1976, Tonka was high in trial 48 times.

On July 1, 1977, the AKC ruled that dogs with utility degrees were eligible to compete for an OT Ch. prefix. Tonka finished on July 23, with 104 points, four more than were needed. But it was a close race, for another Golden Retriever, Topbrass Cisco Kid, owned by Mrs. Pauline Czarnecki of Chicago, a waitress and the mother of three teenagers, finished just a day later. "I drove from 1,500 to 2,000 miles during July, while competing in New York, Vermont, Massachusetts and Connecticut to win that title," said Russ. "Tonka finished in 13 trials and 23 classes, with all scores over 195 and two perfect ones. She had 20 first places and three seconds. If it weren't for the heat and absentees, Tonka would have made it faster. She loves to work and the bigger the crowd, the better her performance. She's a real ham. Applause is like a shot in the arm to her. She's now had six 200-point scores." Since only one dog in 1,500 ever achieves the perfect score, the Golden's record is certainly impressive.

The human part of the team was a comparative latecomer in the sport. "I didn't have a dog until I was 37 years old," Klipple told me. "I was a baker and too busy with my store in Havertown (Pa.). My two daughters were constantly after me to get them a dog. One day, while I was making deliveries, I noticed a kennel. It had Shetland Sheepdogs. I stopped and bought one. I never had been to a dog show but read that one was being held in Philadelphia, so I went. The obedience rings fascinated me. I made inquiries and joined the Philadelphia Dog Training Club." That was in 1947. Klipple proved so proficient at training his

Sheltie, that the next year he became training director, a post he held for 26 years.

Captivator Tam O'Shanter, a Sheltie he owned and trained, had a sensational record. Tam started when a year old by doing the "impossible," getting a perfect score. He repeated at his second outing and then "slipped" to a 199½ for his CD. Continuing for his CDX, he had two more 200's, so that in his first six trials, he had four perfect scores. "At least 95 per cent of all dogs can be trained to a CD," said Klipple, "and 90 percent to a CDX. Owners, however, are pretty stupid. Often they will refuse to correct a dog. It's the people who are problems, not the animals."

Another latecomer to the obedience end of the sport was Mrs. Joe Longo, whose husband, Westchester PGA champion in 1972, was the golf pro at the Briar Hall Country Club. Mrs. Longo, whose career with dogs started in 1944, has had champions in both the show ring and in obedience. Her Great Danes won some great victories and her Boxers, led by Ch. El Wendie of Rockland, with more than 25 best-in-show awards, also achieved fame. "As my dogs grew older, I gradually stopped showing," she said. "In 1967, one of the golfers gave my husband a Poodle, Toby of Rye Top. Toby was pretty pesty around the house, so I took him to obedience school." Toby learned quickly and earned CD and CDX degrees. The Longos then bought a silver Poodle, Tammy of Rye Top, and she went through to a UD. The couple from Harrison, N.Y., have added Poodles to their obedience string and have had great success, with more than 120 trophies on the shelves. Mrs. Longo is an ardent obedience aficionado. "In the show ring, a dog can be absolutely stupid but as long as he's beautiful, he wins points and becomes a champion," she said. "In obedience, a dog must work or get nothing. It's brains, not beauty, that counts."

Another ardent obedience devotee is Eleanor Rotman, a psychologist, a Poodle breeder and obedience judge. "Most people bring their dogs to obedience school because they are having problems with them," she said. "In class, they are taught to gain respect from their dog and learn how to teach the animal. Then it is up to the owner to go home and teach what he has learned. Since we have to live with our dogs, it is our responsibility to educate them to live in our human society. Obedience exercises train a dog to become a worthwhile citizen and companion."

For five years, Susan Wofsey was administrative manager for the editorial department of Bantam Books. So when she decided to buy a dog, she naturally turned to a book to help her decide on a breed. "I wanted a terrier and one small enough to put in a carrier, when I traveled," she said. "I bought a Cairn in a pet shop and brought the pup home. The next morning he was desperately ill. I took him to a vet and for the next six months that's about all we were doing. Before we had Angus the Pooh healthy, I had paid $1,000 in veterinarian fees." Once

Angus was in good health, Miss Wofsey decided to show him. "He won some blue ribbons but didn't enjoy showing," said Susan, "so I decided to try him in obedience. That was something. I just couldn't get him to stop sniffing. It was two years before I could get him to take his nose off the ground and work. And he was stubborn." Furthermore, Angus just wouldn't work outdoors. If it was hot, the brindle would insist on moving into the shade. But Susan is persistent. After three and a half years, Angus has his CD.

Meanwhile Miss Wofsey had acquired another Cairn, a bitch, but this time she went to a breeder for Cairndania Brigrey's Dorey. She soon became a champion and then her mistress started her in obedience. "So few of the judges had ever seen a Cairn that at the trials they would ask me what the breed was," said Susan. In only three months and 11 trials, the little red had her CD. "I did all the training right in my New York City apartment," added Miss Wofsey. "For the CDX, we trained in a parking lot on 65th Street. My friends think that I'm wacky, working with Cairns in obedience. Last year, for example, there were only 19 of the breed in the entire United States, besides my two, who earned CDs."

Now Susan is living in Connecticut where she helped found the Housatonic Valley Cairn Terrier Association.

Linda Siegel and her Siberian Husky, Eu-Mor's Kelev, are a prime example of what can be accomplished in a metropolis, for their obedience training was done in Riverside Park in New York City, and on the roof of their apartment house. The 38-pound Siberian and his 100-pound mistress were attention getters when they did their early training in the park, overlooking the Hudson. "I found it an ideal training ground," said Linda. "Kelev became accustomed to people and other dogs. They never fazed her, when I would give the command to stay. They would pet her and she'd wag her tail and kiss them but never move. Another dog would go dashing by, but again, she'd remain sitting. As a result, when she competed at a trial, nothing disturbed her."

"She's the first dog I ever owned," said the Manhattan housewife. "We brought her home when she was 10 weeks old. Two weeks later, when we were walking, she broke away and ran across Riverside Drive, with me right after her. Both of us narrowly escaped being hit by a car. That was it. I decided then and there, she had to be trained." So one night a week, the two would drive out to Long Island to attend classes from 8:30 until 11:30. "She became a real ham," said Mrs. Siegel. "Whenever there was applause at the school, she would think it was for her and she'd leap up and down." Linda's husband, Marv, an assistant city editor at the *Times,* joined in the act. During a vacation, he built a couple of jumps, so Kelev could go on to train for a CDX.

For four decades Bob Hetherington has been a member of the Bulldog Club of New Jersey. There aren't too many members who have been with the club longer. But Robert is no graybeard. "My father enrolled me as a member when I was four years old,'' said the president of the First Jersey Savings and Loan Association at Wycoff, N.J., who has had Bulldogs as long as he can remember. ''My father liked the breed and we always had a white one. They were strictly pets and never shown.''

It was a natural for Bob to go to Yale, where a Bulldog has been the mascot since 1889. Hetherington was the Eli heavyweight boxing champion for two years. The banker and his wife, Jean, bought their first sourmug in 1962. Carrying on the family tradition, the couple came up with a white Bulldog. ''Our pup wasn't anything spectacular,'' recalled Bob, ''but he did get us out to the shows and we learned enough so that by the end of the year we bought an eight-week-old brindle, Raefair's Pixie of Heatherbull, who definitely was a show prospect.'' Pixie had a litter and one of her five pups, Ch. Hetherbulls' Arrogance, established the Hetheringtons in the world of dogs. The red brindle with white markings, called Harry, proved a specialist for on 14 occasions he took specialties.

''I really brought Harry out too early,'' Hetherington confessed to me, ''but I wanted him to become a champion when he was still a puppy. He missed by just five days but he did finish with four majors, which was quite an achievement. That dog really cost me money. In 1966, I flew Harry to the West Coast for a weekend I'll never forget. I showed him at the Pacific Bulldog Club's specialty in Arcadia (Calif.) and he was named best of 129. I rushed to Western Union and sent telegrams to everyone I could think of. The next day was our national specialty and he was placed over 134. This was the ultimate, so back I went to Western Union to flash the good news. When Harry led 100 Bulldogs at the San Gabriel all-breed show, he had been best of breed three days in a row. That called for a fresh batch of telegrams. Western Union shares should have soared on the New York Stock Exchange.'' Little wonder that the banker's favorite tune those days was, ''I'm Just Wild About Harry.''

But it was another Bulldog, Ch. Hetherbull Arrogant Lazarus, who was to accomplish in obedience what no other champion sourmug had been able to achieve—gain a UD. I was at Providence County in the Civic Center in 1975, when Laz earned his CDX. He had done it in three straight shows, getting a 190½ at Springfield, 187 at Hartford and then a 186 at Providence. His score would have been even higher the third time, except that after completing an exercise and with the crowd applauding, he leaped with joy. ''I had to take a couple of points away because of his antics,'' said Mrs. Edward Bartlett, the judge. ''I finally appealed to the people to keep quiet.'' The ring was set up at the end of the arena and the stands were more crowded watching Laz than they were later in the day when best in show was judged.

The mahogany brindle and white 65-pounder, who gained his breed championship when only a nine-month-old pup, became a UD at Staten Island the next year and the judge was the well-known Mary Lee Whiting of Minneapolis, who had conducted obedience clinics around the country. His score was a very minimal 172. ''For some reason, known only to Laz, in the scent discrimination he chose to drop the articles at my feet," Hetherington told me. "That cost him half the points in the exercise. Fortunately, he did so well on most of the others, he qualified. Laz is a ham and loves to perform. And the spectators love to watch him. More that twenty clubs have asked me to enter him at their trials. I've owned or bred 35 Bulldog champions but the greatest thrill I've had in the sport was taking Laz through to the UD."

Like so many before her, Beverly Qualls acquired her first dog as a Christmas gift. That was in 1966 and it was rather a familiar story; for purchased through an ad in the paper, the Bulldog bitch was anything but a showdog. But then the young woman from Burlington, N.C., showed great perspicacity. She phoned a breeder and exhibitor from Durham, said she wanted a showdog and would like to learn some of the basics about the breed and handling. She bought a six-month-old pup, who promptly, from the puppy class, went winners dog, best of winners and best of opposite. "Although he never finished," recalled Beverly, "I learned a great deal and acquired confidence, so I next bought a year-and-a-half red-and-white, Tha Mac's Short Circuit, and I finished Sparky myself."

Then came Ch. Scarlet O'Hara of Black Watch and Beverly never tires singing the praises of this red and white. "I finished her when she was only 10-month-old pup," she bragged. At Oak Ridge, Tenn., in 1971, the red-and-white sourmug caused more rumblings among Bulldog fanciers than the generators in the nuclear plant there, when she was named best in show. But the real bombshell came a year later, when Scarlet earned her CD in obedience to become the first best-in-show Bulldog ever to accomplish the feat.

"It wasn't easy," said Mrs. Qualls. "We actually worked for more than a year. She knew the exercises perfectly but would move along at her own sweet pace." The day she gained the third and final leg for the CD, there was more applause than at the best-in-show ring later. The same year Scarlet was best of opposite at the national specialty and a portrait was made of her by the Bulldog Club of America.

"With a Bulldog, I feel it is better for the owner to show, rather than a professional handler," she maintained. "The Bulldog has a mind of his own, He's stubborn, and you know him better than any handler."

Obedience Chemistry

Not too many clerics take part in the dog show world and fewer still are judging. So when I looked over a Penn Ridge premium list in 1972 and saw a Rev. Thomas V. O'Connor would be judging obedience, I made a point of getting to his ring. The bespectacled young man was very serious in his work, although he had a cheery smile for each exhibitor and words of encouragement for the tyro. Later, at lunch, I learned he had a busy schedule. During the week Father O'Connor was teaching at St. Peter's Prep in Jersey City, where he headed the chemistry department. On weekends, he engaged in parish work.

Then, as an avocation, he was busy with dogs, either judging the educated set or working with Soft-Coated Wheaten Terriers. At the time the Wheaten was a labor of love, for the breed had yet to be registered by the AKC. It was being shown in the "forgotten" class—the miscellaneous.

The good priest had a rather unusual introduction to the sport. "Every week, I would drive my sister to Greenlawn [L.I.] to the Suffolk Obedience Training Club, where she was training her Wheaten, Little Firecracker," he recalled. "It was boring just playing the role of a chauffeur, so since we had an old bitch, Holmenock's Gramachree, at my mother's house, I decided to take Irish, as we called the Wheaten, to training class myself. Irish was eight years old at the time and only had three lessons when we entered a trial. She gained a leg and in four shows had a CD." That was in 1965. The next year the cleric brought Faraderry Fairy through to a CDX, only the third Wheaten to have achieved that distinction.

In 1970, Father O'Connor received his license to judge obedience. Although his teaching and clerical duties restricted his judging, he was in great demand as an arbiter. "If you can't trust a priest, who can you?" said an owner, waiting to go into the ring that day at Penn Ridge.

The Wheatens were accepted for registration by the AKC in 1973, along with the Tibetan Terriers. Much of the credit goes to the O'Connor family of Brooklyn. The priest's mother, Mrs. Anne O'Connor, imported Gramachree from Ireland in 1957. The dog was shown at Staten Island in 1961, the first Wheaten seen at an AKC event in more than a decade. "The Soft-Coated Wheaten Terrier Club of America was founded on March 17, 1962, with my sister, Margaret, as president," said Father O'Connor. "There were a dozen members." When his sister died, the priest was elected president. The year the Wheaten was accepted the membership had soared to 450 and there were 1,100 Wheatens registered in the club's own stud book.

"Beauty and brains go hand in hand," said Betty Durland, "so when I sell a Cocker Spaniel, I always tell the buyer to take the dog for obedience training. After all, 90 percent of the dogs are going to be house pets, not show dogs, and people want a good companion." The Baldwinsville,N.Y., fancier has had success in both the show ring and at obedience trials. At the American Spaniel Club's specialty, in 1971, Betty received the organization's championship plaque, with the names of 11 Cocker Spaniel titleholders she had bred or owned. And for five years, Mrs. Durland had been training director for the Syracuse Obedience Training Club, where she helped to educate more than 2,500 owners and their pets. She scoffs at the exhibitor who maintains a dog cannot be shown in obedience and breed at the same time. "At Amsterdam N.Y., I was in the obedience ring with Dur-Bet's Headliner and he ran up a 198½, the highest scoring dog at trial," she said. "We then hurried over to the breed ring and he was named best of variety."

As is so often the case, it was an unruly pup—a German Shepherd—that sent Mr. and Mrs. Wesley Buckman of Sinking Spring, Pa., into obedience. "He was so bad, it was almost impossible to keep him around the house," said Mrs. Buckman. When we tried to enroll him in obedience, we were told he was too young." So the Buckmans bought a book on training. He did so well that when he was only 19 months old a club used him for exhibitions. He earned his CD, CDX and UD. The Buckmans then started an obedience school. "We have them for a week or two," said Mrs. Buckman. "When the owners take them home, the dogs have learned the basics—heel, sit, down, come and stay."

"Training You to Train Your Dog" isn't a title on the lights of movie marquees but it has been a smash hit for a dozen years. Invariably it draws the largest viewing audience of any film in the Gaines Dog Research library. In 1979, I learned that in the thirteen years since Gaines films were distributed by the Association-Sterling Films Company, fanciers had seen 45,154 screenings and they had drawn a total audience of 2,421,456. The hit film of the 17 Gaines had at the time, was an instructive and entertaining presentation of the basic principles of obedience training, narrated by Blanche Saunders.

Obedience Sports

A criticism of dog shows is the lack of variety for the casual spectator. Perhaps that is why the obedience rings drew such large crowds. It is something different and easy for the onlooker to understand. Some of the clubs added color to the educated performers. Penn Ridge held an obedience trial to the skirl of bagpipes. The Swingin' Canines of the Utica (N.Y.) Dog Training Club, consisting of eight obedience-trained dogs and eight members of the club, performed a square dance routine.

In 1969, Herbert O. Wegner developed scent hurdle racing and it has swept across the country and Canada. By applying basic rules, any novice-training dog in obedience can be taught the simple rudiments for the competition. In a race there are two teams of four handlers and their dogs. Each team sends its dogs simultaneously over a series of four hurdles. There are four dumbbells and the dog must pick out the one his handler has rubbed up. If a dog should take the wrong dumbbell, he must be sent out again.

At the United Kennel Club's shows at Place Bonaventure in Montreal, in April 1975, which drew a two-day paying total of 44,468, the greatest number to watch dogs in Canadian history up to that time, the scent hurdle racing was the star attraction. Most of the people in the audience had never been to a dog show. At ringside, typing my story, I was a target for questions. "What kind of a dog is that?", "What's the most expensive dog in the ring?" Few understood how a judge made his decision. But they all could follow the progress of the dogs in the hurdle racing and there was wild enthusiasm and applause.

A Five-Minute Training Course

A column I wrote on training brought in one of the heaviest mails I ever received. It was about Barbara Woodhouse of England. At a luncheon, she told me she could train an animal to do the basic obedience commands in five minutes. Then she added that she had trained 16,867 dogs and their owners in her native land. "I give my lessons over a weekend and they last a total of six-and-a-half hours. Most of the time is spent on the owners. The dogs are no problem," she said.

When I appeared skeptical, she suggested I bring two untrained dogs to the hotel, where she and her husband were staying, and let her demonstrate. The hotel was on Central Park South, so I phoned someone I knew who lived a block away and owned a totally spoiled Lhasa Apso. Unable to get a second dog, I stopped a young woman, who was walking her dog, told her how Mrs. Woodhouse said she could train an animal in a matter of minutes and would she permit her dog, a mixed breed she called Sneakers, to take part in the experiment. Ollie, the 18-month-old Lhasa, was already in the room. The Lhasa's greeting was a lunge, with much barking, and Sneakers replied with growls. The young woman was in favor of leaving immediately.

Then Mrs. Woodhouse took over. She pushed Sneakers into a sitting position, looked directly into his eyes, put her face close to his head, praising him in a quiet, confidential voice. Slipping a choke chain on Ollie, she walked him over to Sneakers and ordered him to sit, repeating her performance, ending with praise. She told each to stay and came over to our little group. It had all taken less than two minutes.

Putting the choke chain on Sneakers, the Englishwoman took him into the hall. After an abortive attempt or two to get to his owner, he quietly accompanied Barbara down the long corridor, where she had him lie down, as if for the long stay at an obedience trial. She then left Sneakers and joined us. Several minutes later, she called him and he ran to us. "He would have stayed an hour, if I had wanted," Mrs. Woodhouse assured us. It was a most convincing demonstration.

Unlike most instructors who want pups to be at least six months old, before they accept them for training, the Englishwoman takes them as young as three months. "I also take them up to the age of ten years. I trained a nine-year-old for a movie. She had to learn 13 commands. It took 15 minutes. When you are working with your dog, you should choose a time when you are placid. Bear in mind that a dog picks up your thought by an acute telepathic sense. If you wish to talk to your dog, you must do so with your mind and will power, as well as your voice. If you are in tune with your dog, he will work for you cheerfully and well." Since she puts her face so close to the dog's head, I asked if she had ever been bitten. "Twice," she replied. Perhaps it is fortunate that her husband is a surgeon.

Security Training

That same year I interviewed Joseph DeCosta, who was training dogs for security work. "Before I take an animal who is going to protect the home, I evaluate him," he said. "He must have the right temperament, intelligence, fearlessness and the ability to work. Many dogs are just too high-strung. Physically, I want a strong animal, with a good deep chest. Unless a dog has been trained, he doesn't know what to expect and he's no good except to bark and sound an alarm. Certainly you don't want a dog who is going to leap at anyone who rings the bell and enters the room.

"The security dog must show no sign of viciousness, unless it is provoked, and he must know the difference between a friendly greeting and an aggressive approach. The dog may be leaping in to attack, but a single command will stop him in midair if he has been trained properly. Obedience previously was a hobby for the dog fanciers. However, since 1970, the demand for guard dogs has tripled. Now people are buying and seeking animals for security and personal protection." DeCosta stressed positive control as the key to his training program. "For example," he said, "if a man approaches you with a weapon, or should he raise an iron pipe to strike, the dog will leap without a command, grab the arm and hold on until the resistance stops or he gets a command to release." The training generally lasts from six to eight weeks. DeCosta works alone with the dog for three days and with the dog and owner for two. He finds the work span of the average dog is from 40 minutes to an hour. After that the animal is tired and won't respond to training.

The trainer spends the first two days gaining the dog's confidence. He walks with him frequently, petting and praising him. "By the third day, he's waiting anxiously for me," said DeCosta. "I exercise him in the neighborhood where he lives. The first two words he learns from me are 'No' and 'Stay.' At the third meeting, I start him on a control pattern. I computerize the dog's mind by repetition, so he responds to prescribed commands. Like a computer, if you have set the commands properly, all you do is push the button. You almost can hear him think."

The Pros

Concerned that anyone can set himself up as a trainer of guard dogs, professionals in the field have been flocking to the United States Professional Dog Trainers Association. I wrote several articles about how high standards should be set by the trainers themselves and they were so impressed, they made me an honorary life member.

In 1976, Dick Maller, the president, told me, "Our organization has tripled in the past year. We now have 450 members from 44 states, Puerto Rico, the Virgin Islands, Bermuda, Jamaica, Britain, Germany and Australia. The men in the field realize an organization is necessary to promote legislation that will get rid of the fly-by-night inexperienced trainer. Remember, a guard dog can kill or maim. We also are working with the media, striving to eliminate false advertising."

In order to maintain a high standard, the association certifies its members. An apprentice, with up to a year's experience, is permitted to work only in obedience. A journeyman, with from one-to-five years experience, can take on security training of watch dogs. An assistant master, with from five-to-10 years, adds guard and police dog training. A master, with 10 or more years, is qualified for all phases.

"A professional works basically with a problem dog," explained Maller, "whom the owner is unable to handle. It might be a tiny Yorkie or a giant St. Bernard. The training period generally is three weeks."

The dog is taught basic obedience—heel, sit, down, come, a stand-stay (which is useful if it is raining)—and not to nip, jump or chew destructively. He is also housebroken, taught to walk through traffic and obey simple commands, such as "No" and "OK." The owner is shown how the dog is trained for each command and asked to practice 20 minutes each day with the animal for a month.

Training Psychology

But for training, two New Jersey behavioral psychologists have come up with a most novel approach. They are Dr. Lane Lenard and Dr. Ray Herman, who operate Canine Counseling of Princeton (CCP). "We apply methods of behavioral control and modification that have been scientifically developed and tested in the laboratory and field conditions," said Dr. Lenard, a Ph.D. from Rutgers. "Much of what science has learned about human behavior has come from the behavior of dogs," added Dr. Herman. "It has become clear through this research that the same rules of behavior apply to both dogs and people. The knowledge gained from this research has been applied with ever-increasing effectiveness to people's behavior problems. It is ironic that these scientifically acquired techniques and therapeutic programs had not been available to dogs themselves. It was to fill this need that we created our counseling service."

The two scientists treat both dog and owner, first making a house call and interviewing the entire family. "We ask how the dog has been treated," said Dr. Lenard. "Before long, the various members of the family invariably open up and tell us things that ordinarily would never come to light."

CCP is convinced that the causes of a dog's problems almost always can be traced to the dog's environment. "The best way to handle such problems," asserted Dr. Lenard, "is for the proper changes to be made by the most significant figures in that environment—the dog's owner and other members of the family. So we train the family, as well as the dog. That's why we want the home interview. We see how the animal and family interact. Thus root causes of the problem can be assessed and the proper treatment designed to fit the individual case."

It can take a few hours or perhaps two or three months to remedy a situation. "People all want short cuts," said Dr. Herman. "They feel that if we, or they, snap their fingers the dog will be cured. An animal doesn't acquire a behavior problem overnight, so he cannot be expected to lose that behavior pattern overnight. If people work with just a minimal effort, we can achieve 100 percent success. Most problems can be handled in two or three sessions, with the owner working from 15-to-20 minutes a day."

According to the psychologists, a dog learns by associating what he does with the consequences of that behavior. For example, if he does something that brings pleasure, he will receive food, praise or be petted. Thus he is likely to repeat that behavior in the future. However, if the dog does something and receives no pleasure from it or is immediately reprimanded, that behavior will soon disappear.

The scientists have found that dogs often reflect the owner's behavior. For example, if the children in the family are spoiled, the dog is likely to be spoiled, too. In many cases where the dog is spoiled, the owner isn't strong enough in dealing with his pet. The dog does as he pleases and isn't given a reprimand or reward at the proper time. "Most of a dog's problems stem from general disobedience," Dr. Herman explained, "and will begin to disappear as obedience training becomes more a part of his life and yours."

"When people come to us, frequently they are desperate and on the verge of having their dogs put to sleep," said Dr. Lenard. "We have saved many an animal who is now a good pet."

Schutzhund Training

A further dimension was added to obedience training in the early Seventies when schutzhund work was introduced from Europe. When I was in Austria in 1970, the *Oestrreichischer Kynolohenverband* invited me to the former royal hunting preserve, near Vienna, and staged a demonstration for me. I remember being tremendously impressed watching a Rottweiler climb over a six-foot fence, almost like a cat.

In 1973, I covered the first schutzhund trial ever held in the East and only the fourth in the United States. It lasted three days at a park in Newark, N.Y., and 14 dogs managed to earn degrees. In schutzhund, dog and handler work as a team in tracking, obedience and protection. The classes were Schutzhund A, for beginners, and SchH I, II, and III, with the tests getting increasingly difficult. There was also an endurance event, in which a candidate gaited 12½ miles within two hours and at the conclusion ran through some obedience exercises, including off-lead heeling and retrieving an object over a 40-inch wall. "We were looking for bad hips," said Nero Lindblad, a physicist who was director of the Northeast division of the North American Working Dog Association. "We also wanted the dog to prove he could still work, after such a taxing test."

For the beginners, there were two sections—obedience and protection. The obedience exercises were similar to those for CDX. In the protection phase, the dog had to locate an agitator hidden in a field and just bark. Then, heeling without a lead, he would attack the agitator who had come out of hiding to attack the handler. The animal was hit with a switch but could not show fear. He had to

270

stop on command. When the agitator ran away, acting in a belligerent manner, the handler would send the dog after the man to attack and hold.

For the first degree, the dog, at least 14 months old, had to pass a temperament qualifying test. Tracking was added to the other two phases. In tracking, the candidate followed an unmarked track of a minimum of 400 paces, at least 20 minutes old, and had to find two lost articles. In the second degree, for the tracking, the trail was 600 paces and 30 minutes old. The retrieve in obedience was much more difficult, the animal recovering a 1-pound-7-ounce dumbbell, with a free jump over a 40-inch hurdle and then had to climb a 64-inch barrier to retrieve an article. In the protection phase, the handler left the dog to guard a "suspect" while he "investigated" the hiding place. The suspect would attempt to escape and the dog had to stop him by seizing him. When the suspect hit the dog with a whip or stick, the dog immediately had to attack to prevent further aggressive action. The dog would stop, without command, when the suspect yielded.

For the third and most difficult degree, the SchH III, the candidate had to find three articles on a track 1,200 paces and 50 minutes old. In obedience, he retrieved an article, after climbing a 71-inch fence. The protection trial was similar to the second degree but more difficult, the dog working with two suspects. He was scored on his overall combativeness.

Lauren Myers, a production planner for Corning Glass, who then was North American president, told me, "We have a motto, 'Everything we do is for the dog.' Our clubs are born in the training field, not at council meetings. Take this Finger Lakes group (the club sponsoring the trial). Twice a month members come to Newark from four areas—Rochester, Utica, Ithaca and Elmira—to train. We don't have the word weather in our vocabulary. Dog and handler are exposed to heat, cold and rain. We arrive on a Sunday morning at 8 o'clock and train until sundown. Those owners whose dogs had good scores at the trial have worked from two-to-three hours every day."

Three years later, I covered the first schutzhund trial to be held on Long Island, at Eisenhower Park, East Meadow. It was conducted under the auspices of Working Dogs of America, a division of a German organization and the degrees were recognized by the FCI. Each dog was worked individually. When the animal completed an exercise, Dr. Dietmar Schellenberg of Webster, N.Y., a Ph.D. in chemistry, who judged the two-day event, addressed the spectators and gave a critique of the performance.

The top scorer at the trial was a 14-month-old Rottweiler, Klein Hasso Aller Meiner, owned by Neal Seaman, a psychology doctoral student. "I've been training him since he was six weeks old," said his proud owner. "He's blind in his right eye and still able to follow my hand signals." The Rottweiler earned both his SchH I and II degrees, even though Seaman hadn't trained him in the higher category exercises. "He did so well in the I, the judge suggested I let him try for the higher degree and darned if he didn't make it," said Seaman.

Only one other dog, a 110-pound German Shepherd, Las-Sana's Falkurt Ruff, CDX, earned a SchH II degree. "I've been working with him for 10 months," said his New York owner, Len Messana. "Every Sunday, our Long Island club drills all day at Syosset." Joyce Eusepi, the club's secretary, was the only woman to handle a qualifier, her German Shepherd, Whirldes Dawn, CD, coming through in A. Long Island's president, Shelly Liebowitz, said, "I'm the 'criminal' in the protection phase. I have to wear heavy canvas overalls and a strongly padded sleeve to withstand the attack of the dog, who is trying to stop me." Dr. Schellenberg proclaimed, "We hope with schutzhund work to demonstrate the capabilities of the utility dog. We want a sound body and mind, as well as beauty."

Scotland Yard

For training, however, the most interesting assignment I ever had was a day in Keston, England, where I watched the Scotland Yard dogs, who patrol London, being trained. While covering Crufts in 1976, I saw some of Bobby's best friends put on a demonstration at Olympia. I was so impressed, I phoned Benjamin Wilkinson, chief inspector of the Metropolitan Police Training School, and said I would like to interview him. He invited me to visit Keston. When I alighted from the train at this picturesque English town, there was a Scotland Yard car awaiting me with a moustached British inspector at the wheel.

The dog training school occupies a 24-acre site in a farming area. Wilkinson poured some tea for me and then told me the story in which he has played a leading role. "We have 248 fully-trained dogs," he said, "a far cry from the half-dozen Labrador Retrievers at the start, shortly after World War II." The Labs had been brought in by Scotland Yard to help apprehend muggers and handbag snatchers in Hyde Park. They proved so efficient that a section was set up in 1948. A black Lab, Ben, was particularly effective in the park. On patrol with a constable, the dog would stop and growl. At the policeman's command, he would bound away to search the bushes. When the officer would finally catch up to his four-footed partner, the Lab would be snarling and have a very frightened suspect at bay. Then the dog would sniff around, until he had located the stolen handbag or wallet. Ben had his own technique for felling a fugitive. He would run up, thrust his head between the culprit's legs and topple him.

"Although we had been using Labs, after studying programs in other countries, we decided we should add German Shepherds," said the chief inspector, "and soon we had some 30 or 40 dogs. Now came one of the hardest tasks we faced, selling our program to the force itself. There were many officers who weren't enthusiastic about our having dogs. We had to prove their value in tracking, locating people or property, and working in the dark, pointing up how the animal's sense of smell and hearing is so much more acute than that of the human."

The training school was established in Keston in 1954. The local farmers, proud the site had been chosen, agreed to allow the dogs to run over their lands, giving the school more than 3,000 acres.

"What started as a haphazard program soon ironed itself out. Our training methods improved. Not only did we have the dogs search for hidden persons in the school area but we vanned them into London and had them work in the old buildings along the Thames," said Wilkinson. "Then we found the dogs, which we either had bought or were given to us, weren't meeting our requirements. So, in the late Fifties, Tom Mahler, an assistant police commissioner who was our chief instructor, went to Germany. There he bought a half-dozen brood bitches and a stud dog and that was the start of our breeding program. Now we raise 60 percent of our own dogs. The others, which we get as gifts or buy, we bring to Keston for a month on approval. So vigorous is our training that only one in 20 makes the grade. Training involves both the dog and handler who work as a team. The handler, an officer, has to apply for the service, and we have more applications than there are vacancies. The average man, when we take him, has been with the Metropolitan Police for four years, is married and has a house."

There is a civilian woman engaged in the program. After a litter has been whelped, when the pups are six weeks old, they are turned over to her. She lead breaks them and takes them to Keston to get them accustomed to people and traffic. When a pup is 12 weeks old, he is allocated to a policeman novice handler and goes to live with him. A training program is outlined and one day a month the pup is brought to the school to be checked by a veterinarian and his progress noted. He is getting basic obedience, such as walking on the left-hand side of the officer; sit, down and stay. At seven months, the pup starts to retrieve. When he reaches nine months, the pup and officer report to Keston for a two-week course. Manwork is subtly introduced, where the dog barks at someone concealed in the bushes; basic obedience is increased and tracking begins, with the pup following a ground scent. There are three more monthly visits with the team graded.

At the age of a year, the serious work begins. There is a concentrated 14-week course, with daily lessons from 8:30 A.M. until 3:30 P.M. Tracking is stepped up, with both the distance and time the scent has been on the ground increased. Manwork includes finding and cornering a suspect. Once located, the dog crouches in front of him or circles menacingly, until the constable appears. A full-fledged attack is a last resort, executed on command. The dog is trained to bark an alarm when he has located a fugitive or article and to give chase and stop a suspect.

Then the animals must surmount several obstacles, climb ladders, leap hurdles, crawl through sewer pipes, jump to platforms and slide down, and scale a six-foot wall. For greater heights, the Bobby assists. He bends near the wall, with the dog leaping onto his back and taking off from there to go over or alight on a roof. A dog has been known to clear 12-foot barriers this way.

For the human side of the team, there is schoolwork in grooming, conditioning, learning the diseases of the animal and studying the characteristics of his dog. "We stress handling, for we want the officer to be a good handler," said the chief inspector.

Now the team is considered an operational unit and assigned to a station. However, once every two weeks, for the rest of the dog's working life, he and his partner must report to one of five centers maintained in London. If a weakness has been uncovered, there is corrective training.

The animal remains on active duty with the officer for eight years. When the dog is seven, a 12-week-old pup is added to the policeman's household. The pup's training starts and he takes over when the older dog is retired and becomes a pet for his former teammate.

The staff at the school, in addition to Wilkinson, consists of a deputy chief inspector, six instructors, six civilian kennel men and the young woman who handles the puppies.

In the school's breeding program, all the dogs are X-rayed and must be free of hip dysplasia. "We check the others visually," said the chief inspector. "If they run freely and can keep up with our training programs we are satisfied. Dogs from our own breeding give us few problems. They come from known bloodlines, with good temperament, sound conformation and the natural qualities of a true working dog. We have them from the time they have been whelped and they acquire no bad habits or hangups. That's not true of so many of the others we have to reject. Temperament is a must in police work. We will not train any dog that is suspect. The animal must have a good physique, proportionate to his build. He must like his work. Any dog that is cowed or surpressed is no good for us."

Since 1968, the dogs have been used successfully for prison work, where they are trained to search and chase. "They patrol the perimeters," said Wilkinson, "and since we have placed them at the prisons, breakouts have been negligible."

The chief inspector said that during 1975, the policemen and their dogs accounted for 7,412 arrests, 65 missing persons were located and 224 items of property recovered. In narcotics detection, only the Labradors are used, for their keener scenting ability. Of 765 calls, they located the quarry 370 times, leading to the arrest of 906 persons. "Not a drug raid is carried out today without dogs," said the chief inspector. "They have been invaluable."

At Heathrow Airport, two Labs working with customs officers barked at several burlap-covered crates. These were found to contain footballs, which seemed innocent enough. However, an examination revealed that hashish had been placed in some of the rubber bladders, inside the football. This led to the arrest of six persons and the recovery of a large amount of the drug.

With the wave of bombings in the city—several exploded when I was over for Crufts and all the spectators were searched arriving for the show—a unit trained in the detection of explosives is on call. "The dogs were used 732 times in the year," said Wilkinson, "and did excellent work searching areas where it was suspected bombs had been planted."

Scotland Yard has trained dogs for the United States, France, Italy, Poland, Jordan, Egypt, Bermuda, the Bahamas, Jamaica, and several African countries. On the walls are plaques of appreciation.

But Wilkinson is particularly proud of a special unit sent to the Sinai Desert, under the auspices of the United Nations, to help recover the bodies of 700 Egyptian and Israeli soldiers killed in the 1967 fighting.

"The most modern sophisticated equipment had been used, but none of the bodies had been uncovered," he said. "We arrived with two dogs trained for the work. In the first week, they located 75 bodies, some under eight feet of sand. We sent for another four dogs and within a month all of the other bodies were found. What amazed me was that the dogs left here in February, when it was bloody cold and the next day they were working in the heat of the desert. They made an immediate adjustment. The only problem was in the feeding."

When I asked why he kept referring to the animals only as he and not she, Wilkinson responded, "We only use dogs; less problems, you know."

The queen of Obedience, Moreland's Golden Tonka, Golden Retriever. Tonka became the first to win the AKC Obedience championship title, winning the last of the 100 required points on July 23, 1977. She was America's top obedience dog for 1974, 1975, 1976 and 1978. Owned and trained by Russ Klipple.

Mac, an English Setter, stands at point during a field trial held by the Long Island Bird Dog Club. Owner Ned Brown is seen in background.

Field Trials

CATS AND DOGS proverbially are linked together, but not at the *Times*. Week after week, I'd get calls from irate cat owners demanding equal treatment for tabby. "Why don't you cover cat shows?" they would ask. More or less patiently, I'd explain, "At the *Times* dogs are considered sports, while cats are news. I'll switch you to the City Desk."

In the twenties, there were far more papers around the country than today. In New York, in addition to the *Times, The Herald-Tribune* and *Evening Sun* gave doggy events good coverage. So did the long defunct *Boston Transcript* and thereby hangs a tale. The sports editor of that august paper, a voice for amateur sports, instead of reporting a World Series game, covered a field trial. It reportedly cost him his job. He always maintained he had been right, that a trial is a true amateur event, without the crass commercialism of a professional sport.

He had a point, for the field trial devotee is still another "breed" in the world of dogs. In blazing heat, in bitter cold, in rain and snow, these dedicated aficionados are out running their Pointers, Setters, Retrievers There is a spirit of friendship among them too often missing at the show ring. "We don't charge admission, we have no superintendents and our judges receive no fees," an old-timer explained. "All we want to prove is my dog can find more birds than yours and he can do it more stylishly."

Very much like the obedience enthusiasts the sportsmen and sportswomen—who range in age from teenagers to septuagenarians—applaud when the judges gather at the end of the day to announce their findings. There is no established list of field trial judges as there is for conformation. Instead, each club holding a trial chooses its own judges (usually based on experience) and submits them to the AKC for approval. At the pointing breed trials, they work in pairs, riding for hours behind the dogs, evaluating their performances, and then, after consulting with each other, make their placements. The dogs are judged on style, pace, drive, range, stamina, bird sense, intensity on point and use of the wind and terrain in locating birds.

There is a serenity in the early hours before a trial unique to the sports world. The club officials have been up since the wee hours preparing for the event. Shortly after dawn they can be seen trudging through thickets, straw fields and hedgerows, planting. But unlike the farmers, who are busy with corn, soybeans or wheat, the field trialers are planting quail. The birds, pen-raised, will join the native colony on the grounds. It is quiet, the mist rising from the earth, with only the bobwhite whistle of the quail breaking the morning silence.

Soon the cars carrying the dogs begin to roll into the grounds. If it is a major trial, lasting several days, there is activity in what resembles a gypsy encampment. These are the handlers in their motor homes, with their Tennessee walking horses tethered nearby.

Then there is a call for the first brace, which is sent away promptly at seven o'clock for the trial must be over in daylight. Riding behind the dogs is a colorful procession. There are the two judges, the handlers, the marshals and the gallery. When a dog points a bird, its handler dismounts and fires a blank pistol to show that the animal is staunch and true to shot and wing. A bird is never killed. Indeed, at most grounds in the North, the pointing breed season stops from the end of April until the beginning of September, so the quail, pheasant, woodcock and grouse won't be disturbed in their nesting and will have a chance to multiply.

Hamilton Rowan, in charge of field trials for the AKC, points out that with grounds for hunting steadily diminishing, sportsmen are turning to field trials in increasing numbers. It gives them a chance to run their dogs in competition every week.

The English Setter Club of America has the distinction of being the oldest field trial club in the United States owning its own grounds. On its 286 acres, near the rustic community of Medford, N.J., is the former clubhouse, now a museum, which was the homestead of the Thomas Wilkins family from 1732 until the club purchased it early in this century. It is the second oldest building standing in Burlington County. In it is field trial memorabilia, with oil paintings and prints dotting the walls. Among the trophies is the Blue Ribbon Derby Cup, first offered by Gustave Pabst in 1911, and a huge sterling silver plaque donated by George C. Thomas, the next year. A Kentucky long rifle with a powder horn, a reminder of another era, hangs over a fireplace, along with a print of Count Gladstone, a famous English Setter in 1896. On the grounds is a cemetery in which are buried dogs who formerly ran in field trials and horses that ran behind them. I noticed a pair of matching headstones for David and Goliath.

Jack Laytham, a former president of the English Setter, the American Pointer, the Camden and Wilmington clubs, who retired as a du Pont executive in the Sixties, donated a perpetual trophy, which is now the most prized of those in competition. "When I took over in 1972, the club had dwindled to 22 members," said the white-haired sportsman. "We made a strong comeback and when I turned the club over to John Rosenburg, four years later, there were 87."

I covered a three-day trial at Medford in the spring and there was a variety of weather conditions. The first day began under a blue sky with a scattering of clouds. But as the trial progressed it grew warmer. There had been a protracted dry spell and scenting conditions were not good. The second day saw the temperature soar to 87. The scenting was so bad a dog almost had to stumble over a quail to make a find. A shallow stream ran through the course and this proved a lifesaver, most of the dogs racing in to cool off.

Each brace ran for a half-hour and with the dogs ranging far and wide, they covered more than 10 miles. At noon on the third day, there was a downpour and for the next hour and a half, the dogs had to prove their worth as mudders. "We were wearing raincoats, Paul Fuhrman and Howard McDonald, the judges, told me, "but we were soaked to the skin." Although the event was held on the English Setter Club grounds, there wasn't an English Setter among the 103 entries. German Shorthaired Pointers dominated, with 84 running. So it was no surprise when a Shorthair won the open stake. What was a surprise was that he was competing for only the fifth time. He was Viktridee's Bold Bruno, owned by Bill Grim, an accountant for du Pont, and handled by Mike Allen.

The Long Island Bird Dog Club was organized in 1955, with Ned Brown, its first president. The club's most prized trophy is the Doyle Cup, in competition since 1961. The owner of the winning dog takes home the big silver bowl and keeps it for one year. Six times Brown's English Setters have kept it in his living room. The Long Islanders have their trials at 1,700-acre Southaven Park, near Shirley. In addition to that site, there is the 4,500-acre Navy Cooperative Hunting Area at Ridge, operated by the New York State Department of Environmental Conservation.

Schuyler Gorwin, Suffolk County's Superintendent of Parks, was warm in his praise of the field trialers. "They're out regardless of the weather," he told me. "At Southaven, we are open from sunrise to sunset. During the week only a handful train their dogs. They come early, before going to work, or late afternoon, after they get home. I've seen them working dogs in a pelting rain and in driving snowstorms. They certainly are a hardy lot. We never have any trouble with them. They police the grounds themselves and there's no clean-up necessary when they leave. In the off-season, we plow the land and the club plants acres of rye, millet and sorghum so the birds will have ample feed. During the season, the club releases 75 pheasants every week, which strengthens the native colony."

The big event of the trial, on a day I covered, was the shooting dog stake and it went to a four-year-old liver-and-white Pointer, Elhew Christie, owned and run by a Suffolk County policeman, Paul Fuhrman, who had been a judge at the Jersey trial. He stayed just long enough to learn he had won and then was off. "I'm on the 4-to-12 shift at St. James," he explained. Fuhrman had bought Chris when she was a nine-week-old pup. "When she was four months old," he chuckled, "she was pointing butterflies in the yard. Two months later she pointed her first covey of quail. Chris is a housepet. My two girls and boy dress her up and she plays nicely with them." The Pointer won the Doyle Cup in 1975.

Bob Friedman, who judged the stake along with Jim McGoldrick, was warm in his praise of Chris. "The Pointer's application was faultless," said Bob. "She was always to the front seeking birds. With head and tail up, she was pleasing to the eye. She had two stylish finds and had so much stamina, I'm sure she could have run a three-hour heat.''

McGoldrick agreed with Friedman and added, "When I see a dog frozen on point, it still makes me sit up in the saddle and my hair stands on end. It's a sight one never forgets.''

Like Fuhrman, policemen in their spare time like to run in the field. At one of the last trials I covered, in 1976, the Long Island shooting dog championship, the two major awards were "copped" by officers. Pat Marshall, a retired detective who worked on famous underworld cases when he was with the Brooklyn Homicide Squad, ran his Brittany Spaniel, Canaan Lake Rusty, to the title, and John Gormly, a New York City transit officer, was runner-up with his German Shorthaired Pointer bitch, Hewlett's S. A. Ginger.

Rusty was one of the top bird dogs on the East Coast. The orange-and-white had triumphed in 35 stakes and was both a field and amateur champion. Ginger had been awarded a trophy for having taken more events in 1975 than any other member's dog in the Long Island Bird Dog Club.

Spaniel trials are similar to those for the pointing breeds, except that the dog flushes birds, so they take to the air, instead of pointing them. Spaniels also retrieve the birds. They work much closer, so the judges and handlers follow on foot, not on horseback.

I found retriever trials the most exciting. Few events are more demanding. The dogs are sent through both water and land tests for which they are judged for their natural abilities—intelligence, nose, courage, perseverance, style—and for skills acquired through training—steadiness, control, response to direction and delivery. The dogs are expected to retrieve any type of game under all conditions.

I remember a Long Island Retriever Club meet I covered, when the nation's top retrievers were confronted with fog, relatively warm weather and then cold, biting breezes. Only rain was missing. The amateur all-age open drew 37 entries—five series were called—a double blind, where two pheasants were planted in heavy cover; a land triple, where a dog had to retrieve three birds; a water blind retrieve, where a duck was planted in heavy cover across a pond, unseen by the dog but visible to the handler, who directed the retriever with whistle and hand signals; a water triple and another land triple.

The first two tests, started in fog on the opening day, saw the field reduced to 35. The water blind, on the second day, proved the Waterloo for 15 of the survivors. Only Fld. Ch. Mi-Chris Sailor, a Canadian import owned by Mrs. George Murname, the victor, did his work without the aid of a whistle from his handler, the black Lab swimming high and making a brilliant retrieve. The water triple eliminated nine more, Sailor again proving his prowess, getting three ducks, with dispatch. In the final, he lined all three pheasants perfectly.

Among the retriever devotees, August Belmont, former Chairman of the AKC Board of Directors, is known for his work with Chesapeake Bays and Labradors in the field. But as proficient as he has been training duck hunters, he also has done well in obedience and the show ring.

"It all started in 1957," he told me, "when I bought a six-week-old Chesapeake, Bomarc of South Bay. The pup made history for the breed. He earned a CD in obedience, gained his show title and became an amateur field champion. In the previous two decades only one other Chesapeake ever had become an amateur field champion.

"Bo had his CD when he was only six months and 11 days old. He liked to hunt and I did some shooting over him. He was so good that five months later, I ran him in a derby stake at a trial and he took first place. Still a pup, I took Bo to the Piping Rock dog show. Some friends were showing and asked me to enter the pup to help make a major. Neither of us ever had been in a ring, but it was quite a debut, for Bo took best of breed."

Belmont's great pride, however, was a black Labrador, Super Chief. Soupy, as his owner called him, was "a once in a lifetime dog, one of the greatest Labrador Retrievers in the history of the sport."

The Lab's record substantiates the lavish praise. The Chief's career started at the early age of five months, when he was sent to Rex Carr in California for schooling. And a proficient student he was, winning his first derby when he was only 11 months old. Although Soupy was eligible to compete in derby stakes until he was two years old, Belmont withdrew him from competition seven months later, after he had rolled up 40 points.

The Lab's owner ran him in the national amateur retriever championship in 1967, which he promptly won. The next year Soupy not only repeated the victory but won the national open, as well, the first time this ever had been accomplished.

When Mrs. Belmont was in good health, she was extremely active in the sport. "Louise did a much better job than I," said Augie. "She ran three dogs to both field and amateur championships." A well-known figure in the Wall Street area, Belmont served as chairman of Dillon, Read & Company, when he wasn't working his retrievers. But then his financial knowledge proved useful among the fancy. For years, he was treasurer of the AKC and secretary-treasurer of the National Retriever Club. Augie also was president of the National Amateur Retriever Club.

Driving from a hospital delivery room to walk a dog into a show ring or run a retriever at a trial is routine for Dr. Anna Van Rooy, an obstetrician from Kensington, Md. She has the distinction of having trained the youngest Golden Retriever to earn a TD. She told me that she enjoyed the field work most of all. "But with my profession, I have little free time, since I never know when I'm going to be called. So it is very hard to train."

The physician is from the Netherlands. She came to this country as an exchange student in 1956 after she had completed medical school at the University of Utrecht. "I wanted to see the medical facilities in the United States," she said. She stayed on and trained at a hospital in Bethesda, Md.

Having always had dogs in her native land, she bought a Golden Retriever pup, Lady Butterscotch, and started her in obedience. "She had a CD when she was nine months old," recalled the doctor, "a TD eight months later; a CDX the next month, and a UD when she was 22 months old, a Golden record for a UDT." After Buffy had a litter, Dr. Van Rooy started her in the show ring and she gained her championship with two four-point majors. She didn't begin working in the field until she was three years old and she proved a real triple-threat ace. At the national, in 1972, Buffy won the trophy as the champion placing highest in the trial. One of her pups, Happy Go Lucky of Jolly Way, also made history. The obstetrician trained her and she delivered with a TD, when she was seven months old, the youngest Golden to do so. She's also a UDT.

An international Brittany Spaniel championship was held at Evans Mills, N.Y., in 1971, with 20 dogs qualifying from the United States and Canada. And who was the winner? None other than a city dog, whose weekday training consisted of romps in the then New York University parking lot in the Bronx before his master left for work in the morning. He was Carey's Freckles, owned by John J. Carey, an industrial buyer for Esso International.

"We live in an apartment house around the corner from NYU," Carey told me. "At a picnic, my wife saw a Brit and said she would like one. So we bought Freckles, our first and only dog. We knew nothing about Brits but I read up on the breed and learned it was a good gun dog, so I decided I'd do some hunting. Neither the pup nor I knew what it was all about. I'd drive up Route 22 and we'd tramp through the woods looking for birds. We met some hunters and they told us about field trials. I went to a couple and decided I'd run the dog. We learned by doing. After three years, we managed to get a fourth place."

Other Brit owners, watching Freckles work, prevailed upon Carey to have the dog professionally trained. So at the age of six, Freckles went to "school" for three months. He proved to be a good pupil. In three years, the Brittany had 32 placements. But it was at the age of nine that he really came into his own. He won an open stake in Georgia, gained his field championship at the Southern New England Brittany trial, next led a field of 38 at Hudson Valley and wound up with the international title. Not bad for a nine-year-old who would only get into the field on weekends. The other five days, he either rested at home or romped around at NYU, where he was a great favorite of the students. Maybe some of the education rubbed off.

The next year, Jupp's Trooper Rochambeau, known to his owners, Mr. and Mrs. Thomas Tivnan of Saddle River, N.J., as Beau, became the American Brittany Club's national champion. Beau led a field of 67 over a demanding course in the snow in Lake Murray. The Brit's sire was Lund's Trooper, a show and field champion, who had more than 100 placements.

The Cost of Training Field Trial Dogs

On occasions, I was asked how much it would cost to buy a trained field dog, who could win in national competition. Ed Carey of Woodstock, Ill., who trained more than 2,000 hunting dogs, placed a value of from $15,000 to $20,000 for a prospective Retriever winner. Since it is estimated it costs $1,000 a point on the way to a championship, and it takes 10 points, winning a Retriever title can be a costly business.

The basic training takes three months," Carey told me, "plus two hunting seasons, with additional work during the off-seasons." However, to develop a field trial dog who can win in national competition, much more is required. "There must be continuous work, starting when he's a six-month-old pup, until he is four or five years old, when he reaches his peak," said Carey. "With the tremendous number of entrants at the big trials, only those dogs with the highest performance level will win or place. I was at a trial in which there were 96 dogs in the open all-age. All a dog had to do was look sideways and he was out. There was no such thing as luck. To finish in the top four was sheer skill on the part of the both the dog and handler."

I interviewed Carey at the International show in Chicago, where he staged a demonstration of multiple retrieving with three Retrievers—a Chesapeake, Labrador and Golden. When I asked him to discuss the relative merits of the three breeds, he replied, "The Labs have dominated the competition since the '60s. However, the Goldens came up in the late 1960s, winning and placing at major trials. In the early '70s, the American Chesapeake Bay Retriever Club began to make great strides with its breeding program, with many good young Chesapeakes showing up."

Where There's A Wehle, There's A Way

Then there is the man who is almost a legend among bird dog enthusiasts. He is Robert Wehle, a tall, soft-spoken man, who wears tweeds well. In his rambling green ranchhouse, on his 2,000 acre farm in Scottsville, N.Y., a Rochester suburb, he welcomed us to a delightful afternoon of good talk covering a few of the many facets of this sportsman's life—Pointers, horses, cattle, art, cooking, antiques, ecology. There is a quiet confidence and determination about him. Here is a man who combines vision and dedication with know-how.

Wehle is a rugged individualist when it comes to Pointers. He has defied the AKC standard for the breed and set up his own. "Their standard has already proven its inadequacies insofar as the physical ability of these dogs to perform properly in the field, particularly as to gait, speed, grace and endurance," he explained.

It is pretty hard to dispute with Wehle for his Elhew (Wehle spelled backward) Kennel has been one of the most successful in field trial history. Among its national champions, all carrying the Elhew prefix, were the Pointers, Marksman, Jungle, Zeus, Holly and Huckleberry. A breeding program set up in 1936 by the millionaire, "in which I established conformation and psychological standards designed to produce a strain that would not only win field trials but be pleasing to the eye and satisfy the most discriminating sportsmen as gun dogs," has sent out more than 3,000 Pointers. Fanciers on four continents have bought and hunted with them.

Wehle, a firm proponent of inbreeding or of selective line breeding, pores over pedigrees and rating sheets he keeps on all his dogs before he breeds them. They not only must conform to his conformation standards but they must work in the field for months to evaluate their psychological qualities. Says he, "A top field dog must have not only the physical wherewithal, but the intelligence and desire to accomplish the job." There must be no excess nervousness, shyness or belligerence but an affectionate disposition with a desire to please. Then there must be an acute sense of smell, sight and hearing and the ability to use them to their fullest advantage. This calls for severe and rigid culling over the years. Elhew Marmaduke, one of the best dogs he ever raised, traced 19 times to his original foundation stud, Lexington Jake.

An extremely articulate man, Wehle doesn't exhibit this quality while training. He expresses all commands with short, sharp words, holds them to a minimum and uses them as little as possible. A vocabulary of 15 words, he maintains, is enough to win any championship.

As to breed competition, Wehle says, "The most important gait in a Pointer is running. In the show ring, they never run." Wehle stresses conditioning in his Pointers and he's rigged up a four-wheeled cart to which as many as 16 dogs can be tandem-hitched and driven along the country roads. He caused a sensation at Clayton, N.Y., in 1963, when he appeared for a program of sled-dog races, with a team of Pointers, three of the dogs being national field trial champions. All the other starting teams were either Siberian Huskies, Alaskan Malamutes or Samoyeds. The Pointers did not win that time, but they finished the race.

Later, at Harrisville, N.Y., "one of the longest races this side of Alaska," said Wehle, the conditioning paid off. "It was 14 below zero and there was fresh snow," he recalled. The teams had to race over a 22-mile trail, for two days, with the best elapsed time to count. "We had to cross two lakes, wind through pine groves and through brush. At one two-mile stretch, the visibility was so bad I couldn't see my lead dog." Of 54 starting teams, 14 failed to finish. The Pointers covered the 44 miles in two hours, 49 minutes, 37 seconds—winning by eight minutes. Wehle next took the team to Tamworth, N.H., to compete in the Honeoye Lake races. In his den is the trophy the Pointers won for the sportsman, taking the gruelling event three years in a row.

Robert Wehle is accomplished in many fields. He's a former president of the Genesee Brewing Company, a talented sculptor and painter, horticulturist, chef and collector of antiques. Most of his sculpture, and it's all bronze, is of dogs and they overflow the room he uses as studio, into the den and living room. A striking, rough-surfaced head of John F. Kennedy attracts attention. Some of his work has been exhibited at the Grand Central Art Gallery in New York and it has won awards of the National Arts Society.

On the wood-paneled walls of his den are a half-dozen large oil paintings and a dozen water colors of Pointers. In a greenhouse off the living room are many flowers. "I have them coming up all year," he said. The kitchen, which he designed, encourages good conversation and the drinks which he expertly prepares, unloose the tongue. His culinary specialty: sauerbraten, from an old family recipe. When complimented on his renowned cooking, Wehle replied modestly, "I have more than 30 cookbooks."

His modern kennel buildings and barn resemble a colonial village. "I designed them from several I saw at Sturbridge Village and Williamsburg," he said. His whelping building is fashioned after one at Cornell Veterinary School.

In the past, Wehle was a noted sportsman, who hunted in Europe and took part in African safaris. He now takes a different view. A leading conservationist and ecologist, he looks with alarm on the increasing number of hunters pursuing a decreasing supply of game. "Hunting is an indulgence we no longer can afford," warned Wehle. "We are experiencing an ecological dilemma, not only in game birds but insects, the fauna and flora. I'm opposed to hunting irreplaceable species. The only birds I'll shoot are quail, pheasant and mallards, all of which are easily replaceable. We should not try for the limit. The birds spared by the gun will live to be pointed again."

John M. Olin

Another famous sportsman is John M. Olin, president of Olin Mathieson, known for his gun dogs. He is the founder of the Orthopedic Foundation for Animals, which has the largest collection of radiographs of dogs' hips in the world. When I interviewed him in 1972, the then 79-year-old Olin said, "I've had dogs all my life. My father had Irish Setters and Pointers and from the time I was seven, I'd hunt with him."

Over the years Olin had a variety of hunting breeds but it was the Labrador who drew his greatest accolade. "He's the best all-round retriever there is," asserted Olin and he could speak with authority for he has been active in the field for more than a quarter of a century. He had two national retriever champions, Nilo's King Buck and Martin's Little Smokey, with the former having been used as the model for the United States duck stamp in 1959.

His Nilo Kennels (Olin spelled backward) at the time of the interview had 80 Labs, at Alton, Ill., while on Nilo Plantation, in Georgia, there were 40 Pointers. English Springers and Brittany Spaniels were at Nilo Farm in Illinois. "I believe in using dogs in hunting as a conservation measure," he said. "A good worker reduces your losses immeasurably."

OFA deals principally in hip dysplasia. A central registry has been set up as an important step in controlling and helping to prevent this widespread skeletal abnormality. "The life of a dog is seven times as rapid as a human," explained Olin. "So by studying skeletal problems in canines, we have a speed-up laboratory. Our work should unravel a great many skeletal problems in man."

The Newfoundland Water Tests

Intrigued by the idea of four-footed lifeguards (in France, lifeguards are backed up by Newfoundlands for rescue work), the summer after I retired I drove to a lake in Pennsylvania's Poconos to watch the first Newfoundland Club of America water tests ever held in the East. This is a competition developed by Clare Carr of Manchester, Michigan, and first conducted in her state in 1973. The tests are divided into two divisions, junior and senior, with six exercises in each. The junior leads to a "water" degree, the senior to a "water rescue" title.

In the junior, the exercises are: basic obedience; a go-out where the dog, on the handler's command, goes out to swimming depth and remains until the judge signals the handler for the return; an underwater retrieve; a single retrieve, where a dog must recover an object thrown at least 30 feet from shore; take a line, in which the dog delivers a line to a steward 75 feet away; tow a boat, where the dog pulls a boat 50 feet. For the senior, the tests become increasingly difficult.

The exercises proved so demanding that at the Pocono tests, only two of 15 dogs in the junior trial earned degrees. Both of the senior candidates failed.

When I spoke to the judges—John Van Brandeghen, a former president of the Great Lakes Newfoundland Club, and Bill Hutchins, an obedience arbiter for more than 20 years—they said they were impressed with the enthusiasm of the dogs and handlers. "The hardest part of the training is to find water where one can practice," added Van Brandeghen. "As to the actual tests, we are more concerned with getting the job done rather than with the precision required in an obedience trial. Our great concern is that we keep a dual dog and not one for water work and another for the breed ring."

Canineada

THE CLOSEST RELATIONSHIP in dogdom between nations is that of the United States and Canada. Exhibitors frequently are crossing the border to show, eager to make their dogs champions in two countries. Some great performers have come down from Canada and few will forget Westminster victories of the Old English Sheepdog, Ch. Sir Lancelot of Barvan in 1975, and the Irish Water Spaniel, Ch Oaktree's Irishtocrat in 1979. Judges from the United States frequently are ruling in rings north of the border and their counterparts come from Canada. Indeed one of the AKC all-rounders is Bob Waters, from British Columbia, and Vince Perry's roots trace to Ontario.

For more than four decades Betty Hyslop has been showing in this country as well as in her native land. I remember stopping off at her charming two-century old stone house on the St. Lawrence. For years it has been a landmark on the river in Ontario, so boatmen knew when they saw it they were at Brockville. Only old timers will remember that her Cairndania Kennel in the 1930s and '40s was famous for its Great Danes, and the "dania" part of her kennel name is derived from her early days in the sport. At one time she had five of the giant dogs who were champions in both Canada and the United States. But then she decided the Great Danes were just too big for her to handle, so she turned to the feisty little Cairns.

Most experts agree that Cairndania Cairns are among the best in the world. Betty has more than 40 at the kennel and you get quite a welcome when you arrive at Cairndania. She certainly needs no burglar alarm. Two are English champions and 17 have titles in either two or three countries. Mrs. Hyslop bred 118 Cairns that became American or Canadian champions, or both. Few fanciers have had the success of this Canadian breeder. Her Ch. Pimpernel of Marcia was best of breed at Westminster in 1939. Since then she has had best Cairn at America's most prestigious show 15 times. From 1946 for the next 13 years, every purple-and-gold rosette winner came from Cairndania.

Although the mistress of Cairndania has owned various colored Cairns, her favorite shade is red. The only time she sees red in the ring, when she's not looking at her Cairns, is when a judge fails to give one a blue.

It was in Montreal that I met a tall, white-haired man. He was Jeffrey Carrique, a power in both the Canadian football and dog show worlds. For more than two decades he had been associated with the Montreal Alouettes and he was serving as president of the advisory board for the club which so many times has won the Canadian Football League championship. Carrique was a past president of the United Kennel Club and was coordinator for the two extravaganzas staged in Place Bonaventure, the richest ever held on the continent. "We took a gamble," said the Canadian, "for we offered $55,000 in prize money."

Carrique and his committee did a beautiful job with the exhibition hall, which incidentally had 200,000 square feet of space, compared with 20,400 at Madison Square Garden, where Westminster is held. Although there still was the remains of a storm, which dropped 14 inches of snow on Montreal, inside Place Bonaventure there was a tropical look in the rings, with a half-dozen five-foot potted palms in each.

Although the Canadian is best known for his Shih Tzu, he started with Old English Sheepdogs. "We imported a bitch from England," he said, "and she finished in Canada and the United States. But it's hard to have such big dogs in the city, so we decided to change to a long-coated little dog–the Shih Tzu. The greatest thrill I had in the sport was when Carrimount Chop-Chop, a champion in Canada, the United States and Bermuda, went best in show in Burlington [Vt.]. It had been raining and we left early. When the phone rang and I was told my Shih Tzu had won, I thought someone was pulling my leg. The next day I refused an offer of $7,500 for him."

Sarah Diamond is the Province of Quebec's director to the Canadian KC. The CKC has an entirely different set-up from the AKC, which is an organization of clubs, each represented by a delegate. The CKC has 14,000 members, a president, two vice presidents and 12 directors. The directors are elected by the members from their own province. Mrs. Diamond for four years was head of the powerful judge's committee. Originally she had Boxers, but then turned to Dachshunds. At one time, the Montrealer had 45 miniature smooths or wires. "I haven't shown since 1973," she said. "I'm much too busy with my CKC work and judging."

The women's lib movement in the show world reached Canada much earlier than the United States. Whereas the AKC refused to permit women as delegates until 1974, north of the border the president of the CKC was Hilda Pugh, and in 1975, when I interviewed her in Montreal, she had been the chief executive for six years. The CKC, which was organized in 1898, had two other women presidents, Mrs. Alva McColl and Mrs. Eileen McEachren. "We have 400 shows a year," Mrs. Pugh told me. "We are under the jurisdiction of the Canadian Department of Agriculture. Should we make any change in our by-laws, they would have to be approved first by the department. We are able to really protect the public for should anyone sell a dog without papers it becomes a breach of a Federal act and the offender would be dealt with by the Royal Canadian Police. Whereas the AKC is a private organization, we are a Government agency.''

The top-winning dog of all breeds in Canada in 1975 was a red Chow Chow, Ch. Mi-Tu's Han Su Shang, owned by Fred Peddie and Herb Williams, advertising executives in Toronto. The first time I met the Canadians was at Madison Square Garden, when the Toronto dog won the Westminster group in 1975. Williams had been showing the red dog, and spontaneously picked up the 50-pounder, kissed him and held the dog aloft for everyone to see. The crowd responded with a tremendous ovation for the two. Shang has had a remarkable career. Whelped in December 1972, in his first appearance in a ring, at the age of six months and one day, he was best puppy in show and earned three points. Three months later he won the Canadian national specialty, beating 17 champions. Tommy Joel, who judged, told Williams as he gave him the rosette, "You have no idea how great this dog is going to be and what he is going to do for the breed." A month later, the puppy gained his Canadian title and when he was 13 months old added a United States championship.

Shang's career nearly ended in 1977, when he had to undergo bladder surgery and for six months he wasn't in a ring. But Williams brought him back in March 1978 and showman that the dog is, he went best at the big Detroit fixture. When Shang triumphed at Devon, in October, it was his 56th top award, more than twice as many ever won by a Chow Chow in America. On the way he collected his 226th blue rosette. The red dog, with cream markings, also has taken nine specialties and all of his victories have been gained with one or the other of his two owners handling.

The best Borzoi to have come to the fore in many a year in North America is an elegant white hound, with mahogany markings from Canada. He is Ch. Kishniga's Desert Song, owned by Dr. Richard Meen, a psychiatrist, and Dr. John Reeve-Newson, a veterinarian, from Campbellville, Ontario. I saw the dog and Dr. Meen for the first time at Toronto and was impressed by the way they complemented each other. It was a pleasure to watch them circle the ring—the dog moving with power and grace and his master keeping stride. In January, 1978, the doctor, who is a psychiatric consultant in the correctional system for the entire province of Ontario, flew the hound to Golden Gate, where he took the top honor. Then followed victories at such big shows as International, Bucks County and Bryn Mawr. The Borzoi undoubtedly will have a great influence on the breed's future.

Princess Antoinette (left), president of the Societe Canine de Monaco, attends the Monte Carlo dog show in company with her sister-in-law, Princess Grace, and her brother, Prince Rainier. — *Joe deHoe*

All The World's A Stage

OVER THE YEARS, I covered shows and met exhibitors from many countries overseas, on both sides of the Iron Curtain in Europe and in the Caribbean and South America. I had the first dog story to come out of Czechoslovakia and it won a *New York Times* Publisher's Award, as well as the Dog Writers Association of America Award for the best single feature that appeared in a paper in this country in 1970.

I was the first American reporter ever admitted to cover the General Assembly of the Federation Cynologique Internationale (FCI). It was in Estoril, Portugal, in 1971. Then I reported on the sessions again in Mexico in 1978, when the representatives of 46 nations met for the first time in North America.

As at the United Nations the meetings were conducted in the basic language of the sponsoring country, with simultaneous translations in English, French and German. Whereas in Portugal tempers flared, with one delegation walking out, in Mexico the meeting was relatively calm.

Four shows were held in conjunction with the FCI meeting in Mexico City and there was an ominous note. Thelma von Thaden, the FCI president, had received notes threatening to disrupt the events. Now the shows were being held on grounds under the jurisdiction of the Department of Defense. So the Army had a company of military police rimming the perimeter of the field. It was the first time I covered a show under the eyes of soldiers. As it turned out there was no trouble. Indeed it was more like a fiesta, with the spectators—and for the world show there were 25,000—thoroughly enjoying themselves. With the proceeds of the events going to a fund for soldiers' orphans, the Army reciprocated by erecting a large tent with a restaurant, stage and a section with Mexican artifacts. Colorfully dressed entertainers and bands were brought in from all over the country. Many of the exhibitors and spectators left the rings, from time to time, to sing along with the vocalists. As to the shows, there were entries from 17 countries, representing 128 breeds or varieties, with judges from five continents.

Frequently I had to have interpreters when I interviewed Japanese, French, Germans, Czechs, Portuguese and Italians. Fortunately, my wife, Vera, speaks several languages and she was a tremendous help. I had lots of trouble also understanding a couple of English-speaking judges—Scots and Welsh—so on occasions I would ask them to write the words. They must have considered me an illiterate.

In Italy when I phoned and asked a judge for an interview, he sent someone to look me over before he acquiesced. It amused me, since he apparently envisioned me as the old movie sterotype of an American reporter, with the peaked cap, short-stubbed cigar and a bottle at his elbow.

Crufts

Crufts is a show even the most sophisticated fancier will never forget. Big is the word to best describe it, for it dwarfs any dog event I ever attended. The 1976 fixture was the biggest in the history of the classic up to that time, the biggest since Charles Cruft first staged the all-breed show that bears his name at the Royal Agricultural Hall in London, in 1891.

The 1976 Crufts was held in three huge exhibition halls at Olympia and drew 9,919 dogs. Even though a placement at a championship show had been a requirement, the entry still eclipsed the previous Crufts record by 1,551. There were 32 rings, covering 13 acres, compared to eight rings for Westminster in Madison Square Garden. It was the only show I ever attended where people stood in line all night. There were twenty who formed a queue as soon as the first day's judging ended at 8 P.M. By 5 o'clock the next morning, they had been joined by another 1,000. The doors were opened at 6:30, although judging wasn't to start for three hours. "We wanted to be sure we had one of the 1,500 seats around the obedience ring," a die-hard told me. Admission was one pound ($2.07 at the time). Catalogues were published for each day. The first, which included Toy, Working and Utility (Non-Sporting in America) ran 597 pages and the second, for Terriers, Gun Dogs and Hounds, had 595. Each cost one pound. Asked how many books were sold, the show manager responded, "Oh dear, we don't count them but we know it was 10 tons."

A dominant figure in the British dog world is Air Commodore J. A. C. Cecil-Wright, who was president of Crufts for a quarter of a century. I met him first in Portugal at an FCI congress, where he and Lieut. Comdr. J. C. Williams were the English delegates. A small, slender white-haired man, his gentle manners belied the real Cecil-Wright. Until he retired from the business world, a few years earlier, he had been director of several companies. He also, for a decade, served in Parliament.

The Englishman had a diversified career. While we both sipped sherry, he told me that he flew with the Royal Air Force in World War I. "Between the wars, I was asked to raise an auxiliary squadron," he recalled. "We were weekend fliers and won the trophy as best auxiliary for six of nine years." Too old to fly in World War II, the Briton directed an air squadron.

In dogs, Cecil-Wright was a founder of the Alsatian Club in England. He started to judge in the 1920s and three times named the best-in-show winner at Crufts. In 1973 at the 100th anniversary of The Kennel Club, he stepped down, after having served 25 years as chairman. In 1977 the Duke of Gloucester died, and the 90-year-old Cecil-Wright was chosen to succeed him as President of The

Kennel Club, the first commoner ever to hold the post. In the past it had been reserved for royalty, with the Duke of Connaught having been the first in 1873. "When I was made chairman, I stopped all breeding, showing and judging," Cecil-Wright said.

In the fifties and sixties, he bred thoroughbreds and several carried his wife's silks to victory. "In a very amateurish way, I trained horses," he added modestly. "I was also interested in steeplechasing and rode a winner or two." And what has been the greatest change he had observed in the show world? "Unfortunately, what once was a hobby now has become a business," he lamented. On a more positive note, he cited the enormous growth of pedigreed dogs all over the world.

The Scottish Kennel Club

Only the Scottish KC and the National Dog Show Society of Birmingham, in addition to Crufts, have the privilege of awarding challenge certificates (CCs) for every breed registered with The Kennel Club.

The Scots always have been known as an independent people and that goes for the dog show world, as well. "We are a step ahead of either The Kennel Club or the Welsh KC in that we have a woman holding a major office," opined Ian Butchart, the convener (president) of the Scottish KC. "She's Elsie Montgomery, our vice convener, the first of her sex to be elected to a key position in a major dog club in the United Kingdom. We did a survey in 1975, and found that 65 percent of the exhibitors in Britain are women. Certainly they should have a voice in an executive capacity." The Scottish Club was organized in 1881 and holds two championship fixtures annually—in May and October—on the grounds of the Royal Highland Society in Edinburgh. "Thirty years ago, if we had 1,600 dogs we were mighty happy. Now we draw more than 5,000," observed Butchart. The SKC allots dates for more than 400 events held each year by member clubs. "I've visited as many as five shows in one day in my role of convener," he added.

Mrs. Montgomery, who is well known among the Corgi fanciers in America, was active with Pembrokes for more than 25 years and served as head of the Scottish section of the Welsh Corgi League. The league has some 1,000 members, including many in the United States.

In the office of the AKC president there hangs a bit of Scotland. There's a map of the country, with a matting of the Stewart clan plaid, and a handsome life-membership, presented to the AKC by the SKC.

Welsh Kennel Club

The old adage, "If at first you don't succeed, try, try again," apparently took roots in Wales. "I was one of four to help revive the Welsh KC," noted George W. R. Couzens. "We brought it back in 1968, after a hiatus of 56 years. We applied to The Kennel Club in London for recognition and were turned down. So we tried again, only to be rejected again. The third time, they gave us the go ahead.'' And the Welsh KC has gone ahead full speed. It now runs championship shows, obedience tests, field trials and working trials. Couzens, chairman of the WKC, brought a lot of judicial experience to the position. For years he was a justice of the peace but he had to retire from the bench in 1975, when he became 70. He is also active in England's Kennel Club, where he is a member of four committees.

In the show ring, Couzens was best known for his Bull Terriers. A longtime judge of the breed, he ruled on it three times at Crufts. ''I've also shown and won with Welsh Springers, Irish Terriers, Scotties and Pointers. But I stopped all that in 1972, when I moved up as chairman. Now all I own is a Siamese cat.''

Irish Kennel Club

In the beautiful park in front of the Casino in Estoril, with its multi-colored flower beds and reflecting pools, I covered an international dog show. Typical of Portugal in the early summer, it grew increasingly hot as the show progressed and typical of the Portuguese fanciers, it progressed at a snail's pace. As the sun began to lower and the winds came up, Vera, wearing a sleeveless summer dress, began to shiver. Then from nowhere appeared a stocky, ruddy-complexioned man who, observing Vera, whipped off his jacket and put it around her. ''I'm John Plunkett,'' he said. ''Perhaps this will help your wife, until you can get back to your hotel.'' That was my introduction to the vice chairman of the Irish KC, who had been judging at the show. I invited him to join us at dinner and that evening I had a chance to learn about the dog world in Eire.

''Our club was organized in 1922, and on March 17th, in Dublin, held its first show,'' he remembered. ''We immediately were recognized by Norway and Germany and three years later your AKC agreed to accept our pedigrees. Now we are recognized all over the world. We are proud there is no discrimination between clubs or breeders. We are completely non-political and non-sectarian and there never has been any trouble between fanciers of the north or south in our land. They support each other's shows.''

Plunkett had praise for the specialty clubs, who, he said, have done much for the seven native breeds—Kerry Blue, Irish Wolfhound, Irish Terrier, Irish Water Spaniel, Irish Setter, Soft-Coated Wheaten Terrier and Glen of Imaal. ''Take the Glen of Imaal,'' he said, ''which resembles a small Wheaten, with the head of a Dandie Dinmont. It was almost extinct but through the efforts of the breed club has come back.'' When I asked him which breed was the most popular in Ireland, feeling it had to be one of the seven, Plunkett laughingly replied, ''None of those. You always can count on an Irishman to do the unexpected. German Shepherds lead in registrations, followed by English Cockers and Golden Retrievers.''

Director and secretary of the Irish KC is Denis J. Smyth, a member since 1927. ''I've been in dogs all my life,'' he told me. ''My father had Wire Fox Terriers in a show at Dublin in 1892. When I was seven years old, in 1911, I was showing against grownups.''

Graham Head

Before I ever met Graham Head, I had been told by Maxwell Riddle, the all-round judge from Ohio, that the Australian was one of the greatest arbiters in the world. At Westchester, in 1973, I got to speak with the Aussie. "It's my 10th trip to judge in the United States," Head told me. "In addition, I've worked at all the major shows in my own country and I've judged in New Zealand, Hong Kong, the Philippines, Singapore, Malaysia, Canada, Rhodesia and Kenya." As a breeder, Head had the most successful Labrador Retriever kennel in Australia for a decade starting in 1952. He showed his Labs to victory in the national specialty five years in a row, and he bred 25 champions.

"All of my dogs were trained for the field," he said. "One of my best-in-show Labs was the sire of several field champions. I've always been a strong advocate of a dual-purpose dog. When I began to be active as a judge, I stopped all showing."

The Australian is chairman of the Kennel Control Council, the ruling body in Victoria. He's head of the Royal Melbourne show, the biggest in the Southern Hemisphere. When I met him again in 1976, he spoke about the progress the Royal Melbourne had made over a five-year span. "We had 4,242 dogs in 1970 and 5,680 in 1975," he said. "In that '75 show, which lasted 11 days, there were 300 Afghans, 255 Irish Setters, 239 German Shepherds and 211 Rough Collies. When you consider our population, as compared to the United States, I feel we are doing all right dogwise."

Stanley Dangerfield

It took Phineas Fogg 80 days to go around the world. To Stanley Dangerfield, the English all-rounder who has ruled in rings in this country so many times, it is almost routine to go halfway around the world overnight to judge. "I have traveled as much as 50,000 miles in a year," said the willowy, suave Briton. Dangerfield makes a striking sartorial picture in the ring. Most of the time he is immaculately fitted out by his Saville Row tailor. Then I have seen him at Crufts judging in some rather wild combinations—purple slacks and a lavender jacket.

"I've been a judge for more than a quarter of a century," Stanley told me, "and I've had assignments in 49 countries. From 1953 to 1963, I was chief steward at Crufts." Dangerfield is a familiar figure to many TV viewers and radio listeners in his native land, for he was a commentator on pets. Just after Vera and I arrived at our hotel in London, on a trip overseas, we turned on the TV set and there were some mynah birds carrying on an animated conversation with none other than Mr. Dangerfield.

The lean Englishman, a great raconteur, told Vera that one of his judging highlights was in her native land. "I was at Brno, in 1965, when Czechoslovakia had been thrown open to foreign exhibitors," he recalled. "It was the first time since 1948 that fanciers from the West had been permitted to show their dogs behind the Iron Curtain. There was no problem getting visas and there were no restrictions placed on us. It was a two-day show, held in a huge exhibition hall. There were 150,000 spectators. The crowd was so large, it was almost impossible to move. As far as I know they never picked a best in show. The people weren't there to see the dogs. They wanted to see and talk with visitors from the free countries.'' He added that half of the 2,000 dogs were from Communist countries but none from the Soviet Union. In addition to the host country, there were dogs from Poland, Hungary, East Germany and Bulgaria. Every nation in the West was represented except Spain. ''There were 40 judges, 24 of us from the West,'' said Stanley. ''We visited at several Czechoslovak homes and were treated royally. We were all interested in one subject—dogs.''

Raymond Oppenheimer

For years I had heard Terrier people talk about Raymond Oppenheimer and I had read two of his books. So it was with great anticipation that I went to the Bull Terrier Club of America specialty in Darien, Connecticut, in 1970. I wasn't disappointed when I met ''Mr. Bull Terrier,'' who also is a power in the Kennel Club in London, for the slender, gray-haired Englishman had much to say and said it with emphasis. Since 1935, he has been devoted to the gladiators of the canine world and for years maintained the greatest Bull Terrier kennel in the world.

His first judging assignment in the United States was at Morris and Essex, in 1952. Then he didn't come back as an arbiter for 18 years. He had showed a bitch of his breeding at M&E in 1939 and he wasn't impressed with what he saw in Bull Terriers. In his book, *McGuffin & Co.*, published in 1964, he wrote, ''American Bull-terrierdom suffers from what I would call 'all-rounderitis': that is to say the breed is judged at the vast majority of their shows by an all-rounder, who in at least 90 percent of cases judges them exactly like any ordinary Terrier, i.e., Fox, Lakeland, etc., since he is completely unaware of correct type. This naturally, by a cumulative process, reacts upon the breeders, who tend to show and breed what the judges want. This, in some breeds, might not much matter, But in Bull Terriers, for simple genetic reasons, it is completely disastrous. Bull Terriers are a composite breed of Bulldog and Terrier. The whole art of breeding a good one is in getting the Terrier construction with the Bulldog substance topped off by an outstanding head.''

When I interviewed him at the national specialty, in Darien, where he drew 104 dogs from as far as California and western Canada, the largest number ever assembled up to the time in the United States, he told me, ''I was delighted with the improvement of the breed in the 18 years since I last was here.''

Ormandy, an anagram of Raymond, is the name of the Oppenheimer kennel in Maidenhead, and it has had more than 50 champions. When I asked him which of these was the greatest Bull Terrier he ever had owned, he promptly responded, ''None. The best never was in a show ring. He's Ormandy Superlative Bar Sinister. His name is in the pedigrees of almost all the top winners.''

International golfers will remember Oppenheimer, for he was captain of the Walker Cup team. At one time he held the course record of 70 for Birkdale and had the lowest possible handicap in England, a plus 2. He gave up the Royal and Ancient Game in 1967 to devote all his attention to the dogs.

Monaco

When Princess Antoinette of Monaco, who had been the first woman elected president of the FCI, was named to its board at the FCI meeting in Estoril, Portugal in 1971, she became the first woman to serve as a director in the 60-year-history of the international organization. Sister of Prince Rainier, the reigning monarch of the principality, she is not only one of the most gracious in the European dog show scene but also one of the most efficient. She is head of the Societe Canine de Monaco, having succeeded her mother, Princess Charlotte, who founded the club in 1921. "We are trying to make our show a model for the rest of Europe," Antoinette told me. "I go to shows in England and the Continent, study what is being done and adopt suitable innovations for Monaco."

The Princess had organized an International Dog Show Week of the Mediterranean—at San Remo in Italy, Nice in France and Monte Carlo in her tiny homeland—and I covered the three shows. The first, San Remo, was held in Ormond Park facing a bay in the city whose name is derived from its patron saint, San Romulo. Although the judging was indoors, the benching was outside in a park with magnificent flower beds. Running the show was Barone Rennidells Rena, a delegate of the national dog organization in his country.

Catherine Sutton of Britain headed a panel of 16 judges, and her choice for best was an Alaskan Malamute, Glacier's Storm Kloud, CD, from Sussex, Wis., an international champion owned and handled by Nancy Russell. It was the first time a Malamute ever had been shown in Italy and the eight-year-old and his attractive owner were the favorites of the spectators. The victory drew tremendous cheers, with the ringsiders surrounding Mrs. Russell and the Alaskan.

The Exposition Canine de Nice, organized by the Societe Canine Midi Cote d'Azur, took place in the massive Palais des Espositions. It was the most poorly organized event of the circuit. There were 10 groups, with no best in show, and all the breed winners milled around the entrance gate, waiting to parade their dogs.

The most prized trophy, a cobalt-colored Sevres vase, was offered by the President of the French Republic for the best team bred by an exhibitor.

Following the show, a reception was held for the Americans in the City Hall. Mme. Denise Blancard, the Deputy Mayor of Nice, made a speech welcoming the visitors and expressing the hope they would take back many nice memories and come again. Since none of the American delegation spoke French, Vera was called upon to uphold the honor of the United States. In French (and in what she confided was her first public speech), Vera thanked Mme. Blancard and the club for all the courtesies extended to our countrymen.

The beautiful series of dog stamps issued by the Monacan government.

Monte Carlo was the most lavish of the three fixtures and it drew dogs from 14 countries, including three from behind the Iron Curtain—Czechoslovakia, Hungary and Poland.

"We have come up with a couple of ideas that we hope other clubs will follow," the Princess said. "When we mail our entry forms, we include a health certificate which the exhibitor, when he arrives at the show, must present to our veterinarian. We also set up a display with such pertinent information as 'Buying a Dog,' 'The Veterinarian and the Public,' 'How to Register a Dog.' Until just before World War II, my mother had one of the top-winning Wire Fox Terrier kennels in Europe. I spent much of my childhood getting out of the way of the dogs' teeth."

The Princess worked unsparingly to make the show a success. The night before, she met with all the judges, discussed the assignments, and stressed that the show was to run on time. There was one dog running about as she spoke. It was her Pharaoh Hound, which she brought to the meeting to show me.

The next morning Antoinette met me at the show, looking spry as ever and confided, "I worked on the judges' book until 2:30 A.M., then was up at six to be here and make sure things started on time." The following day was even more trying for her. "I didn't get to sleep until 2:15 and was up three hours later," she said.

But her efforts brought results, for the show ran right to the minute. The benches were white, with red trim, the colors of the principality. There were 230 trophies and 300 medals for the winners. At each ring entrance, there not only was a sign with the name of the breed being judged, but a large drawing of the particular dog, along with the breed standard. One of the American exhibitors quipped, "Too bad we don't have the signs back home; and instead of outside, it might be a good idea to have them inside the rings where the judge could study what he is looking for."

The two-day show was outdoors and indoors. The benching and breed judging was in a park fronting on the Mediterranean, while the group and best in show was in Gardens Hall, erected in 1966 to celebrate the Monte Carlo centennial.

There was quite a ceremony for the groups. To the beat of the drums, smartly dressed hostesses, carrying the flag of Monaco, led the breed winners into the ring. Unlike the United States, where usually there is a different judge for each group, only one, Ivan Swedrup, the very personable Swede who had been his country's representative to the FCI for many years, handled all ten groups. He did it expertly and with great dispatch. For the top award, Judy de Casembroot of England made the decision. She had the distinction of being the only woman to ever take a best in show at Crufts, gaiting her Greyhound, Treetop's Golden Fleece, to the honors in 1956, and then 18 years later juding best at the London classic. Her choice at Monte Carlo was the seal-gray American Malamute Ch. Glacier's Storm Kloud, and once again there was great applause from the ringsiders. Prince Rainier presented the trophy to Mrs. Russell.

Monte Carlo ended on my birthday and I joshingly told one of Antoinette's aides that it must have been scheduled that way. In the evening, the Princess gave a party in the Casino. She sat me at her table. Suddenly the lights dimmed, there was a roll of the drums and the orchestra broke into "Happy Birthday," while, to my great surprise, a cake was brought to the table. This was so typical of her graciousness.

Italy

Italy long has been one of my favorite countries, and a delightful memory is an interview with Commandante Paolo Contini in Florence. As secretary of the judging committee of the Ente Nazionale Della Cinofilia Italiana, the ruling dog show body in Italy, the former Italian naval officer passed on the qualifications for a would-be judge.

A small, slight man, Contini had attended Leghorn, the Annapolis of Italy, and he spoke English, which was a big help.

I was invited to his three-century-old villa, high in the hills over the city of Dante and Michelangelo. "As long as this house has been here, we Continis always have had dogs," he informed me. "My father, who also served in the Italian Navy, had Great Danes and my mother said the first word I spoke was 'dog.'" On the wall of the living room, among the masters, was a portrait, in oil, of Contini's great-grandfather, Augusto, who was a general in Napoleon's army. He, too, had dogs.

We walked through the villa and into the garden. The lights of Florence were just beginning to come on and it was a breath-taking view. I long have been an opera buff and the city below so reminded me of a scene from *Louise,* where the lights of Paris begin to twinkle, that I said this to Contini. The Italian looked at me in amazement. He couldn't believe an American journalist, as he called me, could possibly be interested or know a bit about opera. After that, I could have had anything. He begged me to stay an extra week, attend a dog show and hear some music.

The Florentine told me that like his father, he too had bred Great Danes and over the years a dozen international champions. But then he decided to judge and stopped breeding and showing. "To become a judge in Italy," he said, "an applicant must have been a breeder for five years. Then he has to pass an examination on anatomy and physiology. If successful, he serves in rings under five different judges, each of whom writes a report about his work. He next works a show, with all six members of the judging committee observing. If he passes, he must judge for two years at small events, before he is qualified for championship shows."

The Commandante said Italy was a hunting country and there were nearly as many field trials as breed shows. As a result, at the time, four of the five most popular breeds were of Sporting dogs. He praised the Pointers, which, he said, along with Denmark were the best in Europe. "We are striving for the dual-purpose dog and a gun dog cannot become a bench champion unless he has a minimum of qualifications in the field, as well. A Fox Terrier or Dachshund must work underground. We put a fox in a cage to protect him and then send the dog underground after him. A utility dog, such as a German Shepherd or Doberman, must be able to do police or guard work.''

Italy at one time had no best-in-show judging. However, Contini led the successful campaign to change the system. "From a purely technical viewpoint," he told me, "I feel it is extremely hard to pick one dog as best. But from a sporting angle, and for spectator appeal, I feel it is preferable."

A sharp dissenter was Franca Simondetti of Novi-Ligure, whom I met on the Mediterranean circuit. "I'm entirely opposed to a best-in-show award," she said. "There are far too many breeds for one man to be versed in them all. It is just a question of preference. Some like a big dog, others a small one. I'm just happy when one of my dogs takes the breed. Then I know my breeding program must be on the right track." Signora Simondetti, at the time, was the biggest breeder of English Cocker Spaniels in her native land. In 1972, she bred 90 pups. "I kept a few for showing," she said, "and sold the rest. There was no problem getting buyers. I could have sold twice as many."

Switzerland

Rarely does one see an all-white dog in Switzerland. "The Swiss want to keep everything spotless," explained Mrs. Elsbeth Clerc, a leading Scottish Terrier and West Highland White Terrier breeder. "A dark coat doesn't show the dirt, so you can see why Westies are not too popular. It's the same with the Poodles. It's extremely hard to sell a white, cream or apricot. Black is the favorite." Secretary of the Swiss Terrier Club, Mrs. Clerc stressed the Swiss are largely hobby breeders and that there are comparatively few top terriers. "I visit kennels in England three or four times a year and conformationwise the Scotties there are superior to those I saw at Westminster. But I was very impressed with your Westies. Then the presentation of the terrier in America is so much better than in Europe. In Switzerland, we have no professional handlers, and our exhibitors certainly leave a lot to be desired, when showing their dogs."

France

Mme. Francoise Firminhac in 1958 bought a pair of American Cocker Spaniels to become the first Frenchwoman to register the breed in her native land. "An American had a pair before me," she said, "but he didn't show. His first two were in the studbook, so mine were No. 3 and No. 4. Then for the next seven years, I was the only Cocker breeder in the country. I bought Pinefair Parson, a black, from Mrs. Terrell Van Ingen of Greenwich, Conn., and showed him to best in show at Monte Carlo in 1967."

Since then the tall, elegant Frenchwoman has done much to make the Cocker popular in France and to help the breed gain recognition on the rest of the continent. "I've had my American Cockers at all the big shows in my country, Italy, Spain, Holland and Belgium," she told me. She had as many as 50 Cocker Spaniels in her kennel near Paris, although she has been cutting down in recent years. In the early '70s she said she had 35. "I've had 13 international champions," Mme. Firminac proudly told me.

A frequent visitor at the American Spaniel Club show and at Westminster, she was surprised by the speed of the American judges. "It amazed me to learn that in the United States a judge can have 175 dogs," said the Frenchwoman. "In my country we are not permitted to judge more than 50. I write a critique on each dog and it is published in our Spaniel bulletin. Exhibitors are allowed to ask questions and you can count on at least a half of them doing so."

Belgium

Certainly one of the best known European judges was Mme. Denise Nizet de Leemans of Brussels. For a half-century she ruled in rings all over the continent. in South America, Mexico and Canada. For more than two decades she was the delegate to the FCI and in that worldwide organization she headed the standards commission for 15 years. And whenever a Bichon Frise is seen, the Belgian woman should be remembered, for she gave the breed its name.

"In the United States," she said, "you have far more dogs than we have on the continent, and overall they are excellent. But in many of the breeds, the dogs are just too big. I have another complaint about your shows. I find the judges seem to favor the professional handlers. Except in England, there are few professionals in Europe. The owners show their own dogs and they do it very badly. Excepting England, the Scandinavian countries, the Netherlands and Spain, your rings are much larger than we have abroad. In Paris, where I've judged for many years, they are so small that the show has to run for a week so all the dogs can be judged."

Austria

To many people, Vienna is the waltzing city of Johann Strauss. To the philotherian, however, it is the capital of the central European gun dog world. "For centuries, we Austrians have hunted in the Alps," Walter Hiedl, the president of the *Oestrreichischer Kynologenverbrand,* the equivilent of the AKC, explained to me when I met him in Vienna. "Almost every hunter has his dog to help him find game. We breed dogs to work, not just to sit on the sofa. For example, I have Dachshunds. Every one is a good working dog and has been used on badger and the fox." In the previous 23 years, only 28 of all the gun dogs in Austria became working champions. To attain the title, an animal had to win at least three trials and pass a series of difficult tests. Fourteen of the champions were Dachshunds and three had been bred by Hiedl.

"We strive for a dual-type dog," said the Austrian sportsman. "A working champion cannot gain his title until he has attained at least a 'very good' rating in the show ring. A Dachshund, when he is tested, must work both above and below ground. That's done since a badger will run into a hole and it is up to the dog to keep the animal cornered and then, with a good, long bark, make the hunter aware of the situation.''

Hiedl invited me to his two-century-old charming house on the Danube. On the walls of his trophy room were the horns of a half-dozen chamois bucks he brought down high in the Alps. There also were a few prize pelts of the 148 fox and 53 badgers that he and his Dachshunds had accounted for in a decade.

I was made an honorary member of the Austrian Kennel Club at a dinner at Grinzing to which the leading exhibitors from Austria had been invited. It was a very impressive ceremony. Hiedl told of how the club had 16,000 members. Then, his voice quivering with emotion, he took a pin from his lapel and said, ''Only 16 of our members are permitted to wear this club emblem. You are the seventeenth and the first from America.''

In Vienna, there is a dog museum founded by the late Prof. Emil Hauck, which contains the skulls of 1,200 dogs and traces the history of the *Canis familiaris* through a half-century of research by the educator.

Germany
As recently as 1964, the Doberman Pinscher was 22d on the AKC registration list. In the '70s, with the rise of crime and people wanting a good guard dog, the Dobe came into his own. He crashed into the top ten in 1972, and in 1978 was second, led only by the Poodle. Watching the rise of the breed I was delighted to meet Werner Niermann, at Baltimore, where he judged in 1972. He had been president of the Doberman Pinscher Club in Germany since 1969 and was considered the authority of the breed. It was a pleasure interviewing Niermann, since he spoke English fluently. When I made that remark, he laughed, replying, ''I teach English at a college in Hamm.''

It was particularly interesting to watch the German judge. He went over each entry meticulously and using symbols—(''It's the Niermann shorthand,'' he said)—made notes on each. Then at a meeting of the Baltimore Dobe club, he transmitted his notes and gave each owner his opinions. As president of the national organization in Germany, he is a powerful figure. No Dobe may be bred without the club's approval, otherwise the litter may not be registered.

A native of Rottweil in Germany wouldn't know a Rottweiler of the canine variety by that name. He would call him a *metzgerhund* (butcher dog). And who was the head warden of the 2,400-member *Allegemeiner Duetscher Rottweiler Klub* and the chief judge of the breed in his native land? None other than a master butcher, Friedrich Berger. He told me that in Germany, to insure that the breed is kept up to standard—and he, incidentally, wrote the Rottweiler standard—the country is divided into 16 geographical districts. Each has four breed wardens, with Berger in overall charge. To qualify as a warden, a man must have been a judge for at least five years, have bred three litters and trained two dogs in obedience. A tight leash is kept on the fancier. Before a Rottweiler may be bred, it must have been shown three times, under two different judges, and have been rated either excellent or very good. Until 1973, when puppies were whelped, a warden would examine them when they were four days old. No more than six were permitted to be kept and the warden would suggest which he considered the most acceptable. However in 1973, the West German government ruled no pups could be put down unless they were physically deformed. The club inspects the pups at the end of seven weeks, and those that conform to the standard receive certificates.

Netherlands

Among the organizations that have made me an honorary member is the American Cocker Spaniel Club of the Netherlands. Organized in 1964, it was the first for the breed in Europe. The driving force behind the club was Nell Koning, a frequent visitor to America, since she started to come for the American Spaniel Club specialty in 1974. "Although we are a small country," she told me, "we are a dog-loving nation. Our show in Amsterdam invariably draws 3,000 dogs, and that's more than in much larger countries." Her Cockerbox Kennel has had a great influence on the American Cocker for she has sold dogs to Belgium, France, Germany, Austria, the Scandinavian countries, Italy, Spain, Portugal and India. "I've bred or owned more than 20 champions and it is extremely difficult to win a title in my country," she said. "A dog has to be at least 27 months old. I feel this regulation should be changed."

Sweden

Sweden not only is known for its smorgasbord and its peaches-and-cream-skinned blondes, but also for its very good dogs. On the international canine scene, its most famous representative is Ivan Swedrup, a former captain in the Swedish cavalry, who once rode on his country's horse show team. So it's no surprise that when he is judging, the man from Stockholm stresses movement. Ivan has written several erudite dog books, one of which recently was published in the United States.

We crossed paths at shows in Portugal, France, Monaco and Mexico, four of the 25 countries where he's ruled in rings. Indeed, he has judged on five continents. A veterinarian and a member of Sweden's Royal Veterinary Academy, Swedrup was secretary-general of the Swedish KC from 1945 until 1972, and for 25 years served as secretary of the Scandinavian Kennel Association. For years, Ivan also was Sweden's delegate to the FCI and he and his charming wife, Gunnel, helped to enliven the social events at the meetings. A gentleman, he's a favorite with the exhibitors, especially the women. "He's so nice, it's a pleasure to show under him, even if my dog loses," sighed one.

Spain

I arrived in Spain, the land of the siesta, by bus from Portugal in 1967 and in Madrid went to the headquarters of the *Real Sociedad Central de Fomento de la Raza Canina*. The name was almost larger than the offices, for they consisted of a three-room suite in considerable disarray. I had arranged to meet with Luis Gomez Bea, who not only was the club's president but also was heading the FCI. I had been warned he probably wouldn't be on time, that the club operated on a *"Manana, manana, por la manana."* He lived up to the reputation. Although I had a very tight schedule, the good senor kept me waiting for more than an hour. However, he proved to be articulate and gave me a good picture of the Spanish dog scene. The big Exposicion International Canina had been held shortly before my arrival. Whereas in America we start our big shows at 8 A.M. and finish some 10 or 12 hours later, Madrid's top canine event, staged in the beautiful setting of the Retiro, the largest park in the city, started at 4 o'clock in the afternoon and finished at 8. But it lasted for four days.

The easy-going Spanish owners prefer to keep their dogs home as pets, rather than travel to shows. "Our big problem," said Bea, "is to get people to show their dogs. There are thousands of good hunting dogs who work in the field but we never see them in a ring."

The Czech Terrier, Created and
Officially Recognized in Only 14 Years!

How many of us have imagined creating a dream breed? In Czechoslvakia, I met a man who has actually done it. In only a 10-year span and five generations, he had the Terrier he wanted. In another four years—1963—it was recognized by the FCI as the newest member of the Terrier family.

Of course, it would have taken the ordinary breeder a much longer time but the creator of the Czech Terrier was a top-ranking geneticist with the Academy of Sciences in Prague, who had written numerous oft-quoted articles on animals. He is Frantisek Horak. I not only met him, but studied his charts, saw his kennel and learned from the master what he had done.

The scientist was well known in his country's dog world. Not only was he one of only three all-breed judges in Czechoslovakia, but from 1932 until 1963, he was the nation's leading breeder of Scottish Terriers. For 15 years, Scotties he had bred captured the national titles. But he will be remembered far less for those achievements than as the developer of this massive short-legged little dog. "Unlike so many countries, where the Scottie is just a pet," explained Horak, "in Czechoslovakia we use him for hunting." But the breed had such massive fronts and heavy coats, it was ineffective underground, after it had cornered its prey in a hole. The fox was narrower, and like the sly fellow he is, could laugh at the Scottie, once he wedged himself into a hole. So the scientist decided to cross a Scottie and a Sealyham and come up with a terrier that would have much better hunting qualities.

Frantisek Horak's creation—the Czech Terrier.

"I wanted a dog with a longer leg than either of its progenitors," said Horak, "and a more practical color than the white of the Sealy. Then I was striving to develop a narrow chest for burrowing. I wanted an ear that would give protection from the dirt, when working underground. I also wanted a tail long enough, so if the dog was deep in the hole, you could pull him out." The Czech scientist began his experiment in 1949, breeding a Scottie bitch to a Sealyham dog. Four matings later, the geneticist had achieved what he had envisioned. A pup, Javor Lovu Zdar, was whelped and this silver-blue made history for the breed. Permitted to be exhibited at Leipzig, in East Germany, the Czech Terrier proved the leading attraction of the show.

In Czechoslovakia, the breed hadn't been taken too seriously up to this time, but now it was given a second look. By the time of the fifth generation, there were enough Czech Terriers and they were breeding true, so no more crossing was necessary. Javor became the first champion. Developing the breed had been a costly one for Horak. "By the time I had bred 10 generations," he told me, "I had spent $4,500." And scientists are not that well paid in Czechoslovakia.

Unlike Louis Dobermann, who perpetuated his name by developing a breed, Horak chose instead to immortalize his country in the dog world. The bewhiskered, bushy-eyebrowed Terrier is blue, silver, blue and tan or silver-blue. He's 10½-13½ inches at the shoulders, weighs from 12-18 pounds, and has a tail 7-7½ inches. The coat is long, dense, wavy and silky.

Schnauzers Behind the Iron Curtain

The first Miniature Schnauzer was imported into Czechoslovakia only in 1962 but the breed has had tremendous success. In 1971, I met Dr. Victor Benes, who was president of Club of Schnauzer Breeders. "In 1968, we had 150 members," he said. "Now we have more than 1,000. Our Miniature Schnauzers are the best on the continent, with the exception of their native country—Germany." The physician could speak with authority, for he was an international judge. The breeding of Miniature Schnauzers in Czechoslovakia is no guessing game. The parent club, and each of eight regional bodies, has a breeder adviser. Before a member is permitted to breed a dog or bitch, the fancier must get permission of the adviser. Twice a year in Prague, the "City of 100 Spires" (actually there are 473), and once annually for each of the other two regions, seminars are held at which members bring their puppies. A three-man jury evaluates each pup and judges the success of the breeding. When a dog or bitch becomes four years old, it must be brought to the adviser, who determines whether further breeding will be permitted. "We feel that with such stringent regulations, we can keep the Miniature Schnauzer from deteriorating," said the physician.

Vera and I attended the national Schnauzer specialty in a park in Prague. There were four good-sized rings for the 47 Giant Schnauzers, 44 Standards and 88 Miniatures. Admission was 30 cents. All the Giants were black and were of excellent quality, although on the big side. Among the Standards, the dogs seemed better than the bitches, who had a tendency to be too heavy. The Miniatures were of good quality but lacked the show training of American dogs and were poorly presented, a failing that prevailed in all three varieties. When I inquired the price of a Miniature Schnauzer pup, I was told it ranged from $63, the monthly wage of a cashier at a supermarket, to $125, the monthly earning of a young chemical engineer.

In Prague, most business offices are open from 8 A.M. to 4 P.M., so early in the morning and late in the afternoon, the large parks beneath the Castle become alive with owners walking with their dogs, which are largely purebreds. On a Sunday stroll, I counted 29 dogs, representing 16 breeds, with only three mutts.

I found two other native breeds of Czechoslovakia interesting. The Fousek, which means whisker in Czech, is a bearded hunting dog, 75 pounds and 26 inches at the shoulder. Brown, with white markings, or black, he's good natured, easy to train and he strives to please. The Slovakian Kopov, known as the Black Forest Hound, is 18 inches, about 37 pounds, and is used mostly for wild boar hunting. The black, with tan markings, is temperamental but adjusts quickly. With an excellent nose, he can follow a track for hours, giving voice as he trails.

Japan

For years there were suspicions in the United States about Japanese breeders. Several of our fanciers refused to sell to their counterparts in Japan, even though the breeders across the Pacific offered huge prices for dogs here. So I made an effort to interview Japanese owners and officials to try and present a true picture. I always maintained that since breeders were paying such big prices for dogs, they certainly were going to maintain them.

At the International show in Chicago, I met the president of the Japanese Kennel Club, the 61-year-old Takensuke Kobayashi. I learned the JKC was organized in 1948, and that 24 years later it had 910 member clubs, with a total membership of 110,000. "We are constantly striving to improve our breeds," said Kobayashi. "Many of our Maltese, Boxers, Yorkshire Terriers and Collies have come from the United States. England has supplied us with Terriers and Pomeranians and we went to Germany for German Shepherds." The Japanese follow our system of judging, except there is a seventh group for native breeds. Kobayashi said the sport was enjoying a great boom in his land. Whereas ten years earlier, 3,500 dogs were registered monthly, by 1972 the figure had risen to 15,000. Obedience training was very popular and there were 500 instructors.

Yoshinori Sakai, a director of the JKC, and a judge, here for his third Westminster, said, "Of our top ten breeds, six are Toys." Sakai had his own theory about this. "We are small people physically," he reasoned, "and our houses are small. Consequently, we like small dogs."

His small dog theory was substantiated by Kanji Sakashita, who was serving his seventh term as president of the Cocker Spaniel Club, an affiliate of the JKC. The owner of a Chinese restaurant in Tokyo, he informed me that over the last 20 years, he had imported ten champions from the United States. "I felt it wasn't fair to show them in competition with our own dogs," he added, "so instead, they were only exhibited. Of course, they were used at stud, to improve the breed. Our parti-colors are the best of the three varieties, with red and white the most in demand." The restauranteur stressed that women play a leading role in the Japanese dog show picture. "From 60 to 75 percent of the exhibitors are women," he said.

Japan is having a pupulation explosion. This I learned from a very learned man, Ryou Yamazaki, the president of the Shibuya College of Dog Grooming. "There are eight million dogs in my country. That's one for every 13 persons," he said. Yamazaki opened a school, in 1968, to educate dog specialists, who would be working in various fields. At the time, he said, Japan was importing many excellent animals, but there were few persons who knew how to care for them. If a dog needed grooming, the owner had to go to a veterinarian. There were no professional handlers and dogs weren't being shown to their full advantage. At the beginning his program called for a one-year course. Of his students, 99 percent were women. Graduates opened grooming businesses in a half-dozen cities. By 1974, the program had been expanded, so there were both one- and two-year courses, with the longer training nurses for veterinarians. No longer do owners have to take their pets to be groomed by a veterinarian. Now almost all of the department stores have salons.

Yamazaki is president of the International Dog Education Association, with chapters in Korea, Mexico, Switzerland and England. He brought a plaque, with the organization's insignia, and made me an honorary member. "Through the concern for dogs," he said, "fellowship will develop between men. With the love for animals and nature, we will make a peaceful and well-developed society."

Yamazaki in an effort to promote brotherhood takes his pupils to different parts of the world. Vera and I met a couple of hundred of them at Crufts, where they had flown from Tokyo.

Caribbean Circuit

For many people the islands in the Caribbean are happy vacation grounds and for the dog fancy they have added appeal. Some of the islands have shows and on most one can find dedicated breeders and exhibitors. I interviewed a number and found it encouraging. Where else can one come across a dog barking to the accompaniment of authentic calypso music? The bellwether of the circuit is Puerto Rico, which Columbus discovered during his second voyage to the New World in 1493. I discovered it 468 years later, when I covered my first show on that delightful island.

The members of the Puerto Rico Kennel Club are among the most hospitable I've met anywhere and their shows are such a delight that I kept returning, year after year. Indeed, I was so well known on the island that when I would step off the plane at the San Juan airport, I'd be greeted, "Hola Senor Walterio, it must be dog show time."

Since 1966, Ileana Miller has been president of the PRKC. Proud of her Puerto Rico heritage, she is a goodwill ambassador for the Island. Gracious and graceful, she would have gone far in the diplomatic service, for she exercises great skill in keeping the fiery Latins in the club together. Ileana succeeded her husband, the late Harley Miller, who was a former United States Commissioner for Puerto Rico and until his death a Federal judge.

A dog show on the island is an experience. My first was a bit of a shock. Instead of the lush tropical setting I had visualized, it was held in a high school gymnasium in Santurce. It was hot, the temperature in the 90s and the building was rather run-down. I arrived during the luncheon hour and except for a handful of exhibitors, the place was deserted. But in a few minutes I was greeted by a big, friendly man, who introduced himself, half in Spanish, half in English, "Hola Senor, welcome to Puerto Rico, I'm Alfredo Caselduc, the club treasurer. How about a frozen daiquiri?"

The owners began pouring in, the classes were called, with the announcer over the public address system speaking in both Spanish and English. There was intense rivalry between the members of the PRKC and the Ponce club from the opposite side of the island.

Then for a number of years the show was staged in a far lovelier setting, on the magnificent grounds of the Dorado Beach Hotel. The rings were set up under towering palms and a century-old hucar tree. The show was a fiesta. Entire families attended, had a picnic, and unlike most dog events, stayed until best in show had been decided. Many spectators attended in bathing suits, watched a class or two and then plunged into the ocean.

Like so many exhibitors from the mainland, once they get Puerto Rican sand in their shoes, a variety of rums under their belts, and hear the inviting sound of the ubiquitous coqui at night—little wonder they return, year after year.

Recently the show has been held at Fort Buchanan, through which more than 63,000 Puerto Ricans passed after induction in World War II. The first year the event took place on the military installation it was served by youth as a 12-year-old girl, Jaimi Glodeck, from Severn, Md., showed her West Highland White Terrier, Ch. Keithal Pilot, to the best-in-show trophy. The fact that she was competing against such pros as Bill Trainor, then president of the Professional Handlers Association, and Barbara Partridge, who brought 21 dogs to the show, didn't faze the seventh-grader at all, who said, "I've been handling since I was six."

The guard dog is just as popular in Puerto Rico as in the states. The Latin, too, wants a dog to protect his family and the three most popular breeds are the German Shepherd, Boxer and Doberman.

Among the leading German Shepherd breeders are Joseph Palacios and Luis Maldonado of San Juan. Palacios, who speaks seven languages and is the chief translator for the Puerto Rican government, has a good eye for the breed. In 1966, he went to the Sieger show in Mannheim, Germany, saw a black-and-tan dog and bought him. He was Groll vom Sixtberg. His judgment was vindicated when Groll took best in show at the PRKC fixture in 1968.

Playing a lead role in the club's activities is Lyda Ramirez Fajardo, who was secretary for a decade. When she wasn't stewarding, working on the catalogues, or meeting exhibitors from the mainland and driving them to their hotels and the showgrounds, she was winning rosettes and best in show with her Pomeranians.

Then we have Col. Francisco Badrena, an engineer who plotted a course to success and followed it assiduously. "I bought three top Boston Terriers from a kennel in Iowa," he told me. "But anyone can buy a good dog. My goal is to breed a Puerto Rican Boston, take him or her to New York and win the specialty and then the breed at Westminster." It was an ambitious program and he nearly pulled it off, for a Boston of his went best of opposite sex at the New York specialty.

Badrena is quite a man on the island. An officer in the National Guard, he accepted a $1-a-year job in 1965 as state engineer for the National and Air Guards. Three years later he was awarded a medal for "outstanding work performed in engineering," which saved the Commonwealth $500,000.

A renowned skeet shooter, he participated in six world championships and won 21 medals. In 1966, he flew to Kansas City and left with the Class B 12-gauge world title. He's a collector and in his home has 30 Winchester rifles, all with special stocks; several antique automobiles, and 12,000 lead soldiers, of which 90 percent depict the Napoleonic era.

"In 1969, I won the VIP (an award of the National Capital Collectors of America) in Washington for a diorama of Napoleon in Spain, and I won it again the next year, this time for a diorama of Napoleon in Warsaw," he proudly stated.

The No. 1 man at Ponce is Willie Vicens. He has several firsts to his credit. His Boxer, Mill River's Key Factor, was best in show at the first PRKC show in 1958. Later that year, Factor became a champion in the United States, the first Puerto Rican-owned dog to accomplish the feat. Five years later, Vicens judged a match show at the Miami Boxer Club, the first islander to ever judge on the mainland. Since then he has judged at many of the leading shows in the United States.

"You came up quickly, Willie," I said, when I interviewed the real estate executive. He replied, "You are wrong, it took me many years. I bought my first Boxer from an ad in a dog magazine and paid $80 for her. When she arrived, she didn't even have AKC papers. At that time we had no dog clubs on the island, no shows and no one to help. Those of us who wanted to buy dogs would answer ads in the States and invariably received bad stock. I began reading everything I could about dogs and made up my mind I was some day going to play a part in the sport."

Luck and good stars possibly make a difference. Take Armando Miro, an artist, who escaped from Cuba in 1960 and went to live and work in Miami. Miro works in acrylic and he has created more than 1,000 paintings. A Boxer, Ch. Siboney's Matador of Miro, whom he co-owned with Cirilo Pardo—also a Cuban expatriate now living in San Juan, was best in show at the Puerto Rico fixture two years in a row. Reality was overwhelming for the surrealist artist, when he received the trophy for the second time. Tears of joy streamed down his cheeks as friends congratulated him and shouted "Bravo."

In the relaxed atmosphere of Puerto Rico I met a charming family from the Dominican Republic—the Nelson de Sotos, who insisted that I fly to their island to cover a show. A physician, Dr. de Soto is a former president of his country's Academy of Pediatrics, teaches at the medical school of historic Santo Domingo University, founded in 1538 and the first university in the New World, and is chief of Robert Reid, a huge modern children's hospital. But he still finds time to breed and exhibit dogs, serve as an officer in the Dominican KC and largely through his efforts the club was accepted as a member of the FCI.

The rise of the Dominican club has been spectacular. Dr. de Soto, as adventurous as the Spanish explorer, Hernando de Soto who discovered the Mississippi River in 1541, did a little exploring of his own. Rounding up eight others, he founded the club in 1969. "Once we were accepted into the FCI," said the pediatrician, "there was a surge of interest, more and more Dominicans wanting to buy and exhibit dogs. Furthermore, exhibitors from the eastern part of the United States and Canada began to go to our shows, since they were anxious to gain international certificates and we are closer than Mexico City. So that our members can gain greater proficiency in handling, we give a free course, twice weekly." Who is the teacher? None other than the good doctor.

President of the *Asociacion Canina Dominicana,* counterpart of the AKC, is Dr. Mireya de Schecker. "All our breedings must be approved or no papers are issued," she said. "We had bad experiences at the start with some unscrupulous breeders from the United States, who unloaded inferior dogs on us at premium prices. Germany, on the other hand, charged us enough—from $1,000 to $1,500 for a German Shepherd stud—but they gave us quality dogs. To protect our club members, we worked up an educational program. When someone wanted to buy a showdog, we would advise him. Soon we began to get much better specimens from the United States. German Shepherds are our most popular breed, followed by Dobermans and Boxers."

A hop, swim and jump from the Dominican Republic is a bit of Holland— Curacao. In the bustling, picturesque city of Willemstad is Anne van der Vlis, a woman of distinction not only as a barrister specializing in corporation law, but also as the only breeder of Afghans in the Netherlands Antilles.

Louis Dobermann would have been proud to know the breed he created had crossed the Atlantic and was the most popular on Trinidad and Tobago, two islands off Venezuela. Much of the credit is due Frank Thompson who, when he was senior economist for the Ministry of Planning and Development in Trinidad, did a little planning on his own. Under his guidance, the Doberman Pinscher Club of Trinidad and Tobago has prospered. "We stress breeding a calm, steady dog, rather than an overly aggressive one. I was very fortunate to buy a good black and tan, Damasyn The Honey Buck from Peggy Adamson on Long Island. At an all-breed show in Port of Spain he not only was best of breed, among 59 Dobes, but he went on to best in show." That's planning.

South American Personalities

The diplomatic Dr. Antonio Barone Forzano, a Brazilian physician and veterinarian, is a power not only in his own country's dog show circles but in all Latin America and in many other parts of the world. The rotund little South American certainly does his best to keep the airlines in business for he constantly is flying to either judge or consult with international club officials. When I first met him, he had just flown into New York from Rio de Janeiro, with a stopover in Peru, where he judged. The Brazilian was in this country to try and persuade the AKC to work out reciprocal agreements with South American national clubs, so their dogs could compete here. It was his fifth unsuccessful visit to dogdom's ruling body in the United States. The doctor left to fly to Hungary, Yugoslavia, Italy and Portugal, where he had judging assignments.

313

Until he retired, the physician was public health director for 25 years in Rio. From 1954 to 1957, he headed the veterinarians in the city. He gained international acclaim when he organized a drive in Brazil in which 110,000 dogs were inoculated in 1955.

Asked about dogs in Brazil, the doctor responded, "Our three most popular breeds are German Shepherds, American Cocker Spaniels and Miniature Pinschers. The Shepherds and Minpins are among the best I've seen in the world. The Cockers are of good quality and have excellent coats." He was particularly enthusiastic about two native breeds—the Rastreador and the Fila. The Rastreador looks like an American Foxhound but he is faster. He's bred to hunt jaguar. The Fila, a 130-pounder, is a cross between a Bullmastiff and a Portuguese Mountain Dog.

A little dog bred in New York City was the first Pug to ever take a best in show in Brazil. He was Ch. Shirrayne's Golddigger, whom Tracy Williams bought from Shirley Thomas, the breeder of so many good Pugs over the years and since the mid-seventies an active judge. Tracy, a noted equestrienne, admitted she was more nervous showing dogs than riding. "With a horse, I'm in control," she said, "but with the dogs, I had to learn by watching the others." Digger, who went best at Sao Paulo in his South American debut in 1976, kept right on winning, taking four more top awards. Tracy flew him to New York for the Pug specialty just before Westminster in 1978, and the fawn dog was best, beating 19 other champions. Success breeds success. "When I started to show," said the attractive young blonde, "there was only one other Pug competing in Sao Paulo. Once Digger began to win, I had requests from six Brazilians for puppies."

Venezuela has the distinction of having had the youngest all-breed judge in the FCI. He is Richard Guevara of Caracas and he was approved as an all-rounder by the international body in 1974, when he was 21 years old. At the time he also was the only all-breed judge in Venezuela. "That posed a real problem for me," said Guevara. "The Federacion Canina de Venezuela said I had to be tested and approved by three all-rounders. Fortunately, at our international shows—and we have only two a year, both in June—there were two judges from Canada and Isidore Schoenberg from the United States. They shot questions at me for two days—almost three hours at each session—mostly on breed standards. That's how I became an all-rounder."

Guevara started with dogs when he was eight years old. The boy would go to the kennel of the late Ria Haas, who had one of the greatest Fox Terrier and Poodle establishments in South America. Mrs. Haas took him to the shows and he'd watch the crates. By the time he was 14, she had let him handle a Poodle or two. So he could learn more about the sport, the Venezuelan youth flew to this country and several of the handlers taught him more about grooming and showing. In 1974, he judged his first FCI show, in the Dominican Republic, and the next year he did two in Panama and one in Sao Paulo. "I'm in no hurry," he told me. "I have a few years ahead."

Judges from five continents, L. to r.: Kaumasa Igarashi, Japan; Marie Archer, Australia; Max Riddle, USA; Dr. Antonio Barone Forzano, Brazil; Gordon Archer, Australia; Ivan Swedrup, Sweden; and Jean Servier, France.

Dog show behind the Iron Curtain—Czechoslovakia, 1970. In the foreground are my wife Vera and her brother.

Mexico

South of the border down Mexico way, a transplanted New Jerseyan plays a leading role among the senors and senoras of the dog ring. She is Thelma von Thaden and when I first interviewed her in 1975, she was serving her third year as president of the Federacion Canofila Mexicana, the first woman to be elected to the post. This is the AKC of Mexico and it operates very similarly. There are 32 affiliated clubs, each with its own board and president. Field representatives cover the various shows. At the time there were 52 events held annually in addition to four under FCI rules.

Mrs. von Thaden is an alumna of Upsala College in East Orange, N.J., with graduate courses in psychology at Columbia. She went to Mexico in 1940 as a bride. Long active with dogs there, she bred five generations of German Shepherd champions. "I stopped showing when I became the FCM president," she said. In her Mexico City home she had eight Pembroke Welsh Corgis, a German Shepherd, Golden Retriever, Smooth Fox Terrier, several parrots and canaries and some registered rabbits. She is in great demand as an arbiter in Latin America and also handles a few assignments in this country. This handsome, elegant grandmother, only the second woman to ever head the FCI, showed great skill in presiding over its General Assembly in Mexico City in 1978, and in organizing the four shows and activities over a nine-day period, which went along with FCI sessions.

Dogs in the USSR

Although I never visited the Soviet Union, I did so by proxy. In 1974, Pamela Cole phoned to say she was going. Pam's parents had been prominent German Shepherd breeders and exihibitors and she had been around dogs all her life. I asked her to look over the dog show situation in Moscow and she did an excellent job.

Pam was impressed with the program to develop judges. "Before a fancier may apply for a license," she told me, "he must have trained and shown a minimum of three dogs in both conformation and obedience in the breed or breeds for which he is seeking. Then he must study for one year, attending lectures by senior judges. If approved, the candidate spends another year doing actual ring work, serving as an apprentice under the supervision of senior arbiters. If certified, he becomes a junior judge."

There were five kennel clubs in the Soviet Union in 1974. Each kept its own stud book, litter registrations and managed shows for its particular region. The clubs honored each other's registrations. If a breeder transferred from one city to another, his dogs would come under the jurisdiction of the new club in the area. The five clubs, in order of size, were: Moscow, Leningrad, Kiev, Sverdlovsk and Kharkov. No family living in a city was permitted to have more than three dogs and dogs were allowed in all housing projects.

Being particulary interested in German Shepherds, the American wasn't impressed with what she saw at the show. "The Shepherds were huge," she reported. "The males ran from 28-to-32 inches at the shoulders [the United States standard has 24-26 as the desired height] and most had iron top lines. Whereas the front-end angulation was good, the rear-end was nil. Many were too long in the loin, long-hocked and short-necked for their size. There were no sable-colored Shepherds and only one all-black. The rest had black saddles with pale cream markings, which were too light."

Of the other breeds, Pam was impressed with Airedales and Collies, which she said were also larger than we have in this country. "All the dogs were put down in top condition," she added. "They were well fed. I was told the standard daily diet for a Shepherd was a pound of meat, a pound of fish, a half-pound of cottage cheese, an egg, porridge and macaroni."

German Shepherds are used in the Soviet Union for border patrol, tracking, narcotics and bomb detection work. "I was particularly interested," said Pam, "with the use of the Shepherd in geology. The dogs are trained to smell out certain minerals, such as quartz, and they have found many deposits."

Gun dogs must qualify in the field before being shown in the ring. Toys are required to have basic obedience—heel, sit, down, come and stay—to be eligible to compete in the show ring.

There have been some nice salutes along the way. At top, Walter Chimel, director of the Gaines Dog Research Center, presents the 1971 Fido (dogdom's equivalent of the Oscar) honoring me as "Dogdom's Writer of the Year." Bottom left, John Berry presents me with a special plaque from the Boardwalk Kennel Club, and at right Charlie Westfield bestows one from the Owner-Handler Association of America.

Vera and I survey the impressive overall scene at a Boardwalk Kennel Club show.

A Closing Note . . .

Although it was with considerable apprehension that I covered my first dog show more than a half century ago, I quickly became "hooked"—as have so many thousands of other aficianados. I still get a thrill when I'm at ringside, writing the dog stories. If the day ever comes that I lose my enthusiasm, I will turn in my typewriter.

BIBLIOGRAPHY

ALL OWNERS of pure-bred dogs will benefit themselves and their dogs by enriching their knowledge of breeds and of canine care, training, breeding, psychology and other important aspects of dog management. The following list of books covers further reading recommended by judges, veterinarians, breeders, trainers and other authorities. Books may be obtained at the finer book stores and pet shops, or through Howell Book House Inc., publishers, New York.

Breed Books

AFGHAN HOUND, Complete — *Miller & Gilbert*
AIREDALE, New Complete — *Edwards*
ALASKAN MALAMUTE, Complete — *Riddle & Seeley*
BASSET HOUND, Complete — *Braun*
BEAGLE, Complete — *Noted Authorities*
BLOODHOUND, Complete — *Brey & Reed*
BOXER, Complete — *Denlinger*
BRITTANY SPANIEL, Complete — *Riddle*
BULLDOG, New Complete — *Hanes*
BULL TERRIER, New Complete — *Eberhard*
CAIRN TERRIER, Complete — *Marvin*
CHIHUAHUA, Complete — *Noted Authorities*
COCKER SPANIEL, New — *Kraeuchi*
COLLIE, Complete — *Official Publication of the Collie Club of America*
DACHSHUND, The New — *Meistrell*
DOBERMAN PINSCHER, New — *Walker*
ENGLISH SETTER, New Complete — *Tuck & Howell*
ENGLISH SPRINGER SPANIEL, New — *Goodall & Gasow*
FOX TERRIER, New Complete — *Silvernail*
GERMAN SHEPHERD DOG, Complete — *Bennett*
GERMAN SHORTHAIRED POINTER, New — *Maxwell*
GOLDEN RETRIEVER, Complete — *Fischer*
GREAT DANE, New Complete — *Noted Authorities*
GREAT PYRENEES, Complete — *Strang & Giffin*
IRISH SETTER, New — *Thompson*
IRISH WOLFHOUND, Complete — *Starbuck*
KEESHOND, Complete — *Peterson*
LABRADOR RETRIEVER, Complete — *Warwick*
LHASA APSO, Complete — *Herbel*
MINIATURE SCHNAUZER, Complete — *Eskrigge*
NEWFOUNDLAND, New Complete — *Chern*
NORWEGIAN ELKHOUND, New Complete — *Wallo*
OLD ENGLISH SHEEPDOG, Complete — *Mandeville*
PEKINGESE, Quigley Book of — *Quigley*
PEMBROKE WELSH CORGI, Complete — *Sargent & Harper*
POMERANIAN, New Complete — *Ricketts*
POODLE, New Complete — *Hopkins & Irick*
POODLE CLIPPING AND GROOMING BOOK, Complete — *Kalstone*
PUG, Complete — *Trullinger*
PULI, Complete — *Owen*
ST. BERNARD, New Complete — *Noted Authorities, rev. Raulston*
SAMOYED, Complete — *Ward*
SCHIPPERKE, Official Book of — *Root, Martin, Kent*
SCOTTISH TERRIER, Complete — *Marvin*
SHETLAND SHEEPDOG, New — *Riddle*
SHIH TZU, The (English) — *Dadds*
SIBERIAN HUSKY, Complete — *Demidoff*
TERRIERS, The Book of All — *Marvin*
TOY DOGS, Kalstone Guide to Grooming All — *Kalstone*
TOY DOGS, All About — *Ricketts*
WEST HIGHLAND WHITE TERRIER, Complete — *Marvin*
WHIPPET, Complete — *Pegram*
YORKSHIRE TERRIER, Complete — *Gordon & Bennett*

Care and Training

DOG OBEDIENCE, Complete Book of — *Saunders*
NOVICE, OPEN AND UTILITY COURSES — *Saunders*
DOG CARE AND TRAINING, Howell Book of — *Howell, Denlinger, Merrick*
DOG CARE AND TRAINING FOR BOYS AND GIRLS — *Saunders*
DOG TRAINING FOR KIDS — *Benjamin*
DOG TRAINING, Koehler Method of — *Koehler*
GO FIND! Training Your Dog to Track — *Davis*
GUARD DOG TRAINING, Koehler Method of — *Koehler*
OPEN OBEDIENCE FOR RING, HOME AND FIELD, Koehler Method of — *Koehler*
SPANIELS FOR SPORT (English) — *Radcliffe*
SUCCESSFUL DOG TRAINING, The Pearsall Guide to — *Pearsall*
TRAIN YOUR OWN GUN DOG, How to — *Goodall*
TRAINING THE RETRIEVER — *Kersley*
TRAINING YOUR DOG TO WIN OBEDIENCE TITLES — *Morsell*
UTILITY DOG TRAINING, Koehler Method of — *Koehler*

Breeding

ART OF BREEDING BETTER DOGS, New — *Onstott*
HOW TO BREED DOGS — *Whitney*
HOW PUPPIES ARE BORN — *Prine*
INHERITANCE OF COAT COLOR IN DOGS — *Little*

General

COMPLETE DOG BOOK, The — *Official Pub. of American Kennel Club*
DISNEY ANIMALS, World of — *Koehler*
DOG IN ACTION, The — *Lyon*
DOG BEHAVIOR, New Knowledge of — *Pfaffenberger*
DOG JUDGING, Nicholas Guide to — *Nicholas*
DOG NUTRITION, Collins Guide to — *Collins*
DOG PEOPLE ARE CRAZY — *Riddle*
DOG PSYCHOLOGY — *Whitney*
DOG STANDARDS ILLUSTRATED
DOGSTEPS, Illustrated Gait at a Glance — *Elliott*
ENCYCLOPEDIA OF DOGS, International — *Dangerfield, Howell & Riddle*
JUNIOR SHOWMANSHIP HANDBOOK — *Brown & Mason*
MY TIMES WITH DOGS — *Fletcher*
RICHES TO BITCHES — *Shattuck*
SUCCESSFUL DOG SHOWING, Forsyth Guide to — *Forsyth*
TRIM, GROOM AND SHOW YOUR DOG, How to — *Saunders*
WHY DOES YOUR DOG DO THAT? — *Bergman*
WILD DOGS in Life and Legend — *Riddle*
WORLD OF SLED DOGS, From Siberia to Sport Racing — *Coppinger*
OUR PUPPY'S BABY BOOK (blue or pink)